D1474084

"Jack N. Lightstone is in top form as he guides the non-specialist reader to his vision of the origins of rabbinic Judaism. The author utilizes all his considerable academic and pedagogical talent to create a lucid and cogent introduction to the rabbis of late antiquity and the movement they spawned. In doing so, he contributes to a better, more nuanced understanding of a crucial era in the history of Judaism, Christianity, and Islam alike."

—**Ira Robinson**, professor emeritus of Judaic studies,
Concordia University

"*What Were the Early Rabbis?* addresses intriguing questions and provides stimulating and challenging analyses. The special focus is on the broad emergence of Rabbinic Judaism using social science perspectives but without the burdens of its jargon and always connected to historical and literary contexts. With analytic clarity, Jack N. Lightstone identifies rabbinic culture, its legitimacy, and provides the reader essential ways to understand and study the core rabbinic text, the Mishnah."

—**Calvin Goldscheider**, professor emeritus of Judaic studies,
Brown University

"This book is a very readable introduction to the core profile and expertise of the cadre of the rabbis just before and after the turn of the third century CE, a seminal era in the evolution of the group that later became the most influential institution in Jewish religious and civil life. Jack N. Lightstone skillfully places the early rabbis in their Judean, Middle-Eastern, and Greco-Roman social and cultural settings. Based on sound scholarship, the book adopts an engaging style of an experienced teacher and storyteller."

—**Simcha Fishbane**, professor of Jewish studies, Touro University
Graduate School of Jewish Studies

"*What Were the Early Rabbis* both translates the best of current academic scholarship on the early phases of Rabbinic Judaism and offers non-experts and scholars alike a fresh and insightful approach to tracking these developments. By drawing upon social-scientific approaches, Jack N. Lightstone moves away from a typical focus on individuals and ideas alone to social institutional factors that led to and sustained the formation of a group that over time changed the lives of Jews and others in the West."

—**Joel Gereboff**, associate professor of Religious Studies,
Arizona State University

What Were the Early Rabbis?

Westar Studies

The Westar Studies series offers distinctive scholarly publications on topics related to the field of Religious Studies. The studies seek to be multi-dimensional both in terms of the subject matter addressed and the perspective of the author. Westar Studies are not related to Westar seminars but offer scholars a deliberate space of free inquiry to engage both scholarly peers and the public.

What Were the Early Rabbis?

An Introduction from a Sociocultural Perspective

JACK N. LIGHTSTONE

CASCADE *Books* · Eugene, Oregon

WHAT WERE THE EARLY RABBIS?
An Introduction from a Sociocultural Perspective

Westar Studies

Copyright © 2023 Jack N. Lightstone. All rights reserved. Except for brief quotations in critical publications or reviews, no part of this book may be reproduced in any manner without prior written permission from the publisher. Write: Permissions, Wipf and Stock Publishers, 199 W. 8th Ave., Suite 3, Eugene, OR 97401.

Cascade Books
An Imprint of Wipf and Stock Publishers
199 W. 8th Ave., Suite 3
Eugene, OR 97401

www.wipfandstock.com

PAPERBACK ISBN: 978-1-6667-6247-1
HARDCOVER ISBN: 978-1-6667-6248-8
EBOOK ISBN: 978-1-6667-6249-5

Cataloguing-in-Publication data:

Names: Lightstone, Jack N., author.

Title: What were the early rabbis? : an introduction from a sociocultural perspective / by Jack N. Lightstone.

Description: Eugene, OR: Cascade Books, 2023. | Westar Studies. | Includes bibliographical references and index.

Identifiers: ISBN 978-1-6667-6247-1 (paperback). | ISBN 978-1-6667-6248-8 (hardcover). | ISBN 978-1-6667-6249-5 (ebook).

Subjects: LCSH: Rabbis. | Jewish scholars. | Judaism—History—Talmudic period, 10–425. | Rabbinical literature. | Mishnah—Criticism, interpretation, etc.

Classification: BM175 L54 2023 (print). | BM175 (ebook).

05/31/23

Unless otherwise stated, Scripture quotations are from the Revised Standard Version of the Bible: Old Testament, © 1952; New Testament, 2nd ed., © 1971; Apocrypha, © 1957, by Division of Christian Education of the National Council of the Churches of Christ in the United States of America. Used by permission. All rights reserved.

Contents

Preface

HUMAN COMMUNITIES SEEM ALWAYS to have looked to their past to understand their lives together in the present, and to project their lives into the future. Sometimes they have done so by (re) inventing that past by means of story, myth, and chronicle, focusing on "historical" or, more properly, "historic" moments deemed to be of seminal importance and special meaning for the group.

In the modern academy, in the disciplines of the humanities and social sciences, we often seek to understand our present social, cultural, economic, and political states of affairs in the light of their antecedents as well. Our contemporary societies and civilizations are, in very real terms, significantly the outcomes of seminal moments of earlier societies and civilizations. The latter are part of how we got here and who we are today, as people living with other people in the organized human communities that we have created. And so, the modern, academically informed study of past societies and civilizations is (or ought to be) of interest to a general, interested, and well-read audience, just as much as it is for academics. And it is in this light that I have written the book you are about to read about what the early rabbis were.

This book, then, (1) is intended for and written to be read by a general audience, although my academic colleagues and particularly their students will, I hope, find it useful. The book (2) concerns a particular group, the early cadre of rabbis, that first (self-) formed in the Jewish communities of the southern Levant early in (3) a historical era—no, a historic era—that many academics and many general readers would readily identify as a seminal period for so-called Western society, culture, and civilization. I refer to the first eight or so centuries CE. Permit me to say more about these points in reverse order.

In the West, the first eight or so centuries CE is a period bookended by Jesus' birth, on one end, and the production of the canonical text of the Quran as a consolidation of Mohammed's teaching, on the other end. Immediately before this period, the inhabitants of the Near East and of the lands of the Mediterranean basin worshipped a plethora of local gods, although, as a result of Alexander the Great's conquests, Hellenistic (Greek-like) social, cultural, linguistic, political, and religious norms had made considerable inroads eastward, from Greece and Macedonia across the eastern Mediterranean and into the westernmost parts of the Near East. And from the eastern side of the Near East, Persian rule with its culture and religious movements also had previously made inroads into, while accommodating itself to, Mesopotamian society and civilization of the Babylonian and Assyrian peoples. So, for example, in the year of Jesus' birth, the inhabitants of southwestern Syria might worship Baal and his consort Asherah, Adonis, or Zeus, Aphrodite, and Apollo, or all of them. The inhabitants of Mesopotamia might worship Marduk/Bel and Sarpa-nit/Zarpanitu, or Zeus, or Ahura Mazda.

Simultaneously, both in their homeland, the land of Israel (aka Judea, Judah, Yehud) in the southern Levant, and as minority, ethno-national, diaspora communities scattered around the Mediterranean and Near East, the Jews of Jesus' time adhered to social norms and religious practices, sometimes in a somewhat hellenized mode, that many of their contemporary neighbours considered both stubbornly persistent and overly exclusive. Why? Jews not only tended to shun "the gods," in favor of their one, universal, and imageless deity, YHWH, the God of Israel, but they also denied altogether the very existence of "the gods." Jews, furthermore, adhered to a body of norms and rituals they claimed to be YHWH's will, as represented especially in a document, the Torah, attributed to someone that they deemed to be an ancient prophet without peer, Moses. And as a result, Jews both in the homeland and in the diaspora sought to socially distance themselves from others, when those others among whom or beside whom they lived honored the gods in any fashion.

If, now, we were to fast-forward eight hundred years or so after Jesus' birth, society and culture in the lands around the Mediterranean basin and in the Near East would appear quite changed, and in some respects unrecognizable. True, the legacy of Roman rule (particularly in the areas of law, and civic governance and administration) would be evident throughout much of that landmass. But more startling, after the passage of these approximately eight centuries, the God of Israel, YHWH, was *exclusively* worshipped by the vast majority of the inhabitants of this extensive geography—in cities as far flung as Cadiz, Marseille, Paris, London, Constantinople, Kairouan, Alexandria, Antioch, Damascus, Baghdad, and Susa (today, Shush). The God of Israel was as much revered by Visigothic kings in early medieval Spain as YHWH (aka Allah) alone was extoled by the caliph of Baghdad. The Roman-based law code and Christian teachings of Visigothic Spain as well as Islamic law and theology in Baghdad would equally reflect the influence of the Jewish biblical and postbiblical tradition. And the texts of Islamic prayers and Christian prayers alike would reflect not only themes but sometimes the very language of Jewish hymns. Astounding, when you think about it, is it not?!

Of course, this transformation did not happen because all these peoples had (previously) converted to Judaism and joined the Jewish people. Eight centuries after Jesus' birth, Jews were, at the best of times, treated as second-class residents by both Muslim and Christian authorities. But the fact remains that the founders and leadership of early Christianity, on the one hand, and of Islam, on the other, had quite effectively adopted and adapted the religious culture of the Jews and had used it (in part) to unite the peoples of the Mediterranean basin and the Near East under either the cross of Christianity or the banner of Islam. The early caliphs, ruling as successors to Mohammed, held both political and religious sway in the name of the Jews' God. And the Visigothic kings could be set upon their thrones or deposed by the decision of a national council upon which Christian clerics sat among the nobles, and over which these clerics had undisputed sway in the name of the same God. In the process, the worship of the gods as well as many forms of social and cultural authority associated with the worship of the gods were wiped away in these regions, not just avoided, as the Jews had done. And, at the risk of belaboring the point, our contemporary Western society and civilization is to a very significant degree the long-term results of these transformations.

How may I otherwise characterize this change, if not as the "judaizing" of these non-Jewish populations by the followers of Jesus and Mohammed?! And so, one of the compelling questions that is drawn in the wake of the foregoing account ought, in my view, to be this: What was going on in Judaism and among the Jews over this same, roughly eight-hundred-year period, during which time first Christianity and then Islam was judaizing non-Jews and thereby significantly modifying the society and culture of the West? To begin, let me compare one particularly salient feature of Jewish society around the time of Jesus' birth with comparable institutions of Jewish communal life a century or two after the initial efforts to produce

x
Preface

and promulgate a standardized text of the Quran (which Muslim tradition dates to the mid-seventh century CE).

When Jesus was born in the land of Israel, Judea/Yehud had for much of the previous half-millennium been ruled by a hereditary caste of priests operating, and operating out of, a temple in Jerusalem dedicated to the cult of YHWH. This temple was, at one and the same time, the highest religious and civil authority in Judea, and the chief officer and religious officiant of the temple and of all of its associated institutions and administration was its high priest. Admittedly, from the late sixth to mid-fourth centuries BCE, the then-Persian imperial power appointed a Jewish governor to oversee Judea's administration, and again for an almost century-long period, from the mid-second century BCE until the Roman conquest in the first century BCE, a priestly family, the Hasmoneans, usurped both the high priest's office and crowned themselves kings of the Jews. Nonetheless, from the late sixth century BCE to 70 CE, the Jerusalem temple, its hereditary priesthood, its institutions and administration, and its chief officer, the high priest, constituted the most important, enduring, and authoritative religious and civil-administrative force for Jews in the land of Israel, and the most important moral and religious force for Jews in the diaspora.

Let us fast-forward again to the early eighth century CE. There has been no Jerusalem temple to YHWH for more than six hundred years, and no functioning temple to the God of Israel operates anywhere else either. Gone, too, are all of the institutions, offices, and officers of religious and civil administration associated with the temple. There is no high priest. And while Jews who claim priestly descent are accorded vestigial honors, they may claim no significant authority over religious or civil aspects of Jewish life by reason of their alleged priestly bloodlines. Individual Jewish communities, usually operating as minority "assemblies" (the literal meaning of the Greek term *synagogue*) among a majority population of Christians or Muslims, are administered by local Jewish councils on which sat representatives usually chosen from among the most prosperous local Jewish families. Since prosperity tended to be hereditary, these officers of the community constituted a local Jewish "nobility" (for lack of a better term). But increasingly over the eighth, ninth, and tenth centuries, all Jews, all local Jewish "assemblies," all of their council members and officers, and all of their associated local institutions are subject to a set of norms, over which a local cadre of Jewish "sages" (*hakham*, sg.; *hakhamim*, pl.), the members of the rabbinic "guild" (if I may use that term), have nearly monopolistic sway. On what grounds? Because these Jewish sages have certified one another's mastery of a shared, normative curriculum of study based on specific texts and traditions of their own choosing and/or authorship. (A self-assembled, monopolistic guild of sorts, is it not?) This curriculum of study of a given body of texts was the same for members of this cadre in Cadiz (Spain) and in Susa, and everywhere in between. Yet, each local sage was the assumed/ presumed "master" of his—yes, they were virtually all male—own Jewish community, although they consulted one another in frequent correspondence from one end of this extensive geography to the other.[1]

These Jewish sages addressed one another, and were addressed by others, using the honorific title "rabbi" (a Hebrew term meaning "my master" that connoted "my teacher"). The rabbis were not Jewish priests. They were not Jewish nobility. Nor were they a hereditary caste (although, as was common in the medieval world generally, sons of rabbis often entered the "profession" of their fathers). What rabbis needed to have was the requisite intellectual capacity to master and to constantly revisit their core curriculum, and they had to be able to afford the time to do so. So, they tended not to be paupers. Nor, per se, was rabbi necessarily a salaried profession. And this state of affairs in Jewish communities endured, generally speaking, until the early modern period, when it began to morph.

The cadre of the rabbis as a quasi-guild-like group did not appear *ex nihilo* in the eighth century. Rather, the rabbinic (the English adjective formed from "rabbi") group first formed in the second and third centuries CE. The recognition of their authority over norms of the "Way" (*halakhah*, anglicized as "halakha") to live one's life as a Jew in a community of other Jews built slowly. Only in the medieval period did the rabbis achieve a level of authority that was nearly monopolistic. But inch by inch, step by step, the rabbis' Judaism became all Jews' Judaism—"rabbinic" Judaism.

This, then, was what was transpiring among the Jews *at the very same time* as the Jewish and Gentile associates of the Jesus movement(s) morphed into early Christian assemblies and then into "Christendom," thereby judaizing the Mediterranean lands. And as the rabbis' Way (the halakha) achieved not only greater definition, but greater influence among Jews, it exerted undeniable influence on the development of the Way (Arabic: *sharia*) a Muslim was to live his/her life, when Islam was (re)judaizing

---

1. All this said, it is the case that at least until sometime in the ninth century CE, the principal rabbinic sages, entitled *gaon* (sg.) and *geonim* (pl.), who headed Mesopotamia's several major rabbinic academies enjoyed preeminence in two respects: (1) the interpretation of the texts of the sages' shared curriculum; and (2) the interpretation of the behavioral and ritual norms derived from these texts. Even so, the *geonim* were viewed as first among equals, and local rabbinic sages were the undisputed final authorities in these matters in their communities. Moreover, beginning in the ninth century, the prestige of the *geonim* began steadily to dwindle, until it was all but extinguished several centuries later. See Boyarin, *Traveling Homeland*, chs. 1–2.

the Near East, North Africa, and southern Spain (in many of these regions after Christianity had already done so).

And so, this volume, as its title indicates, seeks to elucidate what the early rabbis were, focusing on *the earliest point at which evidence allows us meaningfully to discern their emergence as a distinctive social formation*, that is, as an organized cadre of sages shaped principally (a) by social interactions with one another structured especially around the study of a common curriculum that they were initially to master and thereafter to continuously study, and (b) by an associated, shared "myth" about the core elements of that curriculum. In my view, that point is sometime in the (late) second century CE and the (first half of the) third century in the land of Israel. This is a period in which, all around the "early rabbis," both in the land of Israel and in adjacent territories, the early Christian assemblies (Greek: *ekklesia*, sg.), in many locales still significantly intertwined with local Jews and Jewish assemblies, rapidly developed. It is the period and region in which (as popular chaos theory likes to say) the flap of the wings of the butterfly caused the whirlwind that several and more centuries later changed the nature of Jewish communal authority, on the one hand, and that "judaized" the Western world via Christianity and Islam, on the other.

I hope that I have now piqued your interest in the choice of topic conveyed in this book's title, *What Were the Early Rabbis?* Of course, I shall have much more to say about this choice in chapter 1. But I should now like to say something about the subtitle of this volume.

This book is billed as an introduction. I mean by this that I did not write this volume for specialists, although the scholarship of many specialists stands behind it (including my own). What follows in these several hundred pages assumes no prior knowledge about the early rabbis, their literature or history, or about rabbinic Judaism. If I assume anything at all, it is a general interest in the historical, social, or religious developments of the first several centuries CE in the lands of the Mediterranean basin and the Near East. As to which specific audiences may find this book of particular interest and why—I have spelled this out in chapter 1 as well. Let me say here, however, that a general readership interested in the history of Judaism, or in the development of early Christianity in context, or in the antecedents of Islam, or in Greco-Roman, Near Eastern culture and society, or (more generally) in the nature of religious institutions and their social formation and transformation should find reading this book a welcome addition to their knowledge.

Because the book is intended as an introduction for nonspecialists, I have written it in a style that is more pedagogical and (at times) even colloquial than scholarly and academic. I use metaphors, and I ask leading and sometimes rhetorical questions to highlight points and to make the writing more conversational. I tell (always historically based) stories, at first glance seemingly tangential in nature, to draw the reader into important topics. (One may think of them as "shaggy-dog" accounts, that is, the telling of a story that seems to wanders far from its principal focus, only to find its way back.) Nor have I exhaustively footnoted this volume, as one would an academic monograph. I have used footnotes to clarify, edify, and to indicate where the reader might find further readings on particular points, as well as to indicate my specific dependence on others' ideas. By contrast, I have only sparingly, but not generally, used footnotes to register the scholarly debates about this or that matter, or to reference the fulsome body of scholarly literature on a subject. Such a level of footnoting is expected in an specialist's publication for specialists, which this book is not. And in a similar vein, the bibliography at the end of this book serves primarily to provide accurate references for publications mentioned in "shorthand" only in the footnotes; so the bibliography is not meant to be exhaustive of the book's subject matter.

And now, the last clause of the subtitle: *from a Sociocultural Perspective.* Why? For several reasons. First, in my own academic work over the course of more than forty-six years, I have melded the perspectives and methods of history, literary history, and literary analysis, on the one hand, with sociological and anthropological perspectives and approaches, on the other. Throughout my career, these approaches have all complemented one another in dealing with the arcane and often historically problematic evidence for the ancient world generally, for the first several centuries CE specifically, and for the early rabbis especially. In other words, unapologetically stated, this is who I am, and that is reflected in this book. That is the first point.

Second, and closely related to the foregoing, I am convinced that what one observes as historical, organized religions (their established belief systems, their institutions, and their associated religious authorities) are not only embedded in their respective societies and cultures, but are constructs of the latter and influence one another's development over time. If you, by contrast, maintain that historical, organized religions as we observe them are revealed, or static, or are sui generis (that is, a thing/ realm apart from others), then reading this volume will expose you to another way of looking at these matters.

My third reason is this. As I will indicate more fully in chapter 1, the evidence at hand makes it notoriously difficult to sort out reliably the developmental history of the early rabbinic group and the roles of its principal, early leaders in that development in the first several centuries

CE. That is not to say that it is impossible to do so.[2] But it is an exercise extensively fraught with methodological hurdles to overcome, and would require a very academically styled book with all of the "ifs, ands, or buts" demanded by the problems inherent in the surviving evidence. So I have chosen another path in this book. I have tried not to present a "movie" of the early rabbinic movement in its first several centuries of development, but more of a "snapshot" of it as close to its inception as available, fulsome, and unproblematic evidence allows. That snapshot is of a group already reasonably well formed socially by the end of the second and mid-third centuries CE. For the rabbis in this snapshot, we may with confidence say what their core, shared curriculum of study was. We have the very document(s) they subjected to lifelong, devoted analysis as rabbis and would-be rabbis, and so we may build a profile of competencies expected of bona fide members of this early rabbinic cadre. Furthermore, we may inquire why this profile "made sense" to members of the cadre, and why it might have made sense (or why the rabbis hoped it might make sense) to the people of the Jewish communities of the land of Israel near the end of the second and in the third centuries CE. These are all issues for which perspectives and approaches of sociology and anthropology are particularly well suited. Why? Because these issues deal with matters of social or group formation and identity, and their sustainability or durability in a larger social and cultural context. Therefore, any reader of this volume who has ever taken an introductory sociology or anthropology course (and I make absolutely no assumptions that any of this book's readers have) will recognize underneath and in between this book's lines a number of fairly standard sociological and anthropological concepts—such as group identity formation, socialization, internalization, routinization, rationalization, legitimation, mythologization, plausibility, authority structures, reference groups, social stratification, elites, etc.[3] That said, I have made every effort *not* to distract the reader with the jargon and technical terminology of the disciplines of sociology or anthropology. Instead I have tried to couch this book's claims, discussions, analyses, and arguments in the most colloquial, conversational, and accessible language that I can muster, given the content of this volume and the concepts that underpin it.

2. Moreover, I have tried to write a (short) history of the early rabbinic movement for a general readership of nonspecialists, to the degree that our evidence reasonably allows. That account may be found in Lightstone, *In Seat of Moses*, ch. 2, extracts of which are presented for your convenience as the appendix to this volume.

3. For those who are interested, a very short, now more than fifty-year-old textbook by Peter Berger, *Invitation to Sociology*, deftly introduces novice students of sociology to most of these concepts.

Let me say something of the "technical" features of this volume. I have already given an account of how I will use (and not use) footnotes and bibliographical entries. Hebrew/Aramaic or Greek letters do not appear in the text. All Hebrew, Aramaic, or Greek words are given in transliteration. Nor have I used one or another of the accepted scholarly systems of transliteration. Instead, I have just tried to reproduce, without diacritical marks and accents, the sound of the words. Translations of passages of the canonical Hebrew Bible and rabbinic literature, whether in Hebrew or Aramaic, are my own. Translations of passages in the Apocrypha and New Testament are based on *The New Oxford Annotated Bible with Apocrypha, Revised Standard Edition*, except where I have specified otherwise. When translating verses from the Hebrew Bible, it is the standard Masoretic text that I am rendering. For passages from the Mishnah, I have used Hanokh Albeck's *Shisha Sidre Mishnah*; for Tosefta, the edition of M. S. Zuckermandel, unless otherwise indicated; for the texts of the Palestinian and Babylonian Talmuds, the standard Vilna editions have been used, in the interest of accessibility.

It is commonplace to refer to the major documents of the early rabbinic corpus using abbreviations. The following abbreviations are frequently used in this volume: m. for Mishnah; t. for Tosefta; JT for the Jerusalem (aka Palestinian) Talmud; BT and b. for the Babylonian Talmud. Other than these, I have mostly avoided the use of abbreviations when referencing early rabbinic texts.

There are several terminological choices that I have made that I ought to explain. Throughout this book I have often used a neologism, "Judah-ites," where others might expect "Jews." Why? First, I do not wish to be restricted by debates about who was a Jew in the various centuries with which this books deals. As Shaya Cohen (in *The Beginnings of Jewishness*) and Lawrence Schiffman (in *Who Was a Jew?*) have taught us, the definition of Jew was not necessarily and always clear-cut in the Achaemenid-Persian period (late sixth to late fourth centuries BCE), Hellenistic era (late fourth to mid-first centuries BCE), and Greco-Roman and Byzantine-Roman times (mid-first century BCE to early seventh century CE). Moreover, I wanted a term that had broader connotations than who might, strictly speaking, be deemed a Jew in the Greco-Roman period. By Judah-ite, then, I refer to all those whose socioreligious culture was primarily (or originally) forged in the "land of Judah" (*yehudah/yehud/yahud*) from the late sixth century BCE, when the territory was ruled by the Achaemenid-Persian empire, to the Muslim conquest in the seventh century CE. Furthermore, Judah-ites held the still-emerging biblical (as well as what later was deemed apocryphal) books of the Hebrew Bible/Christian Old Testament as their authoritative cultural legacy. Moreover, until its destruction in 70 CE, most

Judah-ites viewed YHWH's temple in Jerusalem, its officials, and its institutions as central to who and what they were (even if some Judah-ite groups virulently disputed the policies and practices of those in charge of the temple at any one time). So, in my mind, Judah-ites include the members of the Jesus movement (for a time, at least), some early "Christians," diaspora "Jews" (that is, those who no longer lived in the land of Judah), many so-called "God-fearers," some Idumeans, and (perhaps) Samaritans, as well as any others whom we would conventionally call Jews.

Another terminological issue that I face in this volume is what term(s) to use as the name for the "homeland" territory of the Judah-ites. Most scholars of the Greco-Roman period refer to that territory as Palestine. But Palestine (Latin: *Palestina*) was a moniker invented and used by the Romans as part of their campaign of collective punishment of the Judah-ites in the aftermath of two (failed) revolts (in 66–70 CE and 132–135/6 CE) against Roman rule in the Judah-ites' homeland. Palestine is derived from "Philistine," the people who inhabited the coastal plain of the southernmost region of the Levant near the end of the late Bronze Age and the earliest years of the Iron Age. The Philistines were among the foremost enemies and territorial competitors of the ancient Israelites, and the Philistines were largely subdued by David, at least according to the biblical narrative. So the Romans deliberately chose the name of the Judah-ites' ancestors' mortal enemies as the new designation for the Judah-ite homeland. Few, if any, Judah-ites designated (or preferred to designate) their ancestral homeland by this moniker, even after Rome imposed it. Rather, Judah-ites used three different terms for their ancestral territory: the land of Israel; [the land of] Yehud or Yahud (from the name "Judah," which the Romans latinized as Judea); or simply "the land." Therefore, throughout this volume it is one or another of these three terms that I use.

As is already apparent in the preceding paragraphs, historical-chronological terms inevitably appear throughout this volume—late Bronze Age, Iron Age, Greco-Roman period, Achaemenid-Persian era, Hellenistic times, (Neo-) Babylonian era, to name just a few. As one valued colleague pointed out to me, if one has not read much about ancient history, no doubt this terminology may not be immediately comprehensible and may seem to be a secret language. Moreover, given that the principal focus of the volume is the early rabbinic cadre in the late second and early third centuries CE, why should I need to reference all of these periods anyway? So let me briefly explain and catalogue the systems (plural) I tend to use in this volume to "periodize" the historical time line, and then say something about why I have needed to resort to them.

Historians and archaeologists segment history into periods that seem meaningful to them on the basis of the particular historical evidence they tend to examine. But for the ancient world, there is no one such system of periodization, because what is "meaningful" depends on what one is researching. The history of the people of Israel/the Jewish people in their homeland in antiquity is usually divided into the periods of:

- Era of the tribal confederacy—the last several centuries of the second millennium BCE

- First Temple period—the first half of the first millennium BCE to 586 BCE

- Second Temple period—from the late sixth century BCE to 70 CE, in which year the Jerusalem temple was destroyed by the Romans

- Post-destruction era—from 70 CE to approximately the rise of Islam in the seventh century CE; also commonly referred to as the (Talmudic-) rabbinic period

Thereafter, the medieval period of the history of the Jewish people is generally deemed by historians to have begun.

Moreover, this is not the only system of periodization referred to in this book, or in other works about Judah-ites in antiquity. Another such system refers to the succession of imperial powers whose administrations (and, to a degree, cultures) impinged upon those living in the land of Israel (and/or the surrounding region) in ancient times. As it relates to the substance of this book, the following periods are relevant:

- (Neo-) Assyrian imperial period—latter eighth century BCE, when the Northern Kingdom of Israel fell to the Assyrians and the Southern Kingdom of Judah entered Assyria's political "orbit," to near the end of the seventh century BCE[4]

- (Neo-) Babylonian imperial period—from the end of the seventh century BCE, and specifically from 597 BCE, when the Southern Kingdom of Judah was conquered by the Babylonians, ending before the last third of the sixth century BCE

---

4. You will notice that I do not designate a period of Egyptian rule in the land of Israel. That is not to say that there was not such a period. Rather that period is *largely* finished during the era of the tribal confederacy. During the time of the tribal confederacy and the First Temple period, Egypt remained a major power in the region of the southern Levant, but no longer had sufficient power to conquer and rule large portions of the Levant. Notwithstanding, Egyptian *culture* continued significantly to influence the land of Israel, even beyond the First Temple period.

- Achaemenid-Persian period—from the last third of the sixth century BCE, when the Persian and Mede forces overran the Babylonian Empire, ending near the last quarter of the fourth century BCE when Alexander the Great subdues the Persian Empire, including the land of Israel/Yehud

- Hellenistic period—following Alexander's death in the late fourth century BCE, during which era the land of Israel was subject to either the Ptolemaic-Hellenistic kingdom to the south, or the Seleucid-Hellenistic regime to the north and northeast, concluding with the Roman conquest of the Near East in the decades preceding the mid-first century BCE

- Hasmonean period—an important intermediate period in the land of Israel lasting about a century immediately preceding the Roman conquest, during which time a Jewish dynasty of priest-kings, the Hasmoneans, enjoyed relative freedom from the rule of both of the Hellenistic kingdoms that surrounded the land of Israel

- (Greco-) Roman period—from just before the mid-first century BCE, when Rome conquered the region, until sometime in the first half of the fifth century CE

- Byzantine-Roman period—thereafter and until the Muslim conquest of the land of Israel in the seventh century CE

As stated, the forgoing represents the most commonly used designations for time periods in this book and in most others about the people of Israel/the Jewish people in their homeland in antiquity. However, there is one other system that is sometimes used, one based on a combination of the evolution of human technology in the Near East and eastern Mediterranean basin, and the beginning of history writing in Greece in the fifth century BCE. Thus as regards the people of Israel/the Jewish people, you may see references to:

- Late Bronze Age—the last centuries of which correspond to the era of the tribal confederacy in the history of ancient Israel

- Iron Age—from near the beginning of the First Temple period in the land of Israel until the latter decades of the fifth century BCE, around the time when the first Greek historians begin to write their oeuvres

One practical suggestion I might offer to those who (still) feel at sea when I use such historical-chronological terms is to access or acquire one or several readily available historical time line charts. There are many on the internet, as well as in study editions of the Bible.

Now, why must you, this volume's readers, be subjected to these multiple systems of historical-chronological terms? The answer is related to my view that religions and their institutions are embedded in, and are constructs of, the societies and cultures of their time and place. As I have already written, the early rabbinic group first formed as a reasonably institutionalized entity sometime over the latter second and early third centuries CE in the land of Israel; this is the group (and time period) that constitutes this book's focus. In Judah-ite history this falls within the post-destruction era (from 70 CE to approximately the rise of Islam in the seventh century CE), also commonly referred to as the (Talmudic-) rabbinic period. But society and culture in the land of Israel during the post-destruction era were not sealed off from the world around them; nor had they ever been in the preceding centuries. Consequently, as one would expect, Judah-ite society and culture in the land of Israel in this rabbinic period were also products of what Judah-ite society and culture *had been* before this era. In human societies, the past "makes claims" on the present, as it were. It follows, as you shall see in chapters 5 and 6, that "what the early rabbis were" in the first several centuries of the post-destruction era was significantly influenced by *contemporary* social and cultural forces, extending laterally (that is, in the immediate and adjacent social, political, and cultural geography of Yehud, and beyond in the lands of the Near East and Mediterranean basin), as well as by *historical* social and cultural *antecedents*, extending temporally back in time (that is, by earlier phases of Judah-ite society and culture within, once again, the context of the Near Eastern and Mediterranean lands).[5]

There is a saying: "Success has many parents, but failure is an orphan." As regards this book, the first half of this saying is undoubtedly valid, but the second half is not. Insofar as this book responsibly and cogently presents its subject matter to its intended readers, it is because I have received the advice and help of many supportive and knowledgeable people. I should like to recognize and thank Professors Joel Gereboff, Calvin Goldscheider, and Frances Goldscheider, all of whom graciously agreed to read and comment on the first draft of this book. Their suggestions helped me immeasurably. Dr. Gereboff provided valuable insight based on his four and a half decades of teaching and research in the field of Judaic studies. The Drs.

---

5. In these regards, I take my inspiration from Emile Durkheim's understanding of "social facts." He maintained that the *meaning* of a social fact derives from its fit with, or relationship to, other *contemporary* social facts, as well as its fit with, or relationship to, *historically antecedent* social facts that appear to continue to impinge upon the contemporary situation. See Durkheim, *Rules of Sociological Method*, 74ff.

Goldscheider each brought to bear expertise derived from more than fifty years as academics in sociology; this proved an invaluable aid to, and litmus test for, me, given the sociocultural approach of this volume. The appendix to this volume uses extracts (reproduced with permission) from chapter 2 of my recent book, *In the Seat of Moses*; a first draft of that chapter was, at the time, read by Professor Lee I. Levine, who offered valuable suggestions for its improvement. Drs. David Galston and Arthur Dewey, both of the Westar Institute, have also provided important feedback and sage advice; moreover, without their encouragement and support this book would never have been started, let alone completed and published. My thanks to Christopher Hampson-Curtis for formatting the text for typesetting. I am also greatly indebted to the editors at Cascade/Wipf & Stock for their consummate professionalism. Some of the research for this book was conducted at the National Library of Israel, Jerusalem, and at the libraries of the Pontifical Gregorian University and the Pontifical Biblical Institute, both in Rome. I am grateful for the help of Fr. Etienne Vetö at the Gregoriana and Dr. Adam Wisniewski at the Biblico for facilitating this access. While at the library of the Biblico, I was introduced to Professor Paolo Costa, a specialist in ancient Roman law; he graciously expanded my bibliographical horizons regarding Roman law and Roman jurists. Finally, my work for this volume has been supported by funds from Brock University and has benefited from the unfailing encouragement of my dean, Dr. Carol Merriam (herself a scholar of the literature of ancient Rome). If, however, the book has fallen short, and I am sure there are faults to be found in it, then I am the "single parent" that is responsible. There is no "ducking" it. At such junctures, perhaps my own faults as an academic may have become manifest, or I have failed to heed the good advice of others who know better.

This book was written during the COVID-19 pandemic of 2020-2022. My wife, Dr. Dorothy Markiewicz, to whom I dedicated my most recent book, *In the Seat of Moses*, was and is, as she has been for decades, my constant support, companion, and best friend. During much of the pandemic, Dorothy and I, among other things, longed to hug, kiss, play with, and otherwise keep the company of our grandchildren, Orli, Amit, Erez, and Gabriel. This we were unable to do to our liking, until we had the protection of vaccinations resulting from the efforts of modern science. Until that was the case, not being able to do so was like a constant ache that could not be salved. Video conferencing or socially distanced porch meetings, as joyful as they were, were not enough. We love you all, and to you I dedicate this book as a token of that love.

For Orli, Amit, Erez, and Gabriel

Abbreviations

b.   Babylonian Talmud
BT   Babylonian Talmud
Heb. Hebrew
JT   Jerusalem (Palestinian) Talmud
m.   Mishnah
t.   Tosefta

I

Introduction

IN THE AFTERMATH OF
NATIONAL CATASTROPHE

THE BIBLICAL BOOK OF Lamentations commences with the following
verse:

> How solitary sits
> the city [once so] full of people;
> [it] has become like a widow;
> [once] great among the nations,
> a noble among territories,
> [it] has become subjugated.

In this haunting Hebrew poetry, an ancient author, whom some Judaic traditions identify as the biblical prophet Jeremiah, mourns the devastation
of Jerusalem in 586 BCE by the (Neo-) Babylonian imperial armies. The
Babylonians invaded the land of Israel and the entire Levant at the end of
the seventh century BCE. In 597 BCE, Jerusalem, the capital of the kingdom of Judah, surrendered to the new invaders. But in 587/86 BCE, the last
king descended from David and Solomon decided to revolt. After a hard
siege, Jerusalem fell to the Babylonian forces. Its fortifications, palaces, and
the royal temple to the God of Israel (a temple built centuries earlier by
Solomon) were all torn down. All institutions of *national* civil and religious
self-governance and administration of the people of Israel in the land of
Israel ceased to exist. And the royals, nobles, military leadership, literary

class, temple personnel, and prominent artisans of Jerusalem were herded away to places of exile in Mesopotamia.

Despite this devastation, renewal began in Jerusalem a little more than half a century later, when, after Persian and Median armies overthrew the Babylonians, Cyrus the Great and the Achaemenid-Persian kings who succeeded him mandated the return of control of Jerusalem and its surrounding territory to the descendants of those who had been exiled—all under Persian supervisory rule, of course. What resulted over the next half a millennium, that is, to near the time of Jesus' birth, was a major reframing and refashioning of Judah-ite society, culture, and religion, using (selectively) the heritage of ancient Israel and adding much to it.

During this period of renewal, virtually all of the books of the Hebrew Bible roughly in the versions we possess today were composed as a national literature. Many other literary works were also composed and widely revered, although these ultimately were not included in the canon of Hebrew Scriptures (but were preserved, often in Greek and other translations by the early church).

While the old Davidic monarchy was not renewed, a new Second Temple was built, which became the center for the most important institutions of national civil administration and of the national cult to YHWH, the God of Israel. All of this was under the aegis of the temple's high priest, who oversaw a significant number of cultic personnel, a national judicial and legislative system, and a national civil administration. True, for a brief but significant period lasting roughly from the mid-second to the mid-first century BCE, a priestly family with no Davidic ancestry, the Hasmoneans, reestablished a monarchy (while simultaneously claiming high priestly status). That said, it was the high priest's office and administration that remained throughout at the apex of national Judah-ic life, even after Rome conquered the region in the mid-first century BCE.

In the latter half of the first century CE, history seemingly repeated itself in the land of Israel. In 66 CE, Judah-ites drawn to (or ensnared by) a "national liberation movement" began a revolt against the Roman occupation. The end result was as devastating to Jerusalem and its national institutions of the cult of YHWH and civil administration as the revolt of the last Davidic king against their Babylonian overlords had been more than five hundred years earlier. In 70 CE, rebel-held Jerusalem fell to the Romans, who had been besieging it. As had occurred more than half a millennium before, all of Jerusalem's national institutions, including especially the temple and all of its functions, ceased to exist. Soon thereafter, the last fortress occupied by the rebels, Masada (by the shores of the Dead Sea), fell as well to Roman legions. It was all over.

No doubt some believed that history would repeat itself in another fashion—that by divine providence another national restoration would occur in the not too distant future. Jerusalem would be restored to her people, a Third Temple would be built, and the cult and other institutions administered by a new high priest would resume. Rome was not so inclined, and no new imperial power existed in the region that would immanently overthrow Rome and end its rule in the Levant, as the Persians and Medes had done to the Babylonian Empire many centuries earlier. The seal on the destruction was a second revolt from 132 to 135/6 CE undertaken again by Judah-ic militant nationalists, led by Simon Bar-Kokhba (aka Bar-Kuziba). The immediate impetus to rebel is not entirely clear. Some scholars maintain that plans by the Emperor Trajan (or Hadrian) to rebuild Jerusalem as a "pagan," military, garrison city was the match that lit the fuse. There certainly was such a plan; indeed, it was implemented soon after Bar-Kokhba's forces were defeated. And the city of Aelia Capitolina, with temples to Jupiter and Aphrodite, was constructed over the site of Jerusalem. But whether the plan was devised and adopted as policy by Rome before or after the rebellion is unclear. What was clear to anyone with eyes to see and ears to hear was this. Jerusalem would not be restored to the people of Israel in the near or medium term. None of the Jerusalem temple's institutions of religious and civil administration would be renewed. In fact, Judah-ites were all but banned from dwelling in the city for a time. Indeed, most Judah-ites moved away from the most war-devasted areas and, if they stayed in the land of Israel at all, moved to the west along the coastal plain of the land, as well as to the north in the lower and upper Galilee and the Golan. The *national* Judah-ite world in the land of Israel was in a shambles. What remained largely intact was traditional, local village and town governance and authority. Any renewal to be had, if one could be fashioned, must be reconstituted on this base, upon the unquestionably rich and revered cultural and literary remains of Judah-ite society from the pre-destruction era, and upon the reality of continued Roman rule.

It is precisely in this social, cultural, and political context in the latter decades of the second century CE that the early rabbinic movement, a self-designated, self-formed cadre of scholars and teachers of a specific type, formed in the land of Israel in towns of the coastal plain and soon thereafter in the Galilee. As remarked in the preface, many centuries later, this cadre's intellectual, occupational, and institutional heirs were looked to as the highest authorities for how one should live and act as a Jew in accordance with the demands of Torah. This book aims to elucidate their beginnings, but in a very particular manner, for a certain audience.

This book offers nonspecialists an introduction to the earliest rabbinic movement near and soon after its initial foundation (during the decades leading up to and just following the turn of the third century CE) within Jewish society in the land of Israel. The volume focuses almost entirely on *what* members of the earliest rabbinic movement were by exploring two intertwined sets of questions.

1. What was (were) the shared, collective social profile(s) of members of this group? And what did they seem to think they were (or wish to be)?

2. Moreover, upon what historically, socially, culturally, or politically relevant antecedent and contemporary models might the nascent rabbinic movement have drawn to forge their collective profile(s)? And what might they have thought they were (or should be seen as) like, in their own eyes and in the eyes of others?

Such questions, in various formulations, will recur at junctures throughout the book as important organizational signposts of the volume's subject matter. And later in this first chapter, I will unpack these questions and articulate the value to a nonspecialist readership of posing and addressing these specific queries (as opposed to others) in order to gain an introductory toehold on understanding the early rabbinic movement, including what was "rabbinic" about it (beyond the already stated and somewhat self-evident fact that members of the movement bore the title "rabbi"). Before doing that, however, let me say something about why nonspecialists might be interested at all in better understanding the earliest rabbinic movement. (We specialists, by contrast and by definition, always care intensely about the subject matter of our speciality.)

THE EARLY RABBINIC MOVEMENT: OF INTEREST TO WHOM, AND WHY?

As I have already begun to articulate, the earliest rabbinic movement is a group that

1. First emerged as self-styled "specialists" within Jewish society in the land of Israel under Roman rule after the destruction by Roman armies in 70 CE of Jerusalem and of its central temple of the God of Israel

2. Had attained a reasonable level of organization and shared self-definition as a social formation sometime during the latter half of the second century in the land of Israel (after the failure of the Bar Kokhba rebellion, c. 132–135/6 CE, against Roman rule)

Furthermore, the early rabbinic movement:

3. Had begun by the middle of the third century (if not a little earlier) to articulate a shared narrative that (a) expressed what they were as a group, and that (b) legitimated the role(s) members sought as specialists of a certain type in Jewish society

Indeed, in the mid-third century CE, the movement was sufficiently well self-defined and developed to clone itself to establish a "branch-plant" group (or groups) in Persian-ruled Mesopotamia. How? By the mid-third century, the early rabbinic movement was already attracting would-be members from the lands "between the rivers" (the literal meaning of "Mesopotamia") to apprentice with members of the movement in the homeland, and to export members from the land of Israel (back?) to Mesopotamia. Eventually, due largely to the Christianizing policies and politics of the Byzantine-Roman Empire in the fifth, sixth, and seventh centuries, the Mesopotamian branch, which operated beyond the ken of Byzantine Christian rule, eclipsed its sister, founding movement in the land of Israel. But I am getting not only ahead of myself but also beyond the timeframe of this book's focus.

What, in my view, is so inherently interesting about the earliest rabbinic movement in the land of Israel during the movement's formative period in the second century CE through the first half of the third, and to whom (beyond a more narrowly defined audience of readers for whom this topic is a primary focus of research and study)? That is to say, whom do I believe to be among the more broadly defined, likely interested readers of this book about the early rabbinic group, and why? To answer this question, let me begin not in ancient times, but in the early twenty-first century, our own era.

In our times, almost all Jews who affiliate or identify with one or another institutionalized faction or movement of contemporary Judaism—among them, the ultra-Orthodox (aka *haredi*), Modern Orthodox, Hasidic, Conservative (called *Masorati* in the state of Israel), Reconstructionist, and Reform/Liberal movements—are adherents and practitioners of some *modern* interpretation of rabbinic Judaism.[1] In other words, the

---

1. Yes, even the ultra-Orthodox movements—there are several—of twenty-first-century rabbinic Judaism are modern, no less so than the Reform/Liberal synagogue movements. Like all other contemporary, twenty-first-century forms of rabbinic Judaism, ultra-Orthodoxy, too, represents coherently articulated, shared, and organized Judaic responses to the challenges faced by religious communities in modern, particularly open, and increasingly secularized societies. Those responses are just different than that of the Reform, Reconstructionist, or Conservative movements of Judaism. On a continuum of responses to modernity, ultra-Orthodoxy leans more toward social/cultural distancing from others, even from Jewish others. By contrast, Jews who identify with more liberal streams of modern rabbinic Judaism seek to a

Judaism of today in (almost) *all* of its forms, somehow has its origins in a rabbinic movement that began in the land of Israel in the first several centuries CE. This alone should make that early movement a matter of interest to those who today self-identify as Jews, or to anyone who wishes better to understand modern-era Judaism *and/or its antecedents*, in the same way that the early Jesus movement(s) and earliest Christianity/Christianities of roughly the same ancient period and, in their initial phases, in roughly that same geographical region, the land of Israel and immediately adjacent territory, are at the root of the many forms of contemporary Christianity observed in our current era.

Now I have deliberately devised the last sentence of the preceding paragraph as a "Trojan horse" of sorts. It seeks to entice another group of potentially interested parties to be drawn into the subject matter of this volume, by suggesting that the early Jesus/Christian movement(s) and the earliest rabbinic movement were *sibling* developments. Both movements—a mealymouthed term that permits me to avoid (for now) a more substantive characterization of what they were—proffer *alternative* responses, arising from a *shared* Judah-ic cultural, social, and religious heritage, to roughly the same social, historical, and political environment. The environment was that of the Levant and eastern half of the Greco-Roman world in the lead-up to and/or the aftermath of two tumultuous, dislocating wars fought in the first and second centuries CE in the land of Israel between Roman imperial legions on the one side and, on the other, militant-nationalist Jewish militia bent on freeing the land of its Roman occupiers.

Indeed, the Gospels portray one of Jesus' disciples, Simeon "the Zealot," as someone who was (or had been) associated with such a militant-nationalist Jewish group (Matt 10:4; Mark 3:18; Luke 6:15; and also Acts 1:13). This portrayal plays into the Gospels' deft handling of the question of Jewish messianism and of Jesus' identity as the expected Messiah. How so? Simeon is, at least implicitly, portrayed (like other disciples of Jesus) as knowing or suspecting that Jesus is (or will be) the expected Jewish Messiah. But Simeon's (former?) zealotry would contrast with the Gospels' explicit portrayal of Jesus as rejecting such nationalistic militancy as part of his messianic consciousness. Jesus' messianic mission, according to the Gospels, lies in another direction altogether, a kingdom of heaven that is not (yet?) political.[2]

---

greater extent to blend their participation with and in non-Jewish society and culture with their rabbinic Judaic identity and their lives as Jews. Absent modern, open, increasingly secularized societies, neither option makes any sense, and so both types of responses are distinctively modern.

2. A theme that became central several centuries later to the philosophy and

The early rabbinic movement, too, portrayed itself as standing opposed to armed militancy as the route to bring about the advent of the Messiah, not the least (I suspect) because the two wars fought by Judean militants against Rome in the land of Israel resulted in national catastrophes that devastated the Judean-Jewish population, culture, and economy, as well as the land's central religious, administrative, and political institutions. Rather, resistance lay in remaining faithful to a life lived in accordance with the teachings of the Torah (as interpreted by the rabbinic movement, of course) in Jewish communities that in other respects accepted Roman hegemony (but not Rome's culture or cults)—a not too different kind of "render unto Caesar that which is Caesar's" than the Gospels'. Simply put, the "life lived in accordance with Torah" (a turn of phrase about which I will say more later) placed boundary limits on romanization and hellenization, but not on Roman rule.

So, the earliest rabbinic group's responses to the challenging issues of its time and place may well be read as an emerging alternative to those of the early Jesus followers within, at first, the very same Jewish communal circles as those of the early Jesus movement(s) and of the earliest Christian assemblies. Would not such an alternative response by a sibling Judah-ic movement be enlightening prima facie for anyone interested in the initial steps of what became late antique, medieval, and modern forms of Christianity?! Each of the two movements, then, represents a path not taken by, but patently open to, the other.

There is yet another shared trait of these two sister developments in the land of Israel under Roman rule in the first several centuries CE—relative insignificance and powerlessness. It is easy (indeed, tempting) to view the early Jesus movement as much more significant and influential than it actually was in this early stage, because we (and especially devoted Christians) tend retroactively to view it so, in light of its overwhelming successes and influence from the fourth century on. But that retrojection is an anachronism. There is a similar tendency (especially among committed Jews) to anachronistically retroject to the second century or even the late first century CE the early rabbinic movement's significance and influence as Judaism's (alleged) "savior" in the aftermath of the temple's destruction in 70 CE—again, because of the authority the movement achieved in the early medieval period and its near monopoly over the norms and practices of Judaism thereafter. It is highly likely that beyond a restrained circle of followers/members, neither of these two sister movements mattered all

---

theology of St. Augustine, as expressed in his notion of the "city of God." See Rubenstein, *Aristotle's Children*, 47–87.

that much to those living in the land of Israel (or beyond) in the late first or second centuries CE, whether to Jews or gentiles. Indeed, it is perhaps the case that members/followers of neither movement stood out terribly among their contemporaries. At best, both movements might have been viewed by others as pretentious in their formative stages. Let us call this "the fallacy of misplaced importance" due to anachronistic tendencies retroactively to aggrandize the founders.

Some of my remarks in the previous paragraphs hint at where I might next go to suggest this book to a likely interested readership. Earlier, I noted that both the early rabbinic movement and early Jesus movements were *non-militant* resisters of Roman rule. One notable expression of this resistance was that both the early rabbinic movement and the earliest Christians shared (from their common Judah-ic heritage) a peculiarly virulent rejection of the Greek and Roman gods, along with related aspects of Greco-Roman culture—and this even more so in *both* instances than what one may observe among some other contemporary Judah-ists, who as loyal Jews (in their self-definition) nonetheless embraced more overtly the currents of hellenization and romanization. How well did that resistance work (or not) for both the early rabbinic and Jesus/early Christian movements? How (or to what degree) was such resistance even a realistic option or aspiration in the imperial Roman world, with, among others, its cult of the Roman emperor? Surely, anyone interested in the cultural and political history of the Roman Empire would find both these movements of interest, precisely because they each represent (1) historical tests of the limits of romanization/hellenization (in culture, society, religion, law, or administration), an often avowed goal (among others) of Roman imperial expansion and rule, as well as (2) two different test cases of Roman tolerance for such resistance.

Let me suggest why yet another audience, interested in another epochal time, might find this volume illuminating. In the early seventh century CE, when the Byzantine Christian Roman Empire was arguably at its height, just outside its eastern fringes, and just beyond the furthest extent of what had once been the Roman province of Arabia, Mohammed founded Islam. Early Islam is a religious (and soon thereafter also a religiously inspired political) movement born arguably out of the twin wombs of two specific Judah-ic projects, the rabbinic movement (which by the seventh century boasted increasing influence among the Jewish communities of Mesopotamia and the land of Israel, both adjacent to the Arabian Peninsula) and late antique "Eastern" Christianity. There is no doubt that Mohammed knew Christian and Jewish communities, including "rabbinized" ones, and explicitly articulated his teachings as the completion of God's revelation to the Jewish prophets and to the "prophet" Jesus. It is partly in this sense that Mohammed is revered in Islam as the "seal" of the prophets. Would not those interested, then, in early Islam find value, too, in greater knowledge of the earliest rabbinic movement? After all, the rabbinic notion of the Way (halakha) a Jew ought to live his/her life in accordance with the demands/commandments of Torah is very much comparable to the Islamic concept of the Way (Sharia) a Muslim ought to live his/her life in accordance with revealed Islamic law.

Finally, there is an additional likely readership for this volume, perhaps its most important, potentially interested audience. I have in mind those who seek, more generally, to understand how institutionalized forms of religion and religious authority arise, are framed, are justified, and are significantly transformed over time within communities.

Many religious communities (Jewish, Christian, and Muslim, among them) tend to view contemporary forms of institutionalized religion as stemming somehow from, and coterminous with, the points of origin of the community itself, and often from divine revelation communicated to the founder(s). And change in religious institutions (which almost inevitably happens) is often skillfully framed within the aforementioned faith commitments. I would claim, on the one hand, that such views are indeed important and valid facts about these religious communities' self-understanding and identity. But, on the other hand, I would maintain that these religious perspectives and commitments tend not to be valid observations about the emergence and development (historically, culturally, or sociologically) of religious traditions and religious communities. To understand how religions and religiously informed communities operate we must be able seriously to consider *both* of the foregoing claims in light of the evidence before us.

The formation in second and third centuries CE of the early rabbinic movement provides a case study that allows us to think more analytically about just these issues. How so? The formation of the rabbinic group is not coterminous with the formation of either Judaism or the Jewish people. However one chooses to define and date the latter, it is incontrovertible that the emergence of the rabbinic movement and its slow, centuries-long ascent to power and authority is something *relatively* novel with Judah-ite society. Why "relatively"? Because as novel as the rabbinic movement was, it did not arise ex nihilo (or *ex deo*). Rather, as you shall learn in this book, in forming their own "professional" profile and identity, the early rabbinic group reworks elements of contemporary and antecedent Judah-ite culture and society, all within the social and cultural currents of the preceding half a millennium of the Near Eastern and Mediterranean worlds. That ought to make the early rabbinic cadre, taken as a case study, interesting for readers who seek an understanding of religions generally.[3]

In sum, the earliest rabbinic movement is the ancestor of (almost) all forms of contemporary, twenty-first-century Judaism; and developments of, and within, the rabbinic movement have been the normative interpretations of Judaism for one thousand years or more. The earliest rabbinic movement originates in roughly the same place, time, and religious, cultural, and political circumstances as the early Jesus movement(s) and the earliest Christian assemblies; they are sibling responses to their shared Judah-ic heritage in a time of tumult in the Roman-ruled lands of the eastern Mediterranean region, characterized in large part by forces of romanization and hellenization. And both movements, rabbinic and earliest Christian, are reclaimed and reframed in Mohammed's and his immediate followers' teachings. Anyone interested in any of these topics—the roots of rabbinic Judaism, the context of earliest Christianities, developments in the Roman Empire and the processes (and limits) of romanization and Roman hellenization, or the religious and cultural Judah-ic backgrounds of early Islam—ought to be edified by this volume. But even more fundamentally, and commencing with the very next section of this introduction, our examination of the early rabbinic group offers a case study for readers wishing better to understand the nature and transformations of authority structures and authority figures in institutionalized religions. Indeed, it is for all of these reasons—this entire range of interests—that I have spent my career in the community of other academics with intersecting specialities seeking to better understand the early rabbinic movement, the literature that it produced, and its legacy.

WHY THIS BOOK'S SPECIFIC FOCUS?

Of all the ways one might seek to contribute to a likely interested, nonspecialist readership's understanding of the early rabbinic movement, why do I think that this book's particular approach (characterized by the questions articulated at the beginning this chapter) is a reasonably compelling route? And what does taking such an approach really entail? Let me address these issues in three successive stages, and in a manner that I think will prove both helpful and informative.

3. Indeed, the early rabbinic movement served as one of the case studies appealed to by Max Weber, one of the founders of the modern sociological study of religion, when early in the twentieth century he developed his "ideal types" of religious authority: traditional (e.g., priests); charismatic (e.g., prophets); legal-rational (e.g., members of the rabbinic group).

Rabbinic Judaism—Is There, and Was There, Any Other Kind?

Thus far in chapter 1, I have tended to refer to the "rabbinic movement" (or group). Earlier I characterized "movement" as a mealymouthed term that tells us nothing specific about forms of institutionalization, social formation, or social location. (And "group" is no better in this respect.) But even more important, none of my frequent references to rabbinic Judaism thus far have been followed by any explication of what is distinctively rabbinic about its Judaism. So, let me now say more about the term "rabbinic," as a useful (and, I hope, enlightening) segue to explaining what is compelling about this book's particular focus on what the early rabbis were.

"Rabbinic," the adjective, is actually a modern term that became pervasive in scholarly circles in the nineteenth century and thereafter among modern-era Jewish community leaders in the late nineteenth and twentieth centuries. And while "Judaism" is a modern counterpart to a Hellenistic term *Iudaismos*, the usage in antiquity of the latter indicates that it meant something like "the national or ethnic culture of the Judeans," which is a far cry from how the term "Judaism" is used today as the designation for a (world?) religion. If we were able to ask a Jew of, let us say, the medieval period to name or to characterize his or her way of life as a Jew in a Jewish community, he or she would likely refer not to Judaism but to something like "the life lived together with others in accordance with the Way [*halakhah*] of (the) Torah (of Moses)." (But more on this later in the volume, because it is an incomplete answer, as you will see.) My point is, our hypothetical medieval Jew would likely not use an adjective "rabbinic" to modify anything; indeed, she or he would likely not even use the terms "Judaism" or "movement" as nouns for which any adjective would apply. (After all, does a fish swimming in the sea feel that it is wet?!)

Why, then, did nineteenth-century scholars feel the need to devise and use "rabbinic" as an adjective? They adopted the adjectival term "rabbinic" to modify the noun "Judaism" (understood now to be a religion, in the modern sense of the term), precisely in order to designate the *dominant* form(s) of Judaism from *at least* the tenth century CE in almost all lands with established Jewish communities and, in some locales in the Levant and Near East, earlier still—perhaps since the sixth or seventh centuries. You will recall this historical state of affairs from what I have already written both in the preface and earlier in this chapter. And it is a small jump indeed from using the adjective "rabbinic" to designate what became, and has for over a millennium been, historically *dominant*, to using "rabbinic" as a modifier to refer to what is "normative" Judaism, which in my view is how contemporary Jewish authorities think of rabbinic Judaism.

"Normative" is an equivocal term; that is, it has a double entendre. It can mean something like "historically prevailing," in which usage it comes very close to the scholarly circle's need for the adjective "rabbinic," namely, to be able distinguish rabbinic Judaism from other strains of Judaism, which rabbinic Judaism increasingly supplanted. But "normative" can also convey another sense; that is, especially authentic, legitimate, or authoritative.[4] Modern religious communities, Jews among them, implicitly subscribe to such double entendres. That is, dominant forms somehow *deserve(d)* to be so, because they are presumed to be authentically legitimate and authoritative. And rabbinic Jews, like devotees of other religions, adopt mythopoeic narratives that "prove" (in their opinion) that authenticity. For them, rabbinic Judaism is *authentic* Judaism. However, this is no longer a historical claim, even if it might often seem like one; it is, rather, a theological claim with social and political significance, since at issue is power and authority within a community.

The preceding paragraphs beg several obvious and important questions, even though to properly address them is beyond this volume's specific focus and scope.

1. If rabbinic Judaism became dominant in the tenth or seventh or sixth centuries CE, what (other) forms of Judaism that were not rabbinic preceded rabbinic Judaism's dominance, and/or coexisted and competed with it for supremacy?

2. How are we to situate rabbinic Judaism's appearance, development, dependence upon, and (eventual) ascendency among these other forms of Judaism, the early Jesus movement(s) among them?

3. In what respects, on the one hand, did rabbinic Judaism differ from these antecedent or competing Judaisms; and, on the other hand, to what degree did rabbinic Judaism build open or share important features with these antecedent or contemporary, competing Judaisms?

Of course, one such antecedent Judaism is that represented in the Hebrew Scriptures, and especially in the first five books of these Scriptures (the

4. This conflation of rabbinic Judaism with that form of Judaism that is understood to be *normative* plays out in a number of interesting ways in modern times. E.g., there has been a Jewish community in Ethiopia for centuries, largely (although not totally) isolated from the late antique and medieval streams of rabbinic Judaism. When in the twentieth century a significant number of Ethiopic Jews were airlifted to the state of Israel, the (Orthodox) rabbinic authorities of the state of Israel were initially hesitant to recognize them as Jews.

Pentateuch), which, in one literary state of development or another, Judah-ites between the fifth and second centuries BCE came to acclaim, and have revered ever since, as the Torah of Moses.[5] From that era on, any life lived as a Jew had, arguably, to be firmly rooted (or claim to be firmly rooted) in the teachings, prescriptions, and proscriptions of the Torah of Moses, or one risked being excluded from the Jewish people or (more broadly articulated) the people with a covenant with YHWH, the God of Israel.[6] So, to say that (in whatever century it happened) rabbinic Judaism achieved dominance among almost all Jewish communities, and remained so until and into modern times, is in effect to assert that rabbinic Judaism attained a near monopoly in these communities on defining teachings, prescriptions, and proscriptions claimed to be authentically based upon the Torah of Moses.

Rabbinic Judaism, however, is an abstract concept (invented by nineteenth-century scholars, as I wrote earlier). Abstract concepts do not in themselves proffer teachings, prescriptions, and proscriptions, let alone ones that communities view as prima facie authentic and authoritative. Who or what does? *People do*—people recognized by the community as uniquely authoritative for some reason(s) that the communities accept. And with this recognition we find the segue not only to the next section of chapter 1 but also to the specific focus of the remainder of this volume, the early rabbis (an English pluralization of a Hebrew word, *rabbi*), who are a specific cadre of people, not an abstract concept modified by the adjectival use of the term "rabbinic."

---

5. In saying this I do not mean to imply that the Pentateuch was throughout these centuries (as of yet) a stable, largely unchanging text. Much evidence, including from the Dead Sea Scrolls found at Qumran, indicates that the state of the text of the Penta-teuch was not yet entirely "fixed" when the earlier documents found among the Dead Sea Scrolls were composed (as opposed to copied). See Schiffman, *Reclaiming Dead Sea Scrolls*, as well as his *From Text to Tradition*.

6. I would venture the view that this became tantamount to a normative orthodoxy among Judah-ites and a litmus test of belonging to the Jewish people sometime in the second century BCE. The book of Ben Sira and the prologue to the original Greek translation done by the author's grandson, which I will say more about in ch. 5, attest to this state of affairs. In this regard, I also find interesting Horsley, *Revolt of the Scribes*, 1–18, 21–32, although this issue is not his primary focus.

Not Only Does "Rabbinic" Come from "Rabbi," but Also the Authority and Role of the Rabbi is a Defining Characteristic of Rabbinic Judaism

Now, remember question number 3 several paragraphs back? In essence (if I were to rephrase it) it asks, What is particularly distinctive about rabbinic Judaism in comparison with its antecedents or competitors? My response follows upon the claim with which I just concluded the previous section; people, not abstract concepts (like rabbinic Judaism) proffer authoritative teachings.

The most defining, distinctive, and enduring characteristics of the rabbinic movement and/or rabbinic Judaism are the *profile* and (real or aspirational) *role(s)* of the rabbi *as a Jewish communal authority*, usually among other types of Jewish communal leaders (such as elders on the community's council) in some (even if informal) power-sharing division of responsibilities. So, that which is most distinctive, above all else, about rabbinic Judaism, is the authority of the rabbi. One might initially be startled at (and skeptical about) both the explicit simplicity and the implicit audacity of the foregoing claim. But the matter is, arguably, that simple, as I shall presently discuss. The audacity of the claim will be clear by the end of this book.

Rabbi in Hebrew literally means "my master," in the sense of the Latin word *doctor* (teacher), as opposed to *dominus* (lord).[7] Therefore, the (claimed) mastery of the rabbi is in the realm of the authoritative teacher who *instructs* others and who may have disciples/students, as the famous pagan rhetor/teacher Libanius did in fourth-century CE Antioch in Syria, or as the Gospels denote sometimes Jesus, sometimes the scribes, and sometimes the Pharisees as authoritative teachers (*didaskaloi* and *nomodidaskaloi* in the Greek New Testament) of Israel's norms and values.[8]

7. In Biblical Hebrew the term *adon* is used to refer to the master/lord of a slave or of those of a lesser social class, and is the cognate of the Latin *dominus*. *Adon* is also used as a title or form of honorary address for the God of Israel in both biblical literature and thereafter, again much like the Christian use of *dominus*.

8. See, e.g., Luke 2:46 (*didaskalon*), Luke 5:17 (*nomodidaskaloi*), Matt 23:8 (*rabbi . . . didaskalos*, the designations here being used as modes of address or as quasi-synonyms for Jesus), Mark 12:32 (*didaskale*), Mark 13:1 (*didaskale*).
On whether the early rabbinic movement is a direct development of the Pharisaic movement or of a "scribal class" operating in the period before the Jerusalem temple's destruction by the Romans in 70 CE, a great deal has been written. I shall say much more about scribes in the Second Temple period at various junctures of this book. In ch. 5 I consider more fully the issue of the Pharisees as some sort of antecedent to the early rabbis. At this juncture, however, I would state that the often stated, wholesale identification of the early rabbis with pre-70 CE Pharisees is not, in my mind, a settled question. That there were Pharisees—e.g., Rabban Gamaliel I and possibly Yohanan

As intimated in the preface, the members of the early rabbinic movement addressed one another as Rabbi So-and-So, and have done so ever since. And while rabbis addressed one another (and no doubt welcomed others addressing them) as rabbi, their claim to mastery as authoritative teachers is bolstered by two other terms they used to self-designate as members of their early movement, especially when referring to themselves collectively. One such term is *hakhamim* (*hakham*, sg.), meaning "sages"; the other is *talmidei hakhamim* (*talmid hakham*, sg.), meaning "disciples of the sages." Within Judah-ic culture of the Roman period, such terms could be understood only as a claim to issue (authoritative) instructions or teachings.[9] Indeed, one passage in the early rabbinic movement's first literary magnum opus, the Mishnah (c. 200 CE), places the authority (and honor) of a *talmid hakham* of even the lowest birth status—yes, ancient Judaism had a caste system of sorts[10]—above that of the Judah-ite of highest birth status, namely the high priest of the Jerusalem temple.[11] This is an obvious early rabbinic pipe dream, but it is informative nonetheless.

The honorific "rabbi" (along with several of its closely related titles, such as "rabban," meaning "our master" or "our teacher") has, arguably, a much more ancient and long-standing pedigree in Judah-ic communities than the adjective "rabbinic," a nineteenth-century abstraction. "Rabbi" (or related titles) precedes names on some tomb inscriptions in the land of Israel dating from the late Roman or early Byzantine periods. Many so designated by these epitaphs, as far as we can tell, probably have nothing

---

ben Zakkai (based on m. Yadayim 4:6)—among the founders or proto-founders of the rabbinic movement is in my mind undisputable; that the early rabbinic movement's legal traditions included demonstrably Pharisaic legal positions over against Saddu-cean ones is also reasonably well supported by evidence. But the notion that the early rabbinic movement was, more or less, the Pharisaic movement translated into the late first, second, and third centuries is far from clear. In ch. 5 I will discuss some Pharisaic notions as part of what was "culturally current" for the early rabbis and their contemporary Judah-ites. But it is beyond the ken of this book to attempt fully to sort out the historical relationship of the Pharisaic movement and the early rabbinic movement. For a full, fairly comprehensive range of scholarly analyses about who/what the Pharisees were, see the many essays in Neusner and Childton, *In Quest.*

9. Chapter 5 will discuss, as relevant social and cultural antecedents to the profile of the early rabbis, the emerging tendency in the late Hellenistic period in the land of Israel to meld the image, role, and authority of the scribe and the sage, specifically as authoritative purveyors of instructions deemed consistent with the demands of To-rah. Recent and compelling scholarship on these late Hellenistic developments may be found in the work of Elisa Uusimäki; see her "Rise of the Sage," *Lived Wisdom*, "Maskil," *Turning Proverbs towards Torah.*

10. See Lightstone, "Mishnah Kiddushin 4:1–8."

11. Mishnah Horayot 3:8.

to do with the early rabbinic movement's members, the names of many dozens of whom are known to us from literary sources produced by the rabbis themselves. So, it is hard to know why all of the departed designated in this manner on their epitaphs have been so honored and what was meant by use of the honorific.[12]

There is, however, no such ambiguity at all concerning another early use of the honorific title "rabbi." Those familiar with (the canonical) Christian Gospels will recall that Jesus is sometimes addressed in the Gospel stories by those drawn to him and his teachings as "rabbi."[13] Whether, historically speaking, Jesus was actually so addressed by anyone is beside the point. More to the point is this; these stories in the canonical Gospels provide early *literary* evidence from Judah-ic circles of the use of the term "rabbi" as an honorific—earlier than any rabbinic text. So in the period in which in the Gospel writers composed their texts (in the last several decades of the first century CE and the early second century), one use of the honorific form of address Rabbi So-and-So in Judah-ic circles generally serves (perhaps among other early usages of the honorific) to denote and *accept* the person so addressed as an authoritative source of instruction and wisdom, which is exactly what these Gospel writers seek to communicate about Jesus and his teachings.

In sum, from the earliest era of the rabbinic movement, almost two millennia ago, up to every modern, twenty-first-century form of rabbinic Judaism, a self-selected cadre of persons addressed one another and (eventually) were addressed by other Jews as rabbi (literally, "my master," in the sense of "my teacher"). These sages' adoption of this nomenclature was, in effect, to claim to be authoritative sources for authentic instruction and interpretation. In what? In how to live a life as a Jew in accordance with the demands (or the "Way," the halakha) of Torah. Again, if anything stands out that is unique to rabbinic Judaism in comparison to other types of Judaism

12. S. Cohen, "Epigraphical Rabbis." See Lapin, "Epigraphical Rabbis." In regard to the wider use in Roman and Byzantine times of the use of the honorific *rabbi* as a form of respectful address, I am inclined to consider as a possible parallel the French form of address *monsieur*. In modern times, every male is respectfully addressed as Monsieur So-and-So, even though the term's origins are clearly tied to addressing one's feudal masters (whether lay or ecclesiastic) as "mon sieur" ("my lord"). Not infrequently in societies, in my view, courtesy has involved extending the use of honorifics for addressing one's superiors to addressing one's peers. Among late nineteenth and early twentieth-century Jews of Eastern Europe, in many communities, all adult males were addressed as Reb So-and-So. "Reb" is derived from "rabbi." But clearly a (small) minority of all adult males of these communities were rabbis.

13. See, e.g., John 1:38, 1:49, 3:2, 3:26, 4:31, 6:25, 9:2, 11:8, 20:16; Matt 23:7–8, 26:25, 26:49; Mark 10:51; 14:45. The Gospel of John seems to have a greater penchant for having Jesus addressed as Rabbi Jesus than do the Synoptic Gospels.

since (and even prior to) the advent of the rabbinic movement, it is the role and authority of the rabbi. Such Judaic institutions as the synagogue, communal prayer, refraining from work-related activities on Sabbaths and festivals, dietary restrictions, public readings and exposition of Scriptures, endogamy, ritual purification by immersion, circumcision, and many other aspects of what is commonly recognized as rabbinic Judaism—*none* of this was *invented* by the members of early rabbinic movement.[14] For example, Roman imperial-period Jewish communities in the Greco-Roman diaspora engaged in all or most of this, and they seem never to have heard of (let alone recognized the authority of) a rabbi until (possibly) the fifth century or the sixth century CE. Even so, the members of the early rabbinic movement, as rabbis, had much to say about these Judaic institutions, in their actual or hoped-for roles as authors of authentic, authoritative instruction in the Way (halakha) of life lived in accordance with Torah.

If, then, as just asserted, what is uniquely or distinctively rabbinic about rabbinic Judaism at its inception in the second and third centuries CE is the role of the rabbi, actual or claimed, then one will want to ask, *What were the early rabbis?* So, I will now turn our attention to what I think is the significance of posing precisely this question, as opposed to others.

14. It is commonplace for modern authors writing for the Jewish community's edification to paint the early rabbis as the saviors of Judaism by having modified biblical Judaism in order to adapt to the destruction in 70 CE of the Jerusalem temple and the demise of its cult. Historically, this is patently false. A viable Judaism without recourse to the Jerusalem temple existed in the diaspora (and in all probability even in other districts of the land of Israel) before Jerusalem's destruction. Moreover, diaspora Judaism ticked along quite well after the temple's demise without the benefit of interventions from the early rabbis. Rabbinic influence seems barely to register in the Greco-Roman diaspora until the fifth or sixth century CE. See Lightstone, *Commerce of the Sacred*, "Roman Diaspora Judaism," and "Is it Meaningful."

Although the early rabbis did not invent a Judaism without the temple, they certainly (1) adopted what was largely already established, (2) claimed to be authoritative arbiters of its detailed prescriptions and proscriptions, and (3) further adapted it, when they saw the need. The question remains: For this early period, who was listening to the rabbis apart from disciples of the rabbis? My long-considered answer is this: not that many before the fifth or sixth centuries CE in the Near East and Levant, or the seventh or eighth centuries CE at further remove. After that, the rabbis' authority was significant and well on the road to being nearly monopolistic in Jewish communities. I have more to say about this in ch. 2, when I write about the resisters to "rabbinization" in the early medieval period. See also my *In the Seat of Moses*, ch. 2 (or the appendix to this volume).

Why "What" (Were the Early Rabbis)?

I began this chapter and this book by posing two sets of intertwined questions about the earliest, sufficiently well-documented, self-formed, and institutionalized cadre of the rabbis or, as they referred to themselves collectively, the sages (*hakhamim*, pl.) and the disciples of the sages (*talmidei hahkamim*, pl). Restating those questions differently, this book seeks to explore *what* that group's members' shared, collective social profile and identity was, within the context of Judah-ite society and culture in the land of Israel in the latter second century CE and/or during the first half or so of the third. And as a complement to this first focus on *what* the early rabbis were, I have specified another task; namely, to explore *what other* (antecedent or contemporary) socially and culturally authoritative models may have been drawn upon by the early rabbis or, if not explicitly appealed to by them, might nevertheless have rendered the early rabbis' social identity, professional profile, and specific aspirations plausible and legitimate to a Judah-ite audience. So, why my obsession with "what"? And what is the alternative to this focus?

In this volume, I use "what" as a shorthand or cipher for a particular approach to understanding the earliest rabbinic movement in its nascent or formative period. That approach I differentiate from others, which I will designate by another interrogative pronoun, "who," again used as just a shorthand signal. Let me elaborate.

Imagine that I were writing a book that addressed either of the following questions: *Who* were the founders of the early Jesus movement(s)? Or *who* were the architects of the Roman imperial system of administration and rule? What would the readers of such a book rightly expect? They would certainly expect names of key figures in either instance. But readers would anticipate an account that does not stop there. Readers would want to know something of the *biographies* of these key figures, their *roles* and *actions* in the early Jesus movement(s) and in the emerging and maturing Roman imperial system respectively. And it is a short leap indeed, and a logical one, to expect a fulsome account of the *historical*, institutional development of either the early Jesus movement(s) or the Roman imperial system. In other words, my who questions would elicit studies focussed on biography and developmental history, insofar as the evidence permits one to reconstruct these with either confidence or appropriate caveats.

Now, not only modern authors would produce works of biography and/or history in response to who-like questions about early Christianity or the Roman Empire; importantly for modern historians and biographers, ancient authors did so as well.

Is this not what the canonical Gospels (on the surface) do for Jesus (although via such accounts they also hoped to indicate what they believed Jesus to be and why this mattered)? The book of Acts also addresses issues of biography and/or history in its account of the acts of the first generation of some of the early Jesus movement's leaders, especially Paul, after Jesus' execution. In the fourth century, Eusebius wrote a full-blown *Church History*, providing an account of the church's development under the guidance of key historical figures, viewed retrospectively as the purveyors and architects of Christian orthodoxy, from Eusebius's fourth-century perspective, of course.

So too, there is no shortage of Roman writers from the imperial period addressing issues of *biography* and *history*—who-type accounts. For example, Suetonius, writing in the second century CE, provided his contemporaries and posterity with biographies of the twelve Caesars (*De vita Caesarum*, 121 CE)—about Julius Caesar and the first eleven Roman emperors. Writing during the reign of Hadrian, Suetonius thereby undertakes to document the rise and development of imperial governance from its proto-founder, Julius Caesar, and its officially recognized founder, Augustus (aka Octavian Caesar). Among many other examples, one may also point to Tacitus's *Histories* and *Annals* for accounts of the history of the early Roman Empire, and to Livy's *Ab urbe condita* for a history of the Roman Republic's founding, development, and transition to imperial rule under Augustus. Livy's history is rife with legends of Rome's earliest development presented as history, as well as with idealizations of the principles and shared values of the citizens of the early Roman Republic.[15] These extolled values and principles, in Livy's view, had eroded considerably by the time Augustus implemented imperial rule. Livy, ironically perhaps, depicts Augustus as a restorer of traditional Roman ideals, rather than as the destroyer of the republican system. So in addressing who-type questions, Livy blatantly (but also other ancient historians such as Suetonius or Tacitus) had "axes to grind," just as did the Gospel writers, Luke in his book of Acts, and Eusebius in his *Church History*. All

15. In this regard, I cannot resist mentioning ch. 9 of Robert Graves's famous early twentieth-century pseudepigraphic work *I, Claudius*. Graves writes as if the Roman emperor Claudius were writing his autobiography. Chapter 9 is a gem for any teacher of Roman history or user of Roman-era historians' works, because in it Graves composes a conversation involving a young Claudius and the ancient historians Pollio and Livy. During this fictitious conversation, Livy explains/justifies his tendency to "put words into the mouths" of historical persons, so that they are portrayed as expressing the social and moral values and dispositions Livy believes his histories ought to instil in its readers. In Graves's book, Pollio takes great exception to this form of historiography, and in so doing is effectively cautioning Graves's *modern* readership about what *ancient* writers of "history" are actually doing.

of these ancient authors have (re) constructed events and biographical accounts to serve their respective purposes.

What types of axes are these? These writings are accounts that justify
and legitimate specific social or political formations, the members of which
these ancient authors are addressing in an effort to express and/or shore up
their sense of what they share (or ought to share) as a group. Does this mean
that every historical (-like) or biographical (-like) claim in such ancient writings is necessarily "false history"? No, it does not. But it does mean that the
social or political purposes served by these writings for their respective audiences are the grinders to which their authors put their axes and their "historical facts," false or otherwise. The driver of matters is not the (alleged) facts
adduced in these histories or biographies, but rather the overall explicit or
implicit social or political ends of the histories or biographies, to which the
(alleged) facts render service. And this is, in effect, to recognize that underlying all is the process of social formation. These last three sentences provide
an apt segue from the works of ancient authors to those of modern scholars
using these ancient authors' writings as evidence.

Modern scholars who ask who-type questions that impel towards
scholarship focused on biographical and/or historical accounts must rely,
to a significant degree, upon the accounts of ancient writers, among other
types of evidence, to do their work. And here is the rub! Modern scholars must carefully assess the *value* of what ancient writers provide. How?
First, by understanding the motives, purposes, and intended audiences of
these ancient authors, and the social purposes—and the processes of social
formation—that underlie these ancient writings. Second, by ferreting out
how these ancient authors' perspectives and purposes (may have) affected
their accounts in possibly tendentious ways. And, third, by evaluating the
evidentiary bases or sources used by ancient writers. That is, on what bases
do these ancients claim to know what they claim to know? Just by posing
these three questions, a startling proposition becomes evident: *It is often
easier (and sometimes more appropriate) for modern scholars to use these
ancient writers' works as evidence for the shared views and social identity
of the authors' social circles than to figure out what in their texts amounts
to valid historical claims.* Once again, this is not to say that such ancient
texts are devoid of valid historical claims. Far from it! It is, however, often
a difficult (if not sometimes impossible) scholarly pursuit to sort out what
is historically valid, what are outright fabrications (by the ancient author or
by the author's sources), and what are (somewhere in between) idealized or
stylized portrayals in service of the authors' or the authors' circles' social
or political ends. And that is why, by contrast, modern scholars can safely

approach an ancient text with the confidence that the text serves its author and its author's circle in some meaningful manner.

What now of asking who-type questions concerning the early rabbinic movement from its inception in the land of Israel under Roman rule sometime after 70 CE (likely in the second century) to near the mid-third century CE? On the surface, the modern scholar has both a plethora and a dearth of evidence from the ancient world about the early rabbinic movement.

The early rabbinic movement has left us a significant body of its literature. However, not one document of this extensive literature, written between the end of the second century CE and the beginning of the seventh, provides anything like a gospel, a biography, or a history proffering accounts either of the development of the early rabbinic movement from its inception to near the rise of Islam or of "lives" of its important figures. The first attempt to produce a history of the rabbinic movement, its literature, and its seminal personages is that of the tenth-century rabbi Sherira (bar Hanina) Gaon, the head of one of the major Babylonian-Mesopotamian rabbinic academies. (We will discuss in ch. 2 what Sherira does in his history and to what ends.) So, what literary evidence do we possess from the early rabbinic movement?

The earliest (and arguably, the most influential) text produced by and for the early rabbinic movement's members is the Mishnah, a legal "study"[16] composed in the land of Israel around the turn of the third century CE (let us say, no later than c. 220–230 CE). Other collections and compositions of primarily legal traditions and discussions (formulated, preserved, and/ or brought together over the next four hundred or so years to aid, reflect, or model engaged Mishnah study by the rabbis) stem from the land of Israel and, later, from Babylonian rabbinic circles.[17] By name, the more prominent among these additional early works are the Tosefta (c. 250–425), the halakhic Midrashim (c. 250–425), the Jerusalem Talmud (c. 400 and, its name notwithstanding, produced in Tiberias in the Galilee), and the Babylonian Talmud (c. 600). (In a companion introductory book, entitled *In the Seat of Moses*, I have provided nonspecialists with a "gateway" to understanding these documents.) All of these texts constitute what the rabbinic movement of the medieval and modern eras views as the principal early documents of the halakha, that is, they deal with the "Way" to live and act in accordance with Torah, as interpreted and understood by ancient rabbis.[18]

16. But by no means a halakhic legal "code" in literary terms; but more about this follows in ch. 3. For a more extensive account of the literary nature of Mishnah see my *In the Seat of Moses*, chs. 3 and 4.

17. For an economical survey of these documents see my *In the Seat of Moses*, ch. 3.

18. As noted earlier, in this sense, halakha is a close lexical cognate of Sharia, as

The Mishnah, Tosefta, and the halakhic Midrashim are all under-stood/believed/deemed—the choice of the appropriate verb is, frankly, fraught with methodological issues—by the early rabbis (and by rabbis thereafter until the modern period) accurately to preserve traditions ex-clusively from rabbinic masters living up to c. 220–230 CE. Rabbis who flourished in this period are collectively called the Tannaim (*Tanna*, sg.; from the Aramaic verb root meaning "to repeat/teach") by later genera-tions of the rabbinic movement (and by modern scholars). The Tannaim, understood as the founding (and therefore most authoritative) generations of the rabbis, are distinguished from immediately subsequent generations, the Amoraim (*Amora*, sg.; from the verb root meaning "to say/speak"). The Amoraim are the early rabbinic masters who flourished after the Tan-naim and up to the last decades of the fourth century CE in the land of Israel and the final years of the fifth century in Mesopotamia-Babylonia. The Tannaitic period (and especially the late Tannaitic era, when Mishnah was produced), together with the first several decades of the Amoraic pe-riod (when Mishnah was initially received and studied within early rab-binic circles), is precisely the focus of this book. Moreover, analyses given in the compositions of the two Talmuds regularly adduce extra-mishnaic traditions (that is, traditions not contained in the Mishnah) that the Tal-muds nonetheless portray as Tannaitic, namely, as dating from the same, early period of the rabbinic movement as the substance of Mishnah itself. Many, but by no means all, of these extra-mishnaic traditions in fact have parallels in Tosefta and the halakhic Midrashim.

There is another body of early rabbinic literature that modern schol-ars have in hand. It is the literature of early rabbinic aggada or haggadah. These documents present very short stories, parables, and sayings meant to convey moral lessons, belief stances, and ways of being in the world as a rabbi or a Jew. In some of these documents, like Bereshit (Genesis) Rab-bah, the stories and sayings are portrayed as being rooted in the exegesis of Scripture, and are organized not topically but "scripturally," that is, as if they were expositions of Scripture's verses (often taken in their order). When the latter is the case, such a document is called a work of "Midrash aggada" within ancient and traditional rabbinic circles. Midrash (from the Biblical Hebrew verb root *drsh*, meaning "to search/inquire") is a distinc-tive genre of exposition of Scripture.[19]

---

used in Islam to designate its normative legal tradition.

19. Paul Mandel, in *Origins of Midrash*, convincingly argues that the verb *drsh* (from which the term *midrash* is derived) was not understood within Judah-ite or early rabbinic circles to refer primarily to Scripture-based exposition/interpretation (in which multiple interpretations of Scripture are adduced) until the mid- to late

Many passages of aggada and Midrash aggada contain stories and sayings in which the (alleged) dramatis personae or speakers are rabbis from the formative period ending c. 220–230 CE, that is, Tannaim. And two works of aggada, Avot and Avot de Rabbi Natan, convey aggadic traditions that are presented as exclusively Tannaitic in origin.

Significantly, then, a great many of these Tannaitic traditions of halakha and aggada bear attributions to early rabbis *by name*. Rabbi X says this. Or Rabbi X says this, but Rabbi Y says that. Or the following incident happened under these circumstances, and Rabbi Z acted or ruled in such a manner. From Mishnah (and Tosefta), for example, the names of about ten to eleven dozen early rabbinic figures (Tannaim) are known to us from the formative period of the rabbinic movement up to c. 230 CE—to all of whom halakhic views on this or that matter are attributed. In fact, to *each* of some of these rabbinic personages, such as Rabbi Akiva, Rabbi Meir, Rabbi Judah ben Ilai, or Rabbi Yose ben Halafta (all mid-second century CE), many dozens of views are attributed in Mishnah alone, scattered as they are throughout the Mishnah text. And biographical-like incidents are recounted about many Tannaim in narrative aggadic passages and documents.

At first glance, then, the modern scholar of the early rabbinic movement interested in who-type questions, that is, in matters of biography and history, has a richesse of ancient sources upon which to base her or his scholarship. And indeed, from the mid-nineteenth through three-quarters (at least) of the twentieth century, many renowned historians and intellectual historians of Early Judaism and of the early rabbinic movement undertook such biographical/historical work on the basis of these sources, sometimes interpreted together with evidence of the material culture and/or other documentary evidence of the first several centuries CE in the Levant generally and the land of Israel specifically. To name just a few examples, scholarly biographies or intellectual biographies were produced concerning Rabbi Akiva, Rabbi Eliezer ben Hyrcanus, and Rabbi Yohanan ben Zakkai.[20] And modern intellectual histories of the early rabbinic movement were written;

Amoraic period (*Origins of Midrash*, 289–305). According to Mandel, in Judahite culture before the rabbinic period, *drsh* more broadly referred to the search for oracular divine knowledge and later to the scribes' search for divine knowledge as expressed especially in authentic law (*Origins of Midrash*, 289–93), from which its usage expanded to refer to authentic instruction or exposition, especially on law/halakha, often to an assembled audience (*Origins of Midrash*, 169–288). More will be said about *drsh* as an early rabbinic skill in ch. 4.

20. E.g., Finkelstein, *Akiba*; Gilat, *R. Eliezer ben Hyrcanus*; Neusner, *Life of Rabbi Yohanan ben Zakkai*.

among the most ambitious and erudite of these may be counted those of
Ephraim E. Urbach and of George Foote Moore.[21]

But over the last three decades of the twentieth century a slow-moving
and *still very much uneven* sea change had begun to take place on many
parallel fronts in the modern scholarly use of such early rabbinic sources.
This sea change is the result of evolution on at least three fronts, singly or
in combination:

1. A growing understanding in some academic circles of the fundamental importance of *each* of these ancient texts' authors' purposes and
   literary conventions to any assessment and scholarly use of the content
   of these documents

2. A growing appreciation of the embeddedness of these early rabbinic
   authors in the social, cultural, and literary currents (both antecedent
   and contemporary) outside of the rabbinic circles

3. The articulation and appreciation of increasingly well-formulated
   theoretical constructs in which to view issues on fronts 1 and 2

That this sea change, however uneven, has become increasingly
evident in the modern, scholarly assessment and use of ancient rabbinic
evidence in addressing who-like questions should hardly be surprising.
Why? These same developments had already begun to significantly affect
how scholars of early Christianity used early Christian literature (including,
or especially, the Gospels) in historical research about Jesus and about the
early Jesus movement(s). That sea change began, according to many, with
Albert Schweitzer's scholarship at the turn of the twentieth century.[22] And
it may be traced on a course through Rudolph Bultmann's writings (also
first articulated in the 1920s) on the use of standardized literary forms in
the Gospels.[23] That scholarly-critical trend attained important, more fully
formed theoretical and methodological expressions in the late 1980s; in this
regard, the work of Burton Mack on the Gospel of Mark is exemplary.[24]
Mack's theoretical take and his analyses of the Gospels focus on the reciprocal relationship between Gospel writing and social formation.

---

21. Urbach, *Sages*; Moore, *Judaism in First Centuries*.

22. See, e.g., Cameron, "Labours of Burton Mack," esp. 28, regarding Albert Schweitzer. Albert Schweitzer's ground-breaking *The Quest of the Historical Jesus* was first
published (in German) in 1906.

23. I refer to Rudolph Bultmann's seminal work *The History of the Synoptic Tradition*, first published (in German) in 1921.

24. Mack, *Myth of Innocence*. See also Cameron, "Labours of Burton Mack"; Mack,
"Quest."

Any account of the parallel sea change in the use of early rabbinic evidence for biographical/historical scholarship must certainly mention Jacob Neusner, a prominent and still very much controversial figure, even after his passing in 2016. For Neusner, the process began in 1970, when he published a book, *Development of a Legend,* in which (remarkably) he completely repudiates his own previously published work, *A Life of Yohanan ben Zakkai.* The latter had followed, as I indicated above, an already well-trodden scholarly path of modern historical and biographical accounts of early rabbinism, early rabbinic Judaism, and seminal early rabbinic figures. Of the three fronts of the sea change that I enumerated earlier, Neusner set himself the task of advancing on front number 1, that is, he increasingly advocated for a growing understanding of the fundamental importance of each of these ancient rabbinic texts' authors' purposes and these texts' dominant literary conventions to any assessment and scholarly use of these documents' content.[25] Later, he called this his "documentary" approach and followed that path for the remainder of his lifetime.

Now, this is not the place to write an account of the state and evolution of modern historical/biographical studies of the early rabbinic movement. Nor is it the place to discuss fully the limitations of the use of early rabbinic documents for such enterprises. And it is certainly not to say that early rabbinic literature is devoid of historically valid evidence either about the lives and teachings of early rabbinic figures or about the development of the rabbinic movement. However, it very much *is* to say that in these regards this literature contains a mélange of historical reminiscences, fabrications (that is, legend and myth), and idealizations; and frequently these texts' sources have been reformulated in accordance with the literary canons and conventions governing the documents in which they appear— all this in service to the ends and purposes of their authorships and their authorships' circles. I have written much on this front in other works, at least one of which is intended for a nonspecialist audience, that is, in *In the Seat of Moses,* chapter 2.[26] In that chapter, I undertook two tasks. (1) I laid out the (severe) limitations of our ancient sources for addressing modern scholarly questions about the history of the early rabbinic movement or of the roles in that history of rabbinism's early, prominent figures. Simply put, individual items of "evidence," seemingly proffering material for historical

---

25. I say "increasingly" because you will not find these methodological stances anywhere near fully formed in his *Development of a Legend.* That easily took another decade.

26. Lightstone, *In the Seat of Moses,* 19–57. I address these issues for an academic audience in several publications, among them (and more recently) in ch. 1 of Fishbane et al., *Exploring Mishnah's World(s),* 1–24; and "Naming Names."

or biographical accounts leading to a history of the early movement, suffer from a number of deficiencies, to several of which I have alluded. (2) Based on what I there articulated as the limitations of our evidence, I, nonetheless, proffered my best guess or estimate of what may be responsibly said about the historical origins and development of the early rabbinic movement; that is, I provided my cautious (or perhaps, at times, incautious) rendering in response to who-type questions. And for those who wish to read such an account as background or as a supplement to what is offered in this volume, extracts of chapter 2 of *In the Seat of Moses* appear as an appendix to this book, for your convenience. Beyond that account, I am, in my opinion, unable (and certainly unwilling) to proceed further, for both methodological and theoretical reasons.

So, in order to move forward (with a nonspecialist audience in mind), I take another path altogether in this book. As indicated at the outset of this section of our introductory chapter, I have characterized that path as one that addresses not who- but what-type questions: *What* were the early rabbis? Now, if the available evidence for addressing who-type questions places hurdles in front of one and imposes (severe) limitations on what can responsibly be achieved, why do I think that transitioning to what-type questions will not land us in the same straits for the same reasons? The answer lies in the *way* I wish to address what were the early rabbis. Let me explain, using Burton Mack's lessons from analysis of the Gospel of Mark as a point of departure.

The insights I have taken away or extrapolated from works such as Burton Mack's, *Myth of Innocence*, are these six.

1. As already stated, and as Mack asserts about the Gospel of Mark, some/many texts stemming from and serving ancient groups are part and parcel of these groups' processes of social formation.

Revered *texts* form important bases (in addition to other things, like shared rituals and norms) for the coalescence of a "group life," a shared group identity, and social solidarity/cohesion. Therefore, the group's specific social formation and identity is, in a very real sense, the origin of the text and conditions its content, and *vice versa*. In other words, the social formation produces the text; the text helps (re) produce the social formation. For Mack, this process is characterized as "mythmaking," not in the sense of expressing falsehoods, but rather in fashioning mutually upholding/reinforcing dynamics between text/story, on the one hand, and the requisites of social formation and cohesion, on the other.[27]

27. See Mack, *Myth of Innocence*; Cameron, "Labours of Burton Mack."

To these notions I would marry several others. In my opinion:

2. The formation of groups and the cementing of their sense of mutual belonging requires frequent, structured interactions among members of the group, and the production and institutionalized study of core, revered texts may provide one/some of the important ways in which members of nascent groups interact meaningfully with one another.

3. The social identity of a group must be experienced by the group's members as inherently and particularly credible/plausible and legitimate.

4. To experience that shared sense of legitimacy, beyond that provided by some "foundational" text alone, it is often the case that in service of defining a compelling social identity, the group (explicitly or implicitly) appeals to, or borrows from, established "models of legitimacy" with evident "social currency" in the group's cultural, social, and/or political environment.

That is, the group's self-understanding as a distinctive social formation is rarely created ex nihilo, without reference to any already well-established cultural norms and models that are given a "makeover" in service to their new social formation. Moreover:

5. Those norms and models may be of two sorts: (a) those with *long-standing historical* currency in the group's cultural setting, since the authoritative past is often seen prima facie as legitimating the present; and (b) those with *contemporary* currency, that is, they are (or resemble) an accepted mode of social identity in the group's immediate or larger contemporary social, cultural, and/or political environment.

In a related vein:

6. When individuals seek to join a social formation, with its "characterizing" identity, these persons must feel supported and valued for taking on or mastering the elements of that identity; that is, the individual's efforts, sacrifices, and newly acquired traits or skills must be *concretely recognized and rewarded* by one or more socially immediate and socially relevant "reference groups," persons to whom individuals look for concrete forms of affirmation.[28]

28. In *A Myth of Innocence*, Mack argues that while Mark's author fashions a Jesus "mythology" expressing the social formation and shared identity of a particularly Markan Christian community, Mark's author has had to reply on antecedent sources that reflect alternative mythologizations of Jesus, serving alternative social formations of the early Jesus movements. But it seems to me to be self-evident that each of these alternative mythologizations explicitly or implicitly borrows from or

How do these six insights or propositions translate into my preoccupations in this book—to provide an *interested* readership of nonspecialists with a volume that addresses the question *what* were the early rabbis? Well, we do not possess a "Gospel" of Rabbi X or Rabbi Y. Nor do we possess an early rabbinic history from a rabbinic counterpart of the fourth-century Christian author, Eusebius. But we do have another type of evidence contemporary with the early rabbinic movement, a document with no less a compelling place/role in early rabbinic social formation as Mark's Gospel had within the Markan community's social formation. That document is the Mishnah.

Mishnah (c. 200), as mentioned, is the first (currently extant?) text of the early rabbinic group. Moreover, and as I shall discuss further in chapters 2 and 3, we know without a smidgen of doubt that the devoted, engaged study of Mishnah was arguably *the most important common, inner-group activity of rabbis and would-be rabbis in the early rabbinic movement from the time of Mishnah's production and for the next four hundred years.* More than anything else of importance that I can discern from the evidence, this is what rabbis and prospective rabbis *did together with one another.* Indeed, soon after Mishnah's promulgation, the members of the early rabbinic cadre in the third century CE begin to articulate a legitimating mythology about the origins of Mishnah's content and about the special intellectual pedigree of Mishnah's framer(s). Hence, as the early rabbis' first, shared magnum opus, Mishnah's production and promulgation as a privileged and increasingly mythologized object of devoted study also bespeaks of the attainment of a level of institutionalized social formation of the rabbinic movement, for which there is no earlier, similar, substantive attestation (just as Mark's Gospel is the earliest, substantial evidence about the Markan community). And whatever the literary-historical origins of Tosefta (c. 250–425), the Jerusalem Talmud (c. 400), and the Babylonian Talmud (c. 600), or of their constituent sources, it is undoubtedly the case

---

appeals to models with established cultural currency with Judah-ic and/or Greco-Roman society. So, Mark's Gospel is a mythologization of established, already current mythologizations! And each alternative mythologization presents a Jesus that would be recognized as possessing an air of authentic leadership in the land of Israel and adjacent areas in the first and early second centuries CE: the compelling (reforming) teacher, a new Moses and/or Elijah, the ultimate cult sacrifice, etc. Each alternative, therefore, appeals implicitly to contemporary reference groups, who in the Gospel author's estimate ought to value such a depiction of "what" Jesus is and, therefore, (or so it is hoped) ought to value the Jesus community whose identity is founded on this mythologization. It is not necessary that—indeed, it is beside that point whether— any of these is "who" Jesus actually was. They are "what" he was made out to be by various Jesus-movement communities with various social identities. Mark's version then informed the depictions of other Gospel writers.

that these documents were produced in service of Mishnah study. So even the production of these texts serves to confirm that for four centuries, Mishnah study functioned as a highly valued group, and group identity-forming, activity within early rabbinic circles.

So, to drive home the point at the risk of repetition, Mishnah's production and Mishnah study were *both* socially formative of the early rabbinic movement. And Mishnah and Mishnah study, together with rapidly emerging mythologies about them, are formative of early rabbinic identity *at the earliest stage* for which we have concrete documentary evidence of any kind for and from the early rabbinic movement, that is, sometime in the latter Tannaitic period (and the first decades of the Amoraic era). And so this is the era upon which this book focuses. Consequently, the Mishnah is a kind of founding mythology of the rabbinic movement, and study of Mishnah is a formative "ritual" of early rabbinic identity formation, as well as the occasion for rabbis to come together in groups. For these reasons, a combination of (1) the evidence of Mishnah, (2) the evident demands (or effects) of Mishnah study as a shared group ritual of sorts, and (3) the early rabbis' mythologizations of Mishnah (and/or its content) as a ne plus ultra is our basis for asking and addressing the question: *What* were the early rabbis?

When, in the course of this book, we have in hand some answers addressing aspects of this first question (the tasks primarily of chs. 2, 3, and 4, comprising pt. 1 of this volume), we proceed (principally in chs. 5 and 6, constituting pt. 2) to address the other set of queries which, as I have stated, drive this introductory work. The latter set I may now reframe as what were the historical and contemporary models with social, cultural, or political currency available to the early rabbis, and explicitly or implicitly appealed to by them, in order to establish the *plausibility* and *legitimacy* of what they were, and what they wished others to see them as like? For without a clear sense of the foundations of its legitimacy in their own eyes and (potentially) in the eyes of others, no social formation, let alone one that characterizes its members as masters, sages, and disciples of sages, will long endure. And so, this introductory chapter has returned to the very issues/questions with which it began and that steer the remainder of the book.

I wish to conclude this introductory chapter with the assurances and a commitment expressed at the outset of this chapter and in the preface. This book relies on specialists' scholarly research, some of which is my own, and much of which has been done by others who, over the last three to four decades in particular, have produced compelling works that, by my definitions (even if not theirs), address what-type questions concerning the early rabbinic movement. In these regards, this volume has been significantly informed by the writings of such scholars as Lee I. Levine, Catherine Hezser,

Haim Lapin, Sigalit Ben-Zion, Stuart Miller, Meir Bar-Ilan, Paul Mandel, Elisa Uusimäki, and Richard Hidary, to name just a few of those whose works figure prominently in this volume's footnotes and bibliography. That said, I have expressly committed to you, the readers, to write this book for nonspecialists. I assume no prior knowledge about its particular subject matter, only an interest in better understanding religiously informed communities and/or curiosity about the general time, region, and social and cultural world in which both the early rabbinic group and early Christianity developed under Roman imperial rule in the aftermath of tumultuous social, political, and cultural upheaval in the land of Israel after two failed rebellions against Rome. I promise that there will be few (if any) methodological and theoretical discussions beyond this first introductory chapter, and, to the degree that I can, I will avoid the technical jargon of specialists. And with this said, we shall in the next chapter jump into *what* the early rabbis were.

PART I

What the Early Rabbis Were, Thought They Were, or Wished to Be

Mishnah and the Social Formation of the "Mishnanians"

2

The Myth of Mishnah and
Early Rabbinic Self-Definition

THERE'S SOMETHING
ABOUT MISHNAH

As articulated in chapter 1, this book aims to address questions concerning *what* the early rabbis were as a group in their formative stage up to c. 220–230 CE, a date marking the approximate end of the Tannaitic era, and in the first several decades that immediately followed of the earliest Amoraic era.[1] It is toward the end of this period that the members of the

---

1. As a reminder, *tanna'im* (*tanna*, sg.; from the verb root *tn'*, "to repeat," "to teach," or "to learn") is an Aramaic noun used in classical rabbinic circles to denote rabbinic authorities up to the era of Mishnah's production and initial promulgation; therefore, modern writers call this period the Tannaitic period. Rabbinic literature, furthermore, classifies as Tannaitic *all* teachings attributed to authorities believed to have lived in the Tannaitic period, even when these traditions appear in rabbinic texts and compilations produced *after* Mishnah. Some of these post-mishnaic texts and compilations are believed in rabbinic circles to be *entirely* comprised of alleged Tannaitic teachings; a case in point is Tosefta, which rabbinic tradition attributes to Rabbi Hiyya, a rabbi of the first half of the third century CE, that is, of the generation immediately following Rabbi Judah the Patriarch, to whom the production of Mishnah is attributed sometime soon after Mishnah was produced. (The actual date of the production of Tosefta is another matter entirely.) Tannaitic teachings appearing in documents other than Mishnah are often referred to in classical rabbinic circles as *beraitot* (*baraita*, sg.), an Aramaic term meaning "[Tannaitic traditions that are] outside," that is, "outside" the Mishnah. So in traditional rabbinic circles, Tosefta is considered to be a collection of *beraitot*. *Beraitot* are also routinely adduced as authoritative sources, second in authority only

33

rabbinic movement promulgated among themselves their first collectively produced magnum opus, the Mishnah, a legal study of Torah-related norms, which oeuvre was quickly accepted as authoritative within early rabbinic circles. And, as stated in the previous chapter,[2] for the next four centuries, the devoted, engaged study of Mishnah was the most important, inner-group activity of members of the rabbinic movement.

This central place of Mishnah study in the early rabbinic curriculum is attested by many different types of ancient evidence. Let us start with the fact that the early rabbinic authorships of Tosefta (c. 250–425 CE), the Jerusalem Talmud (c. 400 CE), and the Babylonian Talmud (c. 600 CE) have all organized their constituent materials as a kind of supplement to, and/or commentary and analysis of, a proportion of Mishnah's tractates.[3] Each of these post-mishnaic, early rabbinic works takes the Mishnah tractates' "chapters"[4] and constituent passages in their order as its organizing principle. And in

---

to Mishnah citations, in the compositions that comprise the Jerusalem and Babylonian Talmuds (produced c. 400 CE and c. 600 CE, respectively).

Classical rabbinic authorities and modern scholars routinely contrast the *tanna'im*, the Tannaitic period and Tannaitic literature, with the *amora'im*, the Amoraic period and Amoraic literature. The *amora'im* (*amora*, sg.; from the Aramaic/Hebrew verb root *'mr*, meaning "to say") were, in classical rabbinic parlance, those rabbinic authorities of the generations immediately after the *tanna'im*, up to the latter fourth century CE in the land of Israel (soon after which the Jerusalem Talmud was composed), and up to the end of the fifth century in Mesopotamia-Babylonia (after which the Babylonian Talmud was composed). Both Talmuds' constituent compositions, therefore, contain what its authorships understood to be Tannaitic and Amoraic teachings and traditions, and these authorships usually use specific terminology to indicate that a tradition about to be cited is (believed to be) Tannaitic in origin. All of these distinctions are more fully explained in my *In the Seat of Moses*, chs. 2 and 3.

2. This is more fully argued in my companion volume to this one, *In the Seat of Moses*, 61–67, esp. 65ff.

3. Tosefta treats about 95 percent of Mishnah's tractates, and each of the two Talmuds cover about 60 percent of Mishnah's tractates (although not the same 60 percent).

4. In the above sentence, I have placed the word "chapters" in what are often called scare quotes when referring to the internal divisions of early rabbinic documents. In doing this, I follow the practice of Jacob Neusner. Why do this? For several reasons. (1) Numbered chapter divisions, and even the enumerating of the passages within chapters, of early rabbinic texts seem to have been an innovation of medieval scribes. The earlier practice was to refer to a rabbinic text's principal, internal, chapter-like divisions by the key words in the opening sentence of the "chapter." (2) The enumerated chapter divisions appearing in medieval manuscripts (and perpetuated in the printed editions) sometimes do not coincide with the "chapter divisions" of the ancients or with the logical-topical internal divisions of the text in question. By the way, the same is true of enumerated chapter divisions of the Hebrew Bible. Hereafter, I will no longer place the word "chapter" in quotation marks, unless I mean to designate a logical-topical internal division of a rabbinic text, that is, a "chapter" that does not correspond with how the standard printed editions demarcate enumerated chapters.

the extant manuscripts of each, each names its own tractate after the corresponding Mishnah tractate. In other words, all of these early rabbinic oeuvres reflect, serve, aid, and/or model normative modes of Mishnah study. And one may add to this evidence the attestation of several early rabbinic passages, dating in all likelihood from between c. 230 CE and (at the latest) c. 500 CE, that explicitly list in priority order the core elements of the *ideal* rabbinic curriculum. In all of these passages, Mishnah study invariably appears second, that is, second only to the study of Scripture itself.[5]

Mishnah study (undertaken together with others and/or guided by a mentor) was at the core of the curriculum that made a would-be rabbi into a fully fledged rabbi. And lifelong Mishnah study, and mentoring rabbinic novices/students as one's disciples in the study of Mishnah, authenticated and elevated one's status as a fully fledged rabbi among one's rabbinic peers. So, Mishnah study was a (or *the*) quintessential early rabbinic activity, the significance of which exceeded that of an important intellectual pursuit. Rather, Mishnah study rose to the level of shared ritual (in the most positive sense of the word), that is, a shared practice that symbolized to its practitioners their communality and reinforced key aspects of their group identity.[6]

5. See, e.g., Avot 5:21 (missing in some medieval mss, according to Albeck, *Shishah Sidre Mishnah*, Neziqin, 501), Avot de Rabbi Natan (AVRN version a) 8:1, JT Megillah 4:1, JT Horayot 3:5, BT Bava Metzi'a 33a, BT Ketubbot 50a. Here are the elements of the early rabbinic core curriculum in the order in which they appear in these passages:

Avot 5:21: Scripture, Mishnah, and Talmud

AVRN (version a) 8:1: Scripture, Mishnah, legal midrash, and aggada

JT Megillah 4:1: Scripture, Mishnah, Talmud, and aggada

JT Horayot 3:5: Scripture, Mishnah teachings (*mishnayot*, pl.), *halakhah*, aggada, "the" Talmud, and *ha-tosefet*

BT Bava Metzi'a 33a: Scripture, Mishnah, Talmud

BT Ketubbot 50a: Scripture, Mishnah

So, in all of these passages Mishnah comes second in the curriculum, after the study of Scripture itself. Moreover, these passages either attest or imply that Mishnah's *authority* is exceeded only by that of Scripture (specifically, the Pentateuch). Indeed, Mishnah's superior authority to *all* other rabbinic traditions, whatever the source or genre, is assumed throughout the constituent compositions of both Talmuds.

6. This is demonstrated ably in a short narrative tradition preserved at BT Berakhot 8a. The story depicts a Babylonian rabbi of the early fourth century CE participating in a communal prayer service. At one point in the service, when the Torah scroll was being read aloud to the congregants, the rabbis' students/disciples observe that the rabbi is reciting Mishnah (by heart, it seems), rather than listening to the Torah being reading. In the story, his disciples express surprise, even shock. Upon which the rabbi intimates that Mishnah study is for the members of the rabbinic cadre what the hearing of the public reading of the Torah is for the synagogue participants at large. The Aramaic verb root used in BT Berakhot 8a (and elsewhere in BT) to mean (Mishnah) study is *grs*. Its

It stands to reason, then, that the social identity of the early rabbinic movement, as well as core features of the professional-like profile and skills that made one a rabbi, have much to do with Mishnah study and the (pre) requisites of engaging in Mishnah study. It also stands to reason that the dominant, pervasive traits of Mishnah itself—its subject matter and how Mishnah goes about expressing and developing its subject matter—condition the demands of, and requisites for fully engaged, devoted Mishnah study.

How can I illustrate the cogency of this last claim, which is central to a good deal of this chapter and the next? Quite simply!

Consider that a comprehensive, professional-level understanding of the nuances and meanings of both a Charlotte Bronte novel and Einstein's writings on relativity require significant antecedent education and skills; but they are certainly not the same education or skill requirements for both. What is required is conditioned in each case by the respective traits of the written works of Bronte, on the one hand, and of Einstein, on the other. And no one is born with the specialized requisite knowledge and skills to do justice to either Bronte's or Einstein's works. Different programs of preparatory study are implicated in different disciplines of the academy with a different cadre of academic professionals as one's mentors (and, later, as one's academic peers). The education in literary theory that a professional might bring to the analysis of Bronte's writings is a far cry from the education in astrophysics and mathematics that a very different type of professional would bring to the critical assessment of Einstein's theories.

Now, Einstein was known to have benefited from "thought experiments." Let us try a thought experiment of our own. Imagine that a cadre of specialists formed around the study of Einstein's writings on relativity. Let us suppose these specialists called themselves "Einsteinians" to distinguish themselves from other intellectuals, including other physicists. The devoted study and mastery of Einstein's publications on relativity provided entry to this group. And the lifelong study of these same writings, on one's own and with others, and the tutoring of others in the reading and interpretation of these writings both continued to validate one's belonging to this group of specialists and perpetuated the Einsteinians into the next generation. All of this would reflect or promote a certain level and type of group identity formation, social organization, and social sustainability. Moreover, imagine all this was done because, in the view of the Einsteinians, no other body of knowledge better placed and prepared humanity to understand their place in the universe and to act deliberatively in harmony

---

semantic range in early rabbinic literature is discussed by Hirshman, *Stabilization of Rabbinic Culture*, 75ff.

with how the universe was structured—all this because Einstein's writings were understood by this group to be a near-perfect formulation and completion of many centuries of successive scientific inquiry, and to be the most authoritative basis for further understanding humanity's place in the world. To act in full awareness of the laws of the universe as understood by the Einsteinians was to be at one with the universe and its universal laws. Hence the bona fides of membership in such a group bestowed special status and authority on its members in the general scientific community (if not beyond), *at least in the opinion of the Einsteinians.*

Mishnah and Mishnah study have a comparable place among the early rabbis, with comparable importance (1) for the social/identity formation of the rabbinic group (2) and for their membership's specific skills profile, as well as (3) for the special authority rabbis claimed to possess. As I shall touch upon in this chapter and elaborate upon in the next, Mishnah's content, which is overwhelmingly legal, is of a particular nature, and the way Mishnah expresses and develops that content follows very distinctive formal literary and rhetorical conventions that are different than other forms of discourse and (certainly) unlike everyday speech in the land of Israel in the Roman imperial period.[7] This is why Mishnah study demands an equally specialized education and antecedent skills in order to read, understand, and conduct a professional-level analysis of Mishnah's content. To add an element of serious playfulness to these claims, it would not be a stretch to think of the rabbis of the early third century as "the Mishnanians," the early rabbinic parallel to our Einsteinians.

Again, no one is born with the knowledge and skills that are prerequisites for the careful analysis of Mishnah. Moreover, such (pre) requisites are rarely amassed by individual autodidacts—people studying entirely on their own—cut off from others. And if a group of specialists in the Roman-ruled land of Israel was expected to acquire such antecedent knowledge and intellectual skills, then an organized social formation would probably have existed in which that knowledge and these skills were acquired, honed, validated, and passed on. There is nothing earth-shattering about such a proposition, sociologically, or historically. Indeed, the Roman world of the second and third centuries was replete with occupational and quasi-professional voluntary associations that were an antecedent of the medieval guilds. Moreover, if, as the rabbis came to assert, Mishnah is the most perfect, authentic, and therefore authoritative expression of centuries of Torah scholarship, then, given the rabbis' Jewish contemporaries'

7. Mishnah's principal, most pervasive rhetorical and literary conventions are extensively documented and discussed in ch. 4 of my book *In the Seat of Moses.*

belief that Torah originates in YHWH's revelation to Moses, what could be more important than creating and perpetuating a cadre of experts formed by and for the devoted study of Mishnah, and what could be more appropriate than to attribute to these experts (or, more accurately stated for the early rabbinic period, for these experts to claim for themselves) a special authority over Jewish norms and practice?

Let me, then, sum up the gist of my argument thus far by making two claims that are central to this book's agenda. It follows from the preceding that:

1. Just as the collective production, promulgation, and devoted, ritualized study of Mishnah as an authoritative text bespeak of a social formation that has reached a certain level of development and formal organization, so too understanding the specific intellectual demands of and requisites for Mishnah study ought to tell us much specifically about rabbinic group *identity*, about *what* the rabbis were as a cadre, around the time that the Mishnah was promulgated near the turn of the third century.

To say this is not much different than claiming that the subject matter, modes of thought, and forms of argument in Einstein's writings on relativity tell us not only about Einstein's intellectual preparation but also about the expected intellectual preparation and skills of the cadre of astrophysicists for whom Einstein was writing (or, in our thought experiment, about the Einsteinians). Moreover:

2. Understanding not only *that* the early rabbis at the turn of the third century CE privileged the study of Mishnah but also *why* or *how* the early rabbinic movement *legitimated* Mishnah study specifically as the core rabbinic inner-group activity ought to tell us something relevant and important about how the early rabbinic movement understood the basis for the authority they claimed not only for Mishnah but also *for themselves* as Mishnah experts, that is, for their specific cadre as a distinctive group of self-proclaimed elites *of a certain type* within Jewish society in the land of Israel under Roman rule (and soon thereafter in Mesopotamia-Babylonia under Persian rule).

It is precisely the two assertions of the foregoing paragraph that inform the agenda of the rest of this chapter and the next. Specifically, the first of the two claims will be more fully explored in chapter 3; the second will occupy the remainder of chapter 2. But as regards both—to borrow (and adapt) the title of a movie of several decades ago—it is crystal clear that "there's something about Mishnah," indeed, many things about Mishnah, that are key to addressing the focus of this book, the question *what* were the early rabbis?

So, in the next several sections of this chapter, we shall together address the second conclusion just articulated: that understanding the special authority and legitimacy of Mishnah among the early rabbis was tied to the early rabbinic cadre's understanding of and aspirations (or pretensions?) concerning their own authority as a distinctive group in Jewish society. However, in the great tradition of "shaggy-dog" stories, I begin to examine this topic not with evidence from the turn of the third century CE, when Mishnah was promulgated among the early rabbis, but with a survey of certain features of rabbinic and Jewish communal "politics" near the end of the tenth century CE, and of the place of medieval, rabbinic-authored "historiography" in those politics. Why do I use the term "politics" in this regard? Because we will glimpse some aspects of the organized, institutionalized exercise of rabbinic power, and of detractors of that power, within Jewish society of the medieval era. You and I will then (expeditiously) "peel the onion" in layers back to its core, the late second and third centuries CE, in search of the early elements that were refashioned sometime in early medieval times into a more complete (hi) story about the basis of rabbinic authority and the authority of the rabbis' teachings and literature, especially Mishnah.

HISTORIOGRAPHY, MYTHMAKING, AND LEGITIMATION OF THE AUTHORITY OF MISHNAH AND THE RABBINIC "CLASS": A BRIEF LOOK BACKWARDS FROM THE EARLY MEDIEVAL PERIOD

As I wrote in chapter 1, no ancient writer has produced anything like a biography of any ancient rabbi, let alone a history of the early rabbinic movement. There is no Roman-period Gospel of Rabbi Akiva (like that attributed to Mark about Jesus). We have no ancient *History of the Sages* (like Eusebius's *Church History*), and no *Twelve Founding Rabbis* (like Suetonius's *The Twelve Caesars*), even though early rabbinic literature preserves the names of many dozens of first-century to early third-century rabbis (the Tannaim), attributes legal rulings and teachings to them, and recounts very short stories in which named, early rabbinic figures are the dramatis personae.

Furthermore, as mentioned in the previous chapter, the earliest attempt to craft anything resembling a history of the early rabbinic movement, its institutions, its major figures, and the composition of its literature is from the medieval period. I refer to the lengthy epistle of the late tenth-century head of one of the major Mesopotamian-Babylonian rabbinic academies (yeshivot), Rabbi Sherira Gaon.[8] So, this chapter's discussion of the rabbinic group's self-definitions and self-perceptions in the second and third centuries begins with Sherira's account; for our purposes, his is the outermost layer of the onion.

So why, in the late tenth century, did Sherira undertake this work, when no earlier rabbinic author had done so, as far as we can tell? (Our shaggy-dog story begins.)

Sherira wrote his history in response to a series of queries posed to him by the (rabbinic) sages of the Jewish community of Kairouan in North Africa (in present-day Tunisia). What was Kairouan like in the late tenth century? And what was the Jewish community of Kairouan like? The city had been founded just several centuries earlier by Muslim invaders, who rather quickly established the city not only as a place of trade, and therefore of wealth, but also of high culture. Kairouan was known as a locale in which science and philosophy flourished alongside advanced Islamic studies. One of several, early "universities" in the Muslim world operated in Kairouan in this era, a period in Islam renowned not only for Islamic learning, but also for many areas of knowledge and thought pursued with a "rationalism" not known again in the Near East or the West until the Renaissance and early modern times.

At or near the time of the city's founding, Jews from Egypt and Cyrenaica (present-day Libya) settled in Kairouan, where, among other things, they established a center of advanced Jewish learning. When Sherira wrote to the rabbinic sages of Kairouan, Kairouan had had for over a century a cadre of rabbinic scholars and their students (perhaps in a rabbinic academy, a yeshiva). At the end of the tenth century, when Sherira authored his epistle, neither the Muslims nor the Jews of Kairouan could anticipate that within less than a one hundred years, the high cultural activities of their city, including the tolerance for a thriving Jewish minority's cultural and religious life, would begin speedily to evaporate, when in the eleventh century, other, far more religiously conservative Muslim tribes would conquer Kairouan. But in the late

8. Gaon is not a name or surname but an honorific title used for the heads of several major rabbinic academies in Mesopotamia-Babylonia during the early medieval period. It is from the Hebrew root meaning "loftiness," and I would tend to translate the early medevial rabbinic title *Gaon* as "Excellency." Not incidentally, the early medieval period of the rabbinic movement is referred to by modern scholars as the Gaonic period, because of the special stature and influence of the heads of these several, significant, and large, Mesopotamian-Babylonian academies among rabbis throughout the Near Eastern and Mediterranean lands.

tenth century, Kairouan was still in its heyday, as was Jewish life, culture, and learning, including rabbinic learning, which brings us back to the questions posed by the rabbinic sages of Kairouan to Sherira.

Because neither Kairouan generally, nor its Jewish community, nor its rabbinic sages were a cultural backwater—indeed, quite the opposite is the case—it is telling (perhaps even odd, at first glance) that the rabbinic sages of the city turned to Sherira in Mesopotamia-Babylonia for answers to their questions about the origins and development of the rabbinic movement, of rabbinic teachings and traditions, and of the major rabbinic documents (especially the legal documents) bequeathed to them by the rabbis of late antiquity and the earlier medieval era. Among the several things that we may safely conclude from the fact that they did so is that *they themselves knew of no such history*, as is indicated by the detailed queries posed to Sherira. And given Kairouan's stature as a place of advanced rabbinic learning (which is evident both in the Kairouanese sages' queries and how Sherira responds to them), we may also surmise that the sages of Kairouan knew of no such comprehensive history of the rabbinic movement *because none existed as of yet*. Indeed, we may conclude the same from Sherira's response; he, too, knew of no such historical oeuvre from which to draw his responses, even if he seems to have drawn upon some already existing chronologies, or he would likely have referred to such historiographical works. After all, history and historiography are much more than chronological list-making. Now, why should the sages of Kairouan turn to Sherira? As the head of one of Babylonia's major rabbinic academies (yeshivot), Sherira would normally be sounded on difficult issues, academic and practical, faced by rabbis elsewhere. Why? Because the several major Babylonian academies still enjoyed in the tenth century (but not for that much longer, I might add) an ascendency and authority within worldwide rabbinic circles that centers of rabbinic learning or individual rabbinic scholars in the West did not *yet* have, and that the rabbis of the land of Israel had long ceased to possess.[9]

Now, the Kairouanese sages' questions to Sherira were not articulated in general terms—e.g., please tell us about the history of the rabbis/sages or of the rabbinic movement. Rather, their queries were very specific—roughly a dozen successive, interrelated questions. And the specificities are telling. Let me summarize what I think were the most important issues of concern to the Kairouanese rabbis.

9. For an excellent and readable account of the shift of ascendency in rabbinic learning, first, from the land of Israel to Mesopotamia-Babylonia; and second, from Mesopotamia-Babylonia to the lands of the Mediterranean and southern Rhine valley, and then central Europe (and, finally, in early modern times to Eastern Europe), see Boyarin, *Traveling Homeland*.

They wished, among other things, to know how the core early rabbinic *legal* texts were written and who were their authors, with a focus on Mishnah in particular, but also on Tosefta and the *beraitot* (that is, the allegedly Tannaitic sources, often paralleled in Tosefta, cited by the two Talmuds), and the Talmuds, specifically the Babylonian Talmud. They also sought a chronology of rabbinic authorities and leadership over the centuries (1) leading up to the composition of the Mishnah and, subsequently, the Babylonian Talmud, and (2) after the Babylonian Talmud's composition, down to their own time in the tenth century.

What is this all about? Clearly, the Kairouanese sages wished to be able to establish a *continuous, contiguous chain of instruction through the generations of rabbinic teachers and students* from those rabbis to whom rulings are attributed in Mishnah to the rabbis of their own day, that is, to themselves. We may surmise that the sages of Kairouan believed that being able to establish such a transgenerational chain of rabbinic instruction was a cultural-social and political "requisite" of their own claims to authority in the Jewish community. Such notions of unbroken chains of rabbinic instruction resemble parallel notions of *isnad* in early Islam. *Isnad* refers to specified chains of tradition that link individual *non/extra-Quranic* teachings to Mohammed. The *isnad* for any one such tradition grounds its authority in Mohammed, even though the tradition in question does not appear in the Quran. Remember this notion, because it will be quite germane not only to our examination of tenth-century rabbinic claims about their teachings, but also to third- and fourth-century rabbinic concepts as well. But perhaps the most telling questions posed by the sages of Kairouan have to do with the composition of Mishnah itself (for reasons that will become clearer later), because, as already indicated, Mishnah, a turn-of-the-third-century legal study of Judaic law and practice, was deemed the foundational rabbinic document, seemingly from the moment of its production and promulgation among the early rabbis.

What, then, did the Kairouanese sages seek to know about Mishnah in particular? Permit me to highlight two issues. They wished to know:

1. Whether the Mishnah's *composition* took place over an extended period of time in a process of literary accretion over many generations, with each generation of sages adding to what the previous generation had composed, up to the generation of Rabbi Judah the Patriarch, who (in their view) brought this process to a close; *or* whether, near the turn of the third century, Rabbi Judah the Patriarch (to whom the rabbinic movement in the third and subsequent centuries attributed

Mishnah) composed the whole of Mishnah (all at once, as it were) based on antecedent traditions.

Moreover, the sages of Kairouan wished to understand:

2. Why all of the rabbis (i.e., the Tannaim) that are referred to by name in the Mishnah (or, for that matter, in Tosefta and cited in the Talmuds) as the authorities for this or that ruling are figures who lived *only* in the latter generations preceding, or contemporary with, Rabbi Judah the Patriarch.

In other words, the sages of Kairouan wanted to know why names of *earlier* authorities (e.g., from the first or second century BCE or earlier still) appear either sparsely or (more commonly) not at all in the Mishnah (and, for that matter, in Tosefta and the *beraitot*).[10] To paraphrase the words of the Kairouanese sages, why did the earlier generations leave it to the later generations to compose or articulate the teachings that ultimately found their place in Mishnah (and in Tosefta and the *beraitot*)? A whole lot is either assumed (or many questions are begged) in this query about *who knew what teachings and when*, is it not? Did the so-called earlier generations know these traditions, or did they not? If we suppose that they did, then why no names? Is that not a bit suspicious? And if they did not, as the absence of any names of more ancient sages *might* be taken to indicate, then on what basis did the so-called later generations (whose names *do* appear in early rabbinic literature) ground their teachings? You may already be able to discern what is at stake concerning the authority of rabbinic teachings in these questions. But let us hold these issues in abeyance for the moment. We will return to them at several junctures in this chapter.

Before saying something about Sherira's response, at least two matters beg to be addressed. What occasioned the Kairouan sages' desire/need to have such a history, beside intellectual curiosity and/or not knowing of an already existing historical oeuvre? And why did they wish to have *these specific queries* answered? That is, what has "gotten under their skin"? Let the shaggy-dog story continue!

It is commonly understood that many of the questions posed by the sages of Kairouan were, indeed, not spurred by intellectual curiosity only. Rather, at least one important (and generally agreed-upon) hypothesis about why they wished Sherira to provide such a history is this: the authority of the

10. These are not the only specific questions the sages of Kairouan posed, but they are the ones most germane to this volume. E.g., other questions have to do with why the rulings of some early *named* rabbinic authorities are accepted over the alternative, opposing rulings of their contemporary colleagues.

rabbis, of rabbinic teachings, and of rabbinic literature was under attack in Kairouan (and elsewhere in the Middle Eastern and Mediterranean lands) by a group (or groups) of Jewish elites and literati. In that era, the most notable, organized, Jewish detractors of rabbinic authority were the "Karaites." We do not know whether the Karaities in particular were the basis for the ennui of the rabbinic sages of Kairouan. But underlying the questions they pose to Sherira, it is easy to see some aspects of the Karaites' polemic against the "rabbinites." So, it is useful pedagogically briefly to consider the Karaites and these aspects of the Karaite anti-rabbinic discourse as a foil to what Sherira says in response to the rabbinic sages of Kairouan.[11]

The Karaites had banded together sometime over the previous several centuries (beginning perhaps in early Muslim Babylonia, thereafter in Egypt and beyond). By Sherira's time, the Karaities had attracted a following among a growing minority(?) of Jews bent upon resisting the "rabbinization" of Jewish communities in the Mediterranean basin and Near East. That is to say, the Karaites organized—sometime during the mid-seventh to ninth centuries CE—to stem the advance in the medieval era of the imposition (or voluntary recognition) of rabbis as not only the most authoritative arbiters of Jewish law and practice but also as their exclusive arbiters.

In fact, not that many decades before Sherira composed his response to the queries posed by the rabbinic sages of Kairouan, an Egyptian Karaite scholar, Jacob Qirqisani, wrote a major treatise in Arabic (*Kitāb al-Anwār wal-Marāqib: Kitab al-Shara'i*) on the history of Jewish movements to his day and on Jewish law and ritual practice, to serve as an *alternative* to rabbinic claims, rabbinic legal compositions, and rabbinic traditions and dicta. You do not have to be a scholar of Arabic to recognize the last word of the subtitle of Qirqisani's oeuvre. It is a form of the term "Sharia" and is the exact Arabic cognate of the Hebrew *halakha* (meaning the "Way"). You will remember from chapter 1 that "halakha" is the term the rabbis use in reference to their own pronouncements on Jewish law and ritual practice. Qirqisani, therefore, is offering his readers an alternative, authoritative halakhic text to the halakhic literature of the rabbis, namely and principally, Mishnah, Tosefta, and the (Babylonian) Talmud. And Qirqisani's expansive introduction to his work of Karaite "halakha" provides an alternative history of Judaism. An alternative to what? That is a matter to which I will return later.

The Karaites, then, challenged key aspects of the rabbis' self-definition as a group—of *what* the rabbis thought they were, of *what* the rabbis wished

---

11. Concerning the Karaites, see Fred Astren's *Karaite Judaism*, as well as his earlier book, *History, Historicization*.

other Jews to see them as being, and of the (monopolistic) authority the rabbis claimed for themselves, for their teachings, and for their literature. What, for our purposes,[12] was the principal substance of the Karaites' "attack" on the authority of the rabbis and their literature, and how does considering, however briefly, this attack strategy advance the issues that are central to this volume? Let me very briefly tackle the second half of the question, and then the first half. I say briefly in both instances, because we will cycle back to these matters periodically throughout the volume in different ways.

The substance of the Karaite attack is intended, as already intimated, to strike at the heart of the early medieval rabbis' claims in support of their assumed monopolistic authority over the law and practice of Jews and Jewish communities. Remember that in chapter 1, I stated that over the period of the seventh through tenth centuries, the rabbis' authority over Jewish life and practice was becoming dominant and normative across the Jewish communities of the Near East and Mediterranean basin. But some small and sometimes larger pockets of "resisters" continued to view matters differently. The Karaites were among the more successful (and enduring) resisters. (Indeed, even today some sixty thousand or so Jews still identify as Karaites, most of whom live in the state of Israel.) Therefore, the substance of the early medieval Karaite critique of the rabbinites, taken together with the tenor of rabbinic responses to that critique (like Sherira's answers to the sages of Kairouan), tells us much about the self-perception and self-definition of the rabbinic group as a class of authoritative Jewish elites in the early medieval period. And we, that is, you and I, may then proceed to "peel the onion" further. That is, we may use this as an entry point to tracing matters concerning what the rabbis thought they were (like) back to the initial century or centuries of the social formation of the rabbinic group. So, let me sum up

---

12. I say "for our purposes," because (as Joel Gereboff has reminded me) there are other aspects of the Karaite critique of the "rabbinites" that are important to the Karaites, even though these aspects do not significantly bear upon our discussion here. E.g., among the criticisms leveled by the Karaites at the rabbinites was that the latter often wandered too far from the plain sense of scriptural prescriptions and proscriptions in determining the halakha. In these instances the Karaites preferred a more literal or "plain sense" interpretation of biblical injunctions. This is reminiscent of aspects of the some (alleged?) divergencies of the Pharisees' and Sadducees' halakha in the era before the destruction of the Jerusalem temple in 70 CE (a parallel that some consider evidence of the survival of Sadducean teachings into the medieval period). The distinction is also somewhat akin to the posited divergencies between the Proculians and the Sabinians (the two principal schools or traditions of Roman legal scholarship from the first and second centuries CE, and beyond) in interpreting written (that is, statute) law. See Stein, "Interpretation and Legal Reasoning" and "Two Schools of Jurists." In this last respect, we should keep in mind that Rome ruled the Levant and the Mediterranean lands for centuries, from the first century BCE.

some of the elements of the Karaites' critique of the rabbis' claimed authority, focusing on those Karaite claims that bear most directly on this chapter's concerns. To state matters both concisely and glibly, the Karaite critique of the rabbis may (in part) be summarized as: What/who the heck do you think *you are*, anyway?! Or, what makes you so *special*?!

It was the Karaites' claim that the teachings of rabbis of their day were in fact and in principle no more or less (indeed, sometimes more and sometimes less[13]) authoritative than the teachings of any other well-educated, highly literate, believing Jew's views of the meaning and significance of the biblical tradition for leading a Jewish life in accordance with the demands of Torah. (Does this not sound a bit like the early Protestants' challenge in the sixteenth and subsequent centuries to the Catholic Church's claimed monopolistic authority? To wit, one true believer's well-considered and informed interpretation of the Bible in the quest for understanding what was demanded of a Christian was, prima facie, as valid as another's—which stance not only underpinned early Protestant movements [in the plural] but also spurred a renaissance of Bible study and scholarship.) Moreover, while some of the rabbis' views, according to the Karaites, seem legitimate extrapolations and interpretations of, or supplements to, biblical sources, other interpretations may be equally defensible (or superior). And still other rabbinic teachings, say the Karaites, seem disconnected from biblical texts altogether, or contradict the biblical sources outright. In other words, in either instance, there is nothing *special* about rabbinic teachings just because they are issued by rabbis. And it follows, therefore, that there is nothing, in principle, uniquely special about the rabbis as a group, as a distinctive cadre, class, guild (or whatever is the appropriate designation), the origins of which, say the Karaites, seem, on the evidence of the *names* of early rabbinic figures recorded in rabbinic literature itself, to go no further back than the last decades preceding the destruction of Jerusalem's temple in 70 CE. We are now in a better position to appreciate the implications and significance for this volume of the exchange between Sherira and the sages of Kairouan.

From the questions of the sages of Kairouan (let alone from Sherira's responses), including what is assumed by these questions, we may discern clearly what the contrary rabbinic views—that is, contrary to those of the resisters to a rabbinic monopoly—were concerning the status of rabbinic teachings and the authority of the rabbis. Each rabbi is not just one, believing, literate Jew among others offering interpretations and extrapolations

---

13. "Less" when, e.g., the rabbis' halakha steered further from the plain sense of Scripture's injunctions.

of biblical sources for application to living a life in accordance with To- rah. Rather, each rabbi is part of a distinctively unique cadre of specialists drawing upon, preserving, interpreting, and ramifying a distinctive chain of tradition conveyed faithfully from *hoary antiquity* from generation to generation of *rabbis specifically*—since this is what it meant to be a rabbi in the first place. These traditions were faithfully crystallized in key docu- ments along the way, beginning with and especially in Mishnah but also in Tosefta, in the (other) *beraitot* (extra-mishnaic, allegedly Tannaitic tradi- tions) in the two Talmuds (of the land of Israel and of Babylonia), and ultimately in the Babylonian Talmud (which for Sherira and the sages of Kairouan of the tenth century would have been considered the pinnacle of the literary expression of these traditions).

The Karaites, then, challenged such claims by maintaining (1) that there is insufficient proof/documentation of these claims about some continuous chain of tradition within the cadre of rabbis specifically from ancient times. Furthermore, (2) the evidence from Mishnah (the earliest rabbinic text, and the one touted by rabbis as supremely authoritative after Scripture itself) appears to indicate that most rabbinic traditions are no earlier than approximately the first or second centuries CE, since almost all of the *early* rabbinic figures referred to in Mishnah (or in subsequent rabbinic texts, for that matter) lived in these centuries, not earlier. So it appears, say the Karaites, that the content of Mishnah, the founding rab- binic document, was a rabbinic *invention* of primarily the first or second centuries CE. This is pretty close to calling the earliest rabbinic teachings, and by extension the Mishnah, a kind of relatively late forgery. Relative to what? To the ascribed antiquity of the Hebrew Scriptures and especially the Torah of Moses. Since medieval Jews all but universally believed in the Mosaic authorship of the first five books of the Hebrew Scriptures, there was a rather significant temporal gap between Moses' time and the earliest named rabbinic sages, a gap that the Karaites exploited in their anti-rabbinite arguments. Now, this is precisely what (as we have seen) the rabbinic sages of Kairowan want answers to from Sherira.

We are now very close to discerning what early *medieval* rabbis thought they were as a group from (1) the challenges to their presumed/assumed, special authority over matters of Jewish life and practice, and from (2) the types of responses (in the form of a history of sorts) demanded to counter those challenges. Moreover, we also know not only that no such history was known to the members of the rabbinic movement in the tenth century (even if some chronologies of generations of rabbis were composed and used by Sherira), but also that no such history was known to the tenth-century Karaite detractors of rabbinization either. Because, if the Karaites had known of such oeuvres, they would have argued against the writings of these rabbinic authors, much as "orthodox" Christian writers argued against the writings of "heretical" Christian authors, whose texts are known to us primarily from what the orthodox authors cite from and say about such heretical writings. But Karaite literature does not refer to such rabbinic histories. Rather, the Karaites, as far as we can tell from their writings and from rabbis' responses to the Karaite challenge, cast doubt on *the claims that rabbis tended to make, and had been making for centuries, concerning the basis of rabbinic authority and the authority of Mishnah in particular.* And these claims are already well known to us (and were, of course, known to Sherira and to the sages of Kairouan) from rabbinic literature authored sometime between the mid-third through early seventh centuries and from the constituent Tannaitic and Amoraic traditions embedded in this literature (which Sherira frequently cites). What the sages of Kairouan did not seem to possess, however, were good responses to the Karaites' counter-arguments to those claims.

The foregoing has been a very circuitous route to what I am about to do, namely, to highlight some key aspects of Sherira's answers to the queries posed to him by the rabbinic sages of Kairouan. But as will be clear, the detour will have been worth it, not only when we presently glimpse the tenor of what Sherira writes, especially about Mishnah's composition, but also when later we peel the onion further, as far back as the third century CE.

Sherira's epistle's responses may be characterized as a mixture of (1) chronology and chronicling, on the one hand, and (2) historiography and literary-historical writing, on the other. By the former, I mean something like: Rabbi A trained rabbinic disciples B, C, and D; Rabbi B in turn trained rabbinic disciples E and F, and so on. By the latter, I mean something quite different: Rabbi F composed Mishnah for such and such reason, in the particular language, style, and format that he gave Mishnah, because . . . ; he relied especially on the traditions stemming from Rabbi B because of the following reasons . . . ; and Rabbi B's teachings, like those of Rabbi B's co-disciples, all stem from Rabbi A, whose superiority to his contemporary rabbinic colleagues derives from the following special traits of Rabbi A . . . . As you can readily discern, such an account would provide a *literary-historical* account or *explanatory theory* of why Mishnah exhibits the traits it has. Remember, the nature, pedigree, and the *resulting authority* of Mishnah is undoubtedly key for the sages of Kairouan. Why? Because, as you already know, Mishnah's authority is a kind of initial premise of the argument for rabbinic authority and of the rabbis' shared self-definition of what they were. Remember, "there's something about Mishnah!" Consequently, Sherira's *literary-historiographical* account is (probably consciously) an exercise in social and political legitimation. "Social," because it affirms the basis for the rabbinic movement as a distinctive social group within Jewish society. "Political," in the sense that at stake is rabbinic power within Jewish society. So, Sherira's response is in part an act of historiography—and, given our and his interest in Mishnah, literary historiography—*in service of* mythmaking, since social formation and legitimation is what mythmaking is about, as explained in chapter 1. And the same is true of Sherira's "chronicling," since its purpose is to place Mishnah, the study of Mishnah, and thereafter the study of the (Babylonian) Talmud,[14] which is organized as a kind of analysis of Mishnah, within an unbroken chain of teacher-disciple relationships up to his own day. To put matters differently, in a period in which high-cultured Islamic-ruled society valued rationalism, Sherira is "rationalizing" rabbinic mythmaking by couching the latter in historiography and literary historiography.

Now let me say just a bit about what Sherira says about Mishnah's composition specifically. He is clear that Mishnah is not a text that was composed by accretion over the generations. Rather, it was composed, if not by one author, then by scholars working together under the aegis of one supervisory authority, namely, by Rabbi Judah the Patriarch, over the course of his tenure of office in Roman Palestine in the reign of Judah's imperial patron, "Antoninus," in Sherira's view. If Antoninus Pius (reigned 138–161 CE) is intended, then this is probably between twenty to sixty years too early for the actual dating of Mishnah or of Judah's patriarchy; if the six emperors of the Nerva-Antonine *dynasty* (reigned 96–192 CE) are meant, then Sherira may be closer to the historical mark for the latter decades of the dynasty. But the most likely candidates for Judah's (alleged) imperial patron and "friend" is Emperor Septimius Severus (reigned 193–211 CE, who self-declared as Marcus Aurelius Antoninus Augustus's adoptive son) or Emperor Caracalla (aka Marcus Aurelius Antoninus, co-reigned and reigned 198–217 CE), if we seek a rough time period that coincides both with Mishnah's composition and promulgation, and with Judah's patriarchal authority. But no matter; Sherira is no expert Roman historian, to be sure. He is relying on aggadic (moral-aphoristic) traditions appearing in earlier rabbinic literature that portray a friendship between an Emperor Antoninus and Judah as an indicator of Judah's nobility of rank and of human spirit (*gedulah* and *derekh eretz*). So lofty is Judah's nobility that a Roman emperor would befriend him. In all this, Sherira hangs his claims on earlier rabbinic claims going back as far as the latter third and fourth centuries that assert that Judah the Patriarch formulated Mishnah.

---

14. For an account accessible to nonspecialists of what Talmud does with Mishnah, see my *In the Seat of Moses*, chs. 7 and 8.

Sherira is also clear that the language in which Mishnah's content is cast, is language of Judah's (or of his authorship circle's) choosing, and not (necessarily?) the language of the pool of rabbinic traditions that Judah and his colleagues had at their disposal. In other words, in Mishnah, according to Sherira, the content of antecedent rabbinic teachings and traditions is either recast de novo by Judah and/or his circle, or he has/they have chosen from among various wordings then circulating for individual traditions. And it is this "mishnaic" (re) formulation of matters that thereafter is most authoritative, notwithstanding the parallel and supplementary traditions that are said to be preserved in Tosefta and the *beraitot*.

How does Sherira portray this having happened? He claims that Judah and/or his authorship circle had *recited* before them the many (different) extant versions of discrete, individual rabbinic teachings on this and that subject matter. And then he/they determined what precise wording should be used for each teaching that they incorporated into Judah's Mishnah. So the special qualities of Mishnah must hang upon the special qualities of Judah himself, if Sherira's purposes are to be served. Therefore, Sherira seeks to aggrandize Judah both *as a scholar and as a person* in order to elevate the stature of Mishnah's content, language, and style. And earlier aggadic (one might say, legendary) rabbinic traditions that lionize Judah provide the basis for this aggrandizement.

So, Sherira, as you have just learned, seeks to provide a literary-historiography that legitimates Mishnah as special and especially authoritative, and he has grounded Mishnah's uniquely legitimate status on the special character, skills, learning, and stature of Rabbi Judah the Patriarch, to whom, by the way, the production (in some fashion) of Mishnah had long been attributed by rabbinic tradition. But why does this make Judah and his Mishnah more authoritative *in principle* than, let us say, Jacob Qirqisani, evidently also an accomplished Torah scholar, and *his* halakhic compendium, written just a few decades prior to Sherira's composition? This question, if read as a rhetorical one, is precisely the gist of the Karaites' Protestant-like critique of the rabbinites, is it not? And I continue to maintain that critiques like those of the Karaites underlie the rabbinic sages of Kairouan's anxieties and questions. No wonder, then, that Sherira has more to say about both Judah and Mishnah than I have stated so far. And to say it, Sherira turns once more to earlier rabbinic aggadic sources,[15]

15. Remember, aggada (or haggadah, from the Hebrew root meaning "to narrate") is a genre of rabbinic tradition that intends to impart homiletic, theological, or ideological lessons though the telling of short vignettes about seminal figures or the telling of parables. When Scripture is cited in order to make these lessons appear implicit in Scripture, the resulting rabbinic passages are classified as "aggadic midrash" (*midrash*

which he historicizes in order to rationalize them. Let me show you, because later in this chapter, when we peel the onion further, you will see the logical connection of Sherira's history to much earlier rabbinic mythologizing about themselves, their teachings, and their literature.

How does Sherira to do this? He attempts to historically rationalize a link between Judah and Moses, specifically as it pertains to the production of Mishnah. This is so interesting and important for subsequent sections of this chapter that I want you to see Sherira's language verbatim:

> And heaven prepared a storehouse [of elevated character traits] for Rabbi [Judah the Patriarch], who possessed Torah learning and nobility. And they would defer to him in all locales all the years [of his tenure of office], as we have said [in an Amoraic Talmudic tradition[16]]: "Said Rabbah the son of Rava, and there are those who say, [said] Rabbi Hillel the son of Rabbi Vollas: From the days of Moses until Rabbi [Judah the Patriarch], we have not found [as we find in Judah, such a level of both] Torah learning and nobility in one person.[17]

Citing a passage from the Babylonian Talmud, Sherira has just likened Judah to Moses. But this is only the half of it. Sherira then goes on to assert

---

aggada). Aggadic genres of early rabbinic literature are contrasted in early, medieval, and modern rabbinic circles with halakhic texts and passages, that is, texts and traditions that deal with legal or normative behavioral standards for living a Jewish life. Mishnah, Tosefta, and the two Talmuds are considered to be *primarily* halakhic texts, although embedded in the two Talmuds in particular is plentiful aggadic material. When rabbinic traditions strive explicitly to demonstrate the foundation in Scripture of halakhic teachings, the resulting traditions are called "halakhic midrash" (*midrash halakha*). These distinctions of literary genre in evidence in the literary legacy of the early rabbinic movement are more fully explained in my *In the Seat of Moses*, ch. 3. In rabbinic circles, halakhic texts and traditions were (and still are) deemed to be authoritative in a manner that aggadic texts and traditions were never seen to possess. The former then are normative; the latter are not. This gulf in relative authority (in part) lies behind the much exaggerated assertion that (rabbinic) Judaism is more a matter of *practice* than belief. I assure you that within rabbinic Judaism and rabbinic circles, the disavowal of certain core beliefs would just as likely (or more likely) result in one's exclusion from Jewish society than the failure to adhere to certain normative practices. Indeed, when Maimonides, a preeminent rabbinic authority of the twelfth century, composed his code of Jewish law (the *Mishneh Torah*), the first of the fourteen "books" that comprise the composition was dedicated in large part to normative, core Jewish beliefs, the avowal of which he deemed to be a standard of Jewish practice. In other words, for Maimonides it was halakha to believe (or at least not to disavow) these tenets.

16. See BT Gittin 59a.

17. As a matter of ease and accessibility, I have based my translations on the readily available online text of Sefaria.org, which integrates the two major manuscript traditions of Sherira's epistle.

that in the Tannaitic period, because of the social and political upheavals of first-century Roman Judea, divergent halakhic opinions and differing formulations abounded of what until then remained orally transmitted rabbinic teachings. Judah and/or those working under his aegis/supervision/sponsorship/patronage—I am not committed to which term better fits the historical situation that Sherira imagines to be the case—undertake both to *write down*[18] the tradition and *fix* (or restore?) *its language* in composing the Mishnah, as I have indicated earlier. Now of Judah's Mishnah, Sherira states:

> And in the days of Rabbi [Judah the Patriarch] son of Rabbi Simeon the son of Gamaliel [II], their [differing/divergent formulations of the language of rabbinic teachings] were swept aside and they [re]formulated them and wrote them down [in the Mishnah]. And the language of our Mishnah was *as if* Moses had spoken it in prophecy—and they *likened them* [i.e., the formulated words of the Mishnah] to a sign and miracle.[19]

So Judah is *not* a prophet, and Mishnah is *not* revelation according to Sherira. But *both* Judah the Patriarch *and* "his" Mishnah are *likened* to Moses and to Moses' revelation of Torah respectively—a rational streak in Sherira that historicizes the mythmaking of and about rabbinic tradition that he finds in his sources. But the gist, even rationalized and historicized, is clear: expert and engaged students of the rabbinic tradition cast in writing in Mishnah are studying something so *seemingly* miraculous in formulation as to be *comparable* to Moses' revelation. Chronology then links those who produced Mishnah, c. 200 CE, to the Babylonian Talmud's take on Mishnah, c. 600 CE, and to the rabbis of Sherira's day. *Pace* the Karaites; at least that is what is intended.

What now of the other "burning issues" for the sages of Kairouan, namely, (1) that the earliest rabbinic personages named in rabbinic tradition generally and in Mishnah in particular tend overwhelmingly to have lived in the first and second centuries, and no earlier, and (2) that there is

18. Interestingly, Sherira either does not know of or does not agree with a notion that Mishnah was composed orally. He knows Mishnah as a written text, and it is the status and authority of this text that he is trying to defend. It would not serve his defense if Mishnah existed orally only for several centuries after its composition. Why? Detractors, like the Karaites, would then be able to argue that there is no evidence for Mishnah's existence until several centuries after the career of its alleged author, Judah the Patriarch. Whether or not Mishnah was composed orally has been actively debated by modern scholars. There is, however, a consensus among modern scholars that Mishnah, once composed, was memorized and studied as a memorized text in the initial period after its promulgation (even if/though written texts of Mishnah circulated). I discuss this last noted issue at several junctures in this volume, especially in ch. 4.

19. Emphasis added.

no written evidence of rabbinic teachings that predates Mishnah (c. 200 CE)? This is a problem for the sages of Kairouan, because it may be taken, as it indeed was by the Karaites, as indicating that the earliest rabbinic teachings are the invention of the rabbis of this era. And this may be further borne out by the absence of written evidence of rabbinic teaching before Mishnah's composition near the turn of the third century. In other words, rabbinic teachings have no ancient pedigree—another charge of the Karaites against the rabbinites.

Again, drawing on earlier aggadic rabbinic traditions attributed to Tannaitic and Amoraic sources, Sherira has ready-made, historicized rationales to explain away these inconvenient truths. First, until Mishnah's (written) composition, rabbinic teachings were transmitted *orally*, Sherira "reminds" his readers in Kairouan.[20] That is why no written witness to them is earlier than Mishnah. So much for that problem; again, the solution offered by Sherira is a literary-historicization of what later in this chapter we shall encounter in earlier rabbinic mythmaking.

The fact that few rabbis are named in Mishnah (or in other, later rabbinic literature) who lived earlier than circa the first and second centuries CE is also explained away by Sherira via the historicizing of another earlier rabbinic aggadic tradition. Before the upheavals in the land of the Israel in the first and second centuries, rabbinic scholarship and discipleship were so assiduously carried out in such a stable social, institutional, and administrative environment, says Sherira, that there were no divergent and contradictory halakhic positions on matters, even though rabbinic traditions were orally transmitted in whatever wording the tradent chose to express them. With no divergence of opinion in matters of halakhic substance, there was no need to attribute positions to this or that rabbi *by name*. The detrimental effects on Torah scholarship and rabbinic discipleship of the events leading up to and then following the Jerusalem temple's destruction changed that state of affairs, leading to divergent views on the halakha that then had to be attributed to the individual rabbis who espoused them. So Judah's Mishnah, Sherira says, formulates and preserves anonymous or unattributed teachings, presumably where divergence either does not exist or can be resolved to Judah's satisfaction, as well as *attributed* opinions, where divergences of views stand. Again, Sherira offers historiographical and literary-historical solutions to such challenges to the (monopolistic) authority of the rabbis, just as he did when he stated that literary-historical processes that produced Mishnah resulted in a text *as compelling as* revelation, and that Mishnah's "author," Judah, possessed

20. In other words, it is as if Sherira is a proponent of the modern expression "The absence of evidence is not evidence of absence."

qualities—an exceedingly noble spirit coupled with exemplary Torah scholar
ship—that made him *comparable to* Moses.

Now, I can just imagine—a relatively poor form of historical scholarship, I must admit—what Karaite critics of Sherira's epistle would do with
the foregoing arguments. They might say: You can say repeatedly that Rabbi
Judah was so illustrious that he is *comparable* to Moses and that his Mishnah
is so compellingly perfect that it is *like* relevation, but that does not disprove
our position as Karaites or our critique of the basis for the rabbis' monopolistic claim to power, which rabbis ground on a tradition that goes back to
Mishnah via centuries of Mishnah study. How so? One compelling, learned
scholar's view of the Torah tradition is, in principle, just as valid as another's.
And, moreover, you, Sherira, have just admitted that rabbinic traditions are
grounded in a turn-of-the-third-century text, the Mishnah, the wording of
the constituent passages of which were fixed at that time.

But what if Judah's Mishnah was not lauded by being said to be *like*
revelation but was considered actually *to be* revelation, in the eyes of the
early rabbis? Sherira, it seems, could not bring himself to say so outright.
He lived in an age, region, and time when philosophy and science were en-
thusiastically pursued by Muslim and Jewish scholastics alike. But Sherira's
likening of Judah to Moses and of Mishnah to revelation did not come out
of thin air. Sherira was drawing on what we know to be earlier rabbinic
claims stemming from the third though fifth centuries CE about themselves, their teachings, and their emerging literature. The story continues,
as we peel back the onion some more.

MISHNAH AND RABBINIC MYTHMAKING
IN SERVICE OF EARLY RABBINIC
SOCIAL FORMATION, C. 250–600 CE

In the preceding section, I noted that Sherira frequently references or cites
earlier rabbinic materials, many of which are aggadic traditions (that is, sayings and very short stories conveying a moral, theological, or ideological
lesson). Sherira historicizes these to give them, in my view, a more rational
bent for his time and place, the Islamic world of the tenth century with its
rationalism and scholasticism, at least among many cultural elites. These
earlier traditions, found in rabbinic documents that were composed between c. 250–600 CE, *tended* to make certain claims about the nature, status,
and pedigree of both rabbinic traditions and the texts in which they were
preserved. And in so doing, these aggadic traditions, in the process, made
related assertions (explicitly and implicitly) about the authority of the special

purveyors of those traditions and texts, namely, the rabbis. What are these claims? And what status ought we, modern scholars and critical-analytical readers of ancient literature, assign to them? Again, let me start with the second question and then proceed to the first.

Such claims are the result of the need/tendency of the early rabbinic movement, let us say, sometime in the period from c. 250 CE to 600 CE, to articulate *mythologies* about who they *as a group* claimed to be and about the basis of the authority they professed to legitimately wield. Moreover, such mythologies underpinned the status they claimed for their traditions, teachings, and literary compositions. Obviously, there is a mutually reinforcing relationship between these two requisites: to legitimate their group's authority, on the one hand, and their teachings, traditions, and texts, on the other. After all, rabbis are "produced" by gaining expertise in these texts, especially Mishnah, as I have already stated. But the authority of these documents, Mishnah in particular, rests upon the special authority of those (rabbis) whose traditions are preserved in them, and of Judah the Patriarch (the alleged architect of Mishnah) to whom exceptional qualities are attributed, as we have already seen. In mythologies, such circularities are commonplace; indeed, they heighten their cultural and social effectiveness. So, let me say just a bit more about mythologies and mythologizing.

"Mythologies" is an equivocal term that may mean several different things. One such meaning, often intended in normal, everyday parlance, is akin to fantasies, implying an absence of any historically or empirically valid claims—simply, a fiction, even if an edifying one. A mythology is something we do not believe to be true, at least not *literally* so. (Indeed, we, today, have difficulty imagining that *any* relatively advanced civilization or well-educated, thinking person, present or past, would have ever believed mythologies to be *literally* true—an issue to which I shall return later in this chapter, after I have presented core aspects of the early rabbis' myth-making about themselves.) This is how we moderns tend to think of the ancient Greeks' stories about their gods, although, I would argue, much more is going on in these stories, which leads me to another meaning of myth that stems from modern scholars.

Modern historians and anthropologists of religion use the term "myth" to mean something like "identity-establishing stories" that serve the emergence of "social formations," that is, the emergence of human communities or groups that see themselves as sharing a common past (whether historical, imagined, or some combination of the two), present, and future, within some institutionalized social structure. In this sense, mythologies *may* make history-like claims that are historically true, false, or (more often) some mélange of the two that are often difficult to tease apart and to assign a historical validity rating to, for lack of sufficient evidence to make such judgments. My point is, factual history is not the driver of mythologies (even if historical facts may sometimes be embedded in them). Rather, processes of social formation and the requisites of social formation are the drivers of mythologizing. And other things (conveying historical facts, composing history-like fictions, outright fantasizing) are secondary to and serve this primary function.

So, what are these claims that the early rabbis begin to articulate, clearly evinced in their literature (in my view) sometime in the second half of the third century CE and more fully in the fourth and subsequent centuries, in service of mythologizing about their social formation as a distinctive group within the Jewish communities of the land of Israel under Roman rule and of Mesopotamia-Babylonian under Persian rule? For brevity's sake, I will boil matters down to six such claims of my own formulation, presenting the core rabbinic myth in its *full-blown* state, attained sometime several centuries after Mishnah's production near the turn of the third century.

1. On Sinai, God revealed *two* Torahs to Moses, only one of which (i.e., the Pentateuch of the Hebrew Scriptures) was *written* down; the second was transmitted *orally*, by word of mouth from teacher to student in a continuous *chain of tradition* down through the centuries. Together, the two Torahs—that which was committed to writing by Moses and that which Moses transmitted orally—constitute the *whole* Torah (*torah shlemah*). By implication, to possess only the Hebrew Scriptures, the Written Torah, is to possess an incomplete account of God's revelation to the people of Israel via the agency of Moses.

2. The alleged founders (let us call them the proto-rabbis) of the rabbinic movement (in the first century CE?) occupied a place, indeed, an integral and special place, within this continuous chain of tradition.

3. To be a disciple of a sage, diligently serving (that is, learning from, observing, and mimicking the behavior of) one's rabbinic master, is to occupy a place not only in the reception and preservation but also in the further elucidation and ramification of this tradition. So, the chain of transmission beginning with Moses continues especially through the successive generations of *rabbis* via activities of engaged study, discipleship, and faithful teaching.

4. Rabbi Judah the Patriarch's Mishnah (produced c. 200 CE), the founding document of the early rabbinic movement, represents the *most* accurate and authentic *literary* representation of this process of reception, preservation, further elucidation, and ramification of the tradition of

Oral Torah. Before the production of the Mishnah, the traditions that constituted Oral Torah were, it is alleged, transmitted orally.

5. It follows that the traditions of the rabbis of the generations leading up to the production and promulgation of Mishnah (that is, the Tannaim) are the *most* authoritative of the generations of early rabbis, since it is *their* (oral) teachings that underlie Mishnah, the most authoritative literary expression of Oral Torah.

6. It also follows that the authority of the subsequent several centuries of rabbis (that is, the Amoraim), of the traditions they transmitted, and of the early rabbinic literature composed after the production of Mishnah, is founded above all else on engaged, guided Mishnah study—that is, guided by their rabbinic mentors/teachers—and on the elucidation and further ramification of Mishnah's content.

As I have already intimated, these six claims are *my* articulation of matters based on individual bits and pieces of literary evidence, scattered hither and yon in the documents of early rabbinic literature produced over the several centuries following Mishnah's initial promulgation. One will not find them expressed, as I have done, in six (or any other number) of cohering, fully formed claims anywhere in early rabbinic literature. But I am confident (1) that they accurately come to represent the state of rabbinic ideology sometime before the end of late antiquity; (2) that thereafter they remain core to the late antique and early medieval apologia of the rabbinic movement (such as Sherira's epistle to the sages of Kairowan). And the content of these six claims, taken as a whole, continues to provide the basis for the claimed authority of rabbinic teachings and literature, with one major alteration, until modern times. What is that alteration? Sometime in the several centuries following the production of the Babylonian Talmud (c. 600 CE), the study of it displaced the study of Mishnah as the principal formative activity of rabbis and would be rabbis. The Talmud effectively assumed the position in rabbinic circles of the fullest expression of Oral Torah; I say "effectively," because, *formally* speaking, Mishnah's preeminence endured *in principle*, although Mishnah study ceased to be the quintessential socially formative activity in the rabbinic movement that it had been for four centuries or more from c. 200 CE. Mishnah became subsumed, as it were, in the Babylonian Talmud.

I am, however, getting ahead of myself with this foray into the place Mishnah study occupied in the early rabbinic movement. Let me return to the six claims that emerged, in stages, no doubt, sometime during a three-and-a-half-century period as part and parcel of mythologizing the basis of the rabbinic movement's social formation. Specifically, I would pose three questions, the last two intimately interrelated.

1. How did early rabbinic aggadic traditions themselves express this mythology, as opposed to my systematized reformulation of the six claims presented earlier?

2. Fictional or not, what may have made such claims credible or compelling to the circles of early rabbis?

3. Why might the early rabbis have thought these claims would be credible or compelling to any members of the Jewish communities in which the early rabbis operated as a distinctive group?

SAMPLE, EXEMPLARY AGGADIC TRADITIONS MYTHOLOGIZING THE EARLY RABBIS' ORAL TORAH

Let me provide a taste of the flavor for how several rabbinic traditions embedded in post-mishnaic, early rabbinic literature reflect aggadically the belief in Oral Torah, on the one hand, and, on the other, tie the notion of Oral Torah to rabbinic teachings, Mishnah, and other early rabbinic writings.

Probably the earliest articulation of an unbroken chain of tradition from Moses to the early rabbis (and to the Tannaim specifically) is the prologue to Avot taken together with the organizational shank of its first several chapters. Avot is a late (probably mid-third-century) aggadic addition to Mishnah, which otherwise is an almost entirely halakhic composition. The prologue does not explicitly distinguish Oral from Written Torah. But neither does it speak of *the* Torah (of Moses), that is, Torah with the definite article (*Ha-Torah* or *Torat Moshe*, with the noun in the emphaticus or constructus form), the usual designation for the Pentateuch. Rather, Avot's prologue speaks of a "generic Torah," transmitted via a chain of tradents through the ages. Let me show you the relevant language only from Avot, focusing on the prologue and thereafter on simply the "structuring" language of the first four chapters of the tractate. (The bits left out of my translation—that is, the bits for which I have substituted ellipses—I will characterize as a whole later.)

Avot 1:1–18

Moses received [*qibbel*] Torah from Sinai, and he transmitted [*masar*] it to Joshua.
And Joshua [transmitted it] to the elders.
And the elders [transmitted it] to the prophets.
And the prophets transmitted it to the members of the Great Assembly; they used to say three things. . . .

Simeon the Righteous was among the [last] remnants [of the members] of the Great Assembly; he used to say. . . .

Antigonos of Socho received [it] from Simeon the Righteous; he used to say. . . .
Yose the son of Yo'ezer of Tzredah and Yose the son of Yohanan of Jerusalem received [it] from them; Yose the son of Yo'ezer says. . . . Yose the son of Yohanan of Jerusalem says. . . .

Joshua the son of Perahia and Nittai the Arbelite received [it] from them; Joshua the son of Perahia says. . . . Nittai the Arbelite says. . . .

Judah the son of Tabbai and Simeon the son of Shetah received [it] from them; Judah the son of Tabbai says. . . . Simeon the son of Shetah says. . . .

Shemayah and Abtalyon received [it] from them; Shemayah says. . . . Abtalyon says. . . .
Hillel and Shammai received [it] from them; Hillel says. . . . He [also] used to say. . . . He [furthermore] used to say. . . . Shammai says. . . .

R. Gamaliel [the Elder] says. . . .
Simeon his son [i.e., R. Simeon b. Gamaliel I] says. . . .
R. Simeon b. Gamaliel [II] says. . . .

Avot 2:1–16

Rabbi [Judah the Patriarch] says. . . .
R. Gamaliel [III] the son of Rabbi Judah the Patriarch says . . . ; he [also] used to say. . . . He [furthermore] used to say. [And] he used to say. . . . [And] he used to say. . . .

R. Yohanan b. Zakkai received [it] from Hillel and Shammai; he used to say . . .

R. Yohanan b. Zakkai had five disciples/students, and these are they: R. Eliezer b. Hyrcanus, R. Joshua b. Hananiah, R. Yose the Priest; R. Simeon b. Netan'el; R. Eleazar b. Arakh. He [Yohanan b. Zakkai] would account [thusly] their [his disciples'] laudatory traits. . . .

They [his disciples, each] said three things. R. Eliezer says. . . . R. Joshua says. . . . R. Yose says. . . . R. Simeon says. . . . R. Eleazar says. . . .

R. Tarfon says . . . ; he [also] used to say. . . .

Avot 3:1–18

Akavyah b. Mehalal'el says. . . .

R. Hananiah the prefect of the priests says. . . .

R. Simeon says. . . .

R. Haninah b. Hakinai says. . . .

R. Nehunya b. HaKanah says. . . .

R. Halafta of Kefar Haninah says. . . .

R. Eleazar of Bartota says . . .

R. Simeon says. . . .

R. Dosthai b. Yannai says in the name of R. Meir. . . .

R. Hanina b. Dosa says . . . ; he [also] used to say. . . .

R. Eleazar of Modi'in says. . . .

R. Ishmael says. . . .

R. Akiva says . . . ; he [also] used to say. [And] he [furthermore] used to say. . . .

R. Eleazer b. Hisma says. . . .

Avot 4:1–22

Ben Zoma says. . . .

Ben Azzai says . . . ; he [also] used to say. . . .

R. Levitas of Yavneh says. . . .

R. Yohanan b. Baroka says. . . .

His son, R. Ishmael, says. . . .

R. Zadok says . . . , and so Hillel used to say. . . .

R, Yose says. . . .

His son, R. Ishmael says . . . ; he [also] used to say. . . .

R. Jonathan says. . . .

R. Meir says. . . .

R. Eliezer b. Jacob says. . . .

R. Eleazar b. Shammua says. . . .

R. Judah says. . . .

R. Simeon says. . . .

R. Nehorai says. . . .

R. Yannai says. . . .

R. Mattya b. Harash says. . . .

R. Jacob says . . . ; he [also] used to say. . . .

R. Simeon b. Eleazar says. . . .

Samuel the Younger says. . . .

Elisha b. Avuyah says. . . .

R. Yose b. Judah of Kefar-HaBavli says. . . .

Rabbi [Judah the Patriarch] says. . . .

R. Eliezer HaKappar says . . . ; he [also] used to say. . . .

Before I highlight some salient (and mostly obvious) features of these first four chapters of Avot, I should like to satisfy your curiosity about what all of these named sages are said to have "said"—the missing bits for which I have substituted ellipses. Avot in general, and in particular its first four chapters, attributes to these named sages aphorisms about proper comportment and emotional disposition—what one might call elements of character. This type of instruction is distinct from presenting teachings and rulings about the normative *rules* for living life in accordance with Torah. The former, the content of Avot's aphorisms, is aggada, which genre I have already characterized. The latter, content about normative rules, which occupies almost all of (or the rest of?) Mishnah, is halakha.

Now, many of the aphorisms of Avot 1–4 have a noticeable bent to them, as well as a particular intended audience. They are especially directed to disciples of the sages/rabbis. And a good proportion of the aphorisms deal with how disciples of the sages/rabbis, as opposed to just anyone, are to behave themselves. Therefore, many of the sayings deal with the traits of the ideal rabbinic student of Torah—a kind of Being a Diligent and Worthy Rabbinic Disciple 101. Or, one could think of these aphorisms as a collection of proverbs directed specifically at, and relevant to, the rabbinic novice. There are many good, accessible, modern commentaries on Avot's aphorisms, and you may turn to these commentaries, if you wish. (Warning! As with many premodern societies, the aphoristic wisdom of Avot does not value women's views very much, to say the least.) For our purposes, however, I ask you to remember just two general points about the aphoristic content of Avot 1–4 that deals with this ideal rabbinic student/disciple and rabbinic sage.

1. The would-be rabbinic sage is devoted to the study of Torah—again, not simply *the* Torah [of Moses], that is, the Pentateuch, but this generic Torah—for its own sake.

2. The would-be rabbinic sage serves his—yes, every name listed is male—rabbinic master as an integral, instrumental means of learning Torah.

Here, then, in these two points, derived from a mid-third-century rabbinic text from the land of Israel under Roman rule, one begins to find something of significance of the ethos informing and creating the social formation of the early rabbinic movement. It is a social formation based, in large part, on Torah learning and service to one's rabbinic master/teacher.

What, now, is to be gleaned that is germane to our discussion from the *structuring elements* that we observe in the first four chapters of Avot? Again, let me boil matters down to two salient observations.

1. We are presented with a list of personal names (Moses, Joshua, etc.) and of some alleged Israelite/Judean social institutions (notably, elders, prophets, and members of the Great Assembly), ordered (or intended to be ordered) more or less temporally from Moses in antiquity to the generation of Rabbi Judah the Patriarch and his son(s) in the early third century CE.[21]

21. I must point out an apparent anomaly in the list of authorities. If you go down the list you will notice that Rabbi Judah the Patriarch appears at two different locations in the chain of authorities. One is at the historical tail end of a chain of authorities that goes from Hillel and Shammai through Gamaliel the Elder, Simeon b. Gamaliel I, and Simeon b. Gamaliel II (see the end of Avot, ch. 1, and the beginning of ch. 2). The other location is near the historical tail end of a chain of authorities that again passes through Hillel and Shammai, but then proceeds through Yohanan b. Zakkai and his students (see the middle of ch. 2 to near the end of ch. 4). In other words, we seem to have two lists, both of which proceed from Moses to Hillel and Shammai, which bifurcate after that (Gamaliel the Elder vs. Yohanan b. Zakkai), and which return in both instances

2. Throughout the first two chapters of Avot, we find the recurrent use of either the verb "transmit" or the verb "receive" to characterize the relationship of one generation of tradents to the next.

What may we take away from these two observations about the early rabbinic movement's self-definition of what they were?

First, this generic Torah, to the study of which rabbis and their disciples are to devote themselves, has been transmitted and received by successive generation of students/disciples of it—a chain of tradition—from Sinai (that is, from God), to Moses, and thereafter down the chain to Rabbi Judah the Patriarch and the rabbis of the generation of Judah's son, Gamaliel (III).[22] The rabbis, therefore, are portrayed as the privileged recipients, guardians, and students of this generic Torah revealed by God to Moses. This makes Moses both the first rabbinic disciple (that is, of God) and the first earthly rabbi. And indeed, in numerous (primarily aggadic) passages in early rabbinic texts, from Tosefta (c. 250–425) to the Babylonian Talmud (c. 600), Moses is routinely referred to as "Moses our rabbi" (*moshe rabbeinu*).[23]

---

to Judah. What has happened? Boyarin makes the distinction between the patriarchal family's line of transmission (i.e., from Gamaliel the Elder down to Judah the Patriarch) vs. a specifically *rabbinic* line of tradents to Judah (i.e., Yohanan b. Zakkai down to Judah the Patriarch). Boyarin suggests that the patriarchal family line of transmission was inserted to the rabbinic line of transmission. This, among other things, would have the virtue of "rabbinizing" the patriarchal family, on the one hand, and, on the other, cementing the (would-be?) association of the early rabbinic movement with the aristocratic patriarchal family. See Boyarin, "Diadoche of the Rabbis."

22. There are at least two notable absences from Avot's chain of tradents of Torah: monarchs (or clan/tribal nobles, as a class) and Levitical priests (the alleged descendants of Aaron, again as a hereditary class). If these absences are deliberate, then the underlying message may well be that status and authority achieved by birth are not highly valued by the early rabbinic movement. Rather, status is achieved by diligent discipleship in the mastery of Torah.

23. Let me name just a few sample sources, t. 'Eduyyot 3:4; throughout the halakhic Midrashim; JT Bava Batra 22b; JT Sanhedrin 50a; BT Sotah 13a, 14a; BT Berakhot 7a, 32b, 55a, 55b; BT Ta'anit 11a; BT Sanhedrin 11a; BT Bava Batra 119b; BT Nedarim 38a, BT Sukkah 28a. I will stop there as the list would be interminable. That said, the last mentioned passage, a *baraita* (i.e., a designated Tannaitic tradition) cited at BT Sukkah 28a offers an instructive complement to our current discussion of the "rabbinization" of Moses.

> Our rabbis taught [this Tannaitic tradition]. Hillel the Elder had eighty disciples. Thirty of them were deserving of the *shekhinah* [that is, God's divine presence] alighting on them, like Moses our rabbi. And [another] thirty of them were deserving of the sun standing still for them, like Joshua the son of Nun. [And] twenty [of them were] of middling quality. The greatest among all of them was Jonathan b. Uziel, [and] the junior among all of them was Yohanan b. Zakkai. [And, even so,] they

So, (1) the rabbis of the Roman period have mythologized themselves to be like Moses (that is, recipients and students of God's generic Torah), (2) Moses (the first student/disciple of God) has been remythologized to be like the rabbis of the Roman period, and (3) a special, direct, and faithful line of transmission joins the rabbis to Moses.

Second, since the list of tradents ends with Rabbi Judah the Patriarch and the rabbis of his generation (or of that of his son, Gamaliel III), and because (sometime in the third or fourth century CE) it becomes commonplace to attribute the production (in some fashion) of Mishnah to Judah's agency, then *Mishnah is Torah* (in the generic sense) *from Moses on Sinai*. This syllogistic-like argument may well be one of the reasons that Avot was inserted into Mishnah in the mid-third century. By association, Avot provides Mishnah with a pedigree, that is, with a myth of its origins, which in turn justifies making Mishnah the principle object of devoted, engaged study as a shared formative activity within rabbinic circles. Remember, early third-century rabbis are "Mishnanians," and subsequent generations of rabbis remain so until sometime after the production of the Babylonian Talmud (c. 600).

So, we are making progress in adducing some indicative rabbinic evidence from the mid-third and subsequent several centuries that appears to reflect aspects of my earlier stated six claims that summarize how early rabbis mythologized what they were, in service of (1) creating a viable and distinct social identity for their group, (2) establishing (in their own eyes, at least) their unique monopolistic authority, and (3) justifying the special status of their most important document and object of study (apart from Scripture itself), the Mishnah.

To seal the deal, as it were, I would like to present to you one other indicative/illustrative piece of evidence from early rabbinic literature at JT Megillah 4:1. In this passage from the Jerusalem Talmud (c. 400), the halakhic analysis of Mishnah makes a detour into aggada that speaks directly to aspects of my summative six claims, which characterize what, in my opinion, early rabbis from the mid-third and subsequent several centuries

---

said about him, [that is,] of Yohanan b. Zakkai, that he did not [ever] desist [from studying] Scripture, and Mishnah, *gemara* [that is, Talmud], halakhic traditions, and aggadic traditions.

The inferences of this passage are clear: the greatest of Hillel's rabbinic disciples were worthy of being a Moses, that is, of being the direct recipient of God's revelation. Even the "freshmen" among the disciples never wavered or desisted from the study of the rabbinic curriculum—although, other than Scripture itself, components of that curriculum are an anachronistic retrojection back to Yohanan b. Zakkai's era in the first century CE. (That some sages by reason of their learning are worthy of divine inspiration is a theme that I return to in ch. 5 of this volume.)

tended to say about themselves, about their traditions and their literature, and especially about Mishnah. The Hebrew is in regular font, the Aramaic in italics, and the added emphasis in bold.

JT Megillah 4:1

R. Haggai said: R. Samuel b. R. Isaac went to the synagogue. He saw an open scroll—the [Aramaic] translation [of the Scripture being read aloud by the translator] from the scroll. He [Samuel] said to him [the translator]: You are forbidden [to do this with] materials [lit. words, *devarim*] that were communicated orally [lit. by mouth, *be-peh*]; [rather, only] materials that were communicated in writing [*be-ketav*] [are read aloud] from written [*be-ketav*] [texts].

R. Haggai [said] in the same of R. Samuel b. Nahman: [Some] materials were communicated orally, and [other] materials were communicated in writing, and we [would] not know which are [more] beloved, *were it not for that which is written* [in Exod 34:27b], "For on the basis [*al-py*] of these things [*devarim*], I have established a covenant with you and with Israel." *This says* [that] *those* [materials communicated] orally are [more] beloved.

R. Yohanan and R. Yudan b. R. Simeon [said different things about the just-cited verse in Exod 34:27b, and we do not know which was said by whom]. One said: If you observe that which [was communicated] orally and that which [was communicated] in writing, I will establish a covenant with you, and if not, I will not establish a covenant with you. *And the other said:* If you observe that which [was communicated] orally and that which [was communicated] in writing, you will reap reward, and if not, you will not reap reward [but the covenant endures in either case].

Said R. Joshua b. Levi: [Referring to Deut 9:10: "And YHWH gave to me the two tablets of stone, **written** [*ketuvim*] by the finger of God; **and** on them was [that which] **accorded with** all **the** words [*ke-khol ha-devarim*] that YHWH spoke with you on the mountain out of the fire on the day of the assembly"]—[Scripture does not say just] "on them" [but] "**and** on them"; [not just] "words [*devarim*]" [but] "the words [*ha-devarim*]"; [not just] "all [*kol*] [but] "**accorded with** all [*ke-khol*]"—[indicating that all of] Scripture, and Mishnah, and Talmud, and aggada, and

even what the experienced disciple will teach before his [rab-
binic] master were already spoken to Moses from Sinai.

Before discussing aspects of the passage's content that intersect with
the issues of this chapter, let me provide some relevant context. The first
concerns dating. As already noted, the passage is in a text, the Jerusalem
Talmud, generally thought to have been authored around 400 CE in the
land of Israel.[24] We also see in this passage names of rabbis to whom opinions and sayings are attributed. We have no way of proving the historical accuracy of these attributions. But that said, the rabbinic personages
mentioned were all rabbis in the land of Israel and are believed to have had
careers that range from c. 230 CE (e.g., R. Joshua b. Levi, a younger near-
contemporary of Rabbi Judah the Patriarch), through c. 250 (for instance,
R. Yohanan), to c. 365 (R. Haggai).

The second matter of context has to do with the halakhic issue engendered by the Mishnah analysis that gives rise to this passage in the Jerusalem
Talmud. Normative Jewish ritual involves, among other things, the public
reading of Scriptures in local communal assemblies (the literal meaning of
"synagogue"). Mishnah tractate Megillah proffers a number of legal rulings
on how these public readings are to be conducted. At issue in this passage of
the Jerusalem Talmud is how the public *translation* into Aramaic of the lections of the original Hebrew Scriptures are to be interwoven with the reading
of the Hebrew text's verses in the public assembly's formal ritual. Why were
these Aramaic translations in use in the first place? By the time of the Roman
imperial period, many (perhaps most) Jews of the land of Israel no longer
possessed a knowledge of Hebrew that would have permitted them fully to
grasp the meaning of Biblical Hebrew. Aramaic (along with some Greek) was
the lingua franca of the region. The translation referred to in this passage is
one or another of the Aramaic translations (*targum*, sg.; *targumim*, pl.) in use
in the land of Israel at the time. So what is the halakhic problem with which
this passage begins? Simply this. Is it permitted to recite an Aramaic translation of the prescribed scriptural lection from a *written text* of the Aramaic, as
one *must* do for the scriptural reading itself? With this context understood,
let us examine the cited text from JT Megillah 4:1.

The passage that I have presented begins with a "precedent story" (alleged to have been) cited by R. Haggai concerning the indicative behavior
of one R. Samuel b. R. Isaac. The latter is said to have attended a communal

24. In Tiberias, to be more precise. There has been much debate about whether a
few of the Jerusalem Talmud's tractates were composed a bit earlier in Caesarea. The
debate has no relevance to our discussion. The main modern scholarly proponent of
the Caesarea hypothesis was Saul Lieberman; its principal detractor was Jacob Neusner.

assembly, during which the public reading of Scripture was taking place. Rabbi Samuel noticed a written edition of an Aramaic translation on the reader's table. Rabbi Samuel surmised that the translator was reciting the *targum*, the Aramaic translation, from the written text before him. Samuel immediately forbade the translator from using the written text of the *targum*. Undoubtedly, the precedent story assumes that such written *targumim* were in circulation. It is just that, in Samuel's (or Haggai's) view, they were not to be used in the formal ritual performances of communal assemblies. Rather, the translator was to recite the Aramaic translation by heart from memory. The Hebrew term for recitation by heart from memory is *al-peh* or *be-peh* (lit. "by mouth" or "in the mouth," that is, "orally"). Recitation *al-peh* or *be-peh* is contrasted with reciting while reading from a text, that is, *be-ketav* (lit. "in writing"), which is how Scripture itself is to be publicly recited, namely, from a written text and *not* from memory.

Now, one bit more about Hebrew terminology is worth having in your back pocket in order for us to proceed. It has to do with the Hebrew word *dibrot* (*davar*, sg.). It is a noun based on the verb root *dbr/dvr*, meaning "to speak." So while *davar/devarim* is used in ancient Hebrew (and modern Hebrew too) to denote a number of things, including "thing," "material," "object," "topic," at its heart, in Biblical Hebrew, it means "that which has been spoken," "an instruction," "teaching," or "lesson." Indeed, this is the sense in which it is used in referring to the Ten Commandments (*aseret ha-devarim*). And this is also the sense in which *devarim* is used over and over again in the book of Deuteronomy, beginning with its first verse: "These are the *devarim* which Moses spoke to all [the people] of Israel." Indeed, the entirety of the book of Deuteronomy is portrayed as Moses' final "speech," "lesson," or "instructions" before his death.

This is all the background you need for us to be able to shift our attention to those aspects of the passage that intersect with this chapter's issues. And as regards our specific interests, this passage is remarkably replete with relevant information that attests to our six summative claims about what early rabbis tended to say about themselves, their traditions, and their literature—that is, how they mythologized what they and their teachings and rulings were. Throughout this passage, first a halakhic and then an aggadic distinction is made between those teachings, instructions, or lessons that are given and thereafter conveyed in writing (*be-ketav*) and those that are or ought to be conveyed orally (*al-peh/be-peh*). Scripture is the former (i.e., *be-ketav*). And, formally, *targum* and *extra-scriptural* instructions, lessons, teachings, and rulings are the latter (*al-peh/be-peh*), even though, paradoxically, written texts of these *extra-scriptural* teachings and *targumim* exist, and likely for good reasons (e.g., preservation and consultation), as was the case for the written text of a *targum* that R. Samuel is said to have seen on the reader's table in the synagogue. The remainder of JT Megillah 4:1, namely, those sections that follow the precedent story, takes matters two steps further. Let us, then, proceed step-by-step.

Step 1: The sections of the passage following the opening precedent story proceed on the *premise* that that which has been transmitted orally (*be-peh* or *al-peh*) and that which has been conveyed in writing (*be-ketav*), namely, Scripture itself, are *both* integral parts of a whole revelation of God to Israel by Moses' agency. Both written and oral teachings together comprise the terms of YHWH's covenant. The second tradition attributed to R. Haggai (who is said to be citing R. Samuel b. Nahman), as well as the traditions attributed to R. Yohanan and R. Yudan b. R. Simeon, also *assume as axiomatic* the authority of this divinely revealed, dual written and oral legacy. The "fancy exegetical footwork" we observe is a typical example of aggadic midrash; meaning is extracted from (or attributed to) Exod 34:27b's use of the language *al-py* (which in colloquial English I have had to translate as "on the basis of") and *ha-devarim* (which I have translated as "things"). But *al-py* is just a form of the word *al-peh* (by mouth, that is, orally), and *devarim*, as you already know, is the plural noun based on the verb root *dvr/dbr*, "to speak." So Exod 34:27b is understood "midrashicly" to be referring to God's "speeches" (*devarim*), transmitted "by mouth" or "orally," as the foundation for establishing His covenant. Eureka! Exodus 34:27b is understood to be referring to an Oral Torah that is distinct from and completes the Written Torah.[25]

Now, step 2. Step 2 occurs in the part of this passage at JT Megillah 4:1 attributed to R. Joshua b. Levi, an alleged near-contemporary of Rabbi Judah the Patriarch and his son, Gamaliel III. We have here another exemplar of aggadic midrash, trying to read into Deut 9:10 meanings that on the surface seem not to be there. How? By focussing on word choices that could have (and, presumably, would have) been otherwise, if the surface or plain meaning were all that was intended by Scripture. Again, this is typical aggadic midrash in action. The seemingly superfluous language—[Scripture does not say just] "on them" [but] "**and** on them"; [not just] "words [*devarim*]"

25. Now, I must point out that the "plain sense" of the *whole* verse at Exod 34:27 does not convey this distinction of an oral part and a written part of God's revelation to Moses. The plain sense of Exod 34:27's Hebrew formulation would read the second half of the verse (34:27b: "for on the basis of these *devarim*") in the context of the first half (34:27a: "Write down these *devarim*"). But finding "hooks," however contrived, that justify severing bits and pieces of a scriptural sentence from their context, so that new or additional meanings can be ascribed to Scripture, is precisely how reading Scripture "midrashicly" often proceeds. Midrash is (often) not biblical exegesis or interpretation in the normal sense of the word.

[but] "**the** words [*ha-devarim*]"; [not just] "all [*kol*] [but] "**accorded with** all [*ke-khol*]"—is taken to mean that Deut 9:10 knows of both a revelation that is written and its complement, which is not written. Together, that which is written and that which is not written (but is orally preserved) comprise "[that which] accords with all the words [*ke-khol ha-devarim*]," that is, all of the instructions of YHWH revealed to Moses. Therefore, there is an Oral Torah that was conveyed in "words/speech" (*devarim*) that complements and supplements the Written Torah. But then—and this for us is the critical move that I would call step 2—the teaching attributed to R. Joshua b. Levi goes further. Joshua b. Levi is said to identify this complete dual revelation, written down by Moses and orally transmitted by Moses, as "Scripture, and Mishnah, and Talmud, and aggada." Scripture is the Written Torah; the rest, starting with Mishnah, is Oral Torah (since it was *not written down* by Moses for transmission to successive generations). All of these, "even what the experienced disciple will teach before his [rabbinic] master, were already spoken to Moses from Sinai." The Mishnah herein referenced is "Rabbi Judah the Patriarch's" Mishnah. Talmud is a *genre* or *mode* of Mishnah analysis, since it is unlikely (even impossible) that the Jerusalem Talmud (c. 400), let alone the Babylonian Talmud (c. 600), is being referred to here. Mishnah and Talmud-mode Mishnah study are halakhic in content. Aggada, as you know already, refers to early rabbinic stories and teachings that convey a homiletical, ideological, or theological lesson. So here, in addition to Scripture itself, we see referenced much/most of the early rabbinic curriculum—all of it is said to be Torah revealed to Moses on Sinai, of which only Scripture is understood to have been written at Moses' time.

There are other attestations in early rabbinic literature to the distinction between Written Torah and Oral Torah, of which the rabbis claimed to be the privileged recipients and heirs. It is doubtful that any of these other traditions may be *reliably* dated earlier than what I have just presented. Were the rabbis aware of the irony (if that is the correct term) that they claimed to possess a legacy of Mosaic revelation, an Oral Torah, for which there was (and could be) no ancient evidence, precisely because until their era no one had written down any of it? I think some were aware. And I will end this presentation of early rabbinic sources indicating the early rabbis' mythologizing of their teachings, their literature, their group, and its membership by citing a extract from a composition found in the Babylonian Talmud at BT Menahot 29b. I believe that sense of irony shines through, as you will see. The tradition is attributed to Rav, a first-generation Babylonian Amoraic authority of the first half of the third century.

BT Menahot 29b

R. Judah said [that] Rav said: When Moses went up to heaven [lit. on high], he found the Holy One—blessed be He—sitting and tying crowns on the letters [of the Scripture's text]. He [Moses] said to him: Master of the Universe, who has [made you] delay [revealing Scripture to me by undertaking to so decorate the letters]? He said to him [Moses]: There is a certain man who will live after some generations—and Akiva ben Joseph is his name—who will derive [*li-derosh*] [from] each and every [allegedly decorative] thorn [adorning these letters of the words of Scripture] piles upon piles of *halakhot*. He [Moses] said to Him: Master of the Universe, show him to me? He said to him [Moses]: Turn around. He [Moses] went and sat at the end of the eighth row [among Akiva's students/disciples], and he [Moses] did not understand what they were saying; he grew weary [i.e., inattentive]. When a certain matter came up [in the discussion], his [Akiva's] students/disciples said to him [Akiva]: Rabbi, whence do you [get this teaching]? [Akiva responded]: [It is] Halakha [revealed] to Moses on Sinai. [Upon hearing this answer, Moses'] awareness returned.

Now this aggada may be interpreted in two, but not necessarily contradictory, ways. (1) Moses, after having ascended to heaven from Mount Sinai and then having been miraculously transported to a future time, does not recognize anything being discussed in the study session conducted by R. Akiva, because Moses has *not yet* received on Sinai God's revelation to him of the Oral and Written Torah. Or (2) Moses has risen to heaven after his death on Mount Pisga, that is, *well after having received* Torah (that is, the "whole" Torah, Oral and Written) from God, but nonetheless does not recognize what Akiva and his disciples are talking about (a deliberately ironic twist, as it were). You be the judge, but the reference to a delay in the process of revelation suggests the former interpretation. In either case, this passage from BT Menahot 29b aptly caps our presentation of examples of early rabbinic mythologizing about the divine origins of both their teachings and their own authority as one important foundation of what they thought they were.

Before summarizing and consolidating what has been presented in this chapter about the rabbis' mythmaking about themselves, their teachings and their literature (Mishnah in particular), I wish to return to something I wrote earlier about mythologies and mythmaking. I remarked that not only do we moderns tend to think of mythologies as fantasies, but also we have difficulty imagining that any relatively advanced civilization or intellectually sophisticated members of societies, present or past, would believe their mythologies to be "literally true." Without turning this chapter into a phenomenological study of myth, mythmaking, or myth-believing, I would venture to say that there is ample evidence to suggest that some (or many) thinkers in the ancient world, including the world of the early rabbis, had a complex relationship with their own mythologies. In this regard, let me say something of an ancient Jewish philosopher, Philo, who lived in Alexandria (Egypt) in the first century CE. He was a leading figure in Alexandria's Jewish community; in fact, he participated in a delegation sent by Alexandria's Jews to plead a case before the emperor Caligula.[26] In this sense, Philo may be considered socially and politically mainstream among Alexandria's Jews. Yet, Philo displays what at first glance is a peculiar stance toward the stories of the Jewish Bible (which, by the way, he knows primarily or exclusively in Greek translation). He does not consider many of these stories, particularly about the biblical patriarchs, to be *literally* true but *allegorically* true. That is, he views the language of these stories to be deliberately *symbolic*. Symbolic of what? Of Philo's Middle Platonic understanding of God and the tenants of biblical Judaism. Indeed, for Philo, even many of the ritual injunctions enjoined by Moses according to the Bible amount to "action-symbols" of this Middle Platonic philosophy and ethics. So, according to Philo, why did the (now Platonically redefined) God or Moses, God's disciple, not just dispense altogether with the symbolic language of mythology and give the people of Israel a Torah with "the straight goods," a Middle Platonic view of the world and an associated way of living together with others? The answer for Philo is this: only the intellectual elite (that is, those well educated in Middle Platonic values and philosophy) would be able to grasp it.

Now, Philo was not a rabbi; he lived before as well as outside the geographical ken of the early rabbinic movement. But, more than one thousand years later, one of the most distinguished *rabbis* of the medieval period, Rabbi Moses ben Maimon (aka Maimonides), steeped in the medieval version of Aristotelian philosophy,[27] takes a comparable stance vis-à-vis biblical narrative, biblical injunctions and rituals, *and* rabbinic halakha in his book *A*

26. The case being made was rehearsed (or reconstructed) in Philo's treatise, *Legatio ad Gaium*. The matter was decided, however, by the emperor Claudius, Gaius's successor. Legatio is a treasure trove of valuable information about the social and organizational structure of the Alexandrian Jewish community and about the community's status (and aspirations) within Alexandrian society.

27. Aristotelian philosophy in the medieval period was not "pure Aristotle." Rather, it was heavily tinged with Middle Platonic and Neoplatonic ideas.

Guide for the Perplexed (*Moreh Nevukhim*).[28] Who are the perplexed? They
are the highly educated among Jewish society of Maimonides's day—not only
highly educated in the biblical and rabbinic literatures but also well conver-
sant with the philosophy, science, mathematics (and often also the medical
sciences) of the twelfth century, particularly in Muslim-ruled lands and cities,
where the world's earliest "universities" were established.

If an elite Alexandrian Jew in the first century CE and an illustrious
rabbi in the twelfth century could both exhibit complex understandings of
the mythologies (and even the rituals) of biblical and rabbinic Judaism respectively, why assume that the early rabbis could not have had a similarly
complex relationship with their mythmaking? Do we imagine all early
rabbis to be ancient fundamentalists, believing in the literal truth only of
their mythologies? After all, the early rabbis' midrashic understandings
of Scripture are replete with nonliteral interpretations of the Bible; often
these midrashic takes are themselves rabbinic mythologizations of biblical
mythologizations.

Now, we cannot get into a time machine and ask a sample group of
third- or fourth-century rabbis whether they *literally* believe that everything said by them or their disciples in their study sessions (of Mishnah)
was *actually* already revealed to Moses on Sinai as Oral Torah. Maybe BT
Menahot 29b, the last cited rabbinic passage, is an aggadic expression, a
mythologization of a myth, indicating a recognition by at least some in early rabbinic circles that the myth of Oral Torah could not be taken as *literally
true*. Indeed, the early rabbis themselves frequently point to several allegedly historical sources of their halakha, not all of it, in this view, from Moses. For example, while they view much of rabbinic halakha as grounded in,
and as developments of, biblical law (and therefore, in their view, of Mosaic
origin), the early rabbis often posit a different origin for some of the legal
traditions that they have inherited and recognize as normative. And that
origin is not stated to lie in Oral Torah revealed to Moses, but rather in the
legal edicts issued by a class of "scribes" who, in the rabbis' view, were part
of the official administration of Judea in the Second Temple period (that
is, before 70 CE).[29] (By the way, the early rabbis do not, to my knowledge,

---

28. Composed by Maimonides in Arabic (in the Hebrew alphabet) under the title
Dalalat al-Ha'irin, and in Maimonides's own lifetime, translated into Hebrew under
the title *Moreh Nevukhim* for circulation among Jewish scholars outside the Arabic-
speaking world.

29. On the early rabbis' attribution of parts of their halakha to edicts of "the scribes"
of the Second Temple period (as opposed to positing scriptural authority for these particular legal teachings), see, e.g.: m. Toharot 4:7–11; m. Parah 11:5–6; m. Yevamot 2:4;
m. Sanhedrin 11:3; m. Yadayim 3:2; m. 'Orlah 3:9; t. 'Eduyyot 1:1; 1:3; Sifre Devarim
154:2; JT Sheqalim 5:1; BT Hullin 104a (on m. Hullin 8:1); BT Ketubbot 10a (citing a

make comparable claims about a body of edicts of the Pharisees as a major source of their legal traditions.) These edicts from (lit. "the words of") the scribes, while clearly part and parcel of rabbinic halakha, *do not have the same legal standing* for the rabbis as do injunctions in the Pentateuch. How can this be the case, if (according to rabbinic mythologizing) everything, that is, all halakha and especially all that is in Mishnah, is either based in the Written Torah or the Oral Torah revealed to Moses on Sinai? When, in chapter 4, we discuss antecedents with significant cultural currency to what the rabbis were, I shall say more about this scribal class. But the seed has been planted here. However, more to the point of this chapter's deliberations—like many educated, intellectually sophisticated elite, the early rabbis, too, likely had a complex relationship with their own myths grounding their authority, their teachings, and their literature.

CONCLUSION: THE MYTH OF MISHNAH'S ORIGINS UNDERGIRDS THE RABBINIC MYTHOLOGIZING OF WHAT THE EARLY RABBIS WERE

Here, then, in the exemplary, early rabbinic traditions discussed in the previous section, many of which may be reasonably dated to the third and fourth centuries CE, we have attestations to beliefs, axioms, and assertions expressed by the early rabbis that substantiate the six summative claims I articulated earlier concerning early rabbinic mythologizing. About what did they mythologize? About (1) the basis for their special, even monopolistic, authority as a group, *as a result of* (2) the extraordinary status of their teaching and texts, particularly Rabbi Judah the Patriarch's Mishnah. The rabbis as a group claim for their collective and for their individual members' status to be *exclusive* recipients and guardians of an orally transmitted Torah that is a complement of the Written Torah—both revealed to Moses. So, somewhat paradoxically, one might say that the early rabbis' *texts*, chief among them the Mishnah (c. 200 CE), are *Oral* Torah. You will recall that for Sherira, Mishnah's formulation of traditions was so extraordinarily compelling as to be *like* revelation from Moses, and Mishnah's author, R. Judah the Patriarch, was so accomplished as to be *like* Moses. We could well anticipate what the Karaite's reaction to Sherira's rationalizing in the guise of historiography might have been. They might have said, "So what? How does that change anything in principle?" But for the early rabbis of the third

---

tradition allegedly from Rabbi Simeon ben Gamaliel II).

and fourth centuries, Mishnah was not just *like* revelation to Moses; it *was* revelation to Moses, transmitted orally, until formalized in the language of Judah's Mishnah. In this mythologizing, Judah was not like a Moses; he was a special heir of Moses' teachings through an extraordinary (and exclusive) chain of student/disciples serving their masters/teachers. The devoted, engaged study of the early rabbinic curriculum, and of Mishnah in particular, perpetuated that chain through the generations of rabbinic masters and disciples after Judah the Patriarch's career, through the Amoraic period and into the early medieval era, when the Babylonian Talmud's treatment of Mishnah displaced Mishnah itself as the most important element of the rabbinic curriculum and the most authoritative expression of Oral Torah.

At this juncture, I feel compelled to point out that we (just as did the early and medieval rabbis) find ourselves in an awkward, perhaps paradoxical, place. A *literature* (Mishnah, Tosefta, the Jerusalem Talmud, the Babylonian Talmud, and many other rabbinic texts produced before the rise of Islam), all of which was (eventually) preserved and transmitted *in written form* sometime during the late Roman and early Byzantine eras, is mythologized to be an "oral" tradition. Communities with central mythologies take them seriously, even if they do not always understand them literally. They see them as "true" in some significant sense. They try to *live that truth* as well. Without involving you in an extensive exercise of literary history, which is not the focus of this volume, I must nevertheless point out that the early rabbis (in part) *lived the truth* of Mishnah as the highest embodiment of Oral Torah by highly valuing the committing of Mishnah to memory and studying it together from memory. Sometime in the third century CE, there developed within the early rabbinic movement specialists who were charged with being able to recite (presumably on demand) any section of Mishnah—this as a resource to those engaged in Mishnah study with their master/teacher. Moreover, we know from several passages in the Babylonian Talmud that a certain value was placed on pronouncing halakhic decisions orally, rather than delivering them in writing.[30]

All of this has led modern academic scholarship on the literary history of Mishnah and of other early rabbinic "texts" to consider whether at the turn of the third century Mishnah was actually *composed* orally (like the Homeric epics), and attained written form only later in that century or the beginning of the fourth. Personally, I do not subscribe to the argument that Mishnah was *composed* orally,[31] even though I find compelling the evidence that great

---

30. See, e.g., BT Temurah 14b, with its parallel at BT Gittin 60b.

31. In *In the Seat of Moses*, 65n7, I write:

There has been of late much scholarly debate about the role orality may

value was placed on *memorizing* Mishnah. What I do think is the case is that we are observing in the early rabbinic movement the downstream effects of a community trying faithfully to live its myth.

So, in the agenda of this volume, set out in chapter 1, where do we now stand? Were we able to ask a member of the early rabbinic movement, just after Mishnah's production and promulgation, what are you as a group, we would now be able to anticipate an answer. If we were to ask what makes your group so special, we could also accurately anticipate a response. If we were to further inquire what makes one a bona fide member of your special group, we would already know much that they would likely tell us. And if we were, finally, to probe what activities are the most central to the members of the movement as a group, here, too, we would not be surprised about what they might recount. All of the likely most important answers to such queries, were we able to pose them, have been articulated in this chapter, which is about to be brought to a conclusion.

Here, however, is what we do not know, yet. We do not know what *particular* skills, traits, and (pre) requisites characterize, and are central to, the members of the early rabbinic group. For example, how are these particular characteristic traits different than those of our fictitious Einsteinians? Since we know that following its production near 200 CE, Mishnah study was the most important inner-group activity of the early rabbinic group, then figuring out (1) what the requisites or prerequisites of Mishnah study were, and (2) what skills were engaged and engendered by Mishnah study, would tell us much about the particular normative *profile* of members of the early rabbinic movement. As I intimated earlier in this chapter, divining this profile by looking at Mishnah itself, particularly at what demands Mishnah study makes on those engaged in it, will occupy you and me in the next chapter, chapter 3, of this volume.

There is something else we, as of yet, do not know. Let me sum it up glibly in this question: Why would any Jew in the land of Israel (or in Mesopotamia-Babylonia) in the third and fourth centuries, whether a member of the rabbinic group or not, find the elements of early rabbinic mythologizing about themselves even remotely plausible, credible, compelling, or

---

have played in the composition and promulgation of Mishnah. One exemplary voice of the "oral composition" advocates is Elizabeth Shanks Alexander, in *Transmitting Mishnah*, and "Fixing"; she argues that both Tosefta and Mishnah were composed and initially promulgated via a process of oral performance. I am far from convinced that the evidence bears out the hypothesis that both Mishnah and Tosefta were composed via oral performative acts, as she spells out. To argue the point more fully is beyond the ken of this book's introductory purposes. It suffices that this volume's readers are aware of these debates.

legitimate? In other words, to use my language from chapter 1, what cultural, social, or political *currency* might the elements of the early rabbinic myth
have had in Judah-ic society of the period? There is, indeed, a great deal that
may be said of contemporary and earlier Judah-ic culture and society that
provides meaningful context and valuable currency to what the early rabbis
say about themselves. Let me be clear that context and cultural currency do
not make the early rabbinic mythologization historically true; rather, they
makes it culturally and socially plausible, in the sense that sociologists and
anthropologists use the term. This issue will occupy us later in this volume,
in chapters 5 and 6. But to whet your appetite, I will say that notions of Oral
Torah or oral tradition might not surprise a Pharisee of the first century
BCE or first century CE, even though, as I shall argue, it is overly facile to
identify the early rabbis as Pharisees. The idea of a revelation of teachings
that exceeded, completed, and complemented that which appears in the Hebrew Scriptures, but which were the legacy of only a restrained, even secret,
elite group would not shock the author of 4 Ezra or many of the members
of the community at Qumran. But, as stated, we will wait to broach these
matters. In the meanwhile, in the next chapter, you and I will study some
Mishnah to see what it demands of one as a profile. We will glimpse what it
means to be a Mishnanian as opposed to an Einsteinian.

3

Mishnah Study and the Shaping of a Shared, Early Rabbinic, Professional Profile

"BUT ALWAYS PURSUE THE [STUDY OF THE] MISHNAH MORE"[1]

I N CHAPTER 2, WITH tongue in cheek, I named the early rabbis the Mishnanians and likened them to my fictitious Einsteinians. Why? Because, as already stated, a document that the early rabbis called the Mishnah (from the Hebrew verb *shnh/shny*, meaning "to repeat/teach") was not only the first magnum opus (indeed, the first opus) produced by and for the members of the early rabbinic movement;[2] Mishnah was also the principal object of lifelong, engaged, and devoted study, undertaken together with others, in an early rabbinic curriculum that *formed* rabbis as bona fide associates of their fellows.

---

1. BT Bava Metzi'a 33a.

2. I leave aside the literary-historical question about whether there were one or several proto-Mishnahs, as it has little to no bearing on the arguments made in this chapter or in the volume as a whole. As far as one can tell, only one Mishnah was the most privileged object of devoted study across the early rabbinic movement for four hundred years or more. It is "our" Mishnah—more or less, given the slight "improvements" that will have been made to it. An excellent and concise summary of the early literary history of the text of the Mishnah may be found in Fox, "Introducing Tosefta."

Mishnah remained at the center of the early rabbinic curriculum for about four centuries, after which a turn-of-the-seventh-century composition, the Babylonian Talmud, *began* (over a period of time) to replace Mishnah as the centerpiece of the rabbinic curriculum. However, (even) the Babylonian Talmud was *originally* produced to reflect and model a particular genre of Mishnah analysis. So the production of the Babylonian Talmud, like its earlier counterpart, the Palestinian (aka Jerusalem) Talmud, serves only to confirm what has just been said about the place and significance of Mishnah study for the early rabbis.

To be sure, for the early rabbis, the teachings and injunctions of the Hebrew Scriptures, and particularly the books of the Pentateuch (the Torah of Moses), exceeded Mishnah in authority. However, the study of Scripture did not make one a rabbi. Mishnah study did, even though knowledge of Scripture's content is, as we shall soon see, a requisite of reading Mishnah and of early rabbinic authority. After all, any and all first-, second-, or third-century CE Judean literati, teachers, and officials (like the scribes?) would have known, and would have been expected to know, Scripture well, particularly its prescriptions and proscriptions. What these other learned cadres did not have was the Mishnah, understood, as we have seen in chapter 2, by the rabbis of the third and fourth centuries also to be God's revelation to Moses. So, possession and knowledge of Mishnah set the early rabbis apart as individuals and as a group from potential peers (and competitors), in the rabbis' minds at least. Scripture and knowledge of Scripture, however important and necessary, did not.

Without a doubt, then, we have before us a case of study as a socially formative individual and group activity. Moreover, I also contend, as noted in chapter 2, that devoted Mishnah study was (or became) a *ritual enactment*. Of what? Of early rabbinic mythologizations (1) of early rabbinic teachings, (2) of Mishnah, (3) of the early rabbinic group itself, as well as (4) of the authority the early rabbis claimed for all three.

Over the first half of the twentieth century, a debate periodically ensued among scholars associated with the relatively new fields of the history of religions and the comparative study of religion about the relationship of myth to ritual.[3] To put matters glibly, the debate was about a "chicken-and-egg" problem. Does myth give rise to ritual? Or does ritual give rise to myth? Whichever side one comes down on, there seems one clear upshot:

3. In the United States, the history of religions school was (initially) especially associated with a group of scholars at the University of Chicago; they were influenced by intellectual currents in France and Germany. The comparative study of religion was (initially) especially associated with Harvard, with a prominent transplant at McGill University in Montreal.

myth and ritual are mutually reinforcing phenomena within social forma-tions. Moreover, through time, mutually reinforcing myths and associated rituals evolve in a kind of dialogue with one another. And so it is with the early rabbis' mythologization of their teachings, of their literary produc-tions (chief among them, Mishnah) and of their cadre, on the one hand, and, on the other, their ritualization of Mishnah study.

Mishnah, as you now know, was produced c. 200 CE, and devoted, ritu-alized Mishnah study seems to have characterized the early rabbinic group immediately upon Mishnah's production and promulgation. Moreover, it is hard to fathom why Mishnah was produced at all, if there had not already arisen among the pre-mishnaic rabbis an ethos and practice of the study of early rabbinic teachings, which Mishnah then systematized and formalized in a shared text. Otherwise, why produce a Mishnah and then install it at the center of the early rabbinic curriculum? And why study this Mishnah as a devoted, engaged, ritualized group practice, if some notions of the mythic importance and instrumentality of this practice were not already current among the early rabbis, even though our concrete evidence for early rabbinic mythologizations comes from mid-third to mid-fourth-century sources? So, Mishnah's *very production*, c. 200 CE, bespeaks of a social formation, as well as some mythologization on the part of that group. Once produced, the devoted, lifelong study of Mishnah by members of the group functions as a socially reinforcing ritual activity, which is legitimated by (further?) my-thologization, for which we have clear third- and fourth-century testimony, some of which I have presented in the previous chapter.

By this point, all of the foregoing should be familiar ground to you. You know what it *means* to be a Mishnanian, in the sense of the *mean-ing and significance* the early rabbis attribute to Mishnah and Mishnah study. But you do not yet know what it is to *be* a Mishnanian, in the sense of *what one becomes* via pursuing and mastering engaged Mishnah study. So, I return to a theme first articulated in chapter 2: "There's something about Mishnah." If one "always pursue[s] [the study of] Mishnah *more*" (my emphasis) than any other object of study (as the Babylonian Talmud, Bava Metzi'a 33a, instructs its readers), then one must *become more of something* that is demanded by the requisites of Mishnah study, rather than becoming something else, were some other body of teachings (like Scripture?) to have been the preferred object of study. It is this *becoming more of something* by reason of the preferential pursuit of Mishnah study that I wish to explore with you in this chapter—what it is to *be* a Mishnanian.

Now, as I have hinted at in chapter 2, *what specifically one becomes more of* by reason of lifelong, devoted Mishnah study will likely have been significantly conditioned:

1. By what Mishnah study demands intellectually of its devoted students, given Mishnah's content and literary style

2. By emerging normative modes of, and models for, Mishnah analysis within rabbinic circles

For the *earliest* rabbinic movement that coalesced just before, at the time of, and in the immediate aftermath of Mishnah's production c. 200 CE, the only direct evidence we have for glimpsing what one becomes by being an Mishnanian lies *in the traits of Mishnah itself, because it is precisely these traits that place demands on the devoted Mishnah student.* By contrast, direct evidence for emerging, normative models for Mishnah analysis must be derived or induced from *post*-mishnaic, early rabbinic texts, which were produced between a century and four centuries after Mishnah's initial promulgation. These post-mishnaic rabbinic texts, consequently, tell us about *later, further evolved* Mishnanians, not about our earliest cohort. And it is the latter, the "early" rabbis, with which this volume is primarily concerned.

In light of the remarks of the previous paragraph, in the next sections, I turn, first, to a very broad, general description of Mishnah, since I assume many of you will never have encountered Mishnah or a Mishnah passage. Second, I will articulate what engaged Mishnah study demands *broadly* or *generally* of the devoted Mishnah student, almost as prerequisites, let us say. In the subsequent section, I will give you a sense of what Mishnah study invites/requires its students *to exercise specifically as intellectual skills.* In order to do this, it is helpful to examine with you several representative passages from the Mishnah. These sections taken together will paint a picture of the "professional profile" of the engaged, devoted, lifelong Mishnah student, our earliest Mishnanian. As just intimated, that portrait has two aspects: (1) what one needs *to enter* the practice of Mishnah study; and (2) what *one gets out of* Mishnah study, that is, how the practice would seem to change or shape one.

GENERAL (PRE) REQUISITES
FOR MISHNAH STUDY

Memorization of Mishnah

First and foremost, what is Mishnah? Probably not coincidentally, in 2006, entire sessions at the annual meetings of two major academic organizations, the Association of Jewish Studies and the Society of Biblical Literature, examined exactly this question. So, you can well imagine that answering it is not straightforward, or even amenable to a simple or single response.[4] In chapter 3 of my introductory book, *In the Seat of Moses*, I address this issue as part of an introductory survey of early rabbinic legal literature. As I have already intimated, Mishnah's content is almost entirely legal; it deals with halakha, the "Way" one lives one's life as a Jew in accordance with Torah. The contents of Mishnah are organized topically as "tractates"; these are of varying lengths. In the current standard printed editions of the Mishnah, one finds sixty-three such tractates. One is Avot. In the previous chapter, you will have read that Avot is not halakhic in content; it is aggadic. Moreover, it is likely a mid-third-century CE addition to Mishnah. So, for our purposes, it is the other sixty-two, overwhelmingly halakhic tractates of Mishnah that are of interest. Additionally, the modern printed editions of Mishnah, following many medieval manuscript versions on which the printed texts are based, group these sixty-two tractates of Mishnah under six grand thematic headings called "orders" (pl. *sedarim*): (1) agricultural law; (2) Sabbath, holy days, and festivals; (3) family law; (4) damages, criminal law, and judicial procedures; (5) sacrificial practices; and (6) purity law.

It is likely the case that the current organization of individual tractates under these six grand thematic headings is a medieval scribal innovation. And the medieval manuscript tradition indicates that there may have been some disagreement about which tractates were to be grouped under which grand thematic order, and/or in what sequence. Moreover, as late as the medieval period, there may also have been disagreements about how many Mishnah tractates there were, because some (originally?) longer tractates may have later been divided for the sake of convenience into two (or more?) shorter ones. Yet another likely medieval scribal innovation is the internal division of individual tractates into numbered "chapters" (pl. *peraqim*) and their discrete, enumerated "Mishnah passages" (pl. *mishnayot*)—much like modern printed editions of the Bible, which divide books into enumerated chapters and verses. This innovation, carried into the era of print, allows one, for example, to refer to Mishnah tractate such-and-such, chapter (*pereq*) 3, Mishnah passage (*mishnah*) 2, just as one may refer, let us say, to Deut 23:3 (that is, the biblical book of Deuteronomy, chapter 23, verse 3). This innovation was the "rage" of the time among scribes of Judaic, Christian, and Muslim holy texts. Before this "advance" in scribal practice, Mishnah tractates' chapters (and sometimes also individual constituent Mishnah passages) were referred to by their opening words. (Today, traditional Jews still refer to the major sections of the Pentateuch by their opening word or words, just

---

4. In a recent article I have addressed the methodological issues relating to how one interprets the question "what is Mishnah" (Lightstone, "What Is Mishnah?").

as they continue to name the books of Pentateuch by a prominent word in each book's opening verse.) Does not this earlier method, naming Mishnah's chapters and passages by their opening words, demand of the Mishnanian a considerable familiarity with the Mishnah text, at least some (if not much) of which would have to have been committed to memory for such a method to be usable? Indeed, yes! Let me demonstrate this proposition with a thought experiment, because it may well be the first conclusion we are able to draw about general (pre) requisites of Mishnah study.

Imagine that you and I are disciples/students of our rabbinic master in 230 CE. We are being guided through the intense study of a particular tractate of Mishnah. It is highly doubtful that we all have written copies of Mishnah before us. Moreover, as you read in the previous chapter, early rabbis "lived the myth" of Oral Torah by studying Mishnah from memory. In any case, even if we were sharing a few copies of written texts among us, it would likely be a copy of the single Mishnah tractate under discussion, not a copy of the whole Mishnah. This is akin to the dominant practice in the Greek- and Latin-speaking/reading world of the era of dividing single literary oeuvres into many smaller "books." Usually, each individual book circulated as a scroll, as a matter of convenience and economics. And it is highly likely that the individual books of the Scriptures were also extant in writing as individual scrolls.[5] If our rabbinic master had a fairly large instructional enterprise operating, a *bet midrash* (house of study), our rabbinic master may have also had on hand instructional assistants whose special tasks included having memorized the Mishnah in order to facilitate our learning and our rabbi's pedagogy. Such an assistant (called a *Tanna*,[6]

---

5. The material remains of many Roman synagogues, particularly from the fourth to sixth centuries CE, include a niche and sometimes two niches in the main assembly hall for the books/scrolls of Scripture that were read (and studied) as a matter of practice. Of course, the niches that archaeologists have unearthed are of stone or brick. Any that might have been made of wood, if such existed, would have long rotted away. Some archaeologists have concluded that within these niches were cubbies (generally, made of wood, now gone) in which scrolls of individual books of the Hebrew Scriptures were deposited. Such a practice would be akin to how documents were stored in libraries in the Greco-Roman period, such as in the great library of Ephesus. In other words, the niches of late Roman synagogues were "libraries" of Scripture's individual books/scrolls—the literal meaning of *biblica*, is it not? It is understandable, then, that we do not find Torah scrolls, that is, the entire Pentateuch written on one continuous scroll, in the Greco-Roman Period. This is significant because scrolls produced by Jewish scribes of the Greco-Roman period have survived—indeed, a whole trove of them at Qumran—aka the Dead Sea Scrolls.

6. Such a *tanna* is not to be confused/conflated with the term used for early rabbinic figures from the period up to and including the career of Rabbi Judah the Patriarch and his son(s), that is, around the time of the production of Mishnah, who are refered to as *tannaim* (*tanna*, sg.)—although the matter is, admittedly, inherently confusing for

a "repeater") is a walking scroll, as it were. But leave that, too, aside. In explicating a particular Mishnah passage in the tractate under study, our imagined rabbi refers to another Mishnah passage in some other Mishnah tractate altogether. How does he do this? From what we know from early rabbinic literature, he *might* say:

> As it teaches in *pereq* "He who steals wood," "He gave [the vessel] to artisans to fix, and they ruined it—they are liable to pay [the owner for the vessel's value]."

What our rabbinic master will *not* have been able to say is this:

> As it teaches in Mishnah tractate Bava Qama, chapter 9, Mishnah passage 3, "He gave [the vessel] to artisans to fix, and they ruined it—they are liable to pay [the owner for the vessel's value]."

Our master *cannot* use such a system of reference, because in the early third century CE, no one has yet divided Mishnah tractates into numbered chapters and numbered constituent passages. And how is anyone to know whether a chapter that begins with the words "He who steals wood" is near the beginning of the Mishnah tractate Bava Qama, its end, or its middle, when one has no recourse to a system that numbers Mishnah chapters in sequence? The answer is, and must be, *one must have memorized a lot of Mishnah,* even if one's rabbi's instructional operation is of a size to be staffed with a Tanna or two, these "walking scrolls" (like characters out of the dystopian novel *Fahrenheit 451*[7]). If this is not a *pre*requisite to engaged study and analysis of Mishnah, it is certainly a *general* requisite which one will have satisfied at some point as a Mishnah student. One must have a "passing knowledge" at least of the opening words of Mishnah chapters (and perhaps also Mishnah passages) in their proper sequence *in one's head,* or one would not know which scroll to consult and where to look in that scroll, if one even had a written text handy, which may not always (or usually) have been the case. Hence, my proposition, much memorization of Mishnah was part and parcel of the profile of Mishnanians, even if and when a Tanna (a "walking book") was at hand.

Now, of course, there are many stories, many of the aggadic genre, in *post*-mishnaic, early rabbinic literature that convey the value and ideal of memorization of halakhic traditions in general and of Mishnah passages specifically.[8] These stories appear in documents authored between

---

those as yet unfamiliar with the early rabbinic movement.

7. Bradbury, *Fahrenheit 451.*

8. See, e.g., the well-known and well-regarded monograph of Martin Jaffee, *Torah in the Mouth,* or the more recent one by Elizabeth Shanks Alexander, *Transmitting*

the latter third and end of the sixth centuries CE. Again, we have already discussed in chapter 2 the place of orality in the ethos and ideology of the early rabbinic movement. And orality is integrally tied to memorization, is it not? (Indeed, the argument has been made that the literary style and conventions of Mishnah facilitate memorization, because one often finds in Mishnah passages the type of cadence, balance, alliteration, and assonance that in modern Western society we commonly associate with lyrics or poetry.[9]) My point here, in this chapter, differs subtly but significantly. So let me repeat it. Mishnah study and analysis, from the time Mishnah was promulgated c. 200 as the ne-plus-ultra object of rabbinic contemplation, demanded a certain degree of memorization of Mishnah as either a *pre*requisite or (minimally) a requisite of engagement.

Permit me at this interim point to sum up what you will have learned about what the early rabbis were from this section of chapter 3. We know from post-mishnaic, early rabbinic literature, and have discussed in chapter 2, that memorization of Mishnah was valued. Moreover, we can surmise that, *in part*, this valuing of memorization dovetailed with the emerging third- and fourth-century mythologization of early rabbinic teachings as Oral Torah. But in the thought experiment just conducted, we glimpse that some degree of memorization of Mishnah is also (and perhaps primarily) a general technical *requirement* when one engages in Mishnah analysis.

As a postscript to this section of the chapter, let me make one final point, which paradoxically will drive home the lesson about memorization and Mishnah study. This requisite has been largely (although not entirely) eliminated in modern printed editions of Mishnah (1) by the medieval scribal innovation of enumerating constituent sections; (2) by modern

---

Mishnah. Alexander argues that Mishnah was not only transmitted orally but also composed in processes of oral performance. I think she may have overstated what the evidence supports, as I state earlier. I have discussed these very issues and my own views of them more extensively in the footnotes to my book *In the Seat of Moses*, ch. 4.

9. See Neusner, *Memorized Mishnah*. See also Jaffee, *Torah in the Mouth*, and E. Alexander, *Transmitting Mishnah*. The argument that Mishnah's literary features were intended to facilitate memorization is in part founded on the quite reasonable hypothesis that in real life no one would "speak" the way Mishnah does. So Mishnah's literary conventions that facilitate memorization are not an artifact of how Middle Hebrew was normally used. Nor does Mishnah's literary style reflect Hebrew poetry, which is based on very different literary principles. That said, there is something else facilitated by Mishnah's style that gives it this lyrical (in modern terms) aural quality that is rarely discussed; the style is a highly effective and efficient way of (1) concatenating and permutating putative circumstances that comprise a hypothetical case or a series of hypothetical cases, for which (2) one or several (disputing) rulings may apply. For a more complete discussion of Mishnah's literary conventions and style see my book *In the Seat of Moses*, ch. 4.

printed editions' increasing propensity to insert cross-references in their texts, thus building on this medieval innovation; and (3) by the unprecedented ubiquity in the modern era of printed editions of early rabbinic classics, itself further driven (4) by the increased availability more recently of digitized, key-word-searchable texts of many early rabbinic texts.

Knowledge of Scriptural Underpinnings of Mishnah

As I have stated several times already, for the early rabbis, the Mishnanians, Mishnah is the most authoritative text, the knowledge and lifelong study of which marks one as a rabbi. That said, no early rabbi would deny the supreme authority of Scripture and, within Scripture, the authority of the Pentateuch (the Torah of Moses). The supreme authority of Scripture and especially of the Pentateuch is not just a tenet of religious ideology for the early rabbis. (Indeed, it could not have been otherwise for the members of the early rabbinic movement, because in that era to assert otherwise would have been considered apostasy in any Judah-ic community in the Near Eastern and Mediterranean regions, including in the assemblies of the early Jesus movement.) Even more so, the authority of Scripture's and specifically of the Pentateuch's laws, proscriptions, and prescriptions is presumed in Mishnah's passages. No! "Presumed" does not even begin to capture the matter. The Pentateuch's legal injunctions, although *largely left unquoted* in Mishnah, everywhere constitute axioms, premises, and authoritative data underlying Mishnah's tractates, chapters, and individual passages. So much so is this the case that one would be hard pressed to make sense of a great deal of Mishnah, were one not able *in one's head* to corollate the content of the Mishnah chapter or Mishnah passage under analysis with all of the subject-relevant scriptural verses.[10] And by "make sense" I do not mean "able to grasp fully the implications of." I mean, rather, "often not even *begin*

10. Once again, modern printed editions of the Mishnah have greatly mitigated this requisite. Take Albeck's edition of the Mishnah, *Shisha Sidre Mishnah*, e.g. He provides an introduction for every Mishnah tractate, in which, among other things, he cites in full all relevant scriptural passages that serve as axioms in the tractate. Moreover, his line-by-line commentary of each Mishnah passage will often draw the reader's attention to the relevant verse(s), phrases, or individual words in Scripture that underlie, but are left unquoted in, the passage. Albeck's edition is entirely in Hebrew. A commonly used Hebrew-English Mishnah text with English commentary is that of Blackman; indeed, early editions of Blackman's Mishnah translation and commentary have been digitized in PDF format and may be found online. Blackman's work is highly competent. However, the Blackman edition of the Mishnah did not set out to achieve in English the scope of what Albeck's introductions, commentary, and extensive endnotes have done in Hebrew.

to understand the plain sense of." This is an important distinction. And it is best illustrated by a representative passage of Mishnah itself.

Take for example, Mishnah Horayot, chapter 1, Mishnah passage 1a (or m. Horayot 1:1a). It is the opening "rule-sentence" of the first passage of the first chapter of the tractate in question—a fact that will prove significant.

m. Horayot 1:1a

i. [If] a court instructed to transgress one of the commandments stated in the Torah,

ii. and an individual acted unwittingly on the basis of their word—

iii. whether they acted, and he [or she] acted with them, [or]

iv. whether they acted, and he [or she] acted after them, [or]

v. whether they did not act, and he [or she] acted—

vi. he [or she] is exempt,

vii. because he [or she] depended on the court.

As stated, this is just the first "sentence"[11] of the Mishnah passage. But even this much will suffice to make my point. Keep in mind, this passage, indeed this sentence, *opens* the entire tractate of Horayot, the larger topic of which is the status of decrees of duly constituted courts. As such, *nothing* comes before this extended rule-sentence by way of introduction, background, or context-setting for the passage, for the Mishnah chapter, or for the Mishnah tractate. Let us, then, delve into m. Horayot 1:1a.

---

11. In this section, I have placed "sentence" in quotation marks—what some call scare quotes—because by the standards of modern grammatical English it is not a completely grammatical sentence. This is especially so if one removes the "if" in square brackets, which I have added. One of its oddities is the change in the grammatical subject of the sentences as one progresses to the main predicate at the end. Jacob Neusner (see *History of Mishnaic Law*, pt. 21) called this tendency in Mishnah "apocopation." Mishnah Horayot 1:1a is an example of relatively mild apocopation, rather easily masked by my insertion of "if" at the beginning. Without my "if" at the outset, it looks like the grammatical subject is the court. Yet the subject of the main predicate at the end is "he [or she]" who has acted on the court's say-so—not very good English. But by the standards of mishnaic Hebrew, the first rule-sentence of m. Horayot 1:1a is a perfectly acceptable, even elegant, and certainly grammatically proper one. The implicit rules for mishnaic sentences allow for the concatenation and permutation of alleged/posited circumstances that constitute a hypothetical case or a series of hypothetical cases, for which one or more rulings are said by Mishnah to apply. We shall say a bit more about this in subsequent sections of this chapter. That said, a more complete account of the structure and function of mishnaic rule-sentences may be found in my book *In the Seat of Moses*, ch. 4. Hereafter, I will dispense with the scare quotes around the word "sentence."

The sentence is grammatically complex, even in my English translation, which I have deliberately made as literal as possible (other than to introduce some gender neutrality[12]). It opens with a statement of circumstances—actually, a series of closely related variations of the putative circumstances. A court issues a decree or a judgment, and an individual acts on the court's authority. But the court has decreed something that is forbidden by Torah law. The rest of the sentence answers two unstated questions: What, then, is the liability of the individual actor for his (or her) transgression? Does it matter whether the individual acts with or after the members of the court, or whether the members of the court act at all in accordance with their own (misguided) decree? The answer to the latter question is no! We know that, because one and the same ruling at line vi covers all of the stated permutations of the circumstances. This brings us to the answer to the first unstated question, which again is no. The individual is not liable; he/she is "exempt." Why? Because (as stated at line vii) he/she depended on the court's decree or judgment. But vii in reality introduces nothing new. It merely harps back to part of the posited circumstances stated at line ii; the individual acted on the basis of the court's decree, not on his or her own cognizance. So, line vii of the rule-sentence is a (somewhat redundant, perhaps) explicatory gloss of the rule.

At first glance, all this seems very straightforward and comprehendible, until one asks some basic questions. What is the individual *not* liable for at line vi; that is, of what is he/she exempt? What does "unwittingly" (*shogeig*) add to the posited circumstances that the rest of the language at lines i and ii articulate? Certainly, if the individual acted "because" the court so instructed, one would think that there is nothing "unwitting" about what he or she did. After all, the individual did not act by accident without any intent. The hypothetical person in question *intended* to follow the court's directive, as the explanatory gloss at line vii makes explicitly clear.

I will give you the answer to these questions, and your reaction might rightly be this. From what language in this passage could you have possibly inferred that? Of what is the individual exempt? And in what sense is the term "unwittingly" an apt or even relevant modifier of the individual's putative actions? The answer is this (and take in a large breath): the individual is not liable:

---

12. In Mishnah, the male gender predominates grammatically, unless topically a Mishnah passage expressly deals with women. This does *not* mean that Mishnah considers only men to be subject to the halakha, unless otherwise indicated. But it does reflect the fact that gender neutrality *in language* (and gender equality socially) are foreign concepts to the social world in which the early rabbis lived.

1. For the sin/purification offering of a one-year-old she-goat

2. The offering of which is due when one transgresses *unwittingly* a biblical prohibition

3. For which transgression, if done knowingly or purposefully (*mezid*)

4. The same individual would have been subject to extirpation from the community[13]

Where in the world did all that come from, because it is certainly not found in the Mishnah passage that *opens* tractate Horayot? Well, it comes from Scripture, specifically from Num 15:22–29, largely paralleled in the fourth chapter of Leviticus. Here is where Scripture sets out the penalties for unwitting vs. knowing transgressions of scriptural prohibitions. What might Scripture mean by transgressing a biblical prohibition "unwittingly"? Well, the act might have been done without conscious awareness, or the person may have just been ignorant of the prohibition, in which cases he/she brings a one-year-old she-goat as a sin/purification offering, and all is forgiven. So, for Scripture, transgression unwittingly committed has an "out." Perhaps, we would say today that the person in question lacks "criminal intent," even though he/she committed a criminal act.

Now, m. Horayot 1:1a takes Scripture's "out" one step further; if the individual acted by reason of a court's decree (which, by the way, is action with intent), then one does not even have to offer the designated sin/purification sacrifice. So according to Mishnah, the biblically based halakha in these matters recognizes three levels of culpability (not two, as Scripture prescribes):

Level 1: Willful transgression—penalty is extirpation

Level 2: Unwitting transgression—penalty is a sin/purification offering

Level 3: Unwitting transgression, intentionally based on a court's instruction—no penalty whatsoever

So, m. Horayot 1:1a (and much more in Mishnah tractate Horayot) *ramifies* the biblical law, which itself is *often left unstated in the Mishnah text*. The result, as illustrated by this discussion of the very opening rule-sentence

13. The term "extirpation" is modern authors' attempt to translate the Hebrew term *karait*, "cutting off." *Karait* refers to those numerous instances in which the Pentateuch states that a perpetrator of a designated transgression is to be "cut off . . . from the midst of the people" of Israel. Nowhere does Scripture clearly define what the penalty of *karait* entails. The most likely interpretation involves some form of social shunning or exclusion. The rabbis, however, came to understand *karait* as divine retribution of some sort, rather than a penalty imposed by society.

of tractate Horayot, is that Mishnah is often not intelligible or comprehendible without knowledge of, and reference to, relevant biblical law—this even when (or even though) no references appear in Mishnah to the relevant scriptural verses.

How are novice Mishnah students to know of the need to consider certain specific biblical injunctions or verses when nothing in Mishnah expressly tells us, even as an introduction to its content? They cannot. Or more properly stated, they likely cannot, if left to their own devices without (prior) instruction, or without recourse to an instructor during Mishnah study sessions.

Eureka! Now, you, the reader of this volume, have discovered more about the early Mishnanians' shared group profile. You know that (and how) knowledge of specific verses of Scripture, unstated in Mishnah, is a *requisite* or *prerequisite* of fully understanding even the opening sentence of Mishnah tractate Horayot. And where does one acquire such requisite or prerequisite knowledge? From (prior?) study with a teacher, of course. So, you have just grasped some essential facts (1) about the relationship of Scripture to Mishnah, (2) about one of the requisites or prerequisites for fully understanding the content of Mishnah, and (3) about the necessity of the master-disciple or teacher-student relationship among the group of Mishnanians.

Let me punctuate what I have just said in the preceding paragraph by making another claim. The exercise that I have just undertaken with you, by examining the first rule-sentence of Mishnah tractate Horayot, I could easily repeat using any one of many, many dozens of other Mishnah passages. The result would be more or less the same. What we have discerned about *a* core trait of the Mishnanians via the lens of m. Horayot 1:1a is not an aberration or exception. Why? Because what we have glimpsed in our sample Mishnah passage are some of the *pervasive* traits of Mishnah and what these traits require of devoted, engaged Mishnah students—in this regard, about the acquired capacity to identify any underlying scriptural data, even though (commonly) no reference to, let alone citation of, the relevant verses of Scripture is provided by Mishnah. And I may add, to command this capacity requires (or is at least significantly enhanced by), among other things, memorization of much of the Pentateuch, since that is where almost all biblical law is found.

We are not done with articulating the relationship of Scripture to Mishnah and how this impacts what one becomes in the process of engaged Mishnah study. Earlier in this chapter, I listed the grand themes that define the six orders under which Mishnah's topical tractates are grouped in the extant medieval manuscripts of the Mishnah text. Even at first glance, at least one of these thematic orders should attract attention, namely, the one concerning sacrificial offerings (the fifth order, Qo-dashim). Why should it raise an eyebrow? Well, at the turn of the third century CE in the land of Israel, there is no Jerusalem temple at which to offer sacrifices. The Jerusalem temple was destroyed by the Romans in 70 CE, and Roman authorities would not let it be rebuilt. And the rabbis (and most of world Jewry at the time) seemed pretty much resigned to that state of affairs. As far as the rabbis were concerned, the rebuilding of the temple would have to wait until the coming of the messiah (since revolts against Rome had proven to be national catastrophes).[14]

Now, according to the interpretation of pentateuchal law that by 200 CE had already been normative among the majority of Jews for a while, sac-rifices to the God of Israel could be offered only at the Jerusalem temple. Therefore, as far as these Jews were concerned, no sacrifices enjoined in biblical Scriptures could be offered at all after 70 CE.[15] So most, if not all, of the Mishnah tractates of the Order of Qodashim have "merely theoreti-cal" (rather than practical) importance. Moreover, Mishnah's dealings with

14. At least twice after 70 CE and the failed revolt against Rome in the 130s CE, en-thusiasm erupted concerning the possible opportunity to rebuild the Jerusalem temple. One such opportunity was in the fourth century CE, during the reign of the Roman em-peror Julian ("the Apostate"). Julian, born a Christian, sought to allow non-Christian religions and pagan-associated science and philosophy to revitalize itself. By the same token, he was actively considering allowing the Jews to rebuild the Jerusalem temple. His reign ceased before this could be begun, let alone accomplished. Several centu-ries later, in the throes of the conflict between the Sassanid Persian Empire and the Byzantine-Roman Empire, and just before the rise of Islam and the Islamic conquest of Persian-ruled territories in the mid-seventh century CE, the land of Israel briefly returned to the Persian sphere of the Near East. Discussion ensued to replicate the policy of Cyrus the Great in the latter sixth century BCE, when Cyrus had supported the aspirations of a group of Judean exiles living in Babylonia to return to the land of Judah, to rebuild Jerusalem and its temple, and to repossess their ancestral holdings—events dealt with in the biblical books of Ezra and Nehemiah. The efforts sanctioned by Cyrus and his successors resulted in the so-called Second Temple period and in the production of the books of the Hebrew Bible. The Islamic conquest of the Sassanid Persian Empire precluded the rebuilding of a "Jewish" Jerusalem and its temple, as Is-lam's views and policy about Judaism and Jews (which very much resembled its policy toward Christians living under Islamic hegemony) precluded such a restoration.

15. It is a professional hazard of academic scholarship that for every general asser-tion there are exceptions. We know of two (and perhaps three) "Jewish" temples out-side Jerusalem that operated after the production and promulgation of the Pentateuch. A Jewish temple on the Nile at Elephantine operated into the early Persian imperial period. And a dissenting Jerusalem priest, Onias, founded another one in Hellenistic times at Leontopolis in the Nile Delta. Finally, the Samaritans continued to use an altar near Shekem (today, Nablus); they ultimately opposed the Jerusalem-centrism of the Judeans' interpretation of the Pentateuch, which the Samaritans largely shared with the Judeans. By 200 CE, when Mishnah was produced, only the Samaritan altar site was still in use, although the Samaritan temple itself no longer stood.

sacrifices and matters that require a now nonexistent Jerusalem temple are not limited to the obviously problematic tractates of the Order of Qodashim. Temple and sacrificial matters pervade much of Mishnah's tractates. Much of Mishnah's treatment of festivals involves temple-based rites, as does some of Mishnah's treatment of agricultural gifts and tithes. And the same is true of a great deal of Mishnah's tractates that deal with the halakha of (ritual) purities. The mishnaic treatment of purity halakha often requires purification offerings, and, indeed, much of the purpose served by purity halakha is to protect the temple from contamination. Even the sample rule-sentence examined earlier, m. Horayot 1:1a, assumes an operating temple at Jerusalem. How so? Mishnah Horayot rules that one who unwittingly transgresses a prohibition on the basis of a court's decree is "exempt." From what? A sin/purification offering, which, if he or she were not exempt, would require an operational Jerusalem temple. What do I infer from all of this?

Well, when one studies a society's laws, one reasonably expects to glimpse that society's traditional norms, social structure and institutions, widely shared ethical and social ideals, and (especially) the more frequently occurring "rub points" of upholding those ideals and of making these normative social institutions work. One has only to look at, let us say, Hammurabi's Code (c. 1750 BCE), laws 137 to 143,[16] and one gets a pretty good sense of the how Hammurabi's codifiers try to deal with the rub points in the institution of marriage in Babylonian society of their era. Hammurabi's codifiers are loath to allow faithful wives divorced by their husbands (usually, it appears, because they have borne no children) to leave their marriages without ample financial means to assure their futures—a rub point, if not appropriately managed in law. Or consider, for example, the obvious social rub point attested in biblical law (Num 27:1–11) between ancient Israelite norms concerning gender-based inheritance, on the one hand, and clan/tribal-based land tenure on the other. If daughters are allowed to inherit when there are no sons, and these daughters marry men from another clan/tribe, then the daughters' fathers' lands would eventually pass into the possession of men of the other clan/tribe—reflective of a rub point, no doubt, in ancient Israelite society. The Pentateuch's solution is to require a woman who inherits her deceased father's property (because the father had no son) to marry within her tribe/clan. Such women's sons, who would eventually inherit their maternal grandfathers' lands, have the tribal/clan status of their fathers. So the lands stay within the holdings/territories of their maternal grandfathers' tribe/clans. The societal rub point is mitigated.

16. For a readily accessible English translation of Hammurabi's Code, see the online resources of the Avalon Project of Yale Law School (https://avalon.law.yale.edu/ancient/hamframe.asp).

Admittedly, some laws on a society's books might be obsolete (in the sense that the social reality that they reflect no longer holds), and yet they remain on the books by reason of benign neglect (or because the process to change them is onerous). When I was a child in Ottawa, Ontario, Canada, in the 1950s, a posted bylaw at the beginning of the Interprovincial Bridge that joined Ottawa with Hull (now Gatineau) on the Quebec side of the Ottawa River still read "walk your horses." I had never witnessed horse traffic on the bridge, but I presumed that the bylaw had never been revoked. Was this an instance of "just in case"—after all, I remember milk, cheese, and butter being delivered by a horse-drawn wagon—or of benign neglect? In any case, the bylaw and the sign persisted long after they were obsolete, because their persistence was benign. Who cared whether now nonexistent horse-drawn buggies were still required to walk their horses across the Interprovincial Bridge? So, we might say that the bylaw became an anachronism. But were changes in social values or social institutions to make such obsolete laws really contentious, then efforts would be made to revise or strike them, rather than leave them on the books, even if the processes for revising or striking them were onerous.

Now, what does this brief detour into legal anachronisms have to do with Mishnah and the normative profile of Mishnanians? Mishnah is not a law code by any means (a matter that will be clearer later in this chapter). Mishnah is, however, a legally oriented text. That is what makes it halakha; it is about matters that pertain to the "Way" one is supposed to act in accordance with Torah. And yet, mishnaic halakha is to a great extent (even though not entirely) about a world that is no longer actionable, because key social structures and institutions that mishnaic halakha assumes no longer exist in reality. One might be tempted to say that Mishnah's content constitutes one very big anachronism, just as an Ottawa bylaw continued for a time to require walking *no longer existent* horse-drawn buggies or horses across the span of the Interprovincial Bridge. Yes, many social structures and institutions referred to in Mishnah existed once (before 70 CE in the land of Israel), and at least some of Mishnah's halakha may be *reminiscences* of these social structures and institutions. But we are not facing in Mishnah just an anachronism or two (like the bylaw specifying "walk your horses"). On the contrary, Mishnah is shot through and through with anachronistic references to social institutions that no longer exist. So, we must conclude that this is not the result of some benign neglect resulting in inclusion of legislation of the past; rather, this was the intended plan of Mishnah's framers—a massive elaborated *creative anachronism*.

Consequently, it may be said that the "world" that so much of Mishnah presumes to exist, *exists in the imagination* of Mishnah's framers and of its devoted students *as an ideal*—almost in the Middle Platonic sense of the word. But I have come to the conclusion that even this formulation does not completely capture what lies behind Mishnah. Why? Because the ideal world that mishnaic law presumes to exist does exist for the early rabbis somewhere in (a kind of) reality. It exists in Scripture, and particularly in the Pentateuch's proscriptions and prescriptions, and we may think of Scripture as part and parcel of the world of the rabbis, even if the Jerusalem temple no longer stands. I am increasingly convinced that temple institutions and practices are dealt with in Mishnah, not (only or even primarily) because the early rabbis want to remember them but because they are integral to scriptural law. It is the world of Scripture, as much as or perhaps more so than the world of pre-70 Jerusalem, that is the object of so much of the agenda of Mishnah and, consequently, of the contemplation of the engaged Mishnah student.[17]

And so, we have learned yet another thing about what one becomes *in general* in the process of lifelong, devoted Mishnah study. One becomes a contemplator of the intricacies of the application of halakha as it *would* pertain (as opposed to does pertain) to intricacies of a (hypothetical) world structured in accordance with the demands of Scripture, even though Scripture's world is no longer *fully* operational (or operation-able) in Jewish life. Once again, in yet a different manner, thorough knowledge of Scripture is a general prerequisite or requisite of the engaged Mishnanian. Because to be a Mishnanian means, to a significant degree, to *imaginatively* live via Mishnah study in Scripture's world by contemplating possible rulings for equally hypothetical "rub points" in it. Is that not what m. Horayot 1:1a, for example, does when it considers whether the "unwitting" transgressor is obligated to bring the scripturally mandated sin/purification offering to the temple, if the transgressor was (intentionally) acting in accordance with a court order?

Of course, the foregoing begs an obvious question. To what end all of this legal contemplation of an ideal, scripturally based world? My answer to this question (to the degree that I have one at all) will have to wait until near the end of this chapter, after we have considered more prerequisites and requisites of engaged, devoted Mishnah study, and after I have discussed how lifelong Mishnah study pursued together with others of the rabbinic group may have shaped early rabbis' skills, profile, and collective identity.

17. In my four and a half decades of reading Mishnah as an academic, I have often been struck by the fact that many Mishnah passages deal seemingly de novo with issues in Scripture (that is, legal-exegetical matters), rather than reminiscences of the pre-70 temple, since centuries of actual practice in the Jerusalem temple would long ago have had to have solved these same exegetical issues.

Not (Just) the World Created by Scriptural Law,
but Scriptural World, Version 2.0

In the foregoing sections of this chapter, I have argued that the world imagined in and underpinning individual Mishnah passages and Mishnah tractates is, to a large extent, Scripture's world. And this is the case, even though
much of what constitutes Scripture's world does not exist (and cannot exist)
at the time of Mishnah's production c. 200 CE. In other words, first and foremost, *Mishnah's agenda is what it is because it is Scripture's agenda.* And it is
impossible for the Mishnah student fully to comprehend Mishnah without
an anterior comprehensive knowledge of Scripture's legal content.

I have also admitted, however, that other things lurk behind and
underneath Mishnah passages. These other things are Judah-ite institutions and laws acknowledged by the early rabbis as normative that are *not*
denoted in Scripture. Yet, prior knowledge of them is assumed by, and
necessary to begin to comprehend, much of Mishnah, because here, too,
Mishnah passages do not explicitly provide their reader with any account
of this body of legal knowledge.

What are the bases of these extra-biblical institutions and laws assumed by Mishnah? Earlier, I did not rule out that, in addition to all relevant Scriptural prescriptions and proscriptions, historical reminiscences
or memory of pre-70 Judean life and normative practice may be expressly
reflected in or lurk unstated beneath the surface text of Mishnah. Now,
I will go even further than this. It is highly likely, additionally, that aspects of the life and normative behavior of contemporary Judean society
of the second and early third century CE are reflected or are assumed or
presumed in many Mishnah passages. That is to say, the world assumed
or presumed beneath Mishnah's passages is a creative, anachronistic mix
of (1) the world that emerges from Scripture's laws, (2) putative reminiscences (accurate or not) of pre-70 Judean society, and (3) contemporary
post-70 Judean societal practices and institutions. However, we cannot
rule out that some or much of this assumed/presumed world underlying Mishnah's passages represents (4) the early rabbis' wishful thinking
about what Judah-ic society, institutions, and norms should have been (or
should be), as reflected in the teachings of the several generations of rabbis that preceded Mishnah's production c. 200 CE.

I should note that post-mishnaic rabbinic texts, notably the Jerusalem
and Babylonian Talmuds, often speculate about the origins of some of this
extra-biblical legal system—within (or notwithstanding) an overarching
mythological-ideological frame of Oral Torah said to have been revealed
to Moses at Sinai. Passages in the Talmuds will sometimes maintain that an

extra-biblical law is simply implicit in the scriptural injunction that is its underpinning. Here the extra-biblical law is understood (sometimes implausibly) to be the real and original meaning of the biblical injunction. Or (as we have had occasion to remark in previous chapters) some talmudic passages attribute a body of law to the scribes of the pre-destruction era. Or talmudic passages will postulate that certain pre-mishnaic laws emerged from the legislative assemblies—e.g., the alleged Great Assembly, or the Great Sanhedrin—that the rabbis understood to have existed in Judea over the centuries that preceded Jerusalem's destruction in 70 CE. Or, as I have done in the preceding paragraph, they propose that the early rabbis of the Tannaitic period leading up to Mishnah's production decreed on their own (alleged) authority some of these extra-biblical laws.

The social historian or sociologist who wishes to tease apart these likely sources—or in the case of some Talmud passages, these designated sources—for the societal institutions and norms underlying, and presumed/ assumed by, Mishnah has a difficult task indeed. I have no doubt that some of this teasing apart can be done, although it is decidedly *not* our designated purpose here in this book. That said, permit me an example.

Consider the case of the several Mishnah tractates that deal with the themes, topics, and subtopics related to agricultural gifts to priests, Levites, and the poor. Without question, much of what these tractates do is to work out the implications and to test the application of Scripture's many injunctions concerning tithes, heave offerings, firstfruits, forgotten sheaves, etc. These injunctions, the implementation of many of which (e.g., first grain/*omer* offering and firstfruits offering) assume a functioning temple, undoubtedly and unavoidably are authoritative premises of these several Mishnah tractates, even when/where the relevant Scripture is not cited by the Mishnah. But a number of these Mishnah tractates and their constituent Mishnah passages also assume certain modes of agricultural production, farming technology, and norms for land use or land tenure. Do you think the framers of these Mishnah passages are trying to imagine de novo how all this operated in ancient Israel in biblical times? It is far more likely that Mishnah's framers' assumptions about these things are influenced, if not determined, by their knowledge of contemporary or near-contemporary Judean agricultural practices, or the practices of the recent past. They are far less likely to be trying to imagine ancient technology or some future technology, and far more likely to be reflecting agricultural processes of their own time or nearly so.

Sometimes this imaginative mixture of what is assumed in Mishnah as normative creates dissonances between Scripture's injunctions and the imagined state of affairs. Then, *implicitly*, Mishnah must reimagine its

understanding of Scripture in light of extra-scriptural or post-scriptural assumed or presumed states of affairs and laws. So the underlying world (with
its legal system, its halakha) that is imagined in, and *lurks underneath and
behind*, Mishnah passages and of which the Mishnah student must have
thorough prior knowledge, is *Scriptural World+*, or *Scriptural World 2.0*. This
assertion would benefit from both further explanation and further illustration, because it will provide you, the reader, with some inkling of not only the
nature but also the scope of the body of extra-biblical (or non-biblical, if you
will) law lurking behind the pages of Mishnah.

Earlier in this chapter, I asserted that comprehensive knowledge of
all relevant scriptural law is a prerequisite or requisite of Mishnah study,
because it is the law of the imagined *Scriptural World 1.0*. That law is presumed but often left unstated in Mishnah passage after Mishnah passage.
Now, I have claimed that, additionally, there is *another, complementary*
body of law presumed by, but also often left unstated in, a great many Mishnah passages. It is a body of secondary law that turns *Scriptural World 1.0*
into *Mishnaic-Scriptural World 2.0*. So, the engaged Mishnah student must
have *prior* knowledge (or be taught) this secondary body of law, too, as a
general (pre) requisite in order to make sense of Mishnah. Let me give you
an example that will readily further illustrate this.

Mishnah's tractate on Sabbath law is among the longer ones in Mishnah. That many biblical injunctions (largely uncited by Mishnah) underlie
Mishnah tractate Shabbat is obvious. Among many other biblically specified Sabbath prohibitions, Scripture's law limits movement/travel, even on
foot, on the Sabbath. Exodus 16:29 (my translation) enjoins: "Let everyone
rest in place; no one shall go out of his place on the seventh day." On the
surface, the meaning of this biblical injunction is that one stays at home
on the Sabbath, period. We may quibble about what counts as staying at
home—your house, your property, etc. But the plain sense of Exod 16:29
would seem to preclude taking even a longish stroll on the Sabbath. But
this is not the corresponding Sabbath law that is *presumed or assumed* to
lie behind or underneath the passages and chapters of m. Shabbat/Eruvin.
Mishnah assumes, but does not seemingly need to explicitly rule, that staying at home does not really mean staying at home. Rather, there is a limit of
two thousand cubits (in any direction) beyond which one may not venture
on the Sabbath. That two-thousand-cubit limit, furthermore, is measured
from one's personal space (of four cubits in every direction), if one is caught
outdoors in the countryside when the Sabbath begins, or is measured from
the exterior boundaries of one's dwelling place (if one's dwelling is in the
country), or is measured from the outermost habitations of one's town or
city (if one abides in a settlement on the Sabbath). Without *prior* knowledge

of these rules about the Sabbath limit, one cannot even *begin* to make sense of many of the Mishnah passages in m. Shabbat/Eruvin.

The foregoing illustration could be supplemented with a great many extra-biblical rules assumed/presumed by, but not articulated in Mishnah. These rules constitute a body of law that encompasses a set of truly diverse matters. For example, Mishnah presumes/assumes: synagogues and public readings of Scriptures conducted in them; a system completely unknown in the Pentateuch of local and regional courts and a national court (the Great Sanhedrin of the Chamber of Hewn Stone of the temple compound) that both adjudicate and legislate; marriage contracts (*ketubboth*, pl.; *ketubbah*, sg.) that provide for the support of widows and divorcees; and blessings said before and after eating various types of food. I could fill pages of this book with lists of such laws, institutions, and normative practices. These rules are part of a body of law and a legal-judicial system that are *not found in Scripture* but thorough knowledge of which is, nonetheless, a (pre) requisite of Mishnah study. This extra-scriptural body of law, taken together with Scripture's injunctions, constitutes what I have called *Scriptural World 2.0*, all of which is *assumed* in Mishnah's imagined world.

I realize that many of you will still want to ask where this extensive, extra-biblical body of law assumed or presumed by (but left unarticulated in) Mishnah comes from. Above, I have already specified the logical possibilities for its origins. But the specification of logical possibilities is no substitute for the scholarly research that would turn a mixture of *possible* origins into specific claims about evidence-supported, historically probable ones. Such questions and their attendant scholarly research require earnestly addressing who-type inquiries, which are expressly *not* the focus of this volume, the purpose of which is to pursue what-type inquiries. Specifically, what were the early rabbis? Well, based on the foregoing, we now have even more to say that addresses this what-type question. The early rabbis are Mishnanians who, in order to study Mishnah, must have a prior expertise in *both* biblical law *and* this extra-biblical law even to begin to make sense of Mishnah passages. That is to say, the ardent Mishnah student must have (also) mastered an entire body of *extra-biblical law* that underpins but is not (or is rarely) articulated in Mishnah itself. This, too, is part of the profile of the Mishnanians. And I will venture an additional claim. It is my distinct impression[18] that this body of extra-biblical law and normative practice

18. I say "impression" because I have never attempted to document and count the number of extra-biblical laws assumed and presumed by Mishnah's content and to compare these to an enumeration of biblical injunctions. Medieval rabbinic texts that enumerate or otherwise document rabbinic laws do not usually distinguish between halakha *assumed* by Mishnah and halakha *stated* in Mishnah, even though they

assumed or presumed (but left largely unstated) in very many Mishnah passages may actually exceed in volume the prescriptions and proscriptions of the Pentateuch. That is a lot of prerequisite or requisite knowledge to command (much of it by heart) *before* being able to make sense of Mishnah. No one, again, is born with this knowledge. Nor is it likely that all or most second- and third-century CE Judeans acquire thorough knowledge of this body of law as a matter of course. Such thorough familiarity is the purview of a highly educated group of specialists, among them the members of the early rabbinic group, who (likely) vied with other such highly educated cadres for the social status and roles for which their speciality was meant as a qualification in late second- and early third-century Roman-ruled Judea.

Intellectual Skills Inculcated/Nurtured by Mishnah Study

Near the outset of this chapter, I stated that if the early rabbi is "always [to] pursue [the study of] Mishnah more than"[19] the study of anything else, then in the process of devoted lifelong Mishnah study, the rabbinic disciple of the sage *becomes more of something* than would be the case if some other curriculum were at the early rabbinic movement's core. So, what have you learned to this point about what early rabbis and would-be rabbis become by reason of their focus on Mishnah study? Let me summarize.

In the preceding sections of this chapter, you have seen that some of what the early rabbi becomes is a function of the *general* requisites and prerequisites required for/by Mishnah study. These include:

1. A certain degree of knowledge by heart of the Mishnah text, even if only, at the minimum, to process referencing and cross-referencing Mishnah passages

2. A thorough knowledge of all biblical injunctions, because, although largely left uncited and unreferenced in Mishnah, Scripture's proscriptions and prescriptions everywhere underpin Mishnah's tractates and Mishnah passages, which frequently lack any intelligible context without Scripture's law *in mind*

---

episodically attribute laws to scriptural, scribal, or rabbinic origins. This does not help much, because some of what is said to be of scriptural origin is in fact not what Scripture says but is patently extra-biblical. Some of what is ascribed to scribal origins is explicitly given in Mishnah. And some of what is said to derive from the rabbis themselves does not appear in Mishnah but is assumed or presumed by Mishnah.

19. BT Bava Metzi'a 33a.

3. Thorough knowledge of an extensive, additional body of Judah-ic law and norms not found in Scripture, also left unstated in Mishnah's text, but underlying much of Mishnah's tractates, chapters, and passages

I have characterized knowledge of these two prerequisite bodies of law, that is, (2) and (3), as rules for *Scriptural World 2.0.*

Why do I talk of Scripture's world and not of the social and cultural world that the early rabbis inhabit near the turn of the third century CE? Because, first, many of these rules *are* Scripture's, and, second, these are rules for a world in which the Jerusalem temple, its cult, its personnel and associated institutions, and even the Judean monarchy still function. That world *no longer exists at the time of Mishnah's production*, and it is my distinctive impression, that members of the early rabbinic movement harbour no illusions about these institutions being reconstituted any time soon. Now, why 2.0? Simply, because the rules presumed and assumed in Mishnah for this no longer existent Judah-ic world are not just Scripture's teachings and injunctions but also a substantial body of *additional* rules and norms. So, the Mishnah student, before having set out to analyze Mishnah tractates, will have had to have mastered a body of norms defining a world that at the time of Mishnah's production can, to some significant degree, have existed in toto only in the rabbis' minds as a creative anachronism, as an ideal object of contemplation. So, in part, in satisfying even the general requisite or prerequisites for Mishnah study, one becomes a contemplator of this ideal world.

What more does the early rabbinic novice *become specifically* by actually studying Mishnah's tractates, once the Mishnah student has the *general* (pre) requisites for Mishnah analysis in hand? The answer, as you shall see in this section is this: beyond the (pre) requisite knowledge for understanding Mishnah, Mishnah study demands and therefore inculcates certain *specific intellectual/analytic skills*, which, in the process of mastering Mishnah, become part and parcel of the professional profile of the would-be rabbi, because Mishnah study is a (the?) core, *formative* activity of members and would-be members of the early rabbinic group—of the Mishnanians. These inculcated professional skills developed and honed by Mishnah study are largely a function of the interplay between Mishnah's content and Mishnah's literary conventions. So, let me say more about what Mishnah is (and is not) before proceeding to demonstrate the professional intellectual skills demanded/inculcated by Mishnah analysis.[20]

All along, I have said that Mishnah's content is almost entirely legal; it is a halakhic text. The fact that Mishnah's halakha, or much of it, pertains

---

20. For a more extensive, accessible discussion of what Mishnah is and is not, see my book *In the Seat of Moses*, chs. 3 and 4.

to an imagined, ideal society—an elaborate creative anachronism—does not change this fact. However, Mishnah is decidedly not a law code, even for Mishnah's imagined world.[21] For one, much of what one would expect to be in a law code is simply not there. We have already seen that systems of law are assumed by but left unstated in Mishnah. Moreover, many of the types of cases ruled upon in Mishnah would normally represent exercises to implement codified or normative law for the myriad, diverse cases and circumstances to which codified law or accepted legal norms would have to be applied by judicial authorities acting as courts or arbitrators. No law code specifies or can specify how its rules are to be applied to all possible circumstances and cases. The processes of such applications result in case law. And yet, in my considered view, Mishnah overall is not, generally speaking, a record of Judah-ic case law either (even though one cannot rule out that some actual case law may be recorded in Mishnah). Nor is Mishnah a legal "textbook" for novice law students. Among the most famous legal texts from the Roman imperial period, the *Institutes of Gaius*, written just a few decades before Mishnah, is such a textbook; and Mishnah does not resemble the *Institutes* at all. Moreover, how can Mishnah be thought of as a textbook for early rabbinic legal studies, when so much of the mishnaic legal system is left unstated, even though it is presumed by Mishnah's content? The fact is, I have yet to encounter an ancient legal text that actually does what Mishnah does in any way resembling how Mishnah does it. So, how does Mishnah proceed?[22]

While Mishnah *generally* is *not* recorded case law, it *routinely* specifies circumstances and cases and then proffers rulings for them. Indeed, Mishnah often offers different, diametrically opposed rulings for one and the same case or set of circumstances. At these junctures, Mishnah will, as a literary feature, attribute at least one, and sometimes all, of these opposing rulings to a named, early rabbinic authority. (It is hard to know on what historical or literary-historical basis Mishnah's authors make these attributions, but that is not an issue germane to this chapter or this book.) Sometimes Mishnah provides mini-arguments (basically one-liners) for

21. The earliest halakhic text that does look like a law code, including codifying law for Mishnah's imagined ideal world, is that of the twelfth-century rabbinic scholar Rabbi Moses ben Maimon (aka Maimonides). His code is called the *Mishneh Torah*. Subsequent codifiers of rabbinic halakha proceeded to drop from their codes laws pertaining to institutions that no longer existed, such as the sacrificial cult. Needless to say, the *Mishneh Torah* looks nothing like Mishnah.

22. For a fairly comprehensive account, intended for nonspecialists, of Mishnah's literary features, see my book *In the Seat of Moses*, ch. 4. In Lightstone, "What Is Mishnah?," I have also made the point that Mishnah does not appear to fall into any existing genre of literature, Judah-ite or non-Judah-ite, of the Greco-Roman world.

the opposing rulings, and places these mini-arguments in the mouths of the authorities to whom it has attributed the opposing views. However, most of the time by far, Mishnah does *not* provide such mini-"debates" to explain the reasoning behind the "disputants'" attributed rulings. Equally rarely, a ruling in Mishnah is followed by a very short precedent story, in which a rabbinic authority is said to have ruled or to have acted in a manner that accords with Mishnah's ruling for a case exhibiting similar circumstances. The short precedent story functions as a *warrant* for Mishnah's specified rule. All this said, most of the time, Mishnah provides little or no rationales or warrants for its rulings. There are relatively few debates in Mishnah, despite the very many disputes, that is, passages in which opposing rulings are given for one and the same circumstances. And there are only one hundred or so precedent stories in Mishnah, a small number indeed, given the sheer size of the Mishnah text—sixty-two halakhic tractates in the modern printed editions.

So what does all this add up to (so far)? Well, the most dominant feature of Mishnah is that it defines many hundreds of cases by specifying the circumstance or combination of circumstances for each, and provides a ruling, and often opposing rulings, for each. Commonly in Mishnah, series of topically related cases for consideration are "spun out" by altering first one and then another of the circumstances that together define the case. While some of these specific cases (or cases like them) *may* have arisen in real life in Judean society and been ruled upon by Judean authorities, the literary characteristics of Mishnah strongly suggest that these cases are generated and presented by Mishnah's authors as *hypothetical* ones. Why? In order to specify how the halakha applies, or might apply, or should apply to the *posited hypothetical* circumstances. And if that is what by design is happening in Mishnah, so much the better (or equally valuable) if opposing rulings for one and the same set of circumstances might apply. Why? Because the Mishnah student will have *to consider seriously* that the posited circumstances might reasonably call for one ruling *and/or* its opposite And if the hypothetical circumstances can be slightly varied over and over again to generate a series of cases in order to continue to proffer whether the ruling in question continues to apply, or whether there is a dispute about whether the ruling continues to apply in each newly posited case, well, again, so much the better. How so? Because, I maintain, Mishnah "tests" or "explores" and thereby asks its engaged students to test and explore along with Mishnah's authors, how halakha applies, might apply, or should apply to various and varied hypothetical circumstances posited by Mishnah.

Earlier, I made claims about what Mishnah *is not*. It is not a law code. Nor is it a repository or library of case law. And it is not a legal textbook that introduces its students to early rabbinic halakha, in the sense that Gaius's *Institutes* introduces Roman law to second-century CE would-be jurists. Then, what is Mishnah?

Mishnah, in my considered view, is (perhaps among other things) an *exercise in halakhic application* on a wide range of themes and topics.[23] Mishnah begs/demands that its students *enter into, discern, and even propose the logic (or possible competing logics) of this exercise.* Engaged Mishnah study, at the very least, serves to train halakhic thinking, once one has mastered the prerequisite knowledge needed to decipher a Mishnah passage, chapter, or tractate. This makes Mishnah not a law code but perhaps something more akin to a study book to develop halakhic thinking.[24]

Viewed in this light, it is not to the detriment of the exercise that Mishnah's cases are (often) hypothetical, and its does not matter that the world of Mishnah, the world that I have characterized as *Scriptural World 2.0* is, to some significant degree, an imagined, ideal one—a creative anachronism at the turn of the third century CE, when Mishnah is produced. Rather, in Mishnah passage after Mishnah passage, the Mishnah student is asked to consider the possible halakhic logic that applies to *what-if* cases. As far as the engaged Mishnah student is concerned, *if* that world were to exist and *if* such-and-such circumstances arose, then this is how one would think halakhically in that world about these specific circumstances. Again, the operative objective, in my view, is to model and learn to think halakhically. And, because it is Scripture's world, how much more authentic and authoritative is the skill attained to think halakhically by reason of lifelong Mishnah study, and how much more authoritative (in the minds of members of the early rabbinic group, at least) is the highly developed halakhic thinker?!

To hammer the nail home, let me present a hypothetical, made-up scenario of my own. *If* the Karaites were to have arisen in the third century CE, rather than in the medieval period, to challenge any aspirations of the rabbinic movement to corner the market on halakhic decision-making and arbitration, and *if* the early rabbis were to counter the Karaite challenge by proffering something other than, or in addition to, a mythology of the origins of rabbinic teachings and of Mishnah as Oral Torah going back to Moses (and YHWH), then what might a rabbinic spokesperson have additionally argued in response to their Karaite detractors? Our teachings, and halakhic decisions and arbitrations, they might say, are particularly valid *not only* because our training presumes detailed knowledge of scriptural and

23. Today, we might liken it to a workbook of examples or exemplary exercises covering a range of legal themes and topics.

24. See Goldberg, "Mishnah"; Kraemer, "Mishnah."

extra-scriptural law *but also* (and perhaps especially) because lifelong Mishnah study hones our abilities to think halakhically in a manner that is unmatched by others. That is, our imaginary early rabbinic spokesperson might point to the cogency of the shared profile of the rabbis—a profile the rabbinic cadre guarantees through the rigors of master-disciple-based education and validation, via a curriculum centered on Mishnah study.

Now, there is yet one other pervasive feature of Mishnah that, in my view, bolsters and amplifies what I have just said about the objective/effects (intended, in my opinion) of Mishnah study—the modeling and inducement of highly developed halakhic thinking. A pretty common feature of Mishnah's rule-sentences is that they are often missing lots of words that are essential to making sense of them. The technical way of saying this is this: Mishnah's sentences frequently are highly laconic—they are often replete with lacunae. Mishnah students must *in their heads* fill in these missing bits, just as they must know in their heads applicable biblical injunctions and extra-biblical laws.

It is difficult to say why Mishnah's language is so laconic. It is doubtful that second-century CE Judeans spoke Hebrew in this way (to the extent that they still spoke Hebrew, when Aramaic dominated as the lingua franca). Mishnah's authors may just have been trying to save space. Or, perhaps and more likely, this highly laconic style of Hebrew facilitated memorization of Mishnah.[25] But among the effects of the laconic language of Mishnah upon Mishnah study are undoubtedly these: it places further intellectual demands on the Mishnah student in order to understand (1) the precise circumstances of the case, and/or (2) the exact nature of the ruling, and, therefore, (3) the halakhic logic that results in the ruling or opposing rulings. How so? Because the cases and the rulings have first to be *fully constructed* by the Mishnah student adding the missing bits of language, before, or in the process of, grasping the halakhic logic that might underlie the rule-sentences. There is a kind of "see-saw" mental exercise demanded in this process. One must in one's head fill in the missing bits of language to discern a Mishnah passage's logic, and one must have begun to discern the logic of the passage in order to fill in the missing language appropriately. There is no escaping these reciprocal mental gymnastics in reading many, if not most, Mishnah passages.

Ironically, if this, too, is an intended feature of Mishnah precisely in order to induce this type of mental exercise, it is a feature that has been largely undone by medieval and modern Mishnah commentaries,

25. See, e.g., Neusner, *Memorized Mishnah*; E. Alexander, *Transmitting Mishnah*; Jaffee, *Torah in the Mouth*.

which, admittedly, I (like most modern readers of Mishnah in the secular academy or the rabbinic academy) routinely consult. Absent these written commentaries (and absent they were in the early third century, when Mishnah was promulgated), one needs an expert teacher (a rabbi), until one has become a fully autonomous Mishnah analyst (and teacher) oneself. So, perhaps this, too, was intended by Mishnah's authors. Again, we may glimpse how, due to pervasive features of Mishnah, Mishnah study was *socially* formative of the early rabbinic group, not just *intellectually* formative of individual, lone, would-be rabbis.

FROM THE ABSTRACT TO THE CONCRETE AND ILLUSTRATIVE

The preceding section of this chapter has been a lot to take in. And it is perhaps also difficult to grasp, because so much of what I have written in that section is abstract. Let me, therefore, make matters very concrete and in the process demonstrate the claims made.[26] The most efficient way of doing this for you is to present and discuss a Mishnah passage that I consider completely *normal* for Mishnah.[27] If this passage is normal, then the intellectual skills engendered by coming to grips with it may be said to be normative, in some serious sense, of the early rabbinic movement. And because you have already some initial familiarity with the first rule-sentence of m. Horayot 1:1, let us examine not just the first rule-sentence (1:1a) but the whole Mishnah passage, and then consider as well 1:2a. This time, however, my translation will interpolate in square brackets the additional language required to make m. Horayot 1:1 (and 1:2a) fully intelligible and their halakhic logic more readily explorable.

m. Horayot 1:1

i. [If] a court instructed to transgress one of the commandments stated in the Torah,

---

26. To "demonstrate" is not to "prove." But this book is not a research monograph; it is a didactic volume, and so "demonstrate" or "illustrate" is all I intend to, or can reasonably achieve, here. That said, I will stand by my claim that based on years of Mishnah analysis, it is my impression that what I maintain are (among) the pervasive literary features of Mishnah are valid. See Lightstone, *In the Seat of Moses*, ch. 4; Lightstone, *Mishnah and Social Formation*, ch. 2. See also Neusner, *History of Mishnaic Law*, pt. 21.

27. I have deliberately chosen to use the word "normal" because it is unproductive to start a debate here about what is "typical" or "exemplary." "Normality" is all I need to make my points.

ii. and an individual acted [and transgressed] unwittingly on the basis of their [the court's] word—

iii. whether they [that is, the members of the court] acted [in accordance with their own instruction and transgressed], and he [or she, the individual,] acted [and transgressed unwittingly] with them, [or]

iv. whether they acted, and he [or she] acted after them, [or]

v. whether they did not act [at all], and he [or she] acted—

vi. he [or she] is exempt [from offering the sin/purification sacrifice specified in Scriptures],

vii. because he [or she] depended on the court['s instruction].

viii. [If] a court instructed [to transgress one of the commandments stated in the Torah],

ix. and one of them [that is, one of the court's members] knew that they erred,

x. or [if a private individual who was informed of the court's instructions was] a disciple [of the sages], and he was [himself] worthy [to be ordained] to give [halakhic] instruction,

xi. and he [that is, either of these two types of individuals] proceeded and acted [and transgressed unwittingly] on the basis of their [i.e, the court's] word—

xii. whether they [that is, the members of the court] acted [in accordance with their own instruction and transgressed], and he [that is, either of these two types of individuals,] acted [and transgressed unwittingly] with them, [or]

xiii. whether they acted, and he acted after them, [or]

xiv. whether they did not act [at all], and he acted—

xv. lo, this individual is liable [for offering the sin/purification sacrifice specified in Scriptures],

xvi. because he [that is, either of these two types of individuals] did not depend on [that is, had no need to rely on] the court['s instruction].

xvii. This is the general [legal] principle:

xviii. the one who depends upon himself [that is, who knew or ought to have known that the court erred in its instruction] is liable [for the sin/purification offering, if he/she committed a transgression unwittingly that aligns with the court's decision];

xix. and the one that depends on the court['s instruction, because he/she did not or would not have been expected to know better] is exempt [for the sin/purification offering, if he/she committed a transgression unwittingly that aligns with the court's decision].

Before you, now, is the entirety of the first Mishnah passage of Horayot's first chapter. There is nothing particularly remarkable about the passage by mishnaic literary standards. It ends (at lines xvii–xix) with a statement of general principle, of which the preceding parts of the passage are (only because of the context provided by this general principle) illustrative hypothetical cases. In reality, one could easily have induced the general principle from the rulings that precede it. Mishnah does *not* routinely articulate such general principles, even though they are not rarities either.

One feature that is *not* found in m. Horayot 1:1 is a dispute, that is, the presence of two opposing rulings (at least one of which is attributed to a named rabbinic authority) for one and the same circumstances. As I noted earlier, disputes are a common feature of Mishnah passages. To see a dispute, one need only look at the first rule-sentence of the very next Mishnah passage following the one of I have just translated. Let me, then, show you m. Horayot 1:2a.

m. Horayot 1:2a

i. [If] a court instructed [to transgress one of the commandments stated in the Torah],

ii. and [later] they [that is, the members of the court as a whole] knew that they erred,

iii. and they [then] repealed [their original erroneous instruction]—

iv. whether they [the members of the court, already] brought their atonement offering [to atone for their error],

v. or whether they had not [yet] brought their atonement offering,

vi. and an individual acted [and transgressed unwittingly] on the basis of their [the court's] word—

vii. Rabbi Simeon exempts [that individual from the obligation of bringing a sin/purification offering],

viii. and Rabbi Eliezer [declares that it is a case of] doubt [that is, one does not know whether or not the individual must offer a sin/purification offering, and so must instead bring the "guilt offering made in uncertain cases"[28]].

As you can see, the structure of m. Horayot 1:2a recalls that of m. Horayot 1:1 and repeats much of the latter's language. However, whereas m. Horayot 1:1 has one ruling for each of two sets of specified circumstances, m. Horayot 1:2a has two attributed opposing rulings. Moreover, one of the opposing rulings, that attributed to Rabbi Eliezer, presumes/assumes prior knowledge of yet more scriptural law—this time about the "guilt offering made in uncertain cases." How is it reasonable that two rabbinic authorities would rule differently for the same hypothetical circumstances? In other words, what halakhic logic would allow one to reason first to one conclusion and then to another, opposing conclusion? I will say no more than this: that is certainly a question that m. Horayot 1:2a invites, or even demands, the engaged Mishnah student to ponder, as would be so in the study of all of the many disputes in the Mishnah. That said, let us turn our attention back to m. Horayot 1:1, noting in advance that virtually all that I have to say about it applies as well to m. Horayot 1:2a.

The parts of m. Horayot 1:1 that precede the statement of general principle with which this Mishnah passage concludes fall neatly into two large subsections. They are lines i–vii and lines viii–xvi. The first (i–vii) presents a series of hypothetical cases resulting in one ruling for the entire series—the individual is exempt for the sin/purification offering for an unwittingly committed transgression (for which the penalty is extirpation, if done purposefully, according to Scripture). The second large subsection (viii–xvi) presents a closely related, but materially *different*, series of hypothetical cases, for which series the opposite ruling is given by the Mishnah passage—the individual is liable for the sin/purification offering for an unwittingly committed transgression (for which the penalty is extirpation, if done purposefully, according to Scripture). The underlying, but unstated, scriptural law at Num 15:22–29 and Lev 4 should by now be familiar to you from earlier discussions in this chapter.

Why do I say that we have in each of these two large subsections of m. Horayot 1:1 "a closely related, but materially *different*, series of hypothetical cases"? For three major reasons. First, there is an obvious *substantive* halakhic symmetry to them; they articulate two series of cases, one ruling applying to one series and the *exact opposite* ruling applying to the other. Second, a great deal of the *exact same language in the same order* is repeated in both. Third, and closely related to the former, in each large

---

28. The technical Hebrew term is *asham talui* (the "conditional" or "hanging" or "dependent" guilt offering); see Lev 5:17–18.

subsection the same series of sub-cases is generated in the same order—
"whether they acted and he acted with them, whether they acted and
he acted after them, whether they did not act, and he acted . . ." Notice,
too, how the sub-cases in each large subsection are spun out by simple
permutation and variation of the same, limited number of words: "they
acted," "he acted," "with them," "after them." This type of use of language is
endemic and pervasive in Mishnah. And it almost reminds me of how the
language in the stanzas of folk songs often matches and produces balance,
cadence, assonance, and alliteration. If one were given the assignment to
memorize this Mishnah passage, it would not be any more difficult than
memorizing two stanzas of a folk song.

Another blatant feature of my translation of m. Horayot 1:1 is how
much language in square brackets I have interpolated into the text, language
that is absent in the original Hebrew. This is the direct result of what earlier
I described as Mishnah's highly (and typically) laconic style. Because of the
many intentional lacunae (that is, bits missing *by design*) of m. Horayot 1:1's
Hebrew, I have had to add a lot of language in my translation.[29] And it is
evident that without my interpolations, this Mishnah passage would not be
fully intelligible (or not intelligible at all). Equally important, without the
interpolated language that I have provided, the *halakhic logic* of the large
subsections of m. Horayot 1:1 would not be discernable. (Consider, e.g.,
where I have added the word "unwittingly" in square brackets. Remove the
word and the ruling makes no sense; rather, halakhic logic would dictate
that the transgressor would instead be subject to extirpation.) Without
sufficient intelligibility and without its halakhic logic being discernable, of
what value is this passage to the engaged Mishnah student of either the early
third or the early twenty-first century? After all, it seems clear to me that
developing halakhic thinking is precisely the point of Mishnah study, given
that Mishnah, as argued above, is *not* a law code or even an introduction to
early rabbinic law, as Gaius's *Institutes* are to Roman law!

So why did Mishnah's authors deliberately choose to create such a laconic style of Hebrew for this their magnum opus? I cannot say for certain.
Perhaps it is a by-product, or apes the literary style, of the (memorized?)
traditions that Mishnah's authors may have used as sources. Perhaps, it is

29. I stress "by design," because scholars who work with medieval and ancient manuscripts or inscriptions typically deal with lacunae in these texts. These scholars are the
bulk of people who would use the term "lacunae" in their work. But these are lacunae by
accident, not by design. They are missing bits because the scribe's eyes skipped a word
or more when copying, or the manuscript has subsequently been torn, or has holes in
it, or the clay tablet or stone with the inscription is chipped, resulting in words or letters
missing that were *originally there*. The lacunae in Mishnah are not absent bits that were
originally in the text. Rather, Mishnah's authors composed the Mishnah this way.

Mishnah's authors' attempt to create a Mishnah that can more easily be committed to memory. My considered inclination is to assert that the *actual* laconic language in which the extant Mishnah passages are cast is the language produced by Mishnah's authorship, whether or not it is modeled on the style of received traditions.[30]

All this said, the most germane question for you, the reader of this book is this: What does this highly laconic nature of the language of Mishnah passages *demand* of the devoted, engaged Mishnah student? Well, Mishnah students cannot even *begin* to make sense of this Mishnah passage (or of a very significant proportion, if not most, of other Mishnah passages) without, *first*, mentally, that is, *in their heads*, doing what I have done in my translation by interpolation in square brackets. They, *first*, *must* fill in all the missing but *logically necessary* bits. And, here is the essential point. One cannot fill in all the missing bits without first discerning, or better still, without (re) constructing and making manifest the halakhic logic of the Mishnah passage at hand. This is the intellectual see-saw process to which I referred earlier. On the one hand, the interpolated bits *make* the passage halakhically logical, and, on the other hand, one must come up with a halakhic logic for the passage's rulings in order to appropriately fill in the missing bits. This is not some sort of clever catch-22. It is, in my estimation, purposefully endemic to Mishnah study, because Mishnah's authors could easily have made it otherwise.[31] In other words, reading Mishnah in an engaged manner constantly forces the Mishnah student to exercise halakhic thinking by reconstructing the halakhic logic of Mishnah passage after Mishnah passage. Then and only then can one progress to *probing, analyzing, and questioning the halakhic logic* of the Mishnah passage one is studying, which, in my considered, opinion, was the likely, ultimate purpose of intensive Mishnah study. So, the generalizable intellectual capacity to *probe, analyze, and question the halakhic logic* of things is a skill engendered and honed by the lifelong, engaged study of Mishnah—a defining trait of the Mishnanians. And our brief examination

---

30. This is my inclination, because very often the language choices of particular Mishnah passages are sustained through conceptual chapters of Mishnah (not to be identified necessarily with the medieval scribes' divisions into chapters). This would mean that the language choices are those of the authors of these conceptual chapters, and not those of their individual source-traditions. On this matter, see, e.g., Neusner, *History Mishnaic Law*, pt. 21.

31. One need only look at Maimonides code of rabbinic law, his *Mishneh Torah*, to see how Mishnah-like Hebrew may be used to articulate rabbinic rules (many of them based upon Mishnah) in a manner that is largely devoid of the type of lacunae routinely evident in Mishnah.

of m. Horayot 1:1, a Mishnah passage about which there is nothing un-
usual by mishnaic standards, illustrates this in spades.

How does one learn to do this? Like getting to Carnegie Hall, as the
old joke goes, it takes practice. And it is a practice that requires guidance
to develop and perfect—hence, the master-disciple relationships (and a
little later, sometime over the hundred fifty or so years following Mishnah's
production, the institution of the house of study) at the core of the early
rabbinic, social formation.

This chapter, in sum, has discussed what I consider the most important, defining, shared elements that made the early rabbis part of a
particular social formation near and soon after the promulgation of their
magnum opus, the Mishnah. These elements constitute their common
(quasi-) professional profile: (1) experts in scriptural law (largely committed to memory) and (2) in a large body of extra-scriptural law (also largely
in their heads), as well as (3) experts in, and lifelong developers of, halakhic
thinking, engendered by analysis of Mishnah.

This halakhic thinking entailed the capacity to discern series of major
and minor variations in the circumstances that might make up any hypothetical case and to consider the logic that would reasonably lead to one ruling or
another, given all the relevant, background scriptural and extra-scriptural law
that should come to bear. The intensive study of Mishnah is a lifelong exercise
in attaining and perfecting this profile. It matters not one iota, it seems, that
the hypothetical circumstances presented in a great many Mishnah passages
assume a world that no longer exists, one in which, for example, a Jerusalem
temple with all of its functions and related institutions operates. In fact, if
one intellectually inhabits an imagined, ideal world, then the Mishnanian can
posit all sorts of cases. And since this imagined and ideal world resembles that
to which Scripture's law was meant to apply—so much the better in developing a full grasp of scriptural and extra-scriptural law.

Where do we, you and I, go from here in considering what the early
rabbis were? Since the study of Mishnah, their first magnum opus, was
the center of the early rabbis' inner-group life as a social formation, the
demands Mishnah study made of its students and the intellectual traits
and skills Mishnah studies engendered arguably constituted the *normative*
profile of the early rabbis near and soon after the turn of the third century.
To study Mishnah more than anything else, made the early rabbis' profile
more of what Mishnah study demanded and engendered than something
else. Of this, I have little doubt. That said, two questions nag at me, as they
should at you. (1) Was the Mishnanian profile the *sum total* of the early
rabbinic profile? And (2) what social ends, if any, did the Mishnanian profile serve or intend to serve, beyond it being, of course, an intellectual end

in itself? Because if Mishnah study was pursued for its own sake *only*, then it will certainly have been able to act as the central glue of an arcane social formation, the early rabbinic movement. But with no at least intended, aspirational ends beyond maintaining the inner-group social cohesion of the rabbinic movement itself, one wonders how Mishnah study remained so central an activity for at least four hundred years, setting the stage for the near-monopolistic exercise of authority over the halakha within the Jewish communities of the medieval period. The next chapter of this volume will take up these two questions.

4

Extra-Mishnaic Aspects of the Early Rabbinic Profile

I N THE PREVIOUS CHAPTERS, I described the early rabbis as (primarily) Mishnanians. As Mishnanians, they shared a specific profile of acquired knowledge and analytic skills oriented to expert halakhic thinking. Chapters 5 and beyond consider what in chapter 1 I referred to as the cultural currency of the early rabbis' professional profile. For without such currency, it is hard to understand that anyone in Judah-ic society at the turn of the third century CE (including the early rabbis themselves) would have viewed such a profile as having any value and legitimacy.

Before proceeding, however, to discuss such issues later in this volume, and as stated at the end of chapter 3, there are at this point at least two questions that nag at me (as they should at you). I say "nag," because while I would like to be able to answer them definitively, I am not sure I can do so both fully and responsibly for the rabbinic collective near and soon after Mishnah's production and promulgation as an authoritative text among the rabbis. Here, again, are the two nagging questions, nonetheless. First, to what (intended) social ends, outside of serving to establish a shared social identity within early rabbinic circles themselves, did the early rabbis develop this profile? Second, is what I have attempted to characterize as their shared, self-defining profile a complete or nearly complete account? Let me address these questions in reverse order.

IS THE PROFILE NEARLY COMPLETE?

So, is my characterization of the core elements of shared, rabbinic group identity a complete or nearly complete one? My best judgment produces a three-part response to this question.

1. It is most likely *not* a complete characterization; other elements are probably additional features of *some* early rabbis' profiles near and soon after the beginning of the third century.

2. It is difficult reliably to date such additional elements of their shared professional identity and profile to the period that is our focus, namely, near and just after the promulgation of Mishnah within early rabbinic circles.

3. What I have characterized thus far in this book as the elements of the early rabbis' shared identity and professional profile—complete knowledge (in their heads) of both scriptural and extra-scriptural law underlying Mishnah and ongoing cultivation through Mishnah study of expert halakhic thinking—are (a) most likely the primary, central elements; (b) probably those that most engendered the social formation of the early rabbinic group; and (c) likely the more central elements of the early rabbinic profile that, *in the rabbis' view at least*, qualified them for roles outside of the social enclave of their own group.

That is to say, along with a number of normative beliefs (many of which were discussed in ch. 2), the elements elaborated in chapter 3 may be said to have constituted the group's *normative skills profile* in the era of interest to us. Let me now expand somewhat on this three-part response.

As I have had occasion to state several times in this volume, there is a substantial body of early rabbinic literature that is post-mishnaic and that was composed over a roughly four-century-and-more period following Mishnah's production. As you already know, these documents fall into two broad categories: halakhic literature (c. 200–600) and aggadic literature (c. 250–900).[1] (The former texts are primarily legal in substance, although some contain aggadic sections. The two Talmuds, and especially the Babylonian Talmud, contain collections of aggadic materials, even though both Talmuds' primary focus is legal; they model forms of Mishnah analysis.) Aggadic texts proffer many aphorisms and short stories[2] about both biblical

---

1. The only aggadic text that I would reasonably date as early as the mid-third century is Avot, a late insertion into Mishnah.

2. "Short" warrants some specification. Do not think of "short stories" as anything like what the term means in English literature today. Rather, the short aggadic stories of

and rabbinic figures. Via these aphorisms and stories, values, appropriate beliefs, proper comportment, and an ethos are conveyed, often as lessons portrayed as coded in Scripture's language (in which case, a text is of the genre of aggadic midrash).[3]

I believe that I may safely say that in the early rabbinic movement over the four hundred-plus years that followed Mishnah's production and promulgation, halakhic texts and their study figured much more prominently than aggadic texts. (Indeed, most aggadic-midrashic texts were composed after the composition c. 600 of the Babylonian Talmud, albeit using earlier material in all likelihood.) I do not get the impression that early rabbis would have been "credentialed"[4] on the basis of knowledge of aggadic teachings, even though it is clear that rabbis and would-be rabbis studied and were encouraged to study such teachings. By contrast, no rabbinic candidate would have been credentialed, as far as I can tell, without having mastered halakha and halakhic thinking. By way of illustrating this last point, the Mishnah passage at m. Horayot 1:1b, discussed in the previous chapter, assumes this. Halakhic acumen was a central and necessary

---

early rabbinic literature are usually vignettes that are more likely to be a paragraph or maybe two in length—a brief setting of the scene in several sentences and a depiction of the act of the rabbi—something done or said—in the context of the conditions. These may be longer than the typical length of a legal precedent story found in Mishnah and post-mishnaic legal passages, but a paragraph (or two) usually suffices to bring these aggadic vignettes to their intended conclusion. Sometimes, several such aggadic vignettes about a biblical or rabbinic figure may be strung together, resulting in a composite giving the impression of a more sustained narrative. For examples of the latter, see the extended narratives about Rabbi Akiva (c. early second century CE) in Avot de Rabbi Nathan (Schechter edition), version b, ch. 12, and in version a, ch. 6. See also the extended aggadic narrative about Rabbi Yohanan ben Zakkai (c. late first century CE) in Avot de Rabbi Nathan (Schechter edition), version b, ch. 6., and in version a, ch. 4. These two extended narratives seem to me to be as long as they get in early rabbinic literature, and their lengths are *not* the norm. Elements of both these composite narratives have parallels in other post-mishnaic rabbinic literature. This process of creating the appearance of a more extended narrative is familiar to any academic student of the canonical gospels. But nothing like a gospel of this or that rabbi was ever produced in antiquity.

3. Among the more recent scholarly works on the historical development of midrash is Mandel, *Origins of Midrash*. I am indebted to Joel Gereboff for highlighting for me the importance of Mandel's work on the subject.

4. What could being credentialed have entailed in the early rabbinic movement? We cannot show that the "laying on of hands" (*semikha*) by a rabbinic master upon a disciple, thereby marking the latter as a rabbi, was used in the early third century CE. But as we have already seen in m. Horayot 1:1b, by the turn of the third century, when Mishnah was produced, the notion was firmly established that a disciple of a sage at some point would have been deemed by his teacher to have attained the level of learning to make the disciple "worthy" (*ra-ui*) of independently issuing authoritative, halakhic "instructions" (*hora-ah*).

feature of the early rabbinic profile. But was it also a *necessary and suf-ficient* element? In my view, yes! So what is *additionally* reflected about the early rabbis' profile in aggadic content in which early rabbinic personages (whether of the Tannaitic or Amoraic eras) are the dramatis personae? And where do such additional elements fit?

When such aggadic aphorisms and stories feature early rabbinic per-sonages, the values, belief system, normative comportment, and ethos of no-table early rabbis (some Tannaim and others Amoraim) are either held up as *exemplary* and/or as *exceptional*. If they are exemplary, then their comport-ment, ethos, and talents represent something that is *aspirational* for many or all rabbis and their disciples. When they are held up as *both* exemplary *and* exceptional, their talents are portrayed as achievable only by the very few (an elite) among the members of the rabbinic cadre. It is not always easy to distinguish aphorisms and stories portraying aspirational talent from those conveying exceptional talent. But before discussing further what is conveyed as exemplary or exceptional, I must (despite the focus of this volume, and with apologies) make some important methodological points.

It is very difficult to establish if the talents on display in such aggadic traditions, whether intended as aspirational or exceptional, represent the rabbinic group's culture at and soon after the turn of the third century (when Mishnah was produced and initially promulgated). Why? Because the dat-ing of these aggadic traditions cannot be established simply by reference to the supposed dates of the personages that appear in them or of the tradents "in whose mouths" these traditions are conveyed. One may portray the ex-ceptional talents of Rabbi Akiva (a notable, early second-century rabbi) in a tradition composed in the second, third, fourth, or fifth century (or later still, if one is dealing with much of the literature of aggadic midrash). Cer-tainly the date (if knowable) of the composition of the tradition matters for our purposes. So let us say for the sake of argument that an aggadic portrayal of Rabbi Akiva may be shown to have been first composed in the late second or third centuries, and let us even grant that much of that portrayal results from lionizing and heroizing Akiva (making him an early rabbinic figure of legend). At least such a portrayal tells us something about what *counts* as a rabbinic hero in the late second or early third centuries, the period upon which we are focused, even if it may constitute a legend about Akiva, an early second-century rabbi. Unfortunately, it proves very difficult to date many or even any of these aggadic traditions' compositions to this period, let alone earlier. Tractate Avot, the major aggadic insertion into Mishnah, is likely no earlier than the mid-third century.[5] And as you have ready read in chapter 2,

5. And Avot's composition is probably no later than the early fourth century. Avot's

early rabbinic traditions about Oral Torah first appear in passages attributed to mid-third and fourth-century rabbis (Amoraim) and/or in documents often composed later still. What does this mean for what I have to say in much of the remainder of this chapter? Read what follows with imagined caution signs embossed on the pages.

With these very important methodological caveats in mind, what types of rabbinic talents, in addition to the core necessary and sufficient elements of the shared, halakhically oriented early rabbinic profile, are portrayed as either exemplary (and, therefore, aspirational for many rabbis) or exemplary *and* exceptional (and, consequently, the purview of the very few)? Here are some principal ones that I have observed, articulated thematically in no particular order:

- The rabbi as the devoted disciple (exemplary and aspirational)
- The rabbi as the exemplar of everyday piety (exemplary and aspirational)
- The rabbi as the local sage (exemplary and aspirational)
- The rabbi as mystic/gnostic (exemplary and exceptional)
- The rabbi as a gifted local preacher (exemplary and aspirational)

Let me say just a bit about each theme.

Devoted Disciple

As you would expect from the preceding chapters, discipleship, that is, close association with (even devotion to) one's rabbinic master, was a key element of early rabbinic social identity and group relations within the early rabbinic movement. Why? Because it provided the institutionalized basis for study, and specifically for Mishnah study, as the central process of socialization into the early rabbinic group. As with all institutionalized social relationships, discipleship was governed by espoused norms, values, dispositions, and virtues. In these regards, we are fortunate indeed to have the evidence of Avot, since the composition of its first five chapters dates to a period relatively soon after Mishnah's promulgation as the principal object of study among the early rabbis. One of Avot's sustained themes is the comportment and ethos of the devoted rabbinic disciple, both as a student of Torah/Mishnah

---

presentation of a legitimating "pedigree" for Rabbi Judah the Patriarch and his son(s) is probably indicative of when Avot was composed.

and as an actor in society.[6] Rabbis and would-be rabbis are to be diligent students in the acquisition of Torah knowledge (specifically, we may surmise, the study of Mishnah). They are to limit activities that would distract them from this pursuit. Humility furthers learning. Service to one's teacher is an essential feature of a discipleship of learning. How so? Learning from one's teacher involves not only listening to lessons but also watching the teacher's comportment and imitating it. So, the "quality time" spent with one's teacher in service facilitates this learning by example.

For all this, the circle of teacher and disciples is not some quasi-monastic institution. The rabbinic teacher/master has a family and must make a living "in the world." If you cannot make a living, you do not have the means to devote sufficient time to study. Work and study are mutually upholding activities—"if there is no flour [in the house with which to make bread], there is no Torah [study]; and if there is no Torah [study], there is no flour [in the house with which to make bread]" (Avot 3:17). So, work is to be valued by the disciple of the sage (Avot 1:10; 2:2). The disciples, then, are faced with the obligation, challenges, and necessity of earning a living, being an attentive spouse, being a devoted parent, or caring for one's parents. The challenge is to do all this, and yet not become overly distracted from learning. For Avot, women's discourse in particular is seen as a distraction from devoted study (Avot 1:5; 2:7). (The early rabbinic view of women is largely one that sees them and their speech as too often frivolous—a view obviously rejected by most modern societies.) That said, social or communal responsibility legitimately demands time away from study. For example, the disciple of the sage must stop a study session in order to participate fully in the public, communal celebration of the bride, or to join in the communal cortege honoring the deceased.

Exemplar of Everyday Piety

The rabbinic sage and disciple must behave in a manner that accords with the virtues of piety. On the one hand, what is acquired through study must be made manifest in pious deeds (Avot 1:10; 1:17; 2:2; 3:9; 3:17; 5:14); on the

6. In light of the methodological caveats of the preceding paragraphs, I have attempted to punctuate what follows in the next several paragraphs with references to passages in Avot, although one could equally do so with many (more) references to aggadic traditions in other post-mishnaic, early rabbinic texts, such as the Jerusalem Talmud, Avot de Rabbi Nathan (which is a commentary on, and supplement of sorts to, Avot), and the Babylonian Talmud. Avot's first five chapters are generally held to be a relatively early addition to the Mishnah, perhaps as early as the mid-third century CE (and likely no later than the turn of the fourth century).

other, one is not to profit (monetarily or otherwise) from Torah knowledge (Avot 4:5) or be prideful as a result of one's learning (Avot 1:8). Piety—the "fear of sinning" (Avot 3:9)—like humility (Avot 4:4; 3:1; 1:17; 4:10; 4:12; 5:19) and self-control (Avot 4:1; 2:11–12) are the appropriate ways of being in the world and/or facilitating study. This piety has religious ritual and social-ethical dimensions. The rabbi is to praise and acknowledge God and God's sovereignty through both prayer (Avot 2:13) and, of course, the study of God's revelation. Rabbis pray multiple times daily, sometimes in the synagogue with "the community," and sometimes "communally" in the "study house" with other rabbis and rabbinic disciples. In addition to communal prayer, life's everyday activities, such as eating and drinking, present occasions to express thankfulness for God's blessings. That said, for the disciple of the sage, study together with others is also a form of worship, and a substitute for sacrificial offerings in a post-temple era (Avot 3:2–3) And of course, bearing the "yoke of heaven" by following God's "Way," the halakha, is both a display of loyalty and devotion to the God of Israel and a partnering with the deity to effect the type of society that God is understood to want for humankind. The rabbi's behavior is to bring honor and repute to the God of Israel, to reflect well on the people of Israel, and to reflect well on the cadre of rabbis as a whole and on one's teacher. For example, such things as gambling and (excessive) drinking are forbidden. The disciple of the sage is to keep good company (Avot 1:9; 3:10). Charity and charity work conducted with humility are expected (Avot 5:13). And the rabbi and disciple are expected to observe those purity taboos and ritual purifications that may be practiced without recourse to a Jerusalem temple (sitting in ruins).

At this juncture, I should stress two points. First, it is clear, that the piety of the rabbis was *not* that of asceticism, but rather an ethos of everyday, in-the-world self-discipline; of commitment to family and society; and of devotion to God (all as enjoined by the halakha), coupled with their own group's particular commitment to the study of distinctively rabbinic tradition. Second, when the sages and their disciples endeavor to live up to the standards and norms of their own halakha, they are doing nothing more or less than what they expect every other Jew to do or aspire to do, even though they recognize (and accept?) that many (most?) Jews do not.[7] With the exception of their

---

7. The early rabbis often use the term *am ha-aretz* (literally, "the people of the land") as a label for Jews who either do not share their view of what halakha specifically demands in a given set of circumstances, or who do not know what halakha specifically demands in a given set of circumstances. Much later, the term came to mean "ignoramus," which is *not* its meaning in early rabbinic traditions in my view (although modern translators of early rabbinic literature often render it so). Thus in Mishnah's imagined world, a high priest can be an *am ha-aretz*, and I do not think that Mishnah intends to convey that such a high priest is uneducated or illiterate; rather, he is not educated in

devotion to study and discipleship, they do not see themselves as a class that is defined by a supererogatory set of norms.[8]

The rabbis, then, were to be immersed in society like everyone else; they were in no way sectarians, even if they expected of themselves exemplary faithfulness to the demands of their halakha. Their ethos of study and discipleship was to be pursued as something "on top of" or "alongside" their activities and responsibilities as social actors among other social actors. Indeed, in principle, their learning was not to be the basis for claiming social superiority or for exacting social privileges or economic advantage (although, as we have discussed at great length in ch. 2, their learning was certainly the basis for their claim to possess special authority to decide matters of halakha).[9] Their exemplary piety and actions were to bring repute, rather than disrepute, on the rabbinic group, as well as to enshrine attitudes and dispositions conducive to learning and discipleship. Authority, it would seem, would be *accorded to them* by the community and its leadership by reason of this repute and learning in combination. (Later, by the medieval period, the rabbis were,

---

specifically rabbinic halakha (and/or does not share the rabbis' views on such matters) and, therefore, must be instructed what to do by a rabbinic sage—no doubt part of the creative fantasy/imaginings of Mishnah's ideal world.

8. Some may argue that distinctive dress codes were adopted by early rabbis and their disciples expressly to set them apart socially and to mark them as special. In this regard, Jacob Neusner, working with evidence from the Babylonian Talmud for the rabbinic group in Sassanian-ruled Babylonia, remarks that rabbis wore their prayer shawl (*tallit*) and phylacteries (*tefillin*) all day as a kind of uniform (see Neusner, *History of the Jews*, vol. 4). The earlier Jerusalem Talmud (at JT Berakhot 2:3) cites a precedent story (in which the protagonist is the late first-century rabbi Yohanan ben Zakkai) that is often taken to mean that rabbis wore their *tefillin* (and presumably *tallit* as well) all day. But neither Talmud seems to imply that this is a distinctively rabbinic practice, even if not all (male) Jews either in the land of Israel or Babylonia did so (see, e.g., BT Shabbat 118b). Rather, the implication is that some (many?) (male) Jews did, and many did not. And neither class nor vocation seems to be a determinative factor. Indeed, the same could be said about many halakhic norms (whether by rabbinic standards or not) in Jewish society of the period. Today, observant Jews don *tefillin* for the weekday morning service (with some exceptions, when it is worn for the afternoon service instead). But a recent pattern of behavior may be observed among some students in Jerusalem's traditional rabbinic academies (yeshivot); increasingly one observes them wearing *tefillin* all day, not only in the academies but also in the streets. I view this as an instance of adopting a regalia to identify themselves as yeshiva students generally or as students of particular yeshivot.

9. An often encountered interpretation of Avot 4:5; some contemporary Jewish authorities now shy away from this interpretation of Avot 4:5, since in modern times many rabbis do make a living out of studying the rabbinic classics, being supported by other Jews and, in the case of the state of Israel, also by the state, to do so. The political leaders of the nascent state of Israel were concerned that the Holocaust of World War II decimated the ranks of traditional rabbinic scholarship of Europe, and so decided to finance its revival using public money. This policy once established is difficult to revoke.

of course, much more "forward" in expecting to exercise not only authority but exclusive authority on matters of halakha, as was discussed in chapter 2. The consolidation of Karaite resistance to this claimed monopoly is probative evidence of this later development.)

LOCAL SAGE

Without wishing to slip overly much into who-type historical issues,[10] let me point out that many (most?) rabbis near and soon after the turn of the third century CE lived in what may be called economically second-tier towns in the land of Israel,[11] particularly on its coastal plain and in the lower and upper Galilee. The major metropolises (the centers of power, money and culture), like Caesarea, Sepphoris/Zippori, and Tiberias, possessed significant (majority?) pagan populations in this era. And these cities were the seats of sub-provincial Roman authority and administration. (Only in the last several years of his life did Rabbi Judah the Patriarch move his household and "court" to Sepphoris. And he or his successors then moved the patriarchal court to Tiberias.)

Whatever *formal* authority the early rabbis actually wielded—and it was probably little in the Jewish communities of the land of Israel at the turn of the third century—was (de facto, mostly) directed at Jews in communities in which Roman administration and pagan culture were relatively less blatant in everyday life than in the metropolises, and remained so even after 212 CE, when most free persons in the empire were accorded Roman citizenship. In these second-tier towns' Jewish communities, rabbis and their disciples operated alongside and in the interstices of traditional, local forms of Jewish communal organization, administration, governance, and authority. These latter forms were dominated by a largely hereditary class of local Jewish grandees ("elders"),[12] local councils, courts, and their administrative agents. Many rabbis likely aspired to be among these agents by reason of their particular education. But to aspire to be is not always to achieve to be. Indeed, some rabbis were attached to the court of Rabbi Judah the Patriarch and his successors as agents of his delimited trans-local administration of

10. For what, in my considered opinion, may be said of the history of the early rabbinic movement, the reader may turn to my account for nonspecialists in my book *In the Seat of Moses*, ch. 2, extracts of which appear as the appendix to this volume.

11. See Miller, *Sages and Commoners*.

12. In terms of normative forms of local town governance in the Roman provinces, it is probably quite apt to think of such a group of local hereditary elders as the *decuriones* of their towns.

Jewish affairs in the land of Israel. (The attribution of Mishnah's authorship to Judah the Patriarch bespeaks of some actual or desired level of entente, or patron-client relationship, between the rabbis of the third century and the patriarchate. The litany of names of early rabbinic grandees in chapters 1 and 2 of Avot, which list includes Judah the Patriarch and his son, Gamaliel III, attests to this perhaps mutual desire for such an entente.[13] But by the fourth century, the rabbis criticized the patriarchs as too romanized/hellenized for their druthers—perhaps sour grapes on the rabbis' part for unrequited regard of, and sought for positions in, the patriarchal administration.) Additionally, there were rabbinic sages, such as the mid-third-century Amora, Rabbi Yohanan in Caesarea, who operated in the major metropolises. But this was likely not the norm in this era.

The long and the short of it, therefore, is that most rabbis in this period were not "salaried employees" of the Jewish communities of the largely mid-sized and small-sized towns in which they dwelled. They supported themselves by other (and various) economic activities, as merchants, landowners, skilled artisans, etc. And I have little doubt that many or most rabbis were persons of some substantial means, the type of means that allowed sufficient leisure time to devote to study and to teaching disciples. The late third-, fourth-, and/or fifth-century aggadic lionizing of Rabbi Akiva, an early second-century figure, as a person of dirt-poor roots rising to rabbinic scholarly eminence, serves its literary function to aggrandize him only if such a trajectory from poverty and low birth to rabbinic genius was considered highly improbable, if not impossible.

So, in the main, the early rabbis were not the local governing grandees. Nor did they have a guild-like dominance, let alone monopoly, as agents and retainers of local Jewish communal governance and administration. They were a group of scholars of a particular ilk, possessing as individuals sufficient wealth to be able to dedicate much of their time to their particular type of scholarship. That said, their shared ethos of lifelong study made them among the most (recognizably) learned of their respective Jewish communities.

Later in this chapter, I committed to discuss to what (envisaged) social ends the early rabbinic movement pursued its *particular* brand of study, focussed as it was on Mishnah. Here I wish to make a different point; as relatively visible *local sages*, they *seem* to have been expected to be sources of many types of knowledge, knowledge that we would not necessarily associate with the outcomes of intense Mishnah study. It would *seem* that an intense commitment to knowledge acquisition in one domain

13. Boyarin discusses the significance of this list in "Diadoche of the Rabbis."

(for which Mishnah study was the central activity) correlated with curiosity about and acquisition of cognate knowledge in other domains as well. That is to say, a person who has been trained to devote maximum time to learning may seek to know about more than one thing, if there was a local demand or expectation of such. So, while one might have expected (or the rabbis hoped) that local townsfolk would seek out local rabbis for an opinion about some halakhic-related issue, it is entirely understandable that townsfolk *might* seek out *some* rabbis as a *local sages* about other things. What might those *other* things have been for which *some* rabbis' services/ advice seem to have been sometimes sought?

Before proffering an answer to this question, I must, in the spirit of Murphy's Laws, do something else first. I must first alert you once again to the fact that the evidence for what I will say in response tends to be relatively late, that is, fourth and fifth century, and much of the evidence is from the Babylonian Talmud, and therefore may not accurately or sufficiently reflect the state of affairs in the land of Israel, let alone the third century. That is why in the preceding paragraph I frequently resorted to mealymouthed words, such as "seem" and "might." Frankly, I am hedging the claims I am about to make. So, with these caveats in mind, what are these other things for the knowledge of which *some* rabbis *might* have been approached as *local sages*?

Not a few post-mishnaic rabbinic traditions portray certain rabbis as "go-to" sages for a number of things having little or nothing to do with halakha.[14] (Some) rabbis were known as proficient dream interpreters. In the Roman period Levant and Near East, dreams were thought to reveal the future of the dreamer, a future that might be facilitated or avoided. To have such foreknowledge is to be forewarned, potentially allowing some degree of control over one's future that one might not otherwise have. So dream interpreters provided a valued service, as the biblical narratives in Genesis about Joseph indicate.

According to traditions in post-mishnaic rabbinic literature, some rabbis were experts in demon avoidance and in providing incantations, amulets, and potions to stave off attacks from malevolent spirits. Roman culture in the Near East (as was the case elsewhere) believed demons to be as ubiquitous as they were unseen, and mostly malevolent. But they could be controlled, given specialized knowledge of effective incantations, amulets, and potions. (The Gospels and Acts portray Jesus and/or his apostles as effective forces

14. See, e.g., Hauptman, "Talmudic Rabbi." See also Avery-Peck, "Galilean Charismatic," 149–65.

against demonic powers.[15]) What is more, Jews and others believed that other unseen but benevolent forces could be harnessed in the fight to overcome demonic malevolence; these benevolent forces were the myriads of specialized hierarchies of angels. So with the right words, rituals, and/or potions, the countervailing powers of the appropriate, specialized angelic agents could be directed (indeed, compelled to act) against a correspondingly specialized demon's sphere of malevolence.[16] As local sages, then, some rabbis, it would seem, dispensed such shamanistic services.

Closely related to the foregoing was knowledge about the preparation of potions and medicines to treat illness. Early rabbinic texts treat physicians and surgeons as a highly professional group distinct from the rabbinic cadre. While undoubtedly some early rabbis were themselves (also) professional physicians, some other rabbis seem to have possessed, or were believed to possess, knowledge about physiology, medicines, and other treatments of specific medical conditions. Perhaps one might call this knowledge the type of folk medicine known to a local sage, whose learning spanned a number of domains beyond the rabbinic sage's primary domain of study and expertise.

The rabbi as the local sage, whose knowledge extended to dream interpretation, incantations, amulets, potions, and medicinal remedies was, I

15. See, e.g., the discussion in Chilton, *Rabbi Paul*, 204–7. See also M. Smith, *Jesus the Magician*.

16. Among the cache of early medieval manuscripts found in the latter part of the nineteenth century in a synagogue in Cairo—the so-called Cairo-Geniza documents— was a hitherto unknown Hebrew text called *Sefer HaRazim* ("The Book of Secrets"), after its opening sentence. Many scholars see the roots of the text to be in the second or third centuries CE in the land of Israel. Its presence in a medieval manuscript in Egypt could only have been with rabbinic forbearance, although no reference to rabbinic figures appears in the text. The text provides an account of the angelic "brigades," including the names of the angels in each brigade, for each of the "seven heavens." Each brigade has an area of responsibility, and *Sefer HaRazim* provides wording for incantations and instructions for associated rituals that harness the power of these specialized angels by name to effect results on earth. Many scholars have likened these incantations and rituals to those found among the "Greek Magical Papyri" (PGM), the provenance of which is second- or third-century CE Egypt. PGM is a hodgepodge collection of esoteric materials. *Sefer HaRazim* seems to be a carefully composed work with a clear editorial plan, namely, a guided heavenly journey through the seven heavens, via which migrations one learns angelic lore and how to use it. *Sefer HaRazim*'s account of the seventh heaven, however, seeks to represent and expand upon the grandeur of Ezekiel's and Isaiah's inaugural prophetic visions, about which I will say more in the next section of this chapter. Indeed, imaginative representations of such guided tours of angelic realms to attain special knowledge are reflected in some of the earliest layers of 1 Enoch, which are pre-rabbinic Jewish textual traditions. Therefore, that some early third-century CE rabbis, acting as local sages, would have provided services based on claims to similar knowledge as that represented in *Sefer HaRazim* is entirely plausible, if not probable.

suspect, mimicking the profile of the *likely* many other types of local Jewish "wise ones" who dispensed services to villagers and townsfolk. That is, these rabbinic sages likely had to live up to the expectations their neighbors had of sages in general, and so some rabbis acquired the requisite knowledge and skills to do so. I suspect that something similar may be said of comparable portrayals of Jesus and the apostles in early Christian traditions. For example, Acts (latterly, and significantly for contextualizing early rabbis' claimed prowess, understood by some scholars to be a second-century composition[17]) attributed to Paul superior effectiveness in miraculous arts compared to the sons of Sceva (Acts 19:11–20), and Simon "the Magician" is said to have sought to purchase the gifts of the Holy Spirit from Peter and John, because, it would seem, such gifts afforded demonstrable powers superior to his own (Acts 8:9–24). So, Paul, Peter, or John's superiority, according to Acts's construction of matters, derives not from the "magic" that the competition is alleged to be using but from their invocation of the superior power of Jesus and/or the Holy Spirit, rather than that of other unseen beings. My argument is this: those early rabbis who might have dispensed services expected of a local wise one were not engaging in activity that made one a rabbi, or that made the members of the rabbinic cadre a distinctive group, or that helped establish the shared identity of the early rabbinic movement. Unlike portrayals of Paul healing in Jesus' name, which acts served to solidify an early Christian social identity based on Jesus, early rabbis would not have healed in the name of Rabbi Akiva or Rabbi Judah the Patriarch.[18] Rather, early rabbis were, first and foremost, Mishnanians. Their shared profile and social identity derived primarily from the study of Mishnah, for the traditions of which they provided a divine pedigree (as outlined in ch. 2), and from the general and specific skills that Mishnah study engendered (as discussed in ch. 3).

17. Argued thoroughly by Richard Pervo in *Dating Acts*, and stressed to me by Arthur Dewey in correspondence.

18. Ironically, late medieval and particularly early modern Jews of Sephardic and Mideastern communities did venerate, and pray for the intercession of, famous dead rabbis, particularly those who had lived in the Tannaitic period. This veneration often took place at the alleged tombs of these rabbinic "saints," to which sites they would travel as pilgrims. This practice resembles the ancient practice of Jewish pilgrimage to the alleged tombs of the biblical patriarchs and matriarchs, a practice that goes back to the Hellenistic and Roman periods. The tombs of holy people were seen as gateways of sorts to heaven, through which portals prayers and calls for the intercession of the saint could more efficaciously travel. Such practices in Judaism, then, predate Christianity's veneration of its saints, and even predate the rise of the rabbinic movement. I have discussed this at greater length in Lightstone, *Commerce of the Sacred*.

MYSTIC/GNOSTIC RABBI

When the modern academic study of the early rabbinic movement and of its texts began in the nineteenth century, the resulting dominant image of the ancient rabbi was one of the religious, legal, and moral, scholastic-like rationalist. By the nineteenth century, the study of the Babylonian Talmud had dominated the rabbinic curriculum for more than a millennium. And as remarked earlier in this book, both Talmuds (the Jerusalem and Babylonian) have as their *main* purposes to reflect and/or to model particular analytical approaches to Mishnah passages and their halakhic subject matter—a type of rational dialectics. So the nineteenth-century scholars' image of the ancient rabbi as a moral and legal, religiously grounded rationalist seemed an entirely defensible one. And, importantly, it was also an image that, not coincidentally, suited the social and political task of nineteenth-century European Jews to bring about a rehabilitated, more positive attitude to Jews, Judaism, and rabbis in the decades following Jews' political emancipation in a Europe partly inspired by Enlightenment thinkers. Via this image of the rational rabbi, coupled with a liberalized Judaism, some European Jews sought to dispel many centuries of church-driven antisemitism. The several aggadic stories embedded in the Talmuds and other early rabbinic texts in which some rabbis were portrayed as experts in potions, incantations, demon avoidance, and the like, were either ignored or dismissed as aberrations of what the early rabbinic movement was principally about. And, indeed, there may be a great deal of validity to this, if one views the group identity and self-proclaimed authority of the early rabbis as a distinctive cadre as tied especially to their specific type of halakhic expertise engendered by Mishnah study.

The academics of the twentieth century, however, refused to sweep these "aberrations" under the rug. Not only did the involvement of (some) early rabbis in providing shaman-like services receive increased scholarly attention in twentieth-century scholarship, so too did the involvement of (some) ancient rabbis in mystical, ecstatic, contemplative, and gnostic-like activities. And it is undoubtedly the academic research and writing of Gershom Gerhard Scholem from the 1920s through the 1960s that sparked scholarship into rabbinic mysticism in the ancient, as well as medieval and early modern, periods.

What sparked this new, modern scholarly development, at least as regards the study of the ancient rabbis? Several factors. (1) An emerging European cultural current in the last half of the nineteenth century and the beginning of the twentieth increasingly recognized and appreciated the nonrational basis of religious life and valued religious experience and spirituality. (2) Archaeologists and archivists discovered Jewish mystical/gnostic texts written in Hebrew in manuscripts dating from the (earlier) medieval period, the (so-called Geonic) era of the several centuries following the advent of Islam, when rabbinic authority over the halakha was becoming dominant and nearly monopolistic in almost all Jewish communities. (3) Indeed, in some of these medieval texts the names of several second-century rabbis (pseudonymously) appear as the alleged teachers of these mystical/gnostic traditions. (4) Scholem argued and demonstrated that a number of seemingly obscure, almost unintelligible aggadic passages in post-mishnaic early rabbinic texts (especially the Babylonian Talmud) become far more intelligible when viewed in the light of these medieval Jewish mystical/gnostic texts. Scholem's virtually uncontestable conclusion is that some early rabbis of the post-mishnaic period in the land of Israel and/or in Babylonia must have been deeply engaged in the *type* of mystical/gnostic speculation and practices that are more completely articulated in the medieval manuscripts.[19]

Upon what did this type of early rabbinic mystical/gnostic speculation and practice focus? To address this question, I believe I must pose three subsidiary ones. First, what is reflected in the medieval texts? Second, what themes found in the medieval texts are most clearly reflected in early rabbinic post-mishnaic traditions? Third, can we show that these themes preoccupied some or many early rabbis around the time of, and soon after the promulgation of Mishnah in the early third century, since it is upon this cadre of rabbis that this book focuses?

The medieval texts themselves have provided us with three broad types of mystical/gnostic speculation and practice engaged in by some early medieval rabbis:[20] creation Gnosticism and practice (*ma-aseh breshit*); demiurge-dimension gnostic speculation (*shi-ur qoma*); and chariot-palaces mysticism

19. This argument is laid out in Scholem, *Jewish Gnosticism*.

20. In the popular mind, Jewish mysticism is associated with the kabbalah, of which there are several modern movements. Kabbalah is a Jewish theosophic and mystical movement founded in the thirteenth century in Provence and in Spain. Its earliest literary expression is in a text called *Sefer HaBahir*. But its first magnum opus is in a collation of works brought together under the title *Sefer HaZohar*, attributed pseudonymously to the second-century Tannaitic rabbi Simeon bar Yochai, but now thought by modern scholars to have been the work of Rabbi Moses de Leon. The modern scholarly identification of Moses de Leon as the author of *Sefer HaZohar* and of all of its constituent parts is one of the great "who-dun-it" stories of the modern academic study of the history of Judaism and is associated with the research of Gershom G. Scholem. See, e.g., Scholem, *Major Trends*. The medieval gnostic-mystical texts about which I write in this section all predate kabbalah, certainly by several or more centuries, and the types of gnostic-mystical thought and practice represented in these texts may predate kabbalah by nearly a millennium, as my discussion in this section will make clear.

and practice (*mekavah/merkabah, hekhalot*). The first, creation Gnosticism (*ma-aseh breshit*), provides special knowledge leading to contemplative exercises concerning elaborate configurations and permutations of the twenty-two-letter Hebrew alphabet in the belief that certain configurations were used by God in the creation. I will not here provide the basis in Jewish/rabbinic belief that underpins this, other than to say that the book of Genesis portrays God as "speaking" to effect creation, just as God "spoke" the Torah to Moses. This "word-gnosticism" may be likened to the Gospel of John's notion, expressed in its opening verses, of the primordial nature and power of God's word (*logos*), as well as to the Middle Platonic ideas of Philo of Alexandria, a mid-first-century Jewish philosopher, that God's word (*logos*), rather than God, effected and rules creation, first by creating a Platonic-like world of (perfect) ideas as a blueprint for this physical world.

The second, demiurge-dimension gnostic speculation (*shi-ur qoma*), focuses on speculation about the dimensions of the figure that, in the inaugural heavenly vision of the book of Ezekiel, is enthroned on a chariot drawn by fantastical winged beasts. In the book of Ezekiel that figure is said to be shaped like a (male) human, although the figure is anything but human; it is some divine being representing and acting for God. These medieval Judaic mystical texts proffer grandiose dimensions for this heavenly, human-shaped being as an object of spiritual-mystical meditation.

The third, chariot-palaces mysticism and practice (*mekavah/merkabah, hekhalot*), is also driven by the motive to replicate mystically the spiritual experience of the prophet Ezekiel's inaugural vision (conflated with elements from the inaugural prophetic account in Isaiah). But rather than the mystic contemplating the grandiose dimensions of the figure on the heavenly chariot, chariot-palaces mystical practice strives to produce what is experienced as an out-of-body ecstatic journey through the seven heavens, each conceived as a fortified palace, the gate of which is guarded by angelic soldiers. The ecstatic pilgrim, "those who go down to the chariot" (*yordei merkavah*), requires elaborate spiritual and physical preparation, according to these texts, as well as special knowledge, including of incantation-like words, to effect the journey. This heavenly journey is portrayed as fraught with danger, since the angelic guards will kill the journeying soul of any would-be mystic who does not know the secret answers to the questions these guards will pose before deeming the mystic worthy of passing. In the seventh heaven/palace, the destination of the out-of-body experience, the ecstatic traveler sees and hears the heavenly figure seated on the chariot and the angelic cohorts that serve and praise it in ecstatic hymns.[21]

21. See Davila, "Hekhalot Mysticism and Shamanism"; and Blumenthal, *Merkabah*

Of these three types of early medieval rabbinic (or rabbinized) mystical and gnostic traditions, creation-mysticism is mentioned in post-mishnaic early rabbinic aggadic passages. But it is overwhelmingly the third type, chariot-palaces mysticism, that is most clearly and obviously reflected in the (still admittedly few) often enigmatic, aggadic passages in (primarily) post-mishnaic rabbinic literature that portray ancient rabbis (especially Tannaitic sages, and particularly Rabbis Akiva, Eleazar b. Arakh, and Yohanan b. Zakkai) engaging in such practices.[22] The burning questions for us, given this volume's purpose, are these. First, how widespread was this mystical practice among the early rabbis; that is, are the practitioners of it portrayed as exemplary in the sense of aspirational for the many, or are they exemplary in the sense of the exceptional purview of the very few? Second, whether it is the one or the other, may we reliably date this practice among (some of) the early rabbis to the period around and/or soon after Mishnah's production and promulgation in the early third century? Let me begin with the second of the two questions. Mishnah itself (at m. Hagigah 2:1) places cautionary parameters around rabbis' "expounding" (Heb. verb root *drsh*) upon certain biblical text-based topics, among them the act of creation in Genesis and the account of the chariot in Ezekiel. If Mishnah's wariness applies to the simple reading and straightforward exegesis of these biblical texts, then it is hard to see any point to issuing such warnings. These biblical passages would have been read routinely and interpreted in private and in public assemblies/synagogues (as indeed they still are today in the course of the synagogue service and in traditional preparatory study of the weekly biblical lections). The interpreter-analyst of Mishnah is, therefore, certainly invited to consider that "expound" here means something more esoteric and, consequently, inherently dangerous. The arguably earliest post-mishnaic or extra-mishnaic traditions are those collected in the Tosefta (c. 250–400), which brings together allegedly Tannaitic traditions that serve as an aid to Mishnah study by commenting upon, expanding upon, or otherwise supplementing Mishnah.[23] Tosefta's

---

Tradition, 56–89.

22. Another cautionary methodological note must be registered here. To say, e.g., that chariot-palaces esoterism and mystical practice is reflected in early rabbinic aggadic traditions is *not* to say that *all* of the notions and practices spelled out in the medieval chariot-palace mystical texts were also known and practiced by early rabbis. That would be to court falling prey to anachronistic historical thinking. Moreover, as will be seen in my presentation in the next paragraphs, we do not need to risk engaging in such anachronistic thinking in order to show that *some form* of this type of esoteric teaching and practice was present among some (limited number of) early rabbinic circles.

23. For an account of Tosefta's place among the texts of early rabbinic literature, see Lightstone, *In the Seat of Moses*, ch. 3.

traditions (at t. Hagigah 2:1–2) concerning m. Hagigah 2:1 undoubtedly take the Mishnah passage to be referring to such potentially dangerous esoterism, as do the Jerusalem Talmud's (c. 400) and Babylonian Talmud's (c. 600) use of and elaboration upon traditions that parallel those of t. Hagigah 2:1–2 (at JT Hagigah 2:1 and BT Hagigah 14b–16a). We may be reasonably assured, therefore, that the earliest post-mishnaic traditions—possibly as early as several decades after Mishnah's production—register caution while they lionize those Tannaitic rabbis alleged to be masters of such esoterism. As to the other question, clearly these post-mishnaic texts (and possibly Mishnah too) view such esoterism as the purview of the very few—exemplary but highly exceptional. The implication is that outside of a very restrained circle, such esoterism is a road to madness, heresy, or apostasy, even for rabbis. As much as its few (successful) practitioners are admired, it is clear that such esoteric speculation and practice are *not* meant to be part of the *normative* early rabbinic profile of the Mishnanians.

LOCAL PREACHER

The evidence is nothing short of overwhelming that by the first century CE (if not earlier) local and visiting learned persons regularly delivered homilies or lectures in the synagogue to the community gathered there on Sabbaths and festivals. Similarly well supported by the ancient sources is the practice of thematically linking these discourses to the public reading of scriptural lections during the synagogue assemblies.[24] Was delivering public homilies or discourses an *integral and central* part of the skill set (and self-defined duties) of the early rabbis? For those with a knowledge of *modern* Judaism and the *contemporary* rabbinate, it is all too inviting to assemble the ancient evidence in such as manner as to respond in the affirmative. But a more critical assessment of the evidence supports a much more nuanced response than that. So let me begin to address this topic with remarks about modern rabbis and expeditiously work my way back to our early rabbis.

Beginning in Europe in the 1830s among those liberal Judaic movements committed to adapting Judaism to modern social and cultural currents, rabbis appointed by synagogue-congregations were expected to preach sermons regularly, on the model of Protestant Christian ministers. And it is safe to say, since the 1950s (if not earlier) in North America, the liberal synagogues (i.e., those associated with the Conservative, Reconstructionist, and Reform movements of Judaism) expected their rabbis to be effective and

---

24. The evidence for the preceding two statements is very well presented and summarized in Graves, "Public Reading of Scripture," esp. 480–84.

engaging preachers on Sabbaths and festivals during the communal worship services. Their sermons often followed the designated scriptural readings of the day from the Pentateuch and the Prophets and were usually expected to link something in these readings to the theme of the homily delivered. Preaching, together with the congregational rabbis' pastoral capabilities, more than anything else, it may be argued, were and are in North America the most important factors in their contract renewal, even though local synagogue rabbis were also expected to teach Jewish texts and traditions to their synagogues' lay study groups and to answer any questions posed by synagogue members about authentic Judaic practice and ritual.[25]

Before the nineteenth century, in the late medieval, Renaissance, and early modern periods, preaching happened irregularly in synagogues. Local rabbis typically preached twice only a year, on the Sabbaths preceding the Day of Atonement (around the autumn equinox) and before Passover (just after the spring equinox). These "sermons" were principally intended to remind community members of their halakhic obligations for these upcoming holy days. Indeed, before the mid-nineteenth and twentieth centuries in Europe, rabbis were not employed by their local synagogue at all, even though the local rabbi(s) had a revered place in it. And that reverence was due to them because they were the highest halakhic authorities of their community.

Preaching in these earlier periods, as irregular as it was, was especially the purview of notable, often itinerant preachers, whom the community wished to hear as edifying and inspirational "entertainment," when these gifted speakers happened to be coming to town.[26] These were the rock stars of the Jewish world before the modern period, and they sometimes had a circuit of engagements, as musicians might today. Some were also credentialed rabbis, and many were not. They were highly gifted professional preachers, who were paid for this particular skill.

So, did *early* rabbis, near and just after the turn of the third century, preach, to whom, and about what? And was preaching part of the standard *normative* profile of members of the early rabbinic movement? As with so much in this chapter, "it's complicated." The evidence may at first glance seem abundant but, upon further consideration, is difficult to assess and even more

25. For a revealing, mid-twentieth-century reflection on these issues, see Petuchowski, "Modern Rabbi." The author was on the faculty of Hebrew Union College (now Hebrew Union College-Jewish Institute of Religion), the rabbinical school that trains rabbis for synagogues affiliated with the Reform movement of Judaism. Petuchowski's role at HUC makes his observations all the more poignant. See also Saperstein, "Rabbis as Preachers"; Hoffman, "Professionalization of American Rabbinate."

26. For a comprehensive study of preaching in Judaism in the late medieval, Renaissance, and early modern periods, see Saperstein, *Jewish Preaching*.

difficult confidently to assign to the period that is our focus. And equally confounding, one has to consider the supplementary question: What do we mean by preaching anyway, when talking about early rabbinic skills and practices? Let me begin with the last posed question.

Part of the challenge in addressing this question is terminological/philological. (What did certain words actually mean in earlier eras?) Modern scholars of the ancient rabbis have tended to equate two terms with preaching by members of the early rabbinic movement. One term is "aggada" (or haggadah). As you know from earlier sections of this book, aggada refers to a type of early rabbinic tradition defined by its content. It is not halakha; rather aggada proffers wisdom sayings, parables, and very short stories[27] (often of a legendary-like ilk) about biblical and early rabbinic heroes. The role of aggada is moral, spiritual, and theological edification.

The other term that has been associated with early rabbinic preaching is "midrash." Again, this refers to a genre of early rabbinic and medieval rabbinic traditions and literature, about which earlier parts of this volume have remarked. In this rabbinic literature, characterized by specific literary forms and conventions, midrashic traditions expound upon biblical verses in such a way that the rabbinic teachings conveyed (whether halakhic or aggadic in content) are portrayed as having been derived from layers of meaning inherent in the scriptural verse(s) at issue (although not necessarily at the level of the verse's surface meaning, its plain sense). If that teaching is halakhic in nature, then the tradition is said to be "halakhic midrash." If the tradition is aggadic in nature, then the teaching is classified as "aggadic midrash." As implied, not only individual rabbinic traditions but entire texts may be classified as halakhic midrash or aggadic midrash, when the whole text (or by far the greater part of it) conveys traditions of the halakhic-midrashic or aggadic-midrashic genre. Moreover, these entirely (or nearly so) midrashic texts, as I have previously mentioned, sometimes organize their content by focusing on a particular biblical book, ordering their constituent midrashic traditions according to the sequence of verses in the biblical text, even though not every verse of the biblical book is treated to such an "exposition."

The scholarly consensus view—and consensus is not unanimity—is that those whole texts that are generally classified midrashic-halakhic are relatively early, c. 250–425 CE. On the other hand, the consensus view about the dating of the whole texts that are aggadic-midrashic is that while some may have circulated in proto-versions as early as the fifth century CE, the bulk were produced between the seventh and ninth centuries. That is

---

27. Many of these bear comparison to the *chrea* form in some Greek literature of the Greco-Roman period and to its adaptation by the Gospel writers in their stories about Jesus.

quite a long time after the period of our early third-century Mishnanians. Finally—and this is the bridge to our question about what we mean by early rabbinic preaching—nineteenth and early twentieth-century scholars of the ancient rabbinic movement *tended to associate aggadic midrash, that is, both the individual traditions and the whole texts, with ancient rabbinic preaching.* That is, in the view of these scholars, these traditions and texts (although compiled relatively late) are *highly literary, very formalized* productions with substantive origins in actual (public) preaching by ancient rabbis, both Tannaim and Amoraim (since it is their names that appear in the passages of these literary productions).[28]

On the grounds of this assumed association, the sheer volume of aggadic-midrashic texts (notwithstanding their relatively late dates of composition) might lead one to conclude that a great deal of public preaching was done by ancient rabbis. And so it was concluded by a number of modern scholars in the decades before and after the turn of the twentieth century.[29] But on what *basis* can it be concluded that the content of these many, largely medieval volumes of aggadic midrash derive from *publicly delivered sermons* of rabbis of the Tannaitic and Amoraic periods? Or, to put the matter in other terms, why did these modern scholars *associate* aggadic midrash with early rabbinic preaching in the first place?

The association, in my view, is based on the Hebrew/Aramaic verb root *drsh/darash/derash* and on the linguistic/grammatical relationship of this verb root to several nouns derived from it, especially *darshan* and *midrash*. Let me say more about the semantic ranges of *drsh/darash/derash*, *darshan*, and *midrash*.

Professor Paul Mandel, in his recent book, *The Origins of Midrash*, provides a comprehensive semantic/philological history of these terms'

---

28. For indication that late nineteenth- and early twentieth-century scholars associated the highly literary, aggadic midrashic compilations (which they themselves understood to largely be productions of the early medieval period) with ancient rabbinic preaching, one has only to look at the article "Homiletics" by Kohler and Philipson in the 1906 edition of the *Jewish Encyclopedia*. The editors of the turn-of-the-twentieth-centuiy *Jewish Encyclopedia* took great pains to have the individual entries written by the most eminent scholars of the day, Kohler and Philipson among them. The entry on homiletics clearly evinces all of the associations and trains of thought that I have characterized in this paragraph. Those associations endured relatively unchanged through most of the twentieth century (and for many, beyond). The first prominent, modern scholar to assert this association was Leopold Zunz in a book first published in 1832 under the title *Die Gottesdienstlichen Vorträge der Juden, historisch Entwickelt*, which in its Hebrew translation, *HaDerashot BeYisrael*, remained a mainstay of the modern academic study of ancient Judaism, so much so that it continued to be reprinted well into the mid-twentieth century.

29. See again, e.g., the previous note.

meanings and usages from biblical times to the Amoraic rabbinic era. He demonstrates that over these many centuries, the semantic range of such terms changed dramatically. And importantly for our purposes, it is only in the mid- to late Amoraic era, let us say, at least a century or more after Mishnah's promulgation, that, in Mandel's view, midrash specifically denotes the "production of multiple meanings in the biblical text."[30] And it is the latter meaning of midrash that necessarily is presupposed by, and therefore underlies, the extant traditions and literature of rabbinic midrashic, especially aggadic-midrashic, texts. So let us put aside the once common assertion that in early rabbinic, midrashic literature, particularly those of the genre of aggadic midrash, we find in substance and form something like the sermons *preached* by rabbis of the era of Mishnah's production and the immediately subsequent decades. And as a consequence let us begin, as Mandel does, at the root of the matter with the verb *darash*, except we will focus on the early rabbinic era near and soon after Mishnah's production.[31]

Darash means to "expound" as well as "to search out (the meaning of)." In the latter sense, "to search out," it refers to deep intellectual inquiry into a topic. This specific meaning of the verb has certainly been passed on to nouns (e.g., midrash) derived from the verb, as is evident in the following early rabbinic wisdom saying in Avot 1:17: "The intellectual inquiry [*midrash*] is not the essence, but the action [*ma-aseh*] [that derives from it]." In the former sense, "to expound," the same verb means to declaim (lecture or preach, if you will) before others on the meaning of something, based on one's deep intellectual engagement with the topic.

As just mentioned, the meanings of the rabbinic Hebrew and rabbinic Aramaic verb root *drsh/darash/derash* underlie nouns constructed from the verb. You already know that midrash is one of those nouns, and we have just seen that in Avot 1:17 (and consistent with Mandel's findings about this era) the term clearly does *not* specifically denote the later Amoraic genre of scriptural exposition that gave rise to rabbinic-midrashic

---

30. Mandel, *Origins of Midrash*, 289. Mandel convincingly argues that the verb *drsh* (from which the term "midrash" is derived) was not understood within Judah-ite or early rabbinic circles to refer primarily to Scripture-based exposition/interpretation (in which multiple interpretations of Scripture are adduced) until the mid- to late Amoraic period (*Origins of Midrash*, 289–305). According to Mandel, in Judah-ite culture before the rabbinic period, *drsh* more broadly referred to the search for oracular divine knowledge and later to the scribes' search for divine knowledge as expressed especially in authentic law (*Origins of Midrash*, 289–9), from which its usage expanded to refer to authentic instruction or exposition, especially on law/halakha, often to an assembled audience (*Origins of Midrash*, 169–288).

31. See the previous note for my summary characterization of Mandel's findings for earlier periods.

literature. Rather, midrash refers to engaged intellectual inquiry—diligent study, if you will. This makes eminent sense; you already have learned that the early rabbinic group's ethos was significantly one of study. That said, another noun based on the verb is *darshan* (sg.), which term refers to *someone* who declaims before others upon the meaning of something. It follows (semantically/philologically at least) that a competent *darshan* is one who has engaged intellectually with one's topic (midrash in Avot 1:17's sense), and presumably has the additional skills to engage the audience/listeners in the same. And since the opening chapters of Avot are all about being a student of Torah (in the generic sense), then in accordance with Avot's ethos of being a rabbinic sage, the appropriate topics of a rabbi-*darshan* (insofar as this may be a common element of the early rabbinic profile at all) would be Torah-related subjects (whether aggadic or halakhic in substance). Why am I being coy by proffering the parenthetical comment "insofar as this may be a common element of the early rabbinic profile at all"? Because semantics and philology have done their job for us in clarifying meanings of terms at specific junctures in history. But we must do more before we can legitimately suggest that many, let alone all, early rabbis were (or were expected to be) gifted *darshanim* (pl.), declaimers before audiences, of *their* Torah. So, let us take up this latter matter. Here is what I do think is warranted on the basis of the evidence.

In a textual tradition as early as the turn of the third century CE, some rabbis were understood to have been accomplished public declaimers/preachers (*darshanim*, pl.). An aggadic passage in the (otherwise principally halakhic) Mishnah itself (m. Sotah 9:16) lionizes the early second-century rabbi Ben Zoma for being the last of the truly great *darshanim*. Now, in the mindset of traditional religious societies, the best is hardly ever yet to come but is conceived to have come and gone already. As a historian and anthropologist of religion, I recognize this as an often encountered trope. So, I do not conclude from m. Sotah 9:16 that Mishnah's authors are telling us that no rabbis were *darshanim* after Ben Zoma passed away. Rather, we are being told that no *darshanim* after Ben Zoma were, or will ever be, his equal. That said, Mishnah does not tell us anything about what Ben Zoma (allegedly) declaimed/preached about and to whom. Mishnah assumes that its ancient readers know, but I certainly do not and cannot know.

A tradition cited in the Jerusalem Talmud (c. 400) about Rabbi Meir (a seminal, mid-second-century personage) tells us that Meir is said to have preached regularly on Friday nights to gender-mixed lay audiences in the synagogue in the town of Hamath (JT Sotah 1:4). About what he (allegedly) preached, JT Sotah 1:4 does not say. Moreover, it is not possible reliably to date this tradition to the actual time of Rabbi Meir in the mid-second century or to the time of Mishnah's production about half a century later. But this tradition about Rabbi Meir's regular preaching to a lay audience cannot be dated later than about 365 CE.

The Babylonian Talmud (authored two centuries later still, c. 600) recounts at BT Sotah 40b a story in which the dramatis personae are mid- to late third-century rabbis in the land of Israel. So, it is even more difficult reliably to date the story to the period in which the rabbis in question are believed to have lived. Nonetheless, the story is worth citing, because of its use of terms that we are struggling to understand as denoting early rabbinic preaching.

BT Sotah 40b (Hebrew in regular font, and Aramaic in italics)

 i. *Rabbi Abbahu and Rabbi Hiyya bar Abba happened to be in a certain locale* [at the same time].

 ii. *Rabbi Abbahu expounded* [*derash*] *on aggadic* [subject matter]; *Rabbi Hiyya bar Abba expounded on* [halakhic] *traditions.*

 iii. *Everybody* [in attendance at the latter] *left Rabbi Hiyya bar Abba and went over* [to hear] *Rabbi Abbahu.* [Rabbi Hiyya bar Abba] *was despondent.*

 iv. [Rabbi Abbahu] *said to him: I shall tell you an allegory. To what is the matter comparable?

 v. [It is similar to] two men. One sells precious stones [which are, of course, expensive]. And one sells all sorts of trinkets [which are inexpensive]. Upon who[se merchandise does everyone] pounce? [Will they] not [pounce on the merchandise of] this one who sells all kinds of trinkets?

In this story, *darash/derash* is the verb used to describe both rabbis' expository lectures. Neither of the rabbis is, it seems, in their home town. So they are not surrounded by their regular contingent of disciples or local townsfolk. As the story goes, they happen to be at the same place at the same time for whatever reason, and, as visiting learned persons, the lectures are organized for them. We are not told whether the envisaged audiences in the story are laypeople in the local community or that town's disciples of the sages (if the town had any). But the gist of the story is that whoever the audiences are, they would much rather hear an exposition on aggada (by Rabbi Abbahu) than on halakha (by Rabbi Hiyya bar Abba), to the disappointment and chagrin of Hiyya, whose talk they abandoned. Ouch!

To this point the passage is in Aramaic. The story then switches to Hebrew. Rabbi Abbahu tries to make his colleague, Rabbi Hiyya bar Abba, feel better by telling him an allegorical parable. The gist: most people prefer to acquire the cheap stuff in the marketplace and cannot afford the really valuable merchandise. That is to say, most of the potential audiences for the two lectures/lessons could appreciate only the aggadic content (which, the allegory implies, requires less intellectual expenditure) rather than the halakhic content (which requires far greater intellectual expenditure). The implication, perhaps, is that the envisaged audiences in this story were lay people and not disciples of the sages, who, if present, would presumably have valued halakhic learning above all else. That said, *darash* is clearly used to describe some sort of public-like expository lecture (whether based explicitly on scriptural texts we cannot say), since there are other verbs routinely used in early rabbinic literature to denote "teaching" (e.g., *shanah* in Hebrew or *tana* in Aramaic). The *darshan* may speak about halakahic or aggadic matters, and this story clearly implies that halakhic content is more valuable, even if less engaging for a broader audience.

What do I take from these admittedly varied, widely scattered, and somewhat equivocal pieces of evidence about rabbis as preachers? Here is my best considered estimate on the matter. While the traditions referenced are embedded in early rabbinic texts produced between c. 200 to 600 CE, they all *imagine* that:

1. Some rabbis sometimes preach—they are *darshanim*—and some may routinely do so.

2. Some rabbis are gifted *darshanim*.

3. Sometimes lay audiences are the target audience.

4. Rabbinic *darshanim* may expound on either halakhic or aggadic subject matter, although the latter probably appeals to a much wider audience.

5. *Darshanim* (as the verbal substantive implies) may often ground their presentations in the exposition of Scripture, but there is no indication that this must invariably be the case.

6. Being a regular, gifted *darshan* is probably not seen as part of the standard, necessary, and sufficient profile of every credentialed early rabbi, and, in any case, Mishnah is keen on stressing that the era of the allegedly great *darshanim* ended with Ben Zoma's death in the first half of the second century.

7. The highly formalized and stylized passages of aggadic midrash in the late Amoraic and/or early medieval rabbinic texts of this genre may well reflect little or nothing of forms of actual early rabbinic preaching

in the period just before and after the turn of the third century; rather, these aggadic-midrashic texts are complex *literary* exercises of a slightly later specific genre.

How does one square these impressions derived from a reasonably cautious reading of the early rabbinic evidence, on the one hand, with the extra- and pre-rabbinic sources, on the other, that strongly support the claim that local and visiting learned people regularly declaimed in the synagogue-assemblies about the publicly read scriptural texts of the day?[32] Perhaps this way. Many local and visiting preachers expounded to lay audiences in the synagogue assemblies in the land of Israel in the late second and early third centuries. *Some* of these were rabbis, as one might expect, given that early rabbis were a (but not the only) cadre of wise/learned persons. Those early rabbis who did so, or who did so well, may have been viewed as aspirational examples to their rabbinic peers and students. But the core knowledge and skills both necessary and sufficient to be a bona fide member of the early rabbinic group clearly remained in the area of halakha and halakhic thinking, not in public preaching; early rabbis were, first and foremost, Mishnanians, in my opinion. Halakha and halakhic thinking were the "precious stones" of the early rabbinic profile, as far as the early rabbinic movement was concerned. The ethos of study and discipleship was instrumental in acquiring halakhic expertise through intense, lifelong Mishnah study. Much of the rest was costume jewelry, the "trinkets" in Rabbi Abbahu's allegorical parable, which certainly had a place and appeal if the early rabbis were to draw a wider local audience and clientele amidst competition from other types of wise persons who could dispense folk medicine and amulets, interpret dreams, or preach. And some things, notably esoterism, admirable as its early rabbinic practitioners were deemed to be, were just too dangerous for other than a small elite group among the early rabbis.

With the foregoing, my survey of the profile of what the early rabbis were is concluded. It remains in this chapter to take up the other question with which chapter 4 began: To what social end(s) this profile?

TO WHAT SOCIAL ENDS?

In chapter 1 of this book, I distinguished who-type questions from what-type questions about the early rabbis and their movement. The former concerned the history of the early rabbinic movement and the role that

---

32. See again the excellent survey by Graves, "Public Reading of Scripture," esp. 480–84.

individual named figures played in that history. I argued that because of the nature and limitation of the sources available to us, who-type-questions are difficult to address for the first several centuries of the development of the early rabbinic group. On the other hand, this entire volume is predicated on being able reasonably to address a number of what-type questions about the early rabbinic movement, because we can know a great deal about what members of the early rabbinic group were expected to know; the skills needed to master (and apply?) this knowledge; and other elements of social identity, such as their self-justificatory mythologizations, that bound the early rabbis together as a group. And we can know this, in large part, because (1) we have in hand the Mishnah, (2) we have ample evidence about the singular importance of the Mishnah and Mishnah study among the early rabbis, and (3) we even possess texts (like Tosefta and the two Talmuds) that were produced as aids or models for Mishnah study.

In consequence, that Mishnah study was the centerpiece of the early rabbinic curriculum and that the lifelong analysis of Mishnah was valued by the early rabbis more than the study of any other texts and subjects are, in my judgment, irrefutable assertions, given the evidence. And these claims are not denatured in any way by the fact that, for example, some rabbis, as local wise persons, were sought out for services and talents that other competing types of wise persons also likely provided. What remains to be asked, however, is this: To what end(s) the lifelong, engaged, study of Mishnah, as *the* defining activity of the early rabbinic group? To answer this question may seem like bringing who-type questions back in the room through the emergency exit. And perhaps it is, but only in a limited, very constrained, and controlled manner.

Let me start with a commonsense claim; no one does a lot of a very difficult thing if they do not think that they are getting something out of it. Now, that something may be money or pay in kind, in which case the person's talents fit into some market of the exchange and provision of goods and services, because the talent is *valued* by others. But, that something may be as simple as a sense of personal growth and accomplishment. Yet even here, one's sense of satisfaction of having grown personally and accomplished something important is conditioned by the norms either of one's society generally or of some specific group with which one intensely identifies, in which case, once again, one's hard-won achievements are *valued* by others.

Without in any way intending to sound cynical, the upshot of the preceding paragraph is this. Generally speaking, someone else with whom you identify has to value what you achieve in some meaningful fashion in order for you to value it. In classical sociological analysis, this is called "reference group theory." One needs or expects affirmation from some group in order to be self-affirming. And I would suggest that the more arcane and very difficult the thing to be mastered, the more essential it is to belong to a specific group of like-minded persons or to live in a society that highly values what is to be mastered, given the prodigious time, effort, and (often) expense needed to attain such mastery.

To repeat an important point, this valuing may come in many different forms. The most obvious is that someone will pay you a good living wage or generous fees for your mastery. But there are many other forms of highly effective valuing in addition to this, ones that do not entail making a living (at least not directly) from one's hard-won expertise. In both modern and ancient societies alike, such things as honor, regard, deference, and respect are as valuable, and often more valuable, than monetary compensation (provided, of course, one is able to earn a living by some other means). Honor can have as much, and sometimes more, social value than a paycheck. In the Roman world, even the most wealthy (such as those who belonged to the senatorial class) strove to win *dignitas* by rising through the *cursus honorum*, the hierarchical rungs of public service roles.[33]

Let me illustrate some of the foregoing by referring to an analogous pastime with which all of you probably have some familiarity; that pastime is playing a complicated game, chess, very well. Pay attention in what follows to two pairs of distinctions. The first pair is the distinction between, on the one hand, value accorded by and within a small group of persons who share a particular identity and, on the other hand, value accorded by a wide swath of society at large. The second pair concerns the method of valuing. Is it monetary compensation in a market of goods and services, or is it *dignitas*? Why press these two sets of distinctions about valuing chess mastery, such that the effort to achieve it is worthwhile? Because, as you will see later, we must decide whether the value of the normative profile of the early rabbis falls into the one category or the other, or somewhere in between. Is the reference group the early rabbinic cadre(s) or Jewish communities at large in the land of Israel around and soon after the turn of the third century? Is the normative, distinctively early rabbinic profile recognized by payment of some sort or by forms of bestowing honor? Here, then, is the analogy, chess mastery. In distinctively rabbinic-aggadic terms, chess mastery is our *mashal*, like the story Rabbi Abbahu told Rabbi Hiyya to comfort him.

---

33. Having said this, I cannot deny that great *dignitas* and rising through the *cursus honorum* led to increased economic opportunity. But this was simply not the same economic opportunity as that derived from selling the produce of one's large Italian estate in the marketplace, or importing into Rome large shipments of wheat from Egypt.

As I began to write this chapter, the Netflix series entitled *The Queen's Gambit* was the rage.[34] In it, a young American woman achieves chess mastery of the highest order. Consider that most of the population of North America probably does not care a lot whether you play chess very well. Consequently, North American society at large is relatively indifferent to what you need to do to acquire and maintain that level of play. In fact, some in society, particularly in North America, may even view your pursuit of chess mastery as a little odd and think of you as different, and not in a good way. However, if you join a chess club and spend a great deal of time with members of chess clubs, then you receive a great deal of affirmation for your efforts to play better and better, since playing chess well underlies the identity formation of the group. And the better you play, the more *dignitas*, that is, honor, regard, deference, and status, you are accorded in the *inner-group*, social dynamics of chess clubs—both in your home club and in others. Therefore, even if perfecting one's chess game actually costs you money out of your pocket or has significant opportunity costs (because you could be spending more time doing other things that would improve your financial standing), your chess mastery is the basis for being highly valued. This is reference group theory at work, so to speak.

Now where does one get the time and money to devote so much time to chess and ultimately to chess competitions, since doing well in the latter is the best affirmation of your own abilities and reflects positively on your local chess club? Either you get paid, as an employee or fee-charging professional would, to develop and then exhibit the superiority of your talents. Or, notwithstanding the opportunity costs of spending so much time playing chess, you have other means of self-support, and these means are sufficient to allow you to pursue your chess-playing as an amateur, so to speak. Or is it something in between? (The history of Olympic athletics over the past sixty years has drifted along this continuum from near-complete amateurism to near-total professionalism.) One might have a well-paying job as a lawyer and also get prize money from winning chess tournaments. The prize money may be token amounts at local levels and increase significantly at national and international levels of competition. But, at least in North America, all of this valuing of chess mastery, whether via bestowing honor or a combination of honor and prize money, happens within the highly delimited social sphere of chess clubs and associations. That is to say, the reference group remains the rather restrained number of people who are members of these clubs and associations. Society at large pays relatively little attention and shows relatively little regard.

34. Scott, *Queen's Gambit*.

Now, *The Queen's Gambit*—accurately or not does not matter—depicts society in the then-Soviet Union as having a different attitude than the populace of the United States about chess and those who played it well. Chess is portrayed as a kind of Soviet national passion and pastime, even a national obsession. (Like hockey in Canada?) In the Netflix series, ordinary people closely observed the games played by chess masters in order better to play chess themselves in their normal, everyday lives, not in the enclaved settings of chess clubs. So, in the series at least, the chess knowledge of the Soviet masters was a highly sought-after *commodity* by *many* in Soviet society at large, and Soviet chess masters were portrayed as professionals, in the sense that they were fully supported by the state to play chess well, in contrast to the American chess masters, who were largely self-funded amateurs (who sometimes won prize money or were supported by charitable foundations for international travel). And in the Soviet Union, what was that commodity in concrete terms? It had to do with closely observing the chess moves of competing masters over the course of *multitudinous series of highly varied circumstances, defined by various combinations and configurations of the chess pieces on the board.* Indeed, when the heroine of *The Queen's Gambit* and her Russian opponent are preparing themselves during a requested pause in the game, both she and her opponent (with the help of their respective colleagues) *studied all the hypothetical, possible configurations of pieces that could result from moves that either player might make in what remained of the match, in order to determine for each configuration whether one move or another move was the appropriate one.* (Now, does that not sound a lot like the Mishnanian studying possible configurations of circumstances that define series of hypothetical cases in order to exercise halakhic thinking about whether for each resulting case one ruling or another is appropriate according to the norms and principles of the halakha?) Moreover, upon the conclusion of the pause in the chess game, all of these appropriate responses to hypothetical configurations of the pieces on the board must be in their heads. In fact, *The Queen's Gambit* stresses the heroine's ability visually to imagine configurations of pieces and the appropriate moves, all in her head, even though only some of these configurations would actually occur on the chess board during the remainder of the match. Moreover, outside the building in which the championship was taking place, crowds of ordinary Soviet citizens gathered as each championship player's moves were reported to them. They clearly felt the need to know what moves worked best given these configurations of pieces on the board, in order to apply the knowledge to their own chess-playing.

What would I have you garner from our analogy, our *mashal*? In North America, the reference groups that accord value to the effort of achieving chess mastery are primarily chess clubs, and the valuing of that mastery is primarily expressed in bestowing *dignitas*, honor. In the Soviet Union, supposedly, the reference group that accorded value to chess mastery was a large swath of the population at large, "ordinary folk," because they saw chess masters as providing a valued commodity. Moreover, the Soviet government largely supported the very best chess masters as a kind of full-time professional. Finally, chess mastery involved more than knowing the rules of the game. It involved, among other things, (1) imagining the various combinations and permutations of configurations of chess pieces that *hypothetically might* arise on the board as a result of your own and your opponent's moves, and (2) having thought out in advance the most appropriate next move(s), given the rules of the game and the goal of winning it. If this is the analogy (*mashal*), then in what sense does this help us better discuss the *analogue* (in rabbinic Hebrew, the *nimshal*), namely, the normative shared profile of the early rabbis?

Now, I have argued that notwithstanding *other* elements of *some* rabbis' skills profile (as preachers, dream interpreters, amulet providers, etc.), it is the knowledge and skills required for, and derived from, Mishnah study that are the sine qua non of being a rabbi near and soon after the turn of the third century. That is why I have called the early rabbis Mishnanians.

The lifelong study and mastery of Mishnah undertaken by the early rabbis is another type of difficult preoccupation, one that also demands much time, effort, and (inevitably) financial means in order to do well (because devoting significant time to lifelong Mishnah study must have had considerable opportunity costs). Let us, then, review what doing Mishnah study well entails and what skills it imparts, because this is the defining characteristic not of a chess club with which one identifies but of an association, movement, guild, school—I do not know which term is the more appropriate—of early rabbis.

As you now know, the defining characteristics attained through much effort by members and would-be members of the early rabbinic group formed by Mishnah study, valued and undertaken above all other group intellectual pursuits, are the following:

1. A high level of literacy

2. Expertise in scriptural law, which must to a significant degree be in their heads

3. A mastery of much extra-biblical law, presumed and assumed, but largely unstated, throughout Mishnah, and which also must be largely in their heads

4. Some reasonably extensive memorization of the Mishnah text

5. A type of analytic, halakhic thinking engendered by fully engaging with (a) the lacunae (the missing bits) in Mishnah's language; (b) the meaning and the unstated legal reasoning of Mishnah passages' topically diverse, posited, hypothetical circumstances; and (c) their (sometimes opposing) rulings about legal cases pertaining to an imagined, ideal world

We know that the individual bent on acquiring and perfecting all of this, and who must expend the time and effort and bear the expense of doing so, will rightfully have expected his (the use of the masculine intended) success to be valued and affirmed in meaningful and significant ways. At a minimum, that valuing will have come from other members of the early rabbinic group, particularly from its more eminent members. In modern sociological terminology, this is the individual (would-be) rabbi's *most immediate* reference group, comprising one's teacher and his disciple circle, or (from the mid- or late third century on) one's teacher's house of study and, beyond that, other rabbinic masters' circles. The mere fact that early rabbinic groups persisted from the second century on, coupled with the fact that between c. 200 CE and 600 CE, the early rabbinic movement produced aides to and models for Mishnah study—chiefly Tosefta and the two Talmuds—is adequate indication of the validity of the foregoing claim. Moreover, again at a minimum, the opportunity costs of all of those who devoted extensive time and effort to Mishnah study and Mishnah mastery had to be self-financed by members themselves of the early rabbinic movement.

What we have not yet discussed, but must, is whether, in addition to the early rabbinic circles themselves, there were other significant and meaningful, contemporary, reference groups that valued aspects of the early rabbis' profile, and especially those aspects related to, and derived from intensive, highly engaged Mishnah study. In these regards, let me pose a number of leading questions to guide your thinking about the remainder of this chapter. In the land of Israel in the latter second and third centuries, was early rabbinic mastery, and especially that related to Mishnah study, pursued in a social and cultural environment more akin to achieving chess mastery in mid-twentieth-century North America or, alternatively, in the Soviet Union? In other words, who, if anyone, outside of the early rabbinic circles themselves greatly values the Mishnanians' profile as a commodity in a market of skills and knowledge? And if there are elements of Judean society at large that do, do they express that valuing by payment (including paid positions) or by according *dignitas* to the early rabbis? Finally, if indeed the Mishnanians' skills profile is in demand by many in Jewish society, are there other, competing persons or groups offering something like the same talents proffered by the early rabbis? And are these others "outselling" the rabbis in this "knowledge-skills marketplace"? Let me be clear, in asking about possible competitors, I do not mean competing groups who offer specifically *Mishnah study-honed* expertise, because the latter characterizes members of the early rabbinic group in particular—but something like what early rabbis' knowledge and skills offered.

With these leading questions now top of mind, I have a confession to make. I cannot answer these questions with any high degree of certainty, because the evidence at hand is both relatively scant and ambiguous. (Moreover, since by far most of the evidence comes from early rabbinic literature, much of the evidence is self-serving or represents wishful thinking.) But I do have my best "guestimates" and impressions based on that evidence and on about four and a half decades of my struggles with it.[35] What follows, then, are those well-considered impressions; *caveat lector*, "let the reader beware."

I am going to begin by putting all of my hunches on the table as four claims, and then circle back to say more about some of them.

> *Claim 1*: In this early period of the rabbinic movement's development, the primary, most meaningful reference group for the specifically Mishnah study-engendered knowledge and skills of the early rabbis as halakhic thinkers was the membership and leadership of the early rabbinic group itself.
>
> *Claim 2*: Notwithstanding claim 1, *some* others in Judean society outside of early rabbinic circles themselves valued and sought out the early rabbis for their expertise in halakhic thinking, since Jewish society at large in the Roman-ruled land of Israel did aspire to live a life in accordance with Torah. That said, there is little to no evidence indicating that it was the early rabbis' halakha specifically or exclusively that Judean society at large sought as a commodity.

Based on claim 2 (if indeed it is correct), it would follow, in my estimation, that other (non-rabbinic) "experts" and traditional authorities (also) proffered opinions and judgments on living a Jewish life in accordance with Torah to individual Judeans and to Judean authorities and their associated administrations who sought out such expertise. These others, in aggregate, likely outsold the early rabbis in this market in the late second and third centuries CE. It is likely only in the late fourth century and (more probably)

---

35. Again, the reader may wish to turn to this book's appendix, which brings together extracts of ch. 2 of my book *In the Seat of Moses*.

in the fifth century that the early rabbis' halakhic expertise (and therefore *their* halakha too) *began* to become more dominant in the social/cultural environment of the Judean Jewish community. (Indeed, you will remember from ch. 2 that the rabbis' near-total monopoly over halakhic matters was achieved considerably later still, over the course of the seventh to tenth centuries, sparking resistance movements, such as that of the Karaites.) In sum, claim 2 implies that in the third century, Judean society at large was not (yet) as significant a reference group for early rabbis' specifically Mishnanian-related profile as the early rabbis undoubtedly wished it to be. With this in mind, let me continue with a third claim.

> *Claim 3*: Consistent with claims 1 and 2 (and, indeed, the evidence suggests) that few early rabbis made a living, so to speak, in society at large by offering their specific expertise as Mishnanian halakhacists.

Avot 4:5, referred to earlier in this chapter, seems to make a virtue of this situation, when Avot enjoins that rabbis not make their Torah/halakhic knowledge a tool from which to profit. Mishnah itself (at m. Bekhorot 4:6) prohibits anyone (whether a rabbinic sage or not) sitting as a judge from taking a salary, and the discussion of this Mishnah passage in the Babylonian Talmud (at BT Bekhorot 29a) cites alleged Tannaitic traditions that apply the same principle to teaching or dispensing rabbinic instruction. That said, it is entirely feasible (and seemingly permissible, on the strength of m. Bekhorot 4:6 and the alleged Tannaitic traditions cited at BT Bekhorot 29a) that some early rabbis may have received honoraria (token payments for their time and/or out-of-pocket expenses), when they acted as arbiters in Torah legal disputes for those Judeans who did seek out rabbis for their halakhic thinking. Moreover, such honoraria may also have been paid when rabbis, as local wise ones, interpreted dreams or provided amulets and potions.

I have one more claim to put forward, one that indicates a countercurrent to those I have already articulated.

> *Claim 4*: Notwithstanding claims 2 and 3, some (few?) rabbis were accorded positions by reason of their halakhic expertise in the administration of the Jewish patriarch of the land of Israel, and some (fewer?) may have found positions in the administration of local town-governing institutions.

Later in this section, I will say more about both patriarchal and local administration. At this juncture, however, I will say that it is indisputable, in my mind, that the early rabbis near the end of the second century and first half of the third century saw the patriarchate as an important (and much sought-after) reference group for their halakhic expertise. In fact, the early rabbis viewed the (early) patriarchs themselves as high-ranking rabbinic colleagues. This is borne out by, among other things, (1) attributing the authorship of Mishnah to Rabbi Judah "the Patriarch"; (2) the integration in Avot, chapters 1 and 2, of the patriarchal lineage into the rabbinic chain of masters and disciples going back to Moses; and (3) the attribution of a number of early rabbinic traditions to early patriarchal figures addressed as Rabbi So-and-So. In other words, the early rabbis treat the early patriarchs as *both* empowered nobility *and* "true-blue" rabbis. The relationship between the early rabbis and the Jewish patriarch of the land of Israel seems to have unravelled significantly over the course of the fourth century. By the mid-fourth century, the rabbis were highly critical of the direction of the patriarchate, which the rabbis perceived as increasingly hellenized and romanized.[36] This was anathema to the early rabbis, who styled themselves as a cultural (although not a political) resistance movement to hellenization and romanization.

Permit me, now, to elaborate somewhat on these claims by adding some "color commentary." That, as stated in claim 1, a/the primary reference group for early rabbis was the early rabbinic movement itself is as easily understandable as it is documentable. I shall, therefore, not elaborate much further on claim 1, other than to refer you to the earlier section of this chapter that discusses the ethos of discipleship as an aspect of the early rabbinic profile that is strongly reflected in the aphorisms of Avot. What is discipleship, if it is not making one's rabbinic master/teacher the immediate representative of one's reference group, namely, the rabbinic movement generally?

Claims 2, 3 and 4 take us *outside* the inner-group life and social dynamics of the early rabbinic movement itself. These claims concern the role of others, that is, other than members of the early rabbinic group, and of other institutions in late second- and early third-century CE Judean

36. My thanks to Lee I. Levine, who in conversation with me stressed the importance of this observation. There is some irony in this, since early rabbinic traditions seem to forgive Rabbi Judah the Patriarch's and his sons' hellenization/romanization as a necessary compromise required by their familial duties as the highest-ranking Jewish interlocuters with non-Jews and with the Roman administration. The renowned fourth-century Greco-Roman (and pagan) professor of rhetoric Libanius, then resident in Syrian Antioch, maintained a correspondence in Greek with his contemporary Jewish patriarch in the land of Israel, a direct descendant of Judah. There is little to nothing in the surviving letter that does not reflect the Greco-Roman sensibilities of the (pagan) social elite. But again, more on the patriarchy later in this chapter. Perhaps the rabbis of the fourth century, in contrast to their forebears of the turn of the third century, were less forgiving of the hellenization/romanization of these later patriarchs because the latter were seen by the rabbis as less (or no longer as) patronizing of the members of the rabbinic movement as the rabbis expected.

society as (potential) socially relevant reference groups for the valuing of the early rabbinic profile, and specifically for the Mishnanian-related elements of that profile.

Claim 2 simply maintains that evidence does *not* support the hypothesis that the early rabbis and their particularly rabbinic halakha were a *dominant* force in Judean society in the period in question, even if *some* Judeans sought them out for their expertise in halakha and for other services. We may reasonably surmise that this was somewhat frustrating for the early rabbis. After all, they, understandably, believed that *their* halakha represented legitimate Torah teachings, and, therefore, those who thought and acted otherwise were in error (even if they were not actually apostates or heretics in the rabbis' opinion). In fact, in my view, when the early rabbis' literature uses the Hebrew term *am ha-aretz* (lit. "people of the land"), they seem to mean not only what the phrase says literally, "country folk" or "country gentry," but also "someone not schooled in rabbinic halakha" or "someone who *innocently* does not recognize the (sole) legitimacy of rabbinic halakha." It is in one or both of the latter two senses that Mishnah (at m. Horayot 3:7) hypothesizes about circumstances involving a high priest (that is, the highest born among the highborn) who is an *am ha-aretz*, and a *mamzer* (one born out of an incestuous or adulterous relationship) who is a rabbinic disciple of a sage. And so, early rabbinic texts tacitly recognize that most of the people of the land, that is, most Judeans, neither know nor practice the specifically early rabbinic "Way" of living a Jewish life in accordance with Moses' Torah, notwithstanding their sincere avowal of Torah.

Claim 3, in a similar vein, maintains that little to no evidence is to be found that being a rabbi in the third century directly resulted in making a living. So, while the early rabbis of this period appear to be members of a professional (-like?) association (for purposes of training, self-regulation and credentializing its membership), they did not (yet) function as a professional guild that controlled a market slot in their domain of expertise.[37]

37. Lest one think that this is an inherent social contradiction, it is easy to dispel such a view. One need only look at disciplines in modern colleges and universities. Some are professional, that is, the post-secondary credential is explicitly linked to a "occupational guild." But most programs are not professional. Yet here, too, a highly structured credentializing process is in place ensuring that the candidate for the degree has acquired the knowledge and intellectual skills required for the credential. Society values these credentials, too, but does not as a matter of course "slot" those with these credentials into a corresponding place in the occupational market.

The early rabbis fall somewhere in between. I am of the opinion that they thought that their "credential" *ought* to slot them into the market, but this hope was unrequited. So, the early rabbinic movement credentialed their "graduates" nonetheless, hoping for (or working toward) the day when matters would be different. Mishnah itself tacitly recognizes this "in-between" situation. Mishnah's idealized society, in

Claim 4 especially needs elaboration and contextualization, because understanding claim 4 additionally requires more to be said about the administrative and social organization of Judean society at the time. And this, in turn, demands a detour into another shaggy-dog story on my part.

The last half of the second century CE and the first half of the third was a period of change and transformation in Rome's administration and governance of its empire, and no less so in the land of Israel. Moreover, in the land of Israel itself, this was also a period of considerable migration of non-Jews into what had previously been an overwhelmingly Jewish (even if partly hellenized Jewish) population, both prior to the Roman conquest about two and a half centuries earlier and during the first one to two centuries of Roman rule.

Rome's goals in the eastern Mediterranean, Levant, and Near East were multifaceted. These goals were political and economic, and they were also cultural. Augustus and his successors aimed to impose a Pax Romana (Roman peace) on Rome's still expanding empire by Roman military dominance and the imperial administration.[38] These sought/served to create what for its time was an extensive economic and trade zone in the Mediterranean. And the extension of many aspects of Roman law[39]

---

which the Jerusalem temple and its administration (still) function, has rabbis standing by, as it were, to give rulings and instructions to officiants and officials. But at the same time, Mishnah imagines, as it does at m. Horayot 1:1, officially established courts issuing judgments and instructions contrary to Torah law. How so? Because they are not constituted of, or advised by, rabbis. Immediately post-/extra-mishnaic rabbinic sources would seem to indicate, moreover, that "stand-by" early rabbinic advisers, let alone rabbinically constituted bodies and processes, were not the norm in late second- through third-century Judea.

38. To clarify matters, in the initial period of the empire, some Roman provinces (generally the "older" ones) remained the administrative purview of Rome's senate; other provinces were ruled by the emperor and his administrative cadre. The distinction allegedly had to do with how pacified and romanized a given province was at the time that the Roman Empire was founded by Augustus. Over time, the imperial administration assumed responsibilities for all provincial governance. The eastern provinces were within the emperor's jurisdiction from Augustus's reign on.

39. The imposition of Roman law outside of the city of Rome itself (and sometimes even in the city) was a complex matter. Roman law was made up of two fundamental categories of rules: statutes and edicts. The former were rules dully adopted by an Assembly of the People or an Assembly of the Plebeians (for statutes applied only to the Plebeian class). Edicts did not have the official/formal status of statutes but were authoritative (re) interpretations, extensions, and (de) limitations of statute law. Initially, edicts were derived from the praetors responsible for the operation of the legal and justice system of the city of Rome; by the late Republic, praetors received "advice" from the senate to change or add edicts, just as the senate would offer such advice to the Assembly of the People to change or add to statute law. By extension such advice was also offered by Rome's highest magistrates, and in the Roman imperial

and a hybrid Greco-Roman culture in the Levant and Near East helped to cement culturally and socially that which was initially achieved militarily and administratively.[40] (Remember my remarks earlier. The early rabbis were prepared to acquiesce to the political and administrative agenda of Rome, but they resisted the cultural one.)

During the mid-second to mid-third centuries CE (further) changes were advanced by the Romans in the eastern part of the empire generally, including in the land of Israel, with the migration of many "pagan gentiles" into Judea. Three of these changes are worth noting for our specific

---

period eventually became the near-exclusive prerogative of the emperor (served by a cadre of imperial administrators with legal expertise), whose advice eventually was understood to be edicts in their own right. But the distinction between statute and edict is not the only one that is germane. Rome's civil law (*ius civile*) applied initially only to Roman citizens, and sometimes extended to noncitizens permanently residing in Rome. As Rome's hegemony expanded first in Italy and then beyond, Rome needed a legal framework for law and justice involving people who were not Roman citizens and (often) not permanent residents of Rome, if only (initially) to regulate affairs involving noncitizens. To meet this requisite, Roman authorities developed an *ius gentium*, essentially "law for (foreign) people" under Roman administrative jurisdiction. It is believed that this law was mostly developed by edict (as opposed to statute). So, when the Roman emperors eventually assumed a near-total monopoly on issuing edicts, the imperial administration held effective control over all lawmaking, a state of affairs amply represented in the Theodosian and Justinian codes of the early fifth and sixth centuries CE. By the turn of the third century in the Levant and Near Eastern territories of Rome, what layer of Roman law applied would have largely been that established by imperial edict, informed by what by then was more than half a millennium of Roman legal tradition. The granting of Roman citizenship in 212 CE to nearly all free inhabitants of the Roman Empire did not seem to change this state of legal affairs; that is to say, law was essentially the issue of the emperor's "edict" (even if it was often substantially informed by exiting statutes, earlier edicts, commentaries of the jurists, about which I will write much more in ch. 6). After 212 CE Assemblies of the People in Rome were not passing statute law to be applied to newly minted Roman citizens in the land of Israel, nor (of course) did the millions of newly minted Roman citizens around the empire get representation in Assemblies of the People, since by this time "law based on imperial edict" was the normative state of affairs, notwithstanding, as just noted, the influence of earlier statute law and edicts on imperial edicts.

40. In this, the early Roman Empire trod the path first blazed by Alexander the Great in Asia Minor, the Levant, Egypt, and the Near East. Alexander's goals were significantly undermined by the division of his empire among his companions/generals, whose successors then struggled with one another for territory and hegemony. That said, the Romans embraced the already significant inroads of hellenization in the East, adding a layer of romanization (but little latinization). Alexander (and his successors) founded "independent" Greek cities in the East governed by an elite descended from Greeks and Macedonians (initially significantly drawing upon populations of demobilized veterans and their Near Eastern wives). Rome tended to retain/reconfirm the rights of these Greek cities, and the Romans added to them a number of new independent cities founded as Roman *colonia*, similarly first settled by Roman veterans, and given "Latin rights."

purposes:[41] (1) urbanization, urban expansion, rebuilding urban infra-structure, and the strengthening and further empowerment of *local* urban governance and administration; (2) the professionalization of the Roman *provincial* administrative cadre using more local talent and experts, in-cluding hiring more legally trained professionals into the ranks of the civil service from the late second century or early third century onward; and (3) the significant revamping in 212 CE of the legal status of Roman subject-peoples by extending Roman citizenship to (almost) all free inhabitants of the Roman Empire.[42] What was the impact of these types of developments, specifically as concerns the land of Israel and its Jewish population? And what does this mean for the early rabbis' actual or hoped-for reference groups valuing their distinctive profile, particularly that associated with intense, lifelong Mishnah study?

Before the beginning of the third century CE in the eastern empire, Rome had begun increasingly to devolve autonomous responsibility for local administration to municipalities themselves, which exercised this autonomy and responsibility within a frame of provincial administration. Now in these respects, do not think of the jurisdictions of cities and towns as ending at the city or town wall, or at the last rows of houses or buildings of the municipality. Rather, Roman authorities defined the jurisdiction of a city or town as including its hinterland of farmland and villages, and even smaller towns in its vicinity—what today we might think of as an entire county with its principal urban center as a local seat of governance and administration for this more extensive territory. So in effect, the imperial administration was downloading the governance and administration (as well as any associated costs) of a great deal (indeed, most) of the landmass of Rome's provinces to municipalities writ large. The imperial provincial administration retained responsibility for *inter*-municipal infrastructure, security and regulation, collection of taxes/tribute to fund these and the emperor's operations in Rome, and (further) required that certain public "services"[43] to the imperial provincial administration be provided regularly by those living in the municipalities—this in addition to those services that city officials rendered to the municipality itself. Examples of services to the province might include such things as billeting Roman troops, or provid-ing transport for the imperial administration.

41. I discuss this more fully in the last chapter of my book *Mishnah and the Social Formation*, esp. 187–200.

42. See above, n39.

43. The Roman term for these public services was "liturgies."

So, how did these "cities" operate? With what autonomy? Who ran them? What were their responsibilities? Here Rome adopted and adapted the models it had in hand. One was how the city of Rome itself had traditionally been run. The second was how the Macedonian-Greek cities of the Hellenistic period (before the Roman conquest) operated and in many cases continued to operate after the Roman conquest. The third was the operation of the Roman *colonia* settled by Roman military veterans, which model drew on the first two.

The Macedonian-Greek cities, the Roman *colonia*, and eventually all the major municipalities in the region were typically accorded "constitutional charters," granting them independence in many jurisdictions, and confirming the structure, power, and responsibilities of the city's institutions of governance and administration.[44] In the case of Macedonian-Greek cities in the East, such constitutions had been granted by the Hellenistic kings who succeeded Alexander the Great, that is, long before the Roman conquest.[45] These charters tended to be reconfirmed (with appropriate changes) by the Roman authorities after Rome's conquest of the East. The city of Alexandria in Egypt provides an apt example of this state of affairs, both before and after the Roman conquest of Egypt in the first century BCE. In the case of Roman *colonia* in the eastern empire, these constitutional charters were, of course, initially granted by Rome itself. Over time, the main articles and principles of all of these municipal constitutional charters tended closely to resemble one another. That is to say, over the course of the late second through fifth centuries CE, the nature of municipal government and administration in the eastern half of the empire (and also in many places in the western part), as well as the relationship

44. Some of these cities retained their charter status within the feudal system of medieval Europe; these municipalities were known as "free" cities. This tradition of urban self-rule also lived on in the form of the several municipal "republics" in the Renaissance era, e.g., Florence.

45. The apocryphal book 1 Maccabees attributes part of the kerfuffle in the first half of the second century BCE that led to the Maccabean revolt against the Seleucid-Hellenistic king to the attempt by a pro-hellenization party of some Judean-Jerusalemite elite to secure such a constitutional charter for Jerusalem, in order to make it an autonomous Macedonian-Greek city. First Maccabees does not explain where the true-blue, ethnically Greek-Macedonian Jerusalemites were supposed to come from, since this tended to be the basis for having such charters. Rather, the author of 1 Maccabees, writing as an apologist for the Hasmonean dynasty, states that these pro-hellenization Jews were in the process of "turning themselves into" Greeks, an endeavor justifying the Hasmoneans' military struggle and (eventually) their seizing control of the temple administration and the governance of Judea, which ended only with the Roman conquest in the first century BCE.

of local municipal government to the imperial provincial administration, became fairly uniform across Rome's territorial reach.

Chartered, constitutional municipalities were governed by a city council, on which tended to sit a class of municipal grandees.[46] City council was presided over by its president, and various council members assumed the city's magistracies (secretaries of state, so to speak, each with oversight over and responsibility for an aspect of the municipality's operations). Council also designated those who were to provide requisite services. Seats on council and naming council members to magistracies were in many municipalities originally subject to elections by the people. However, as will be more evident below, traditions of Greek-like city democracy had eroded well before the third and especially fourth and fifth centuries CE.

As just noted, each municipal magistracy had an administrative jurisdiction. One might be oversight over and enforcement of local regulations concerning the city's marketplace(s). Another might have responsibility for public buildings, like the basilica, or the local temples, the local academy (which tended to serve the wealthier classes), the council building, the amphitheatre, stadia, or public baths. Other magistracies might oversee the port and its physical infrastructure, or the potable water and sewer system, or the local justice and court system. And remember, the responsibilities of council and council members not only included what happened within the boundary of the principal town or city but also extended to regulating and administering the municipality's entire hinterland territory and its embedded villages and smaller towns.

Funding for all these activities and responsibilities came from levies approved by council—tariffs of various sorts, if you will. But major projects or major restoration of infrastructure could not be funded by tariff or taxes. These major costs relied on benefaction—gifts by individual people, prominent families, and membership associations. Moreover, members of council, especially those council members who assumed magistracies and services, were expected to be leaders in benefaction. And more than this, those occupying the magistracies or providing services were expected to pay out of their own pockets outright for deficit spending in their respective domains of civic responsibility. *Dignitas* (honor) was acquired by taking on these magistracies, on the one hand, and by benefaction to one's city, on the other. Both the wealthiest and the not-so-wealthy, as individuals, families, or through their associations (such as occupational guilds), could earn

46. This is clearly reflected in edicts from the third century included in Justinian's *Code*, bk. 10, title 32. These may be viewed, in the excellent English translation by Fred H. Blume (with his annotations), on the University of Wyoming's website at http://www.uwyo.edu/lawlib/blume-justinian/ajc-edition-2/books/book10/book10-32rev.pdf.

dignitas by means of acts of benefaction. Take Ephesus on the western coast of Asia Minor as a case in point. Anyone strolling through the archaeological remains of Ephesus will encounter along his or her route dozens of inscriptions honoring the city's benefactors, including on occasion the recognition of gifts to this provincial city by the elite of Rome itself.

What did the foregoing mean for those who sat on the city's council, and how and why were they named to council? Seats on the city council and associated appointments to magistracies were accorded to the city's wealthiest and to their descendants, since wealth tended to be familial and pass from generation to generation. No one else could afford the financial burden of these positions. In other words, cities were run by, and were the responsibility of, what can be described only as a class of local, dynastic, wealthy nobility—at least by the local standards of what amounted to wealth in the immediate region.[47]

Birth, therefore, counted, if not for everything, then for a very great deal. And the ranks of the wealthy/noble families of any locale during this period of Roman rule likely included many families that had been local (wealthy) nobility well before the Roman conquest. By the later Roman imperial period, let us say, by the fourth and fifth centuries CE, wealthy/noble families, from generation to generation, were essentially *chained* by Roman edict to their duties as local municipal council members and, therefore, to appointments to magistracies. These families were known as the class of local municipal *decuriones* (from the term *curia*, "council"[48]), and they and their descendants effectively became transgenerational prisoners of their municipal duties. There are many reasons for the demise of the Roman Empire, first dramatically in the West in the fifth century, and thereafter in the East by slow contraction over the centuries. But one of those factors was the eventual impoverishment of the class of local *decuriones* as a result of generations of essentially forced benefaction to fund their municipalities' operations and infrastructure.[49]

---

47. Again, aptly represented in the edicts from this period preserved in Justinian's *Code*, bk. 10, title 32. See also Rosenfeld and Perlmutter, *Social Stratification*, 1–24, 141–80.

48. Those referencing *decurion* in a Latin lexicon will most frequently encounter it as a Roman military rank—the commander of ten soldiers ("sergeant" if you will). This sense of *decurion* is, obviously, merely a homonym of the word referring to the class of municipal "nobles."

49. Edicts in bk. 10, title 32, of Justinian's *Code* are consequently forced to deal with exigencies arising from the impoverishment of decurial families. These families sought to shed their status among the *decuriones* in order to "unchain" themselves from the associated financial burdens.

Above, so to speak, local municipal governance and administration (overseen by local grandees), was, as I remarked earlier, imperial provincial administration. Provincial administration had oversight, by definition, over that for which the municipalities had no jurisdiction, as well as for general security in the province and for amassing taxes for provincial operations, the emperor's central administration, and Rome itself. Who would keep the network of Roman roads in good order? Who would keep travelers along them free from banditry? Who would contain piracy on the sea routes of trade and transportation? For frontier provinces, who would guard the borders and repel invaders? Who would ensure that the legal framework for the entire province was consistently applied? This, among other things, was the responsibility of the province and its administration. But as long as municipalities operated within the bounds of the Roman *framework* for law, order, taxation, and provision of required services rendered to the province and empire, municipalities were largely free to run their cities and their associated territories according to rules and regulations of their own adoption, under the jurisdiction of their local councils, on which sat their hereditary local "nobility."

For the land of Israel, let me now call this class of local nobility—what Roman authorities came to call *decuriones*—by the names Judean/Jewish sources seem to use. Let me call such local, municipal grandees, "elders" (*zakayn*, sg.; *zekaynim*, pl.). And I will refer to the most eminent and long-standing among these local and regional hereditary nobles as "princes" or "patriarchs" (*nasi*, sg.; *nesi-im*, pl.), as in Rabbi Judah the Prince/Patriarch, to whom the early rabbis attributed the authorship of Mishnah. But in mentioning Rabbi Judah the Prince/Patriarch, I am getting a bit ahead of myself, for I must bring our shaggy-dog story to its end by making one last point, in order, subsequently, to return our focus to the land of Israel and the early rabbis within it.

The use by the Roman imperial administration of these municipalities writ large to do most of the "heavy lifting" of governance and administration of a Roman province's territorial landmass has, for our purposes, an interesting side benefit. And I think it likely that this side benefit was foreseen and intended by Roman imperial rulers. Namely, local culture, and traditional, local rules and norms could (within reasonable limits set by Roman policy) be allowed to continue and even flourish at the municipal level. Notwithstanding Rome's policy of hellenization and romanization, the empire included a variety of cultures, each with their own traditional rules, norms, and religions. Hellenization and romanization might constitute a "layer" over traditional life and eventually modify and modulate it, especially in the larger, more important urban centers.

But underneath that layer of hellenization/romanization, antecedent traditional cultures persisted locally, especially so in the countryside, villages, and smaller towns of a municipality's jurisdiction. And as much as urbanization increased in this period, this constitutes a *relative* increase in city dwellers; the vast majority of folk still lived in more agrarian settings. (That is why, when the Roman imperial administration of the fourth, fifth, and sixth centuries began, first, to promote Christianity and, second, seriously to wipe away the worship of the gods, those who worshipped them were called *pagani*, "pagans," the Latin for "country folk." The history of the semantics of the meaning of *pagani* seems to me to be akin to the semantic shift in the meaning of *am ha-aretz* from "people of the land" to, in the early rabbis' view, "Jews either unschooled in or who do not recognize the exclusive legitimacy of early rabbinic halakha.")

The detour of our shaggy-dog story is concluded. You now have sufficient contextual information pertinent to claim 4, which offered my considered opinion on where the early rabbis, given their particular expertise as Mishnanians, likely fit, or aspired to fit, in the organizational and administrative structures in the land of Israel just before and just after the turn of the third century.

As already noted, Judea in this period had a mixed population of Jews and largely pagan gentiles. (Followers of Jesus in Judea at this time might have been either Jewish or gentile, depending upon the dominant ethnic makeup of the local community.) Moreover, early rabbinic legal traditions recognize that some cities and towns in the land of Israel are majority gentile (and pagan), with a Jewish minority, while others are majority Jewish, with a pagan gentile minority. Jewish towns and cities are assumed in Mishnah and in alleged Tannaitic traditions to be operated in accordance with Judah-ite traditions and norms (although *not* necessarily rabbinic halakhic ones, as the early rabbis certainly would have preferred). Pagan gentile towns and cities in the land of Israel followed the hellenized cultural norms and practices of the larger Levantine/Syrian region. The remains of the material culture of the land of Israel in the Roman period are entirely consistent with the foregoing scenario. Indeed, Rome's particular design for and use of highly localized municipal governance and administration was (intended or not) peculiarly well suited to allow this patchwork of Jewish and non-Jewish settlement in Judea to work.

That said, this system of highly localized governance and administration of relatively extensive municipal territories does present a challenge for the Jewish population of the land of Israel. Traditional Judah-ite culture, social norms, and religious practice assume a relatively high degree of pan-local or trans-local coordination and communality. For example, it was highly desirable that the calculation of the Jewish calendar be agreed upon trans-locally; otherwise, holy days would be celebrated on different days in different Jewish settlements. Or take norms about family and personal status; a Jew or Jewess should not count as being married in one Jewish town but single in the next. Moreover, one would ideally wish court judgments, undertaken in accordance with Judah-ite norms about many things, to be accepted as legitimate in neighboring Jewish municipalities, notwithstanding the fact that most people in antiquity rarely traveled very far. And one could think of many other similar areas of Jewish life and social organization where such pan-local coordination and harmonization is not just desirable but almost essential.

It is obvious that Roman provincial authorities were entirely unsuited to assure this level of pan-municipal coordination of practice in Jewish towns and cities—whatever the degree of harmonization deemed desirable. Before the destruction of the Jerusalem temple in 70 CE by the Romans, the Jerusalem temple administration, given its many centuries of legitimacy and authority among Jews, performed these functions in the land of Israel within the frame of Roman imperial provincial rule. In the immediate aftermath of 70 CE, nothing really existed in Jewish society in the land of Israel that took up the temple institutions' "national" roles in these regards. That lacuna was partially addressed in the late second and/or early third centuries. And perhaps not coincidentally, this is also the very period of the consolidation of the group that we have been calling the Mishnanian rabbis. So what emerged by way of pan-municipal governance and administration, and with what (and by whose) authority, to fill this gap? Moreover, why might one suspect that this development is related to the social formation of the early (Mishnah study-centric) rabbis?

Much as the group of the early rabbis aspired formally (and exclusively) to perform this pan-municipal coordinating function with their specific halakha and halakhic expertise (as, indeed, they later did in the medieval period and thereafter to early modern times), that aspiration was (as claim 2 asserts) *not* substantially fulfilled in the second or subsequent several centuries CE. So, who or what did fill this gap, if anyone? Sometime in the late second or early third century, by design, acquiescence, or benign neglect (it is hard to say which), but ultimately with Roman sanction and license, a prestigious Jewish "patriarch/prince," working with local municipal leadership and administrations, began to fulfill some or many of these pan-local functions for the Jews of the land of Israel.[50] Indeed,

50. There has been considerable academic debate about what precise authority the Jewish patriarch of the land of Israel exercised over what domains of Jewish life in Roman Judea. We cannot know the complete list of domains with certainty. Appelbaum

for the next two centuries, the person/office of *the* Jewish patriarch of the land of Israel enjoyed considerable prestige among Jews of the Roman Empire generally, not just in the homeland where he exercised his principal

---

lists some of them generically in *Dynasty of Jewish Patriarchs*, 1–2, as does Levine, "Jewish Patriarch," para. 2. On the foundation of earlier scholarship on the Jewish patriarchate by Levine in "Status of the Patriarchate," I compiled my own summative and categorized list in my book *Mishnah and the Social Formation*, 189–90, which list I reproduce in full here:

1. representative to imperial authorities;

2. focus of leadership in the Jewish community;

    2.1 receiving daily visits from prominent families;

    2.2 declaration of public fasts;

    2.3 initiating or abrogating the ban (*herem*);

3. appointment of judges to Jewish courts in Palestine;

4. control of the calendar;

5. issuing enactments and decrees with respect to the applicability or release from legal requirements, e.g.:

    5.1 use of sabbatical year produce, and applicability of sabbatical year injunctions;

    5.2 repurchase or redemption of formerly Jewish land from gentile owners;

    5.3 status of Hellenistic cities of Palestine re. purity, tithing, sabbatical year;

    5.4 exemption from tithing;

    5.5 conditions in divorce documents;

    5.6 use of oil produced by gentiles;

6. dispatching emissaries to diaspora communities;

7. taxation: both the power to tax and the authority to rule/intervene on the disposition of taxes raised for local purposes by local councils.

Items of the foregoing list are attested in early rabbinic literature, and, with respect to some items, also in Greco-Roman legal and literary sources. That said, I would mention one additional power of the patriarch attested in Greco-Roman sources, according to Goodblatt, *Monarchic Principle*, 132–39; that is the authority to appoint and to dismiss local Jewish grandees from their municipal posts (see my *Mishnah and the Social Formation*, 190). Finally, one may turn to the third-century Christian writer Origen (*To Africanus*) for a complaint that the Jewish "ethnarch" (his term for patriarch) of the land of Israel was exceeding what Origen understood to be the authority *given him by the Romans* in judging and executing capital cases. To my knowledge, we have no other attestation to such a patriarchal power, so I am inclined to view Origen's accusation as attempted vilification of what to him was an "uppity" Jewish noble who fancied himself to be a client king of Rome.

powers. Jews living in the Mediterranean lands outside the land of Israel viewed the Jewish patriarch's role as a kind of limited restoration of Jewish home rule in their ancient homeland, and they recognized the patriarch's capacity to act as an interlocuter for the interests of all Jews living under Roman rule. Moreover, not only did Judean Jews pay levies to support the activities of the patriarchate, diaspora Jewish communities in the Roman Empire also raised funds at the behest of the patriarch's agents/emissaries to underwrite the operations of his office.

Leaving aside the debates about the date of origin of the Jewish patriarchy,[51] by the early third century CE, that is, in the time ("reign" might even be apropos) of Rabbi Judah the Patriarch/Prince (*ha-nasi*), the office and administration of the Jewish patriarch of the land of Israel was already established, well organized, and viewed as authoritative and legitimate in its spheres of responsibility, not only by the Jews but (importantly) also by the Roman imperial authorities, notably from the time of the Severan emperors (particularly Septimius Severus and Caracalla) on. It appears to me that in the third and fourth centuries, the Romans thought of the patriarchate as "having a foot" (so to speak) in pan-municipal, provincial administration and (consequently) seem to have granted the Jewish patriarchs honors, titles, and privileges akin to members of the now expanding (and therefore diluted) Roman senatorial class and other members of the imperial (as opposed to local) nobility.[52] Moreover, as with all nobility of the era, and like the class of local municipal *decuriones*/elders, the patriarchate was dynastic, passing from father to (usually the eldest) son.[53]

51. Modern scholars have placed the origins of the Jewish patriarchy at various historical junctures and associated its founding with several earlier figures, such as Hillel (first century BCE, possibly into early first century CE), Rabbi Gamaliel (I) the Elder (first century CE), Rabbi Yohanan ben Zakkai (first century CE), Rabbi Gamaliel II (late first to early second century CE), Rabbi Simeon ben Gamaliel II (mid-second century CE). Each one of these, and some others to boot, has been designated by one historian or another as the founder of the patriarchal office and dynasty. However, I agree with the current scholarly consensus that the Jewish patriarchy in the land of Israel emerged near the end of the second century, making Rabbi Judah the Patriarch/ Prince the first of a several centuries-long dynastic succession of Jewish patriarchs. The question of the emergence of the Jewish patriarchal dynasty is well researched and discussed in Appelbaum, *Dynasty of Jewish Patriarchate*, esp. 9 and all of ch. 2. See also Appelbaum, "Rabbi's Successors." A useful bibliography of the major modern academic research publications up to about 2012 concerning the Jewish patriarchate may be found in Appelbaum, *Dynasty of Jewish Patriarchate*, 1n2. For a very concise, readable, academically sound, and recent (2018) account of the history of, and evidence for the Jewish patriarchy and its powers, see Levine, "Jewish Patriarch."

52. See Rosenfeld and Perlmutter, *Social Stratification*, 1–24, 141–80.

53. Appelbaum, *Dynasty of Jewish Patriarchate*, esp. 9 and all of ch. 2. See also Appelbaum, "Rabbi's Successors."

My claim 4, articulated earlier in this section, situates the early rabbis and their (somewhat unrequited?) aspirations as purveyors of halakha and highly honed halakhic-thinking in this three-story administrative-legal organization of the land of Israel: local municipal governance (of/by Jews), the Jewish patriarchate of the land of Israel, and Roman imperial provincial administration. To the extent that the early rabbis (acting just before and after the turn of the third century *like* a professional cadre) operated, or aspired to operate, as officials or authorities *outside* of the enclave of their immediate early rabbinic associations/circles, where would they have done so, or have sought to do so, within this three-level, administrative-legal structure? What further potential reference groups valuing their rabbinic-specific expertise in halakha were out there in the social landscape? One potential level was among the cadre of professionals of the Roman province of which the land of Israel was a part. There is no evidence that early rabbis had or aspired to places, qua rabbis, in Roman provincial administration of the land of Israel. So, none of claims 1 to 4 addressed this potential sphere.

You now know that another (potential) level was, of course, that of local communal life generally, and of local municipal administration and rule by elders/*decuriones*. Claims 2 and 3 in combination asserted that *some* rabbis were sought after by locals not only for services as wise persons but also for halakhic opinions, decisions, and dispute resolution. However, we have little evidence that (many) early rabbis, as a result of their rabbinic training and credential, had a place in local municipal-community administration. Rabbis, qua rabbis, were not *generally* officers, agents, appointees, or employees of local government and administration (even if some persons who had rabbinic credentials were also part of the class of local leaders). And the citable exceptions to this assertion, serve, in my opinion, to support the general claim. To put matters simply, this is not where/how early rabbis, as rabbis, made a living. In fact, it is probably more accurate to say, as I intimated earlier, early rabbis did not generally earn their livelihood from their rabbinic expertise, even if they were sometimes sought after for that expertise.

That leaves us to say more about the early rabbis' relationship as rabbis with the Jewish patriarchate, the orientation of our claim 4. Here I will say, "It's complicated." You will remember from chapter 2 that Rabbi Judah the Patriarch and his sons, one of whom, Gamaliel III, succeeded Judah as patriarch, were all viewed by the early rabbis as part of the early rabbinic group. Early rabbinic texts convey teachings in their names, just as they do for other early rabbis. Avot placed these members of the patriarchal dynasty in the chain of rabbinic and proto-rabbinic masters and disciples going back to Moses. And, most dramatically, the early rabbis attributed the authorship of their central, formative text, the Mishnah, to Rabbi Judah *the Patriarch*. Clearly the early rabbis were, or wished to see themselves and/or have others see them as highly favored by the Jewish patriarchs and patriarchy of the third century. What is difficult to know is how much of this was reciprocated by the patriarchs, and specifically by what range of means? So let us look at that possible range.

Insofar as the patriarchate had a Judean-national-like council or court of its own, rabbis seemed to assert that they should sit on it by reason of their specifically rabbinic halakhic expertise—a post-destruction Sanhedrin, as it were. But we cannot discern with much certainty that such a standing council/court existed or, if it did, that rabbis, qua rabbis, had exclusive rights to its seats (as opposed to, let us say, members of noble families associated with the patriarchy). We think that the patriarch exercised the authority to make some appointments at the local administrative level—for example, judicial appointments. But we cannot discern that the patriarch appointed primarily, let alone exclusively, members of the early rabbinic cadre to these posts, although some rabbis were. We know that the patriarch sent emissaries to Jewish communities to effect his duties there and to collect funds. But we cannot discern that rabbis, qua rabbis, were primarily (let alone exclusively) appointed as the patriarch's apostles, although some rabbis were. So the close association of the early rabbinic cadre with Judah the Patriarch and his immediate descendants is clear, but the result was not (entirely, largely?) what one would expect, or what the rabbis pined after. The upshot of this, to my mind, is the following: (1) as regards patriarchal appointments, I strongly suspect that nobility combined with client-like association with the patriarch counted for more than rabbinic credentials on their own; and (2) much as the patriarchs were (or may have been) associated with early rabbinic learning and credentializing, they were politically not prepared to impose specifically rabbinic halakha on local Jewish communities and their leaders by appointing primarily (let alone exclusively) rabbis to patriarchal and municipal offices within the patriarch's ken.

With regard to appointments to local municipal offices and responsibilities of local councils, elders, and holders of magistracies, it is my opinion that what I have said about the rabbis vis-à-vis the functions of the patriarchate applies again, *mutatis mutandi*. Rabbis, qua rabbis, were not primarily (let alone exclusively) sought out for appointments by reason of their specifically rabbinic halakhic expertise, even if they were not systematically excluded from these as a result of their rabbinic credentials. For the higher municipal functions, local nobility probably turned to their own and to those closely associated with the noble families (their clients, if you will?). If some of these were rabbis, fine. If not, also fine.

In all, one might say that the rabbis were a professional-like cadre well suited to many posts and functions in which what I have characterized as advanced halakhic thinking was highly relevant. But the evidence suggests that they were not the only such persons in Judean society; others had similar knowledge and expertise, just not specifically rabbinic halakhic knowledge and expertise. Individual rabbis made their living doing whatever, and they must generally have been wealthy enough to devote so much of their time and effort to study. So the cadre of the early rabbis lived on, even flourished, attracted novices, and so continued to develop and prosper as an association with a well-defined profile and group ethos. By the time the patriarchy in the land of Israel collapsed over the fifth and sixth centuries because of changes in Roman policy in a now Christianizing empire, the rabbinic movement was sufficiently strong and prestigious to assert itself, and to insert itself into Jewish communal life in the face of competitors. With these developments, specifically rabbinic authority and specifically rabbinic halakha began to make the serious inroads that prefigured the near exclusive power and authority of the rabbis over halakhic matters that they achieved over the seventh to tenth centuries.

In this chapter we have completed the discussion of the professional profile of the early rabbis and have considered who and what within Jewish society near and after the turn of the third century were reference groups valuing the specifically rabbinic profile. In the next two chapters, I leave behind the issue of reference groups in order to consider matters of social and cultural currency, as initially defined in chapter 1. In other words, why would anyone, or why would the rabbis have expected anyone, in Jewish society near the turn of the third century to view the rabbis' distinctive group profile as having currency? This broaches matters that social scientists would call questions of "plausibility" and "legitimation," of which mythologizing is only a part (because the existence of myths in a society begs the question of why that culture would view the precise elements of its myths to be particularly compelling).

PART II

What Did the Early Rabbis Think (or Might Others Have Perceived) They Were Like?

5

Elements of Judah-ite, Homeland Culture That Underpin the Early Rabbinic Profile

Y OU ARE WELL AWARE by now that this volume about what the early rabbis were is framed by two additional, closely related questions. (1) What did the early rabbis think they *were* (or wish to be)? And (2) what did the early rabbis think (or might others have perceived) they were *like*?

In response to the first question, chapters 2, 3, and 4 (part 1 of this book) constructed a shared profile that characterized the members of the early rabbinic cadre and that, consequently, provided the early rabbis with a shared identity as a distinctive social group (of self-proclaimed elites) within Jewish society of the land of Israel. By far the most commonly shared aspects of that identity are those elements required for and derived from devoted, engaged, lifelong Mishnah study. These elements include (but are not exhausted by):

1. Comprehensive knowledge of Scripture, especially its prescriptions and proscriptions

2. Command of an additional extra-biblical system of seemingly authoritative civil, criminal, and religious-ritual law

3. The expertise, which I have characterized as advanced halakhic thinking, to apply the foregoing to complex, posited, hypothetical circumstances, as reflected in Mishnah and as honed in Mishnah analysis

Additionally, the early rabbis:

4. Promoted memorization of this knowledge and even of the Mishnah text itself

Moreover:

5. The early mythologizing of the early rabbinic group attempts to give this shared profile generally, and Mishnah specifically, an unassailably authoritative pedigree as Oral Torah revealed to Moses by YHWH.

That is why I have invented the name Mishnanians as a handy moniker for the members of the early rabbinic cadre in the land of Israel near the end of the second century CE and into the third.

The second question that frames this book asks why anything in this profile would/should have an air of cogency, plausibility, and legitimacy, either in the minds of the early rabbis themselves or in the minds of the Jews among whom the early rabbis lived and over whom the rabbis hoped to assert their authority in matters of the halakha. In other words, what cultural currency did, would, or might this early rabbinic profile have had? For without such currency it would have been difficult for the defining, core elements of the early rabbinic profile to have meant much of anything to anyone. In this chapter and the next, I will search for the bases for such currency in the Judah-ite homeland culture, both preceding and contemporary with the early rabbinic movement's formation, and in the Greco-Roman world and among diaspora Jews outside the land of Israel.

Now, to some degree, chapter 2's account of the mythologization of Mishnah and of Mishnah's author(s) has begun some of the spadework concerning the currency of the core elements of the early rabbinic profile. How so? That mythologization provides, as just mentioned, a *pedigree* for the body of knowledge that is said to characterize early rabbinic expertise *and* to be perfectly embodied in Mishnah's text, by alleging that both are grounded in God's revelation to Moses of Torah generally, some of which Moses committed to writing and some of which he passed on orally. As you have learned, Moses is (re) depicted in the first chapter of Avot as both the first disciple (that is, of YHWH) and the first human teacher of this body of knowledge. Moses is thereby (re) fashioned as the first disciple of a sage (*talmid hakham*) and as the first rabbi/sage, at one and the same time. Then, by reason of an alleged, many-centuries-long chain of masters and disciples beginning with Moses "our rabbi," the rabbis of the Mishnah claim to have "received" this knowledge. And the most lionized of these latter figures, after Moses himself, is "Rabbi" Judah the Patriarch, to whom the authorship of the Mishnah is ascribed.

The myth just summarized appeals to a number of elements that the early rabbis clearly believed ought to have high currency in their immediate social and cultural setting—such as Torah as YHWH's revelation, and Moses as the privileged recipient of that revelation. Anyone familiar with the first five books of the Hebrew or Christian Bible (that is, the Pentateuch) would find such notions familiar. And anyone of Jewish (or even Christian) background would be familiar with another moniker for the Pentateuch, the Torah of Moses. Moreover and importantly, just about any Jew (and follower of Jesus) in the second and third centuries CE would not only be familiar with these notions but also fervently assent to them. Indeed, for a Jew (and a Jesus follower) of the second and third century *not* to avow these tenets would be accounted as heresy or apostasy by almost all of their fellows. So the irrefutable currency of these tenets by the second and third centuries CE at least *partially* grounds the early rabbis' mythologization of what they are (or claimed to be), namely, disciples of Moses and privileged recipients of revealed Torah.

That said, the truth of the matter is this. The Pentateuch (1) does not even designate itself as a whole as the Torah, and (2) says nothing (explicit?) about the existence of an Oral Torah as its complement. Nor (3) does the Pentateuch depict Moses as the first rabbi (or the first rabbinic disciple); rather, Moses' titles are "the man of God" (e.g., Deut 33:1) and the "prophet" who speaks with YHWH "face-to-face" (Exod 33:11). In fact, (4) the Pentateuch knows of no "rabbis" at all, and (5) neither does any other book of the Hebrew Bible (or book of the Apocrypha and Pseudepigrapha of the Hebrew Bible/Old Testament). Rather, the civil, cultic, and moral authorities mentioned in the Hebrew Bible generally or in the Pentateuch specifically are: charismatic prophets; hereditary priests; hereditary Levites; hereditary clan princes; dynastic kings; local (hereditary?) elders, judges, and officers; army commanders (largely clan nobles); and royal or temple scribes. No rabbis! And since, from sometime in the fourth or third century BCE onward, the books of the Hebrew Bible (or such as there were in the fourth or third century BCE) constituted the most authoritative social and cultural artifact of Judah-ite life, we have a problem. On what *additional* socially and culturally credible foundations does the early rabbinic profile and its accompanying mythologization stand as social constructs with currency? And how might these have been made to stand on these foundations? Part (indeed, a large part) of the answer to these perplexing questions is prefigured in chapter 2. And I will give it in one word, scribes (*sofer*, sg.; *sofrim* pl.). You will remember from chapter 2 that the early rabbis characterized a swath of halakhic ordinances that did not appear in the Bible as "the words of the scribes" (*divrei sofrim*). What are these scribes, and why might the early rabbis have "latched onto" them as antecedent authorities for some extra-biblical halakha? In order to elaborate, permit me to introduce to you some ancient Israelite and Judah-ite scribes.

SCRIBES IN ANCIENT JUDAH-ITE SOCIETY: PREFIGURING THE EARLY RABBIS

Meet Shaphan, Son of Azaliah, Son of Meshullam, the Scribe

There are many individuals mentioned by name in the Hebrew Bible. But considering that the biblical narrative attempts to construct a culturally meaningful and significant account of Jewish/Israelite experience alleged to have spanned a part of the second millennium BCE and a little over half of the first millennium BCE, the number of people mentioned by name is really not that big. So when a name does appear in the Bible, we should at least take note of how biblical authors portray the role of the named protagonist. Prepare yourselves for another shaggy-dog story!

I am sure that most of you have never heard of Shaphan the scribe, or if you have once read his name, no longer recall who he is said to have been or what he is portrayed as having done. You will find Shaphan mentioned several times in the narrative of 2 Kgs 22.[1] There, he appears as a high-ranking official and administrator acting as the chief civil servant coordinating the policies, projects, and actions of Josiah, king of Judah, and of Hilkiah, high priest of YHWH's temple, during the latter decades of the seventh century BCE. In that capacity, Shaphan is put in charge of the king's initiative to renovate and restore the Jerusalem temple. He is given oversight over the treasury of the temple to pay for the work and over the contracted skilled labour. Shaphan, therefore, is no slouch; he operates as a trusted official and administrator at the highest levels of power and authority in the kingdom of Judah. He is no (mere?) secretary. (The Hebrew Bible has another designation, *mazkir* [recorder], for such a role in the kings' courts.) Since Shaphan is first introduced with his patronymics (*x*, son of *y*, son of *z*), Shaphan is portrayed as a scion of prominent lineage, which would likely mean a wealthy patrimony as well. And his duties bespeak of a superior education, high literacy, numeracy, and administrative skills. These are relatively rare commodities in the kingdom of Judah in the latter decades of the seventh

---

1. And in its "reworked" parallel at 2 Chron 34.

century BCE, when King Josiah reigned. This was a time when few people could read, and even fewer could write. The higher the level of education sought, the higher the level of literacy required to seek it, and the greater the wealth needed to provide the leisure time to study.

Shaphan is not the first such scribe encountered in the text of the Hebrew Bible. Another is Seraiah the scribe, who is mentioned (in 2 Sam 8:15–18) in a list of the chief officials of King David's civil, military, and religious administration's "cabinet." But Shaphan is of particular interest to me because of his alleged direct participation in what the biblical authors portray as the most remarkable and noteworthy aspects of King Josiah's reign.

The narrator of 2 Kgs 22 alleges that during Josiah's renovation of the temple, "the book of the Law" was found in the "house" (of YHWH)—not *a* book of law, or *a* book of laws, but *the* book of *the* Law (*sefer ha-torah*). Hilkiah gives the book to Shaphan, who reads it. (Interestingly, there is no indication that Hilkiah himself has read it before submitting it to Shaphan.) Only after Shaphan has himself read the text does he take it to King Josiah, and Shaphan reads it aloud to Josiah. The king is despondent upon hearing the content of "the book of the Torah" (for that is henceforth the moniker by which I shall refer to it[2]), because (to use the vernacular) it is apparent to the king that by the norms set out in the Torah, "they have been doing it all wrong." Josiah assumes the demeanor of the sincere penitent. Yet, the king feels that something more must be done to confirm the authenticity of the discovered text. He commands some of his ministers, Hilkiah the high priest and Shaphan the scribe among them, to consult Hulda "the prophetess." Without, it seems, reading the text, she confirms by her oracular gifts that the norms and instructions set out in the discovered book of the Torah are genuinely YHWH's commandments and that the severe collective punishments set out in the book of the Torah for transgressing these commandments will inevitably befall the kingdom of Judah. On this information, King Josiah devotes himself to a comprehensive religious reform, not only among the population of the kingdom of Judah but also among the populace of the adjacent

---

2. In the next chapter, 2 Kgs 23, Josiah has all the leaders/elders of Judah and Jerusalem gather in the temple precinct and, the narrator says, he himself reads the book aloud to them. Rather, here the book is referred to as "the book of the covenant" (*sefer ha-brit*). Modern scholars refer to a specific collection of laws in the book of Exodus as the book of the covenant, because at the end of this mini-law-code, the biblical authors have Moses refer to it by that name. I see no substantive connection between Exodus's book of the covenant and the use of the term in 2 Kgs 23. In contrast, as I shall shortly explain, there are a great many substantive connections between the book of Deuteronomy and the reforms undertaken by Josiah, supposedly in light of the contents of the book of the Torah said to have been found in the temple and transmitted to Shaphan by Hilkiah.

territory of what until the late eighth century BCE had been the Northern Kingdom of Israel. By reason of his penitential stance, the inevitable collective punishment foretold is "postponed" until after Josiah's reign, not too long after which the kingdom of Judah is conquered by the Babylonians (605–597 BCE), Jerusalem and its temple are destroyed (586 BCE), and the flowers of Judah's society are deported (597 and 586 BCE).

So, Shaphan the scribe was what we might call "a significant player" in this narrative, second only to King Josiah, and on par with Hilkiah the high priest. That said, the significance of the characterization of Shaphan the scribe *for you*, the readers of this book about what the early rabbis were (or thought they were), derives from the larger social and cultural significance of the narrative of 2 Kgs 22–23.

Based on the reforms that Josiah is said to have undertaken in light of the contents of the book of the Torah that Shaphan read to him, some scholars have asserted that there is a strong family resemblance between the contents and ideology of the biblical book of Deuteronomy specifically and the narrative about Josiah, Hilkiah, and Shaphan. More than any other book of the Pentateuch, it is the spirit and policy of Deuteronomy that is evident in Josiah's reforms. Consequently, one scholarly view is that some "proto-version" of Deuteronomy (although not the book as we have it now) is the book of the Torah that legitimated Josiah's reforms. And there are other elements that link the story of Shaphan the scribe, Hilkiah the high priest, and King Josiah with Deuteronomy. Remember that I earlier asserted that the Pentateuch never refers to itself as a whole as the Torah or the Torah of Moses, although most Jews from near the end of the third century BCE on would likely have referred to the Pentateuch (in its textual state at the time) by this moniker. (And in any case, the Pentateuch, more or less as we know it today, does not yet exist in Josiah's time.) But remarkably, at several junctures, Deuteronomy refers to its own content in its entirety as "this [book of the] Torah" (e.g., Deut 1:5; 4:44; 17:18; 27:3; 31:9–11). No other book of the Pentateuch does this. Moreover, Deuteronomy clearly ascribes this Torah to Moses (e.g., at 4:44); demands that any future king make, possess, and consult a copy (at 17:18); and entrusts a copy of the Torah to priests (at 31:9–11). Notably, of all the kings and high priests mentioned in the narratives of the books of 1 Samuel, 2 Samuel, 1 Kings, and 2 Kings (a narrative covering more than four centuries of personages), it is especially Josiah and Hilkiah who enact policy explicitly on the say-so of injunctions said to be written in the book of the Torah—just as Deuteronomy enjoins.[3] This narrative about Josiah's reign in the latter seventh

---

3. The biblical authors depict a predecessor of Josiah, King Hezekiah, as pursuing

century BCE registers among the earliest attempts to make something called the book of the Torah the constitution of a Judah-ite monarchy. And it is Shaphan the scribe (who is not a monarch, or a priest, or a prophet) who is the intermediary in all of this. It is he whom the narrator portrays as reading and assessing the book of the Torah before Hilkiah or Josiah do. And it is Shaphan who reads the book of the Torah to Josiah, inspiring him to repent, to consult Hulda the prophetess, and then to enact the wholesale religious-cultic reform of Judah-ite and Israelite society.

This image of the scribe as an expert in the book of the Torah (of Moses) and as operating at or near the apex of the administration of Judah-ite social, political, and religious institutions seems further developed and enhanced in the figure of Ezra (fifth or fourth century BCE[4]), as initially portrayed in the biblical books of Ezra and Nehemiah (composed and successively revised over the fourth, third, and perhaps even into the second centuries BCE).

Ezra as a Prototype of Authority in Judah-ite Society

Readers of the Hebrew Bible are introduced to the figure of Ezra in the seventh chapter of the biblical book bearing his name. At Ezra 7:1, Ezra is first presented with his lineage—a long line of male ancestors of priestly descent going back to Aaron, Moses' brother. After establishing Ezra's pedigree as a priest, the biblical text describes (at Ezra 7:6) his credentials in the following language:

> This is Ezra, who came up from Babylonia [to Jerusalem and the land of Judah]—and he is a scribe [*sofer*] fluent [*mahir*] in the Torah of Moses, which YHWH, the God of Israel, had given [to his people]; and the king [of Persia] gave to him [Ezra]—because the hand of YHWH was on him—all that he requested.

Ezra's qualifications are further supplemented a few verses later (at 7:10) in this manner:

---

about a century earlier what these authors also view as a positive religious policy. But nowhere in the narrative of Hezekiah's acts is Hezekiah said to be acting in accordance with the book of Torah or any written sacred text.

4. The discrepancy in the dates for Ezra's career hinges on whether it is the Persian monarch Artaxerxes I or Artaxerxes II who commissioned Ezra to administer the land of Judah (see Ezra 7:1). Arguments have been proffered for both by modern scholars.

For Ezra had prepared himself to analyze [*li-drosh*, from the verb *darash*] the Torah of YHWH, and to enact and to teach in Israel both statute and judgment [based on these analyses].

With these credentials (and lineage) stated, the biblical text "reproduces" the alleged letters patent in Aramaic (7:11–26) that the Persian monarch had given Ezra to establish and specify his commission and authority. For our particular purposes, here are some salient extracts from the alleged text of the monarch's missive of commission.[5]

And this is a copy of the letter that the King Artaxerxes gave to Ezra the priest and the scribe—a scribe of the content of the commandments of YHWH and of his statutes for Israel.

[From] Artaxerxes, king of kings, to Ezra the priest, a scribe of the law [*data*] of the God of heaven. . . . Inasmuch as you [Erza] are dispatched from before the king and his seven ministers [as our agent] to examine [the state of affairs of] Judah and Jerusalem in accordance with the law [*data*] of your God, which is in your possession. . . .

All that Ezra the priest, the scribe of the law [*data*] of the God of heaven asks of you [the recipients of this letter in the land of Judah], expeditiously let it be done. . . .

And you, Ezra, in accordance with the wisdom of your God [*hakhmat elahakh*] that you possess, appoint magistrates and judges, that they may judge all of the people of Beyond the River—[let them] all [be appointees that] know the laws [*datei*] of your God; and [insofar as there are among the appointees those] that do not know [these laws sufficiently well], you [Ezra] shall instruct them [accordingly]. And anyone who does not act [in accordance with] the law [*data*] of your God, and the law [*data*] of the [Persian] king, let judgment expeditiously be enacted upon him, whether execution, whether exile, whether confiscation of assets, or imprisonment.

Now, for our purposes, it does not matter one iota whether this text of Artazerxes's letters patent to Ezra is genuine. What does matter is that this is how Ezra and the grounds of his authority are portrayed by editors of the biblical book(s) of Ezra-Nehemiah. Why? Because it is this portrayal that

5. Why is this letter (allegedly) from Artaxerxes in Aramaic? The Persians adopted Aramaic as the administrative language of their empire (1) because it was already well installed as such in the Middle East as a result of the Assyrian and Babylonian Empires that preceded it, and (2) because the Persians at the time had no comparably sophisticated method of writing their own language(s). The insertion of the Aramaic text of the letter into a Hebrew narrative serves to convey a sense of the authenticity of the letter. Whether the text of the letter is genuine is another matter altogether.

becomes enshrined in Judah-ite culture via the biblical text centuries before the advent of the early rabbis.

According to this portrayal, Ezra is both a new and an old type of (supreme?) authority within Judah-ite society. He is a member of the priestly caste; indeed the text states that he is the son of Seraiah,[6] the last high priest of the Jerusalem temple at the time of its destruction in 586 BCE by the Babylonians, and the great-grandson of Hilkiah, the high priest during the reign of King Josiah.[7] Taken at face value, that would make Ezra a close relative of the officiating high priest in Jerusalem of his day. Yet in the biblical book(s) of Ezra and Nehemiah, Ezra is not portrayed as assuming regular priestly duties at all. Rather, he is depicted as issuing orders and instructions to the temple priesthood, as well as to everyone else in the land of Judah. He does this not as a king, prince, elder, prophet, or priest, all well-known types of social authority in ancient Israelite society. Rather, Ezra does so as something else, as a new type of supreme authority in Judah. What is that type? Ezra is a scribe who is an expert in "the [book of the] Torah of Moses" (Ezra 7:6; *torat Moshe*), which is referred to multiple times in Artaxerxes's letter as "the law of the God of heaven" (Aramaic: *data di-elah shemaya*) or "the law of your [that is, Ezra's] God" (Aramaic: *data di-elahakh*).

Genuine or not, Artaxerxes's letter of commission makes it quite clear that the latter credential, expertise in the Torah, not Ezra's priestly lineage, is the primary reason for Ezra's appointment. Ezra's (high) priestly caste status probably afforded him greater opportunity to master the Torah; but that is another matter, to be taken up later. Moreover, Ezra is charged with the task and authority to implement that Torah, the Law of his God, in the land of Judah (or at least to do so in a manner that also lies within the boundaries of Persian imperial legal policy, the law of the king, as noted at 7:26).

Here, then, we have a scribe, Ezra, who is much more than a senior administrative officer of the temple or the royal court, as was the case with Shaphan, who plays a role in King Josiah's education in and implementation of the book of the Torah (2 Kgs 22–23). King Josiah is clearly in charge; Shaphan serves him. By contrast, Ezra *the scribe* is the supreme authority in Judah, because as a scribe of the highest accomplishment, he is the chief expert in and chief interpreter of the Torah of Moses, the Law of his

6. Not to be confused with the aforementioned Seraiah the scribe in the court of King David c. 1000 BCE.

7. Of course, the accuracy of this statement is dubious, since if Ezra's governorship occurred during the reign of Artaxerxes I, then Ezra (at best) might have been the grandson of High Priest Seraiah. And if we are dealing with the reign of Artaxerxes II, then all the more so is the time interval problematic. As noted, and worth repeating, this Seraiah is not to be confused with Seraiah the scribe of King David's administration.

God—again, not law, or laws, but *the* book of *the La*w. His authority is depicted as including appointing worthy persons to all senior civil posts (but,
it seems, not priests to the various priestly posts) and to teach and instruct
these officials in the way to fulfill their duties in accordance with the Torah.
What a change from earlier periods of ancient Israel!

What for our purposes is the upshot of this? Well, in this depiction of
Ezra, his qualifications, and the resulting authority, conveyed in a fourth-
to-second-century BCE text that becomes part and parcel of the land of
Judah's biblical writings, are grounded the elevated civil and religious status and authority of a Judah-ite cadre of scribes as a professional guild-like
group of the highest order. "Membership" in this cadre is not based on
elevated lineage (even though many members, like Ezra, may possess it
and have had greater educational opportunities by reason of it[8]) but on
study of and expertise in a specific text, that is, the book of the Torah of
Moses, the Law of God, on the knowledge of which this cadre of scribes
has, or might claim to have, a monopolistic-like "lock."

While I have more to say about Ezra and about the cadre of scribes
that postdate him in Judah-ite society of last two centuries BCE and the
first century CE, I would like you to anticipate, even now, where I am going
with this by saying "How like (aspirations of) the early rabbis!" Substitute "Oral and Written Torah and Mishnah" for "the book of the Torah of
Moses" and the *likeness* is evident, in my view. The well-established image of the cadre of scribes in the several centuries preceding the Jerusalem
temple's destruction by the Romans in 70 CE, provides cultural currency
for the profile of the early rabbis, because the latter may be seen (by the
rabbis themselves and/or by their contemporary Jewish communities in
the land of Israel) to be like the former. But having anticipated where we
are headed, let me get back to the journey of getting there.[9]

8. See Bar-Ilan, "Scribes and Books."

9. The argument (if that is what it is) of the foregoing paragraph and the next several
pages accords, in my view, with the findings of Elisa Uusimäki, to whose scholarship
Joel Gereboff directed me. Let me, then, characterize the main elements of her research
relevant to this book. Uusimäki concludes that the cultural/social image of the sage in
Judah-ite society in the period immediately preceding the rabbis is an "idealization"
resulting from the cultural confluence of three preexistent profiles, namely those of the
Greek/Hellenistic sage, the Judah-ite sage (*hakham* or *maskil*), and the Judah-ite scribe,
and the linkage of this idealization specifically to exemplary knowledge of Torah and
of exemplary proper behavior that accords with Torah. In her essay "Rise of the Sage,"
1, she writes: "The conception of the sage as an idealized figure and object of emulation
originates from the classical Greek world, but it becomes integrated into the Jewish discourse on wisdom and the good life in the later Hellenistic period," when, of course, the
authority of the Torah of Moses had become the most important ground of all norms.
See also Uusimäki, *Lived Wisdom*, and "Maskil." The self-image of Joshua/Jesus Ben

Who Is Joshua/Jesus Ben Sira the Scribe?

Where may we turn next to find social and cultural successors of figures like Shaphan and Ezra—figures the *portrayal* of which may have provided currency for the early rabbinic movement? Now, in part, the answer to this question has much to do with the political history of the land of Judah/Yehud over the several centuries following Ezra's career. While we have a dearth of narrative literary traditions for this period of the history of Judah/Yehud after Ezra and Nehemiah—indeed, the ancient historian, Josephus, writing near the end of the first century CE, struggles somewhat to fill this temporal gap—it is evident that during these several centuries the high priest of the Jerusalem temple was the highest civil and religious authority of the land of Israel. Moreover, once the Pentateuch, more or less as we have it today, was identified as the book of the Torah of Moses, it was the high priest who was the chief custodian of it and the highest arbiter of its content and meaning. That said, it is also the case, in my estimate, that a cadre of scribes (many of priestly descent and some not), modeled on the figure of Ezra, acted as the principal scholars of the Torah, and the major administrators of Torah law within civil society under the high priest's "national government."

Only as a result of the successful Hasmonean revolt against Seleucid rule in the second century BCE did a monarchic dynasty, but now associated with the priesthood and the office of the high priest (not descent from David), reemerge in the land of Judah. But, it would appear, Hasmonean rule, too (and later Herodian administration as well), was exercised through the agency of the cadre of scribes as experts in Torah law.

Where may we glimpse the ethos of these scribe-scholar-sage administrators? Let us consider two such sources. One source, the Christian Gospels, derides the scribes who work for the priests and the scribes in the service of the Pharisees. These scribes (and sometimes their "employers" too) are (mockingly?) characterized as experts in the Law (that is, the Torah of Moses and its interpretation and application).[10] At these many junctures,

---

Sirah the scribe, to which we will presently turn, seems to me to be the consummate image of the confluence that Uusimäki depicts.

10. The Gospel of Luke shows a decided tendency to use the phrase "doctors [i.e., teachers] of the Law." See, e.g., Luke 2:46; 5:17; 11:45–46, 52; 14:3; see also Acts 5:34, in which passage Gamaliel (the Pharisee) is so characterized. In the Gospels, scribes are routinely characterized as both experts in the teachings and the law of the Jewish people, and as authoritative, honored functionaries in local and national administration in the Jewish homeland, who have "met their match," in both knowledge and moral standing, in Jesus and, therefore, who allegedly participate in the conspiracy to silence him. Here is just a smattering of relevant, illustrative Gospel passages: Mark 8:31; 12:38–39 (parallels Luke 20:45–46); 14:1; Matt 9:3; 16:21; 23:1–7, 27–28; Luke 9:22.

the authors of the Gospel texts wish to emphasize both Jesus' authority and his distinctive approach to the Law. The Law should serve people's needs—Jesus' approach—rather than people serving the Law's (and the legal experts', that is, the scribes', needs).

This polemic, for that is certainly what it is, works for its intended audience from a literary-rhetorical perspective only if the image of scribes as competent and respected (and obeyed?) "doctors of the Law" is a highly plausible, well-recognized characterization.[11] The image must "ring true," for the valence (the value equation) of that characterization to be changed via polemical rhetoric from positive to negative. That is often how (and why) polemics work. But the upshot of this brief discussion of the Gospels' anti-scribal polemic is this. Remove the polemical shift in valence from positive to negative, and one is left with an attestation in early Christian literature from the end of the first century CE to the importance of the cadre of scribes as experts in the Law, the Torah, of YHWH, which Scripture is also sacred to the members of the early Jesus movement. This scribal class are not the priests, even though many are probably of priestly descent, and they are not the Pharisees, even though some may be of that sectarian persuasion. Rather, they are high-ranking, well-educated, and authoritative legal experts who are *retainers* of the priestly caste and of the sectarian, politically active Pharisees.[12]

The other relevant pre-rabbinic source that I should like briefly to discuss on this topic is the book of Ben Sira, the author of which was a scribe living in Jerusalem several centuries after Ezra. Here, then, we have a scribe writing about what being a scribe means to him.

The book of Ben Sira was composed in Hebrew probably in the early second century BCE, just decades before the Hasmonean revolt. The Hebrew text eventually fell into disuse, and, consequently, until the modern discoveries of ancient manuscripts, the Hebrew version of the book survived only in part. Why did the original Hebrew version fall into disuse? When the early rabbis set the parameters of the canon of their Hebrew Bible, they did not include the book of Ben Sira in the collection, even though Ben Sira was well known and very much beloved by the early rabbis. Indeed, rabbinic literature sometimes quotes (in Hebrew, of course) from Ben Sira

11. Caricatures, which is likely what the Gospel writers are providing for polemical purposes, work only when the caricature builds upon actual characterizations.

12. For a quite comprehensive discussion of the sources concerning scribes in Judah-ite society in the several centuries preceding and following the destruction of Jerusalem by the Romans in 70 CE, see Bar-Ilan, "Scribes and Books." On the "political-action" orientation of the Pharisees before 70 CE, a good account for nonspecialists may be found in Neusner, *From Politics to Piety*.

as if it were Scripture.[13] That said, the book of Ben Sira did survive in various translations, the first of which was the Greek translation done by the author's grandson, a Judean émigré to Alexandria. And, in translation, the book was preserved by Christians among the books of the Latin Vulgate and Christian Apocrypha to the Old Testament under the titles "The Wisdom of Sirach" and "Ecclesiasticus." Today, most imprints of the Christian Old Testament with Apocrypha will contain this work.

Now from the grandson's prologue to his translation of his grandfather's work, we may discern many things about the ethos and institutionalization of the cadre of scribes in the land of Judah in the early second century BCE. The grandson of the author, Joshua/Jesus Ben Sira, the scribe (*sofer*), depicts the latter as a wise sage (*hakham/maskil*), whose wisdom (*hokhmah*) is grounded in his study of "the Law and the Prophets and the other books of our fathers." This phrase is significant, because it reflects the emerging tripartite division of the Hebrew Scriptures into the Law (*torah*), the Prophets (*nevi-im*), and the (other sacred) Writings (*ketuvim*). According to the grandson/translator, Joshua/Jesus' mastery of these texts and their meaning lies at the heart of the grandfather's (self-assumed?) mandate to write about, and to teach others, the wisdom he has acquired. And this mandate, as we shall see, includes the establishment of a school to educate the next generation of scribes to serve Judah-ite society.

Now, much of the book of Ben Sira is reminiscent of the biblical book of Proverbs. In fact, a number of aphorisms in the latter have topical parallels in the former. In the book of Proverbs one acquires wisdom (*hokhmah*) and becomes as a sage/wise one (*hakham/maskil*) by learning and internalizing these aphorisms for leading the good and virtuous life. This philosophy of what it means to be a sage is also reflected in Ben Sira. Take, for example, the following verse.

---

13. The reasons for the exclusion of Ben Sira from the rabbis' biblical canon are technical, in my opinion. In my view, one of the criteria used by the early rabbis in deciding which books to include and which to exclude had to do with *their* understanding of the date of a book's authorship. They included no book that they understood to be written later than the careers of Ezra and Nehemiah (that is, no later than what *they* dated to the fifth century BCE). The rabbis viewed Ezra and Nehemiah as capstone figures and understood their time to mark the end of the era of prophecy. Of course, modern scholars know that some of the books of the Hebrew Bible were in fact written later than the fourth century BCE. But the early rabbis did not know that. They made these judgments as best they could, based on the assumptions (or knowledge) under which they operated. Although it appears that the book of Ben Sira was much beloved by them, the rabbis could see that its content indicates that the book was authored several centuries later than their "capstone" era.

> Do not slight the discourse of the sages, but busy yourself with
> their maxims; because from them you will gain instruction and
> learn how to serve great men. (Ben Sira 8:8)

In other words, the aphoristic teachings of the sages prepare one for
public service.

But Joshua/Jesus Ben Sira repeatedly overlays this ideology with
something more that is not generally characteristic of the biblical book
of Proverbs. Throughout Ben Sira's text, wisdom is repeatedly said to be
grounded specifically in the Law/Torah, its study, and the faithful observance in daily life of the Law's demands. I have already stated that in the
prologue, the grandson/translator explicitly grounds his grandfather's
credentials to write and to teach in scholarship of the Scriptures. And in
the body of the work, the author himself writes:

> Reflect on the statutes of the Lord, and meditate at all times on
> his commandments. It is he who will give insight to your mind,
> and your desire for wisdom will be granted. (Ben Sira 6:37)

> Let your conversation be with men of understanding, and let all
> your discussions be about the Law of the Most High. (Ben Sira
> 9:15; capitalization of "Law" added)

> The man who fears the Lord will do this, and he who holds to
> the Law will obtain wisdom. (Ben Sira 15:1; capitalization of
> "Law" added)

> All this is the book of the covenant of the Most High God, the
> Law which Moses commanded us as an inheritance for the
> congregations of Jacob. (Ben Sira 24:23; capitalization of "Law"
> added; parallels/cites Deut 33:4)

> He who devotes himself to the study of the Law of the Most
> High will seek out the wisdom of all the ancients, and will be
> concerned with prophesies. . . . He will reveal instruction in his
> teachings and will glory in the Law of the Lord's covenant. (Ben
> Sira 33:1, 8; capitalization of "Law" added)

Clearly, then, the acquisition of wisdom and insight derives not simply
from the maxims of the sages, but also and especially from Torah study
and its analysis—and, of course, from its genuine-hearted observance and
application as well, as indicated in the following passages.

> All wisdom is the fear of the Lord, and in all wisdom there is the
> fulfilment of the Law. (Ben Sira 19:20; capitalization of "Law"
> added)

> A wise man will not hate the Law, but he who is hypocritical
> about it is like as boat in a storm. And a man of understanding
> will trust in the Law; for him the Law is as dependable as an
> inquiry by means of the Urim. (Ben Sira 33:2–3; capitalization
> of "Law" added)

For the author of Ben Sira, who is it that acquires this wisdom based on Torah study? And where does one acquire it? This high level of education is the purview of a cadre of scribes, who have the leisure (read: wealth) to devote themselves to learning. Someone who must dedicate their time and energy to making a living cannot afford the time to study.

> The wisdom of the scribe depends on the opportunity of leisure;
> and he who has little business may become wise. How can he
> become wise who handles the plow? (Ben Sira 38:24–25)

The locus of the pursuit of such higher learning is in the academy of master scribes, such as that of Joshua/Jesus Ben Sira himself. The author is clearly unabashed in his recruitment efforts, and he does not shrink from mentioning that the tuition is significant, but the subsequent return on investment greater still.

> Instruction in understanding and knowledge I have written in
> this book, Jesus the son of Sirach, son of Eleazar of Jerusalem,
> who out of his heart poured forth wisdom. . . . Draw near to me,
> you who are untaught, and lodge in my school. . . . Get instruc-
> tion with a large sum of silver, and you will gain by it much gold.
> (Ben Sira 50:27; 51:23, 28)

The book of Ben Sira circulated widely among highly literate Jews both inside and outside the land of Israel. That is why the Hebrew text was translated into Greek by the author's grandson. And that is how it gained considerable currency among early Christian literati as well. It is clear why the early rabbis were drawn to the text of the book of Ben Sira, even though they had to exclude it on technical grounds from their canon of biblical Scriptures.[14] The text, among (many) other things, extols a life of Torah learning and what is derived from it as a principal, shared attribute of the cadre of scribes/wise ones. Ben Sira aptly illustrates the assertion made in the recent scholarship of Elisa Uusimäki that in the land of Israel

14. Why do I say "technical grounds"? Had Jesus/Joshua Ben Sira pseudonymously attributed his book to some Judah-ite figure whom the early rabbis believed to have lived before the period of Ezra and Nehemiah, as that is the period the rabbis identified as the era of the prophets, then I have little doubt that this work would have been included and preserved within the rabbinic canon of Scriptures.

in the late Hellenistic era the ideals of the Greek sage and of the Judah-ite scribe (*sofer*) and wise one (*hakham/maskil*) converged to produce the figure of the Torah scholar, whose behavior, too, was exemplary, because it accorded with the demands of a life lived in accordance with diligently acquired Torah knowledge.[15] And as a Judah-ite novice scribe, one begins one's self-transformation to become such an exemplar by learning at the feet of—indeed, by "lodging" at the school of—an expert scribe/wise one. Certainly, this is an apt cultural antecedent to the ethos of discipleship that is evident in the early rabbinic movement, as attested, for example, in Avot. If, then, the early rabbis might appear to themselves, and wished to appear to others, to be like something with well-established cultural currency in Judah-ite society, then they are like scribes/wise ones; rabbis were:

1. Experts in the Law, the halakha

2. Devoted to its lifelong study (not only in Scripture but also and especially in its incarnation as Mishnah, of course)

3. Aspiring purveyors of authoritative opinions over the "Way" (halakha) one lives one's life in accordance with Torah

4. Exemplars of such a life lived

Indeed, as you have read in chapter 2, the early rabbis refer to their collectivity as the *hakhamim* (sages/wise ones) and as disciples of the *hakhamim*. And the early rabbis ascribe a swath of extra-biblical law (that is, law that does not appear in the Pentateuch or derive directly from its interpretation) to teachings from "the words of the scribes" (*divrei sofrim*), which, together with halakhic pronouncements deemed to be of strictly rabbinic provenance, are part of Oral Torah, a revelation of which the early rabbis claimed to possess (exclusive?) intellectual mastery. This, of course, begs another question. Are there any cultural antecedents in pre-rabbinic Judah-ite society to the early rabbis' notion of Oral Torah itself? The answer is both yes and no, as is so commonly the case, and has to do with Judah-ite conceptions of revelation in the era of, and just prior to, the consolidation of the Mishnanian sages as a group.

15. Uusimäki, "Rise of the Sage"; *Lived Wisdom*; and "Maskil."

SUPPLEMENTAL (SOMETIMES SECRET?) REVELATIONS RESERVED FOR THE WISE: CULTURAL ANTECEDENTS THAT PRE-FIGURE THE EARLY RABBIS' ORAL TORAH

A "Stew" of Cultural Perceptions and Beliefs about (Ongoing) Revelation as the General Antecedent and Contemporary Cultural Context for the Early Rabbis

The complexity of the issue at hand warrants an introductory "flyover," so that I may refer back to elements of it as this section of the chapter progresses. In the late Hellenistic and early Roman eras, Judah-ite concepts of revelation were complex and diverse.[16] There was no simple or singular response to a question like "What counts as revelation?" Nor was there to the query "Who (in the past, present or future) are authentic sources or recipients of (new) revelation generally or of (new) revealed law specifically?" And if one were to ask "Does veneration of the Law/Torah of Moses (which eventually in the Second Temple/Hellenistic period became the moniker for the Pentateuch) imply that other Israelite prophets, such as a Samuel or a Jeremiah or an Ezekiel, were not and cannot be understood to be sources of revealed Torah law?"—again, no one answer is possible. Rather, with regard to these questions and other related queries that might be posed, the evidence represents a range of ideas and ideologies, some complementary, some contradictory. And it was this stew of perceptions and beliefs about revelation, its sources and its purveyors, that constituted the antecedent and contemporary religio-cultural environment within which, and sometimes against which, the early rabbis first asserted their claims about their special Torah knowledge and halakha expertise (even before the rabbis' fully formed ideology of Oral Torah was framed in latter third and/or fourth centuries CE). Let me, then, separate out some of the ingredients of this stew, just as a point of departure and as a rehearsal for this section of the chapter.

Let us begin by considering Judah-ite notions of prophecy as a case in point. As intimated above, by the time of the Roman conquest of the land of Israel in the first century BCE (if not already well before), virtually all Judah-ites would identify the Pentateuch (more or less in the form we have today) as *the* Torah of Moses. The Pentateuch itself, notably the book of Deuteronomy (18:15–22; 13:1ff), struggles with the issue of prophecy after Moses. It acknowledges that prophecy continues after Moses' death, but one must distinguish a true prophet from a false one using certain specified litmus

16. See, e.g., Sommer, "Did Prophecy Cease"; and Jassen, *Mediating the Divine*, 1–24.

tests. (I will spare you an account of the criteria.) Deuteronomy specifies no end-date for prophecy, but Deuteronomy (4:2; 12:32) also enjoins that *no one* must add anything to, or remove anything from the (that is, Deuteronomy's) Torah, which is depicted as Moses' summative instructions to the people of Israel at the end of his life. Deuteronomy seems to be saying that YHWH will continue to reveal matters to prophets, but the permitted scope of these matters is already set by the Torah revealed to Moses. When the Pentateuch as a whole was promulgated (and accepted) as Scripture *and* as Moses' Torah, Deuteronomy's proscription against changes in "Moses'" legal dictates was extended to all of the Pentateuch's instructions.

So, in principle, can post-Mosaic prophets (or anyone else, for that matter) be understood to have issued (new) laws in God's name? Some Judah-ites quite reasonably thought not, on the basis of Deut 4:2 and 12:32. And yet[17] a number of late Hellenistic and early Roman Judaic texts among the documents discovered in the mid-twentieth century at Qumran (aka the Dead Sea Scrolls) clearly understand the "classical," post-Mosaic, scriptural prophets to have been *lawgivers*, not just law-*repeaters* and exhorters to do YHWH's will. Moreover, some Qumran texts perceive the leaders of their own sectarian community, which we moderns now call the Dead Sea Sect, to be ongoing recipients and teachers of (new) revelation, including laws, by virtue of these leaders' inspiration by YHWH's spirit. These documents simply hesitate *explicitly* to designate these leaders as prophets, in deference to a belief that the era of classical prophecy (although not ongoing revelation) ended centuries earlier. Yet, interestingly, the Qumranians do not hesitate to condemn the sect's contemporary enemies/adversaries as those who consult "false prophets."

Alex Jassen convincingly argues that while some of these views represented in the Dead Sea Scrolls about ongoing revelation may be idiomatic beliefs of the Dead Sea Sect, many, in his opinion, seem to reflect ideas with wider currency among Judah-ites of the late Hellenistic and early Roman periods. That is to say, a not insignificant number of Judah-ites maintained that revelation continues in various forms in their own time and sometimes results in new divine law, even though many of these same Judah-ites would not have classified these revelations as being on par with classical prophecy, and certainly not the equivalent of that deemed to have been revealed to Moses.

17. For what follows in the next several sentences, I am indebted to the work of Jassen, *Mediating the Divine*. It is futile to specify the specific pages in his extensive analyses upon which I rely, since what follows in this and the next paragraph distills the results of his book as a whole.

By comparison, the Gospel writers are not so reticent to use the term "prophet" as a descriptor of Jesus. The author of the Gospel of Matthew (21:10–11) sees no problem in depicting welcoming crowds in Jerusalem designating Jesus as "the *prophet* from Nazareth in the Galilee" (my emphasis). It is safe to conclude that this Gospel's first intended readers would not have perceived such an assertion by Judah-ites of that era to be nonsense or out-and-out heresy; revelation continues and some see its purveyors as prophets. That said, the Gospel of Matthew does exercise some caution in these regards; the author of Matthew (5:17–20) has Jesus say that his mission is not to abolish or even change the Law, a position that appears to reflect guardrails set by Deuteronomy for "true" Israelite prophets. And yet, it is undeniable that the Gospel of Matthew (like Mark and Luke) depict a Jesus whose specific views on (some) important points of halakha differ from those of the Pharisees and scribes (aka doctors of the Law); Jesus' halakha is not theirs (just as some of the Pharisees' halakha differs from that of the Sadducees and the Dead Sea community). Does the authority of Jesus' version of the halakha rest upon his status as a prophet to whom matters of the Law have been revealed? The Gospel chooses to remain mum on this issue. But, as has just been remarked, some of the Dead Sea Scrolls are not at all reticent to acclaim their leaders as recipients of new revelation regarding legal/ritual practice, even though these texts refrain from calling their leaders prophets. Finally, Paul in his Epistle to the Galatians (see, e.g., 1:13–15) appears to claim that he himself has been a recipient of revelation, not about the Law (of which Paul claims to have been a devoted student and practitioner), but rather about the approaching end of times, Jesus' role, and its meaning for the attenuation of that very Law for followers of Jesus. Nonetheless, Paul's "prophetic self-consciousness" is clearly on display.[18]

As regards the rabbis' notions concerning prophetic revelation, the consensus view of rabbinic authorities in the mid- to late Amoraic period (BT Bava Batra 12a–b) is that prophecy (or at least classical prophecy) ended around the era of Ezra with the careers of Haggai, Zachariah, and Malachi. Indeed, the Amoraic rabbis appear to use this notion to justify what is included and excluded from their biblical canon. No book *believed* by the rabbis to be written after Ezra's era, no matter how appropriately edifying, is retained in their canon.[19] Moreover, as you have already learned, the mid-third-century rabbinic authorship of Avot clearly understands *torah* (in a generic or general sense of the word) as that which was revealed

18. I am indebted here to correspondence with Arthur Dewey.

19. That is why, e.g., Ben Sira and 1 Maccabees were excluded. On the rabbis' biblical canon, see Lightstone, "Rabbis' Bible"; see also Neusner, "Rabbis and Prophecy."

to Moses and *only* to Moses. And yet, the scope of the early rabbis' *torah* clearly is not limited to that which is written in the Pentateuch, but, as discussed earlier in chapters 2 and 3, includes a great deal of extra-biblical teachings deemed revelatory in status, of which Mishnah is said, from the third century CE on, to be the highest embodiment.

In sum, thus far, as regards (1) normative concepts of revelation in Judah-ite culture just before and at the time of the Mishnanians, and (2) how the early rabbis' notions of their *torah* (in the more general sense) would be perceived to fit within that culture, once again, I must say, "It's complicated!" Let me, therefore, put on the table my own summative views on these matters piece by piece, assertion by assertion. As I proceed, remember that the task at hand is to explore how the rabbis' claims about the authority of their own teachings would be perceived as having sufficient cultural currency to seem plausible—at least to the rabbis themselves and (they would have hoped) to other Judah-ites as well.

Emergence of a New Framework Concerning Revealed Law between the Late Seventh and the Late Fourth Centuries BCE

It is undoubtedly the case that Judah-ite society in the last century BCE and the first century CE understood that the revelation of YHWH's teachings to his people did not begin or end with God's revelation to Moses. Rather, the by then well-entrenched biblical books depict a number of heroic figures said to have received God's teachings and instructions, beginning with the biblical depictions of Adam, Noah, and Abraham. And according to Judah-ite Scriptures, after Moses, generations of prophets from Deborah and Samuel to Malachi (if not beyond) proffered YHWH's oracular teachings and instructions to the people—representing more than another half a millennium of prophetic vocation and revelation in ancient Israel, according to the biblical tradition. That said, something culturally (and socially) fundamental happened between the late seventh century BCE (that is, in King Josiah's time) and the end of the fourth century BCE (namely, in the aftermath of the reforms associated in Scripture with the policies of Ezra and Nehemiah). And what happened resulted *thereafter* in a "new" allegedly normative ideology about when, how, and to whom YHWH revealed/reveals *what type* of teachings. From that point forward, every bona fide Jew had to operate culturally within the framework of these reforms, or more accurately stated, had to develop a conceptual "work-around" that (1) gave the plausible appearance of staying within the framework but (2) allowed for meaningful ramification and development of teachings, including teachings about law, deemed to be revelation. Indeed, is this not what the early rabbis' mythologizations, described above in chapter 2, did?! But I am getting ahead of myself again. So let me describe the principal elements of this novel, *allegedly* normative framework and then point to evidence that prefigures the early rabbis' own work-around (since, as I shall presently argue, the rabbis' approach to this issue seems to be, as intimated above, one of a "family" or "variety" of such approaches in evidence among Judah-ite groups).[20]

20. My own education on these matters has been substantially augmented, on Joel Gereboff's recommendation, by reading Jassen, *Mediating the Divine*. I have generally avoided lengthy footnotes about modern scholarship on topics related to this volume's discussions. However, a substantial note on this topic will be edifying to many readers of *What Were the Early Rabbis*? Moreover, this note permits me to make some claims on an educated hunch that I am not ready to commit to in the body of this book's text.

Jassen very briefly encapsulates his own findings in the most general terms in his review of Cook, *On the Question of the "Cessation of Prophecy"* (Jassen, "Stephen L. Cook," 452), where Jassen remarks:

> Of all the Second Temple period material, Josephus' writings perhaps best attest to the twofold reality that some Jews in the Second Temple period believed that prophecy was still active *and* that it differed considerably from the [classical] prophetic heritage found in the Hebrew Bible. . . . Josephus' . . . distinction [Prophecy vs. prophecy, if you will] . . . reinforces the notion that prophecy was no longer understood exclusively in terms of the prophets of ancient Israel.

Turning to Jassen's own book on the topic, *Mediating the Divine*, there are several points of intersection between Jassen's conclusions and the claims I make in the following pages of this chapter. So permit me to state here in their own right Jassen's principal points as I interpret them and as they concern this chapter. (1) Prophecy continued to flourish in the Second Temple period (that is, from the late sixth century BCE to 70 CE), but (2) its modalities/forms changed as well. Chief among these changes, according to Jassen, is the view that (3) exegesis of texts, including exegesis pertaining to legal norms, is a form of prophetic revelation. (4) This particular modulation of what may count as prophetic revelation is particularly evident among the Qumran texts (aka the Dead Sea Scrolls), but not exclusively so. The other modality of ongoing revelation claimed by the Qumran community's leadership, according to Jassen, is (5) "sapiential revelation"; the wise, by virtue of their lifelong engagement in study, experience their new insights, including about Judaic law, to be the result of divine inspiration. Thus far, unadulterated Jassen; now me, in light of Jassen.

As I shall have occasion to mention later in this chapter, the Qumran text often referred to as the Community Rule has novices seeking entry into its exclusive community swear an oath of allegiance to abide by the teachings of the Torah of Moses as well as to those teachings "revealed to the sons of Zadoq, the priests [of the community (*yahad*)]." In other words, according to the Community Rule, the priestly founders/ leaders of the sect have been and continue to be recipients of revelation, the content of which supplements and complements the content of the Torah of Moses. Jassen's point, it seems to me, is that one of the modalities by which these priestly authorities "receive" their revelation is exegesis (in other words, study and analysis) of Scripture.

(How very Protestant Christian?!)

Why the prominence of priestly leadership at Qumran, despite the community's self-distancing from the Jerusalem temple, where priests may perform their vocation? In Qumran's sectarian texts, priests have a special prominence in the community. In my opinion, this has to do both with (1) the history of Judah-ite society since approximately the fifth century BCE, and (2) the specific circumstances several centuries later that appear to have resulted in the founding of this sectarian community. For almost the entirety of the Second Temple period in the land of Israel, the priests of YHWH's temple, and especially the high priests, were the highest arbiters and interpreters of Torah norms. This is reflected, among other places, in the biblical passage at Deut 17:8–13, which depicts priests not (only) as cultic officiants but as part of a supreme court system issuing legal directives and judgments. That place of eminence continued to be the case among the Qumran sectarians, because, in their view, the Jerusalem temple had been "hijacked" by "evil" priests, and the leaders of the sectarian community were the true priestly preservers of the temple's heritage, even if they could not offer sacrifices in their place of self-exile from Jerusalem.

Why may (some) Judah-ites of the late Hellenistic and early Roman era, the Qumranians among them, have perceived continuing revelation, including revelation about legal matters, to be "alive and well" but mediated by scriptural interpretation *and/or* devoted sapiential/wisdom learning? On a strong hunch (and at this point, that is all it is), I am inclined to merge Jassen's findings with those of Mandel, *Origins of Midrash* (discussed earlier in this book at ch. 4, n3 and n30), about the history of the meaning of *darash/midrash*. Mandel shows that until the Amoraic rabbinic period, *darash* did not explicitly or principally refer to the attribution of multiple meanings to Scripture (which is what the mid- to late Amoraic rabbis meant by *midrash*, according to Mandel). Rather, before that era, *darash* referred to a deeply engaged, analytic examination of a teaching, and by early rabbinic times (the era of the Mishnaninans) *darash* also referred to exposition/declaiming before others upon an authentic (especially) halakhic teaching based upon deep critical examination. My hunch, to put all this together, is that in the several centuries preceding the advent of the Mishnanian group, to *doreish* (a participial form of *drsh*) an authoritative Judah-ite tradition (sometimes one in Scripture, sometimes not found expressly written in Scripture) was somehow to further the disclosure of YHWH's revelation, even if it was not, strictly speaking, classical prophecy. The upshot: (some) deeply informed analysis (sometimes, but not always) of Scripture by (some particularly learned) sages/authorities is (new) revelation—a kind of prophecy—and, as regards halakhic matters specifically, functions as a work-around of the Deuteronomic and post-Deuteronomic limits placed on prophecy by a "Moses only" ideology. Something about the authority and competence of the sage-*darshan* combined with the authenticity of the tradition analyzed produces something like prophetic revelation. It would take further research to transform this hunch into a warranted historical claim. But I do not find such a claim inconsistent with Jassen's findings.

As to the rabbis' mythologizations in the third and fourth centuries CE (discussed above in ch. 2) that their extra-scriptural teachings and especially Mishnah constituted Oral Torah received from Moses via a chain of master and disciples through the ages—I am inclined to see this as a kind of harmonization of opposites or a squaring of the circle of antecedent Judah-ite views that held that classical prophecy may have ended centuries earlier, but prophecy and revelation did not. Conceptually and ideologically, the rabbis' solution is both very radical and quite conservative at one and the same time. How so? Everything halakhic begins and ends with YHWH's revelation to Moses

The "Moses-Centrism" of the New Framework and the Early Rabbis' Halakha as Revelation

There are at least six major, basic tenets of the aforementioned normative framework, two of which bear especially on our specific task. Let me first list them all.

1. There is only one god, YHWH; therefore only YHWH is to be worshipped.

2. There is only one altar at which sacrifices to YHWH may be offered; it is the altar at the temple in Jerusalem.

3. There is only one caste that may offer sacrifices to YHWH at the Jerusalem altar on behalf of others; it is the caste of "Aaronite" priests, namely those who trace their patrilineal descent to Aaron, Moses' brother.

4. Judah-ites may marry other Judah-ites only (which includes those who have assimilated to Judah-ite society);[21] this is usually referred to as the principle of endogamy, and its primary purpose is to ensure that "foreign" culture and religious cultic practices do not infiltrate Judah-ite culture and religion.

5. There is only one prophet to whom YHWH has revealed the Law/Torah; that prophet is Moses, and that revelation is contained in the book of the Torah of Moses (*sefer torat Moshe*), which several centuries before the early rabbinic movement's formation became wholly identified with the Pentateuch (the first five books of the Hebrew Scriptures, more or less as we have them today).

6. YHWH revealed his word to his select group of "true" prophets but revealed no (new) laws to them after Moses; that said, (classical) prophecy ended sometime around the careers of Ezra and Nehemiah.

Both the biblical and archaeological evidence about ancient Israel confirms that none of these six tenets were normative in Judah-ite society and culture before, let us say, sometime in the fifth or fourth centuries BCE. Hezekiah, king of Judah in the latter eighth century BCE, makes a stab at

---

(a "conservative" stance); yet that revealed halakha continues to develop and be ramified in early rabbinic teachings and halakhic analysis, and the result of this, too, is revelation (a "radical" stance).

21. Only later on does this evolve into a formal system for conversion, on the one hand, and, on the other hand, the adoption of a norm among Jews that matrilineal descent determines one's status as a Jew (but not one's caste status within the ranks of the Jewish people).

imposing some of them. On his death his reforms dissipate in the face of established practice. Josiah, king of Judah in the latter seventh century BCE, institutes reforms aligning with many of these tenets. (The account of Josiah's reforms does not specifically harp on endogamy, e.g.) His immediate successors reverse his policies. But within 200 or 275 years, that is, after the governorships of Ezra and Nehemiah in the land of Judah/Yehud, these six tenets become either "substantially"[22] normative or "official," defining characteristics of Judah-ite social, cultural, and religious identity.[23]

Of these six fundamental tenets, it is the last two (concerning Moses and the Torah, and prophecy/revelation generally) that are of particular interest to us, given the topic of this book and this chapter. Why? Because these last two tenets, which amount to a kind of ideological Moses-centrism, bear directly upon the early rabbis' mythologization of their teachings as Oral Torah and as revelation, and upon their claim that the Mishnah (which the rabbis attributed to the authorship of Rabbi Judah the Patriarch) is the most perfect expression of that Oral Torah. Let me explain.

As you have learned, the rabbis (1) claim (exclusive?) authority to offer directives that accord with the halakha, the "Way" to live one's life in accordance with Torah, and (2) nurture and promote their special expertise in halakhic thinking, engendered in particular by mastery of Mishnah and its lifelong study and analysis. You have also learned that there are (pre) requisites that must be satisfied in order to read, interpret, and analyze Mishnah. One must have a complete command of all of the legal content of Scripture (especially the Pentateuch), and one must have prior knowledge of an entire body of *extra*-biblical Judah-ite law, that is, law *not* found in Scripture, but which, nevertheless, underpins Mishnah at a great many junctures, and which the early rabbis assume nonetheless to be (almost equally) authoritative. Some of that extra-biblical law the early rabbis attribute to the words of the scribes (about whom this chapter has already said much). And other extra-biblical halakhic teachings are deemed to be rabbinic ordinances. Do you see the problem as yet? Let me phrase the issue as a question. How can there be *any* valid extra-scriptural/extra-pentateuchal law at all, given tenets number 5 and 6 of the normative framework just articulated? The answer is: on the face of it, ideologically or theologically, there cannot be.

22. I use "substantially" in the sense that the term is used by building contractors, when they refer to a building project as "substantially complete"; they mean "mostly" or "almost" complete.

23. Of course, one can point to exceptions to the norm. Aren't there always?! E.g., Jewish temples operated for a time in Elephantine and in Leontopolis/Heliopolis (both in Egypt), seemingly with Jerusalem's acquiescence, are two such exceptions. Both were inoperative by the time of the early rabbis.

Why? Let me spell it out. All Torah law comes from YHWH via Moses and only Moses, and that law is *wholly* contained in the Pentateuch (understood to be the book of the Torah of Moses), to which nothing may be added or removed; this is new normative tenet number 5. Other prophets may exhort the people in the name of YHWH to follow his commandments, but prophets other than Moses may issue no new Torah laws, and classical prophecy ended, in any case, after the career of Malachi (just before the governorships of Ezra and Nehemiah?); this is new normative tenet number 6. If Torah law is that which was revealed to Moses, and if the Pentateuch is the book of the Torah of Moses, where (in principle) might any authoritative, extra-biblical/ extra-pentateuchal law come from?!

As we have already discussed, there is ample evidence that many or some Judah-ites in the land of Israel in the late Hellenistic and early Roman eras "found a place" for ongoing revelation, while still formally assenting to new tenets 5 and 6. And I am inclined to entertain, but cannot prove, the proposition that initially (that is, near the turn of the third century CE, when Mishnah was produced) the early rabbis thought of their devotion to study and to halakhic analysis as a kind of ongoing revelatory experience. Why? Because it is clear that other learned Judah-ites so considered their own deep engagement in learning. Take, for example, what Ben Sira (an extra-biblical author seemingly beloved by the early rabbis and other Judah-ite intelligentsia) says about the accomplished scribe who has become wise (*hakham/maskil*) through diligent study:

> If the great Lord is willing, he [the scribe] will be filled with the *spirit of understanding*; he will pour forth words of wisdom of his own and give thanks to the Lord in prayer. The Lord will *direct his counsel and knowledge*, as he meditates on his mysteries. (Ben Sira 39:7–8; emphasis added)

Without saying that an accomplished, learned scribe (like himself) is a prophet, Ben Sira is certainly asserting that such a one may be worthy of receiving divine inspiration that will inform and ground one's teachings and counsel.[24] And therefore, the production, promulgation, and devoted study of Mishnah by the early rabbis *may* have *initially* been so conceived as well. And the Mishnanians *may* have similarly perceived the status of their claimed rabbinic and proto-rabbinic forebears, that is, as persons whose learning warranted the bestowal by YHWH of a spirit of understanding.

24. Jassen, *Mediating the Divine*, 313. The notion that (practical) wisdom may result from the bestowal of the divine spirit recalls Exod 31:1–3, where the chief builder of the desert Tabernacle, Bezalel ben Uri ben Hur, who is not described as a prophet, nevertheless is said to be the beneficiary of such a spirit.

A (subsequent?) more fully formed solution to the problem (for the early rabbis, at least) is their myth of Oral Torah, which came to be articulated by the Amoraim sometime over the several centuries following the production of Mishnah, as we have discussed in chapter 2 of this book. That is, on Sinai, YHWH revealed the *whole* Torah to Moses, *some* of which Moses was instructed to write down (*be-ketav*, i.e., Written Torah = Pentateuch), and *some* of which Moses was instructed to pass on orally (*be-peh*, i.e., Oral Torah) through generations of teachers and disciples down to the early rabbis, of whom Judah the Patriarch, the alleged author of the Mishnah, was said to be the most accomplished. This more fully formed myth about the authority of rabbinic teachings is certainly more Moses-centric in form (even if not in practice)—a more ideologically safe or more satisfying proposition, perhaps.

Now, let us again recall the task at hand. It is to address the question "Why would anyone in late second, third, or fourth-century CE Judah-ite society find such mythologizations even remotely plausible; what currency would they have?" Well, in large part such a claim might have currency, because, *generally* speaking, notions of extra-biblical/extra-pentateuchal revelation of law that complements the written law of the Pentateuch seem to have already been entrenched in *some* swaths of Judah-ite society before the emergence of the early rabbinic group. For these Judah-ites, as you already have learned, revelation did not *entirely* end either with Moses, or with the classical prophets, or, as regards Torah law, with that which is written in the Pentateuch. In *various* ways, such views were deemed to fall within the constraints of what I have called the (new) normative framework as work-arounds, the rabbinic ideology of Oral Torah being just one. Admittedly, we cannot know just *how* widely held such ideas were in Judah-ite society before, or at the time of, the advent of the early rabbis. But we can say, given my earlier made remarks, that such notions were espoused by some *who themselves would have believed these ideas to be plausible to (many?) others.*

One could reasonably terminate here this discussion of Judah-ite cultural antecedents to the rabbis' claims about the divinely grounded authority of their halakhic teachings. However, there remain at least two *additional* notions that we might usefully examine. One I shall characterize as "(sometimes secret) revelations to the wise" (of a type that differs from Ben Sira's sensibility of being divinely inspired). These "revelations" are often, although not always, married to the phenomenon of pseudepigraphy, that is, writing under someone else's name. The other is the notion of normative (that is, of revelation-like status) "ancestral traditions," which Josephus adduces to explain how the "philosophy" of the Pharisees, a prominent group of the last several centuries before Jerusalem's destruction by the Romans, differs from that of their contemporaries or adversaries. These phenomena, too, function as work-arounds for the constraints brought about by new normative tenets 5 and 6, and, as you will see, provide additional meaningful context for understanding early rabbinic mythologizations about their *torahs*.

Revelations to the Wise and Retrojective Pseudepigraphy

Remember the Karaites? They were the group of resisters that coalesced sometime after the seventh century CE to challenge the rabbis' claim to monopolistic authority over the halakha. One of the Karaites' critique of the rabbis was essentially this: "What 'Oral Torah'?! You rabbis have derived (much of) your halakha from your scholarship of Judah-ite legal traditions based in the Pentateuch, which process is, in principle, the purview of *any* well-educated Jew. But you rabbis are (additionally) claiming to possess some sort of exclusive (secret?) revelation that no one else but your rabbinic and pre-/proto-rabbinic forebears possessed. This claim is historically incredulous!" Well, the truth is that the early rabbis' claim may not be historical—after all, it is a mythologization. But by the standards of Judah-ite culture in the several centuries preceding the formation of the early rabbinic movement in the second and third centuries CE, the early rabbis' claim is not incredulous at all, because it is not *wholly* unique or novel. The notion that some elite subgroup among the Judah-ites possessed a special or secret revelation, of which other/most Jews were (largely) unaware, seems to have been almost commonplace in the period immediately preceding the advent of the early rabbinic group.[25] The rabbis' notion of Oral Torah was, in fact, only a somewhat unique variation on a fairly common theme or, rather, device, as I shall now explain. That device combines two elements: (1) what I will henceforth call "retrojective pseudepigraphy"; and (2) sometimes special or secret knowledge reserved for a restricted group of the wise (*hakham*, sg.; *hakhamim*, pl.) or the enlightened (*maskil*, sg.; *maskilim*, pl.). Let me explain and elaborate.

Simply put, pseudepigraphy means writing under a pseudonym; an author writes something but hides his/her authorship by attributing the work to someone else—sort of the opposite of plagiarism. Retrojective pseudepigraphy entails choosing as a pseudonym for one's writing some (allegedly) historical figure who lived earlier, before the actual author's time. So, for example, I might write a play and attribute it to William Shakespeare. Why

25. Recall Jassen's scholarship on the matter; see above, n20.

would I do so, and on what justification? There might be many responses to such a question, not all of them patently illegitimate.

Of course, from a literary-historical perspective, the most important case of retrojective pseudepigraphy in ancient Judah-ite society and culture is the attribution of the authorship of the entire Pentateuch to Moses.[26] For the ancient Judah-ites of the period just prior to the early rabbis, this *came to be the accepted meaning of* the notion of the "Torah of Moses" or of "the book of the Torah of Moses"; namely, that Moses authored the Pentateuch.[27] Now, the Pentateuch, more or less as we have it today, was likely fashioned about half a millennium before the Mishnanians' era. But a historical Moses would have lived many centuries earlier than the period in which the Pentateuch was produced. There is a historical irony to this, is there not? In the several centuries just *after* the time that prophecy is said officially to have ended as an established social and cultural institution in Judah-ite society, the Pentateuch is (more or less) completed, and its authorship is retrojectively attributed to the "greatest" of the Israelite prophets, Moses. (This is in and of itself a work-around of new normative tenets 5 and 6.)

The attribution of the authorship of (almost) the entirety of the Pentateuch to Moses is not the only example of retrojective pseudepigraphy in ancient Judah-ite sacred literature. Scholars know that various parts of the book of Isaiah were composed by different authors at different times, but the entirety becomes attributed to Isaiah. Parts of the biblical book of Daniel were obviously written by different authors living after Daniel would have lived (if indeed he is a historical figure at all). But these parts are put "in his mouth" as Daniel's prophetic visions. In this manner, prophetic visions authored after the "official" end of prophecy, after Malachi's

26. Well, almost the entire Pentateuch. E.g., the early rabbis attributed a few bits to Joshua.

27. Early rabbinic literature states unequivocally that Moses authored the Pentateuch (except, as mentioned earlier, a few bits they attribute to Joshua); see BT Bava Batra 14b–15a. But this is hardly the only plausible meaning that might be given to the notion "the Torah of Moses" (*torat Moshe*) or "the book of the Torah of Moses" (*sefer torat Moshe*). The lexicography and grammar of ancient and Middle Hebrew allow for at least two other interpretations: (1) "the [book of the] Torah *from* Moses"; and (2) "the [book of the] Torah *about* Moses." In the first, the book is said to *contain* "the teaching" (*ha-torah*) of Moses. In the second, the book is *about* Moses' career, including an account of his "teaching" (*torato*). In neither interpretation, allowed by the Hebrew, is it necessarily implied that Moses wrote the Pentateuch but only that much of its important content is from/about him. Of course, historically speaking, these two additional and possible translations of the normative Hebrew terms still involve "retrojective pseudepigraphy" of a significant sort, since the legal content of the Pentateuch is still attributed exclusively to Moses. Again, in any case, the early rabbis (and most other Judah-ites) did not seem to go this route.

career, are attributed to a personage, Daniel, who is alleged to have lived in Babylon before Malachi. Instances of retrojective pseudepigraphy in ancient Judah-ite society and culture before the advent of the early rabbis are so numerous that whole books can (and have) been written about pseudepigraphically authored/attributed Judah-ite texts.[28] Indeed, almost all of ancient Jewish apocalyptic writing (that is, alleged prophetic visions of a cataclysmic "end of times" followed by a "new world" reserved for "the just") are retrojective pseudepigraphical writings. And this includes the apocalyptic sections of the latter half of the biblical book of Daniel, which are the only apocalyptic (as distinct from eschatological) visions to have been retained in the canonical Hebrew Scriptures by the rabbis. Evidently, one can declare the era of prophecy to be over, but that does not mean that prophetic or "vision" writing ends. It continues, but gets attributed to a figure who fits within the declared boundaries of the era of prophecy, that is, the period ending with the career of the prophet Malachi.

"Public" Scripture vs. "Secret," Extra-Biblical Revelations to the Wise

The rampant use of retrojective pseudepigraphy provides us with half of the Judah-ite cultural phenomenon under discussion. An almost ubiquitous, accepted Judah-ite literary device, retrojective pseudepigraphy, including retrospectively attributing teachings to Moses, may have served to give cultural currency to the rabbis' claim that their teachings came from Moses, including those that do not appear in the Pentateuch. But recall (or, more accurately, imagine) this Karaite, anti-rabbinic harangue: "But how is it that no one before you rabbis seems to know a number of your allegedly Mosaic, extra-biblical teachings? This must rank as the *best-kept secret* in the history of Judaism. Your claims are inherently implausible!" We may confidently doubt that the rabbis thought them patently implausible, or thought that they would appear ridiculous to other Judah-ites. Why? It is time for us to discuss the notion of special or secret revelations to the wise (*hakham*) or

---

28. As interesting as the topic is, I will skirt questions like: What type of authorial consciousness underlies the phenomenon of retrojective pseudepigraphy? Do these authors simply aim to perpetrate fraud? Or do they believe that they are legitimately "channeling" in some fashion the figures in whose names they are writing? In any case, the phenomenon is so ubiquitous in early Judaism (and perhaps one might say, in early Christianity as well) that I suspect some sort of yes to the second question is appropriate. That said, we cannot enter the psychological state or consciousness of people long dead, especially if they have chosen not to describe that consciousness, as Ben Sira does in ch. 39 of the book he authored.

the enlightened (*maskil*), another concept commonly encountered in pre-rabbinic Judah-ite literature, culture, and society.

Let me begin by rehearsing yet again what I have called the more fully formed, early rabbinic myth of Oral Torah elaborated in the latter third and fourth centuries CE. God revealed to Moses a "whole" Torah, some of which Moses wrote down (in the Pentateuch), and some of which Moses transmitted orally through a chain of masters and disciples to the early rabbis' immediate forebears. It is this whole Torah, both Written and Oral, of which the early rabbis are the self-acclaimed experts, and of which the Mishnah is said by the rabbis to be the most perfect textual expression. Why "oral"? Well, because it involves entire bodies of law *not* found in the (very much written) Pentateuch. If this additional body of God's law *had* been written down, it would have had to have appeared in the Pentateuch in order to satisfy fundamental, normative tenet 5 (stated earlier), would it not? The solution, then, is that this legal tradition, which does *not* appear in the Pentateuch, *did* stem from God's revelation to Moses, which he passed on as oral teachings. Others who *might* have received these extra-biblical teachings via this oral chain of transmission dropped the ball along the way (to badly mix metaphors). Not so the rabbis, so the rabbis themselves say. So, in the early rabbis' view, Oral Torah was not secret, really, it was largely lost and, therefore, unknown, except to the rabbis, of course.[29]

Why might this notion seem plausible? In part, because Judah-ite society in the several centuries preceding the early rabbinic movement's formation was replete with (alleged) ancient revelations that only the few possessed, because they had (allegedly) been kept secret, supposedly on YHWH's instructions. These ideas about special or secret revelations, as you are about to see, are "close cousins" to the rabbis' claims about their Oral Torah, as well as to the early rabbis' self-designation as sages/wise ones (*hakhamin*).

To begin, let me take you back to apocalyptic "vision literature" in ancient Judah-ite society and culture, which literature I earlier adduced as examples of retrojective pseudepigraphy. Very few of these apocalyptic visions of the end of times, involving a future (Armageddon-like) reckoning for the wicked and a redemption of the just, made it into the canonical Hebrew Bible. As I stated earlier, the latter chapters of the biblical book of Daniel

29. And even the rabbis were worried about they themselves "dropping the ball" in the confusion brought about by the two revolts against Roman rule in the land of Israel, which (the rabbis say) is why Judah the Patriarch chose to compose Mishnah—namely, to (re) establish the correct version of the teachings of Oral Torah. This early rabbinic rationale for Judah's efforts is repeated by Sherira in his response to the queries of the sages of Kairouan.

are exceptions that prove the rule.[30] But there are many other examples of noncanonical apocalyptic texts written by Judah-ite authors of the immediately pre-rabbinic era that have survived. And besides being examples of what I have called retrojective pseudepigraphy, most also display another motif. That is that certain revelations are to be kept secret, or more accurately stated, are to become the purview of a future and restrained group of wise or enlightened persons, who are exclusively equipped to understand the meaning and significance of these revelations.

Several times in the apocalyptic parts of the biblical book of Daniel, Daniel is told to "seal up" his account of his prophetic visions. In other words, the text portrays Daniel as having written down what he saw and heard in his visions and then, upon divine instruction, to have secured its content for a future time and for a privileged readership that would understand matters as they were meant to be understood. Take for example, the following verses:

> And the vision [*mar-eh*] of the evening and the morning that was spoken [*ne-emar*] [to you]—it is true; and you [Daniel], seal up [*setom*[the vision [*ha-hazon*]. (Dan 8:26; trans. my own)

> And you, Daniel, seal up [*setom*] these matters, and seal up [*hatom*] the book until the time of the end. (Dan 12:4; trans. my own)

> Go, Daniel, for the matters are doubly sealed [*setumin ve-hatumim*] until the time of the end. [In the interim period,] many shall cleanse themselves, and whiten themselves, and refine themselves, but the wicked ones will have made themselves [more] wicked; and all the wicked will not understand [the matters revealed to all when unsealed], but the enlightened [*ve-ha-maskilim*] shall understand [them]. (Dan 12:9–10; trans. my own)

This motif—revelation, sealed for some future time and for special recipients who will fully grasp its intent—becomes a commonplace theme in Jewish apocalyptic literature written in the period just preceding the advent of the early rabbinic movement. And, at the risk of overstating matters, all exemplars of this literature display retrojective pseudepigraphy to boot.

Another such Judah-ite (partly apocalyptic-themed) text is 4 Ezra (comprising chs. 3 to 14 of the apocryphal book 2 Esdras, which is included in some Christian collections of the Old Testament). Fourth Ezra

---

30. The apocalyptic chapters of Daniel seem to have ridden on the coattails of the first half of the book, and thereby made it into the rabbinic canon of biblical Scriptures.

was likely written in Hebrew or Aramaic near the end of the first century CE, about a century before Mishnah's composition. The original Hebrew or Aramaic text of the work has not survived, again because 4 Ezra did not "make the cut" when the early rabbinic movement defined the parameters of their canon of the Hebrew Bible. But 4 Ezra was among the many Jewish texts adopted (in translation) by early Christians, who then added two more chapters at its beginning and two more at its conclusion to give the new whole (2 Esdras) a decidedly Christian slant.

As the name 4 Ezra implies, this Jewish first-century CE work is attributed by its author to Ezra, the fifth/fourth-century BCE figure now so familiar to you. And the principal personage throughout this author's text is also Ezra. But the Ezra of (most of) 4 Ezra is not characterized as the scribe of priestly descent, which is his profile in the biblical books of Ezra and Nehemiah. Rather, the Ezra of 4 Ezra is a prophet, and some of his alleged prophetic visions are decidedly apocalyptic in theme and/or literary form.

Now, given this volume's particular issues, it is the last chapter of 4 Ezra (= 2 Esdras 14) that stands out. And I have no doubt that you, my volume's readers, will by now immediately recognize why as soon as the relevant passages are presented. What follows are a selection of passages from the chapter in question, and if you have never before read 4 Ezra but have any familiarity with the biblical book of Exodus, your jaw is about to drop.

> On the third day, while I was sitting under an oak, behold, a voice came out of the bush opposite me and said, "Ezra, Ezra." And I said, "Here I am, Lord," and I rose to my feet. Then he said to me, "I revealed myself in a bush and spoke to Moses, when my people were in bondage in Egypt; and I sent him and led my people out of Egypt; and I led him up on Mount Sinai, where I kept him with me many days; and I told him many wonderous things, and showed him the secrets of the times and declared to him the end of times. Then I commanded him saying, "These words you shall publish openly, and these you shall keep secret." (2 Esd 14:1–6)

Now, God tells Ezra to exhort the people:

> Reprove your people, comfort the lowly among them, and instruct those that are wise. (2 Esd 14:13)

But Ezra expresses to God his concern that

> the world lies in darkness, and its inhabitants are without light. For thy law has been burned, and so no one knows the things which have been done, or will be done by thee. (2 Esd 14:20–21)

So the Ezra of 4 Ezra makes a request of God.

> If then I have found favor before thee, send the Holy Spirit into
> me, and I will write everything that has happened in the world
> from the beginning, [and] the things that were written in thy
> law, that men may be able to find the path, and that those who
> wish to live in the last days may live [and not be destroyed for
> lack of knowledge of the law]. (2 Esd 14:23).

Ezra's concern is addressed by YHWH with the following instructions.

> He answered me and said, "Go and gather the people, and tell
> them not to seek you for forty days. But prepare for yourself
> many writing tablets, and take with you Sarea, Dabria, Selemia,
> Ethanus, and Asiel—these five, because they are trained to write
> rapidly; and you shall come [back] here, and I will light in your
> heart the lamp of understanding, which shall not be put out un-
> til what you are about to write is finished. And when you have
> finished, some things you shall make public, and some things
> you shall deliver in secret to the wise." (2 Esd 14:23–26)

This chapter of 4 Ezra (14 of 2 Esdras) then ends with this account, beginning at verse 42.

> And the Most High gave understanding to the five men, and by
> turns they wrote what was dictated [to them by Ezra], in charac-
> ters that they did not know. . . . So during the forty days ninety-
> four books were written. And when the forty days were ended,
> the Most High spoke to me, saying, "Make public the twenty-
> four books that you wrote first and let the worthy and the un-
> worthy read them; but keep the seventy that were written last, in
> order to give them to the wise among your people. For in them
> is the spring of understanding, the fountain of wisdom, and the
> river of knowledge." And I [Ezra] did so. (2 Esd 14:42–48)

Astounding! Ezra is the new Moses. The "calling" of Ezra by a voice issuing from a bush echoes the biblical account of Moses' calling. Ezra receives
God's complete revelation over a forty-day period (like Moses, as narrated
in Exodus), which divine teachings Ezra's appointed scribes write down.
Why this renewed revelation to Ezra? Because, according to 4 Ezra, Moses'
original has allegedly been destroyed (supposedly in the cataclysm of the
destruction of the Solomon's Temple by the Babylonians in 586 BCE). But
there are new motifs in these passages in 4 Ezra that are not just repetitions
of the narrative of Exodus. Moses' original revelation is said here to have had
a publicly proclaimed/published part and a secret part. And so the revelation

to Ezra is said to have resulted in ninety-four books, only the first twenty-four of which are to be made public. The other seventy are transmitted only to the wise. I will not dwell on the attempts to identify these seventy books. (Such attempts, in my mind, if not entirely futile, do not take us very far.) The first twenty-four probably refer to the collection of Jewish Scriptures in the author's time (that is, near the end of the first century CE), which by tradition (in some circles, at least) was set at this number of books. But the gist and importance of this passage for this volume is clear. A late first-century CE Jew understood that God had revealed a revelation in two parts, first to Moses and then to Ezra, "the second Moses." The first part comprises the written Scriptures known to the (Jewish) public at large; the second (larger) part is another body of revelatory teachings reserved for a select few, whom the text denotes as the wise. Why? Because only the wise have the wherewithal to handle it ("for in them is . . . understanding").

How far a cultural/ideological leap is it from the views represented in 4 Ezra about a dual (written) revelation, part of which is reserved for the wise, to the early rabbis' mythologization that they are the privileged sage-custodians (hakhamim) of an Oral Torah from Moses that complements and completes Moses' Written Torah? Not a far leap at all! The early rabbis' mythologization of the basis for their privileged knowledge and authority has clear antecedents in Judah-ite society, within which notions are already circulating about a dual revelation, only part of which (the Scriptures) is known to the Judah-ite public at large. The myth of Oral Torah would not have seemed that implausible to the early rabbis' hoped-for clientele. After all, how much more or less plausible is (1) an alleged oral transmission among the wise of a supposed second part of Moses' revelation than (2) a written transmission that is kept secret by and for a cadre of the wise?! If the author of 4 Ezra supposed that a Judah-ite audience should be receptive to his notions, then the early rabbinic authors of their myth of Oral Torah could have supposed likewise.

Scripture Plus the Pharisees' Ancestral Traditions

As I intimated above, yet another work-around for normative tenets 5 and 6 that predates and prefigures the early rabbis' mythologizations of their extra-biblical teachings and of Mishnah's origins as Oral Torah is that of the Pharisees, who are said (by the ancient Jewish historian Josephus) to have insisted on the legal validity/authority of their ancestral traditions—again, laws and practices not found in biblical Scriptures. So, who (or what) were the Pharisees? On the strength of evidence provided by Josephus, and by the Christian Gospels and the book of Acts, the Pharisees were an active and seemingly increasingly influential religious party in (or with influence upon) the administration of the Jerusalem temple and Judean society in the last century and a half BCE and the first century CE.

According to Josephus, the Pharisees' influence over Judah-ite law and practice was such that in the early first century BCE, the Hasmonean priest-king Alexander Jannaeus fought a civil war with rebels said to be loyal to Pharisaic teachings.[31] Jannaeus put down the revolt and conducted mass executions of Pharisees and their families.[32] Jannaeus was succeeded by his widow, Salome Alexandra, who restored the Pharisaic party's influence.[33] It is likely that it is because of this enduring prominence that, as a rhetorical device, the Gospels' portrayal of Jesus' authority is contrasted with that of the Pharisees (e.g., Matt 9:14; 15:1–9; 23:23 // Luke 11:42). The device works only because the Gospel writers assume that their intended readership understands the significance of the Pharisees (along with the importance of the priestly class, of course) in Judah-ite society of Jesus' time. Acts's identification of Gamaliel as a Pharisee (in Acts 5:34–39) and of the apostle Paul as an *ex*-Pharisee (in Acts 26:5) relies on similar assumptions about Pharisaic influence in the land of Israel, as does Paul's own appeal to his Pharisaic roots and education (e.g., in his Epistle to the Philippians 3:5–6). But what is the relevance of the Pharisees to this chapter's discussion?

Among those things advocated by the Pharisees, according to Josephus, is the legal validity of ancestral traditions of practice or customs that supplement the laws found in the Pentateuch.[34] For those of you who have already read books about early Christianity and early Judaism, or if you are already familiar with the Gospels, you will probably expect this discussion of the Pharisees' ancestral traditions to be the pinnacle of this chapter's account of Judah-ite social, cultural, and religious trends that prefigure and underlie the early rabbinic movement, their halakhic teachings, and their notion of Oral Torah (that is, early rabbinic law not found in the Written Torah).[35] So, let me put all my cards on the table right now. Here are three

31. Josephus, *Antiquities* 13.298.

32. Josephus, *Antiquities* 13.372–383.

33. Josephus, *Antiquities* 13.400–404; 18.15.

34. Josephus, *Antiquities* 13.297, 404; 17.41. For a very concise but cogent treatment of Josephus's references to the Pharisees' ancestral traditions, see Goodman, "Note on Josephus."

35. E.g., Ben-Zion, *Roadmap to the Heavens*, 102–14, is adamant that the Pharisees were *the* immediate and most important forebears of the early rabbinic group. As you will see, I think the evidence demands that claims to this effect need to be much more qualified.

claims that I stand by concerning the Pharisees as precursors to the early rabbinic movement.

1. I think it is likely, and perhaps even undeniable, that Pharisaic ideas and practices—their ancestral traditions—substantially informed and survived in the early rabbinic movement and its halakha, although not always or necessarily because these ideas and practices came exclusively from the Pharisees. However, it is too often the case that this first claim, which I would characterize as a qualified, warranted conclusion, functions as an unwarranted premise, in ways that I shall explain shortly.

2. I also think it highly likely, if not undeniable, that a number of the prominent, early founders of the early rabbinic group were Pharisees. However, as with the first claim, it is too often the case that this second claim, which, again, is a qualified, warranted conclusion, functions as an unwarranted premise. The early rabbis of the second and early third centuries CE were likely not (just or only) reworked Pharisees; Mishnah and immediately post-mishnaic rabbinic documents hardly ever refer to Pharisees and hardly ever portray an early rabbi as being a Pharisee. I shall return to this point a little later.

3. While the Pharisees' notion of the legal validity of extra-biblical "ancestral traditions" (Josephus's term) is part of a family of ideas circulating in some swaths of Judah-ite society that may have provided the early rabbis' notion of Oral Torah with an air of plausibility.[36] No

36. In fact, I am inclined to view Josephus's appeal to ancestral traditions when characterizing the Pharisees as building upon two cultural phenomena that would plausibly have been relevant to Josephus. One has to do with Josephus's Roman patrons. The Roman legal system accommodated two categories of laws, Roman "civil law" and "laws of the nations" (that is, of groups that were not Roman citizens). Romans touted their superiority, but they also respected traditional, ancestral, legal systems of other nations, when these were faithfully and consistently maintained and applied (within the overarching framework of Roman governance, of course). Josephus, therefore is in essence "recommending" the Pharisees to his Roman patrons, which may also be why Josephus, a priest, claims to be a Pharisee. The other phenomenon that may be at work here is one analyzed by Sivertsev in *Households, Sects, and Origins*, esp. 272ff. Sivertsev maintains that until the late Hellenistic period, Second Temple-era Judah-ite law and ritual practice remained significantly a matter of household or clan tradition, viewed within each household or clan to be authentic, authoritative, and (somehow) divinely sanctioned, and complementary to the centrally promulgated laws and practices stemming from the Jerusalem temple priests and from the Pentateuch. According to Sivertsev, in the latter part of the Second Temple era, associations and "membership" or allegiance to them began to take the place of household allegiances, and these associations became the new loci of ancestral traditions. Such developments would go a long way in contextualizing both the Pharisees' and the early rabbis' self-understanding

ancient text attributes to any Pharisee a belief anything like the early rabbinic concept of Oral Torah.

For me fully to justify these three claims about the early rabbis' relationship to the pre-rabbinic Pharisaic movement is beyond the scope of this book and would itself require a book-length discussion. That said, the identification of the early rabbis with the Pharisees is so entrenched in the mind of the well-read public interested in ancient Judaism and early Christianity that I feel compelled not only to summarize briefly my stance in support of the three claims just made but also, and especially, to explain what I mean in asserting that claims 1 and 2, which are qualified, warranted conclusions, sometimes/often function *inappropriately* as premises.

Claims 1 and 2, taken together, assert that early rabbis are significantly influenced by Pharisees, and some of the earliest rabbinic figures undoubtedly were Pharisees. *But* the ensemble of early rabbis was not just the wholesale continuation of the Pharisees. The sole passages in Mishnah in which any early rabbi is implied to be a Pharisee are two successive pericopae in m. Yadayim 4, in which Rabbi Yohanan ben Zakkai is portrayed as defending two specific, expressly Pharisaic legal positions on uncleanness against Sadducean/Boethusian critics. Other passages implying that Yohanan is a Pharisee are grounded in those two pericopae in m. Yadayim. There is not much more than this, as far as early rabbis being *designated* in early rabbinic literature as Pharisees!

Let us consider, by way of example, another vector commonly followed by those who assert a near-wholesale identification of early rabbinic halakha with Pharisaic practice. It concerns purity rules, generally, and their application to meals (taken together[37]), specifically. Now, there are a number of passages in Mishnah, our core early rabbinic text, concerning persons designated as fellows (*haver*, sg.; *haverim*, pl.). These fellows eat all (or some?) of their meals *together* in a state of cleanness normally incumbent upon a Judah-ite participating in the (and by the rabbis' time, no longer functioning) sacrificial cult of the temple in Jerusalem. Such fellows, according to Mishnah, are also careful to eat produce for which the priestly gifts and tithes have already been designated. Many modern scholars have assumed not only (1) that all early rabbis practiced these "fellowship" rules (sometimes or all of the time) but also (2) that before the advent of the early rabbinic movement, these fellowship rules were quintessential,

---

that their associations were the faithful "keepers" of authoritative legal traditions and practices that complemented those of the Pentateuch.

37. I specify "together," because even those who are unclean must eat, of course. So, what we are talking about is "table fellowship."

distinguishing markers of Pharisees (only). On what basis? Because the Gospels brand the Pharisees as showing *excessive* concern for the rules of uncleanness and tithing, in contrast to Jesus' alleged, more human-centered approach to the demands of Torah Law. Ergo, early rabbis were Pharisees, full stop. However, the Gospel evidence is a flimsy basis for asserting that fellowship meals eaten in a state of priestly-like purity are a quintessential, distinguishing feature of members of the Pharisaic religious party. In fact, the Gospels' treatment (and critique) of the Pharisees implies that many Judah-ites kept some form of purity rules when eating regular meals. And, furthermore, there is no pre-rabbinic evidence about Pharisees' fellowship meals. On the other hand, the sectarian group at Qumran on the Dead Sea coast—the group that left us the Dead Sea Scrolls—certainly did use such "pure fellowship meals" as a central feature of their group life and piety. These sectarians at Qumran were most likely a group that schismed from the Sadducees (who virulently opposed the Pharisees), and the Dead Sea Sect's literature, it has been argued, reflects a Saducean legal legacy. One way or another, one cannot assert that pure table fellowship per se was a distinguishing marker of the Pharisees.

So why have some concluded that pure table fellowship was a particular marker of the Pharisees, and why have I chosen to drone on about this? Well, if you take the position that the early rabbis are the wholesale continuation of the Pharisees and that early rabbinic law and practice is, therefore, Pharisaic law and practice, then pure fellowship meals are a (distinguishing) Pharisaic practice that survived in the early rabbinic movement. This is a "backwards" or "circular" argument! And I wanted you to see this as an example of the type of problems that frequently have haunted thinking about the Pharisees' historical relationship to the early rabbinic movement. Let me now make the broader point, concerning which the case of alleged, quintessentially Pharisaic pure fellowship meals is an example.

As the preceding suggests, it is unwarranted simply to see the early rabbis as the continuation of the Pharisaic group, despite the highly probable influence of the latter on the former. Nevertheless, the near total identification of the two groups was commonplace in modern scholarship. Indeed, so entrenched was this view among modern scholars until at least the 1970s (and, arguably, beyond[38]) that many routinely wrote about "Pharisaic-rabbinic Judaism," seemingly obliterating any distinction between the two groups. This often resulted in inappropriate use of evidence to "fill in" the profile of the Pharisees. How so? Well, for example, what (relatively little) we are told about the Pharisees in pre-rabbinic texts (such as in the Gospels

---

38. See Ben-Zion, *Roadmap to the Heavens*, 102–14.

and in Josephus's writings) was, in the writings of these scholars, *rampantly supplemented* by what (substantially more) we know about the early rabbis from their literature. So, following this modus operandi, if you want to know more about actual Pharisaic practice, attribute early rabbinic halakhic positions to the Pharisees. That, in my opinion, is a serious problem, based, as I have said, on circular reasoning: the Pharisees' traditions (about which we have little evidence) are the same as the early rabbinic halakha (about which we have a lot of evidence), because the early rabbinic halakha is the wholesale continuation of the Pharisees' legal traditions. As cultural-historical reasoning goes, this is simply "not kosher"!

Why should the foregoing concern us, given this book's discussion? Well, one result of such (mal) practice, was this: the early rabbinic notion of Oral Torah was routinely said to have originated with the Pharisees and was said to be the real meaning of Josephus's Pharisees' ancestral traditions. But this whole scholarly edifice is a "house of cards," the foundation of which is (1) a historical reconstruction of who the Pharisees were that is based on an illegitimate "mishmash" of evidence, and (2) a warrantless, near-total assimilation of the early rabbinic movement with the Pharisaic movement, of whom the early rabbis are inappropriately said to be the wholesale continuation.

In my view, what is left, once the house of cards collapses, are my three rather more restrained claims. And it is in light of these claims that we may now bring this discussion of Pharisees to a conclusion. As I maintain in the first half of claim 3: the Pharisees' notion of the legal validity of extra-biblical "ancestral traditions" (Josephus' term) is one example of a family of ideas circulating in some swaths of Judah-ite society that may have provided the early rabbis' notion of Oral Torah, passed down (the literal meaning of "tradition") through a chain of teachers and disciples according to Avot, with an air of plausibility.

So where do we stand in our discussion? In the preceding pages, I have served up the stew comprised of Judah-ite concepts about ongoing and/or supplemental revelation. Why specify "ongoing"? Because by the late Hellenistic and early Roman periods, an "official" ideological framework proclaimed that the era of classical prophecy had ended several centuries earlier. In what sense do I use "supplemental"? Various Judah-ite groups recognized the (divinely sanctioned) authority of extra-scriptural teachings, including teachings about Judah-ite law and religious rites that do not appear in the Pentateuch (which by the late Hellenistic and early Roman eras was wholly attributed to Moses, in what had become a highly Moses-centric ideological environment). With such a cultural background in view, it is plausible that the earliest rabbis viewed the outcomes of their intense study as being divinely inspired; at least, that is my *speculative* hunch. When, over the third and fourth centuries CE, the early rabbinic group articulated their more fully formed ideology of an Oral Torah transmitted by God to Moses, and thereafter taught by generations of teachers to their disciples down to Judah the Patriarch, to whom the production of Mishnah is attributed, the early rabbis' claims would have been made against a well-established cultural background that valued Moses-centrism but gave standing in several ways to post-Mosaic, extra-pentateuchal traditions, including halakhic teachings.

If my presentation of the ingredients of this stew is the meal I have served (to press the metaphor), I do have a dessert to offer. It takes the form of evidence in patristic Christian literature from the third to fifth centuries CE that rants about "second" or "repeated" teachings viewed (inappropriately, as far as these Christian writers are concerned) by contemporary Jews as authoritative. Why is this evidence "tantalizing"? Let me explain.

The Jews' Second/Repeated (Teaching) (deuterosis, sg.) and Its Teachers/Repeaters (deuteroseis, pl.) According to the Early Christian Fathers

Now, would it not be advantageous to know that pre-rabbinic conceptions of an authoritative body of extra-biblical teachings were in fact widely understood and accepted by some significant proportion of the Judah-ite community generally (that is, outside of early rabbinic circles themselves) *at the very time* that the Amoraic rabbis of the third and fourth centuries CE developed and propounded their myth of an Oral Torah, of which the rabbis claimed particular (exclusive?) mastery? What a gift of evidence that would be! Unfortunately, with few exceptions, the surviving texts authored by *Jews* in the land of Israel for the late second and subsequent several centuries CE are ones produced by the early rabbis themselves.

That said, in this period, there *is*, however, a group of authors who are (usually, and perhaps uncritically, understood to be) non-Jews for whom Jewish culture, tradition, and ideas are, nonetheless, critically important. I have in mind early Christian patristic writers, who, on the one hand, rely on Jewish teachings and texts as an authoritative basis for Christian belief and practice, and, on the other hand, progressively define Christians' distinctive identity apart from that of the Jewish people. And, lo and behold, a number of third- and fourth-century Christian authors, some of whom had strong ties to the land of Israel, comment on especially learned Jews possessing and acknowledging the authority of a body of supplementary, extra-biblical teachings that the Jewish masses do not possess for lack of higher education.

These patristic writers, who include Origen (first half of the third century), Eusebius (early and mid-fourth century), Epiphanius (latter fourth century), and Jerome (late fourth and early fifth century), refer (mostly in Greek) to this body of teachings as the Jews' *deuterosis* and designate the learned among the Jews who know these teachings as the *deuteroseis*. The following passages from the writings of Eusebius will serve as examples. Speaking of education and learning among the Jews generally, Eusebius states:

> For which cause also among us those who are newly admitted and in an immature condition, as if infants in soul, have the reading of the sacred Scriptures imparted to them in a very simple way, with the injunction that they must believe what is brought forward as words of God. But those who are in a more advanced condition, and as it were grown grey in mind, are permitted to dive into the deeps, and test the meaning of the words: and these the Hebrews were wont to name "Deutero-tists" (*deuteroseis*) as being interpreters and expounders of the meaning of the Scriptures.[39]

And again:

> And among the Hebrews also it is the custom to teach the his-tories of the inspired Scriptures to those of infantine souls in a very simple way just like any fables, but to teach those of a trained mental habit the more profound and doctrinal views of the histories by means of the so-called Deuterosis and explana-tion of the thoughts that are unknown to the multitude.[40]

In another work, Eusebius even identifies the well-known ancient Jewish historian Josephus as one of the "learned" among the *deuteroseis* of Jews, in order to justify supplementing what Eusebius reads in Scripture from Josephus's writings.

> This is what the Book of Kings establishes. But Josephus care-fully studied the additional *comments of the expounders* [*deu-teroseis*] as well, and a Hebrew of the Hebrews as he was, hear his description of the events of those times.[41]

Eusebius lived much of his life in the land of Israel, as did Origen, a church father of the previous century. Origen, too, uses the term *deuterosis* as a syn-onym for authoritative, extra-biblical Jewish tradition. And Epiphanius, the

---

39. Eusebius, *Praeparatio Evangelica* (trans. Gifford), bk. 12, ch. 1.
40. Eusebius, *Praeparatio Evangelica* (trans. Gifford), bk. 12, ch. 4.
41. Eusebius, *Proof of the Gospel* (trans. Ferrar), bk. 12, ch. 4; emphasis added.

late fourth-century Christian writer based in Cyprus, explains that the Jews' ancestral traditions, referred to in Matt 15:2, is their *deuterosis*.[42]

Is the use of the Greek term *deuterosis* generally, or its use as an explanation of what is meant by the Pharisees'/Jews' ancestral traditions (or, "traditions of the elders," *paradosin ton prebyteron*) in the Gospel of Matthew, significant for our discussion here? Probably yes. And here is why. *Deuterosis* derives from the Greek for "two" and carries the connotation in these patristic authors' writings of "second," "secondary," or "supplemental." So, Eusebius, Origen before him, and Epiphanius after him understand that among the Jews there is a second, secondary, or supplemental body of authoritative teachings that the especially learned among the Jews possess.

Eusebius, in fact, names the late first-century Jewish historian Josephus as one such learned person—"Josephus carefully studied the additional *comments of the expounders* [*deuteroseis*] as well." And Eusebius does this for a particular reason. He wishes to justify supplementing what the Bible says about Ozias (aka Uziyahu), king of Judah, with material from Josephus's work. Appealing to Josephus's study of the *deuterosis* permits Eusebius legitimately to conflate Josephus's narrative and the Bible's narrative, because the *deuterosis*, in the possession of especially learned Jews, is understood by Eusebius to be as authoritative as the content of the Scripture itself. In order to confirm that Eusebius understood this supplementary, second, or secondary but nonetheless authoritative tradition to be *extra*-biblical, we need look only at the original Greek phrases that the English translator, Ferrar, had in front of him. The Greek reads: *tas exothen ioudaikas deuteroseis*—literally, "the outside Judaic *deuteroseis* (pl.)." "Outside" of what? In context, what is clearly meant is "outside" of Scripture, that is, extra-biblical.

In light of the foregoing, a number of questions occur to me. First, what is understood to be the range of content of this *deuterosis* in the minds of these early Christian writers? Well, if one considers Eusebius's use of Josephus to supplement biblical narrative, then part of the *deuterosis* is narrative material. When one considers the use of *deuterosis* to explain the Gospel of Matthew's reference to the Pharisees'/Jews' ancestral traditions (Matt 5:2), then part of the *deuterosis* concerns proper practice, that is, Judaic law.

Second, can we understand the early Christian use of *deuterosis* to imply that these authors understand it to be an oral tradition? I do not think so. Eusebius appeals to Josephus's very much *written* work as *deuterosis/deuteroseis*.

Third, do these early Christian authors associate knowledge of the Judaic *deuterosis* with early rabbis in particular? Well, neither Eusebius nor

---

42. See Horbury, "New Testament," 6–9.

Origen do. However, by the time one gets to, for example, Jerome, who was active at the end of the fourth century and first several decades of the fifth century, one sees a tendency to associate the *deuterosis* with a few notable early rabbinic figures mentioned in the Mishnah and in other allegedly Tannaitic rabbinic traditions. Jerome, for example, mentions as prominent authorities of the *deuterosis* personages whose names clearly are hellenizations/latinizations or transliterations of the names of Hillel, Shammai, Akiva, and Judah (either Rabbi Judah b. Ilai or Rabbi Judah the Patriarch?).[43] What do I make of this? Origen, Eusebius, and Jerome all spent significant periods of time in the land of Israel. But it is not until Jerome that the *deuterosis* is clearly attributed to early rabbinic luminaries by name. To me, this suggests that by the end of the fourth century CE and/or the beginning of the fifth century, rabbis had become a more prominent cadre among the well-recognized, highly educated class of the land of Israel. Therefore, as reflected in Jerome, it was the rabbis' *deuterosis/deuteroseis* that was increasingly known to others (and appears to have been sought out by Jerome in his effort to gain expertise in the Jewish Scriptures and interpretive tradition).

What is the upshot of all of the foregoing for this chapter's objective, namely, to explore what social or cultural currency the early rabbis' notion of an Oral Torah (that supplements and completes the Written Torah) might have had in Juhah-ite society of the third or fourth centuries CE? We do not see evidence for an established pre-rabbinic ideology of an oral transmission of extra-scriptural teachings originating with Moses. That said, we have seen evidence for a family of notions and ideologies that assert that an authoritative body of teachings, known to the wise and often understood to be revelation, supplements and completes the content of Scripture. The early rabbis' ideology seems clearly to fall within the set of this family of notions—enough to give that ideology an air of plausibility, at least for those inclined to become clients of the early rabbis' teachings, instructions, and arbitrations of their Judaic lives.

43. See Horbury, "New Testament," 6–9. Perhaps it is at this point that Mishnah, which also derives from the (Hebrew) term for "two," "second," and "repeat," becomes associated in the minds of early Christian writers, like Jerome, with the *deuterosis* referred to by the likes of Origen and Eusebius.

6

Elements of Greco-Roman, Near Eastern, and Diaspora Jewish Culture and the Currency of the Early Rabbinic Profile

L ET US TAKE STOCK of where we are at this juncture. Part 2 of this volume focuses on the second of two questions at the heart this book. That second question was: What did the early rabbis think (or might others have perceived) they were *like*? In chapter 1, I discussed the importance of this line of inquiry. Permit me briefly to rehearse that discussion here.

The early rabbis established a profile of particular expertise, grounded in a specific scholarship, Mishnah study, that characterized members of their newly fashioned group. Elements of that profile, along with the early rabbis' seminal literary creation, the Mishnah, were mythologized as rooted in a tradition transmitted (orally) via an alleged, many centuries-long chain of master-teachers and their disciples. Elements of this myth of the chain of tradition are clearly evident in early rabbinic sources by the mid-third century CE. The chain, according to the myth, began with Moses ("our rabbi"), whose master-teacher was God, and continued to Rabbi Judah the Patriarch, to whom the authorship of Mishnah is ascribed. Together, the profile and myth are intended to establish the rabbis as *the* authorities in the realm of Judaic teachings, especially in matters of halakha, the "Way" one is to live one's life in accordance with Torah, in both its written (that is, scriptural) and oral components. Neither birthright (as in the case of kings, clan nobility, local elders/chieftains, and the Levitical/priestly caste) nor charismatic/prophetic gifts have anything to do with that authority, even though the biblical Scriptures consistently reflects and validates just these authority figures. Rather, lifelong scholarship (of the right kind with the right kind of teacher) does. With a few notable exceptions that prove the rule, the Judah-ite biblical texts do not tend to place scholars at the very apex of systems of power and authority. Rather, highly literate, highly educated persons play "supporting roles" to those in power by reason of their birth or charisma. So, in essence, our second question asks: Why would the profile and myth of origins of the early rabbis' expertise be expected to have an air of plausibility for the rabbis themselves, or for Jews at large in the land of Israel in the late second or third centuries CE? Put in other terms, why might the early rabbis' claims and profile have had currency in the social and/or cultural context of Roman-ruled Judea?

In the previous chapter, and notwithstanding what I have just said about biblical norms, you and I began exploring answers to this query by considering a number of well-attested cultural/social roles and shared Judah-ite ideas that prefigured the early rabbis' profile and their claims to possess special, authoritative knowledge. We saw that this early rabbinic profile and the rabbis' mythologizations seem to fit into a family of already existent roles, notions, and ideologies evident in pre-rabbinic Judah-ite society. This family of roles and notions would have lent credence to the plausibility of the early rabbis' normative profile and justifying myth. (And we may well speculate that, simultaneously, the social upheavals of Judah-ite society resulting from the two failed revolts against Roman rule probably went some way in shaking the foundations of more biblically traditional forms of power and authority in Judea, just as did the Babylonian destruction of Jerusalem in 586 BCE.) So where do we go from here? The answer lies in considering that Judah-ite society and culture, both at the time of the early rabbinic movement's formation and during the many centuries that preceded the advent of the early rabbis, were and had always been part and parcel of social and cultural currents of the lands surrounding it.

It Is a Big (and Small) World after All!

The early rabbinic group was not only part and parcel of Judah-ite society and culture of the land of Israel in the Roman imperial era. The early rabbis and other Jews in their homeland were part of Near Eastern/Mediterranean society of the time. In fact, since ancient times, the land of Israel (like the rest of the Levant) was located, for good and for ill, at a strategic crossroads or boundary. Limiting ourselves to land routes for the moment, consider the fact that the land of Israel constituted a kind of narrow highway between Asia Minor and Egypt, and between Mesopotamia and Egypt. Why "for good *and* for ill"? For good, because the land of Israel during the Bronze and Iron Ages was at a nexus of cultural exchange between the relatively more developed civilizations of Eastern Asia Minor (the Hittites), Mesopotamia (Sumer, Babylon, and Assyria), and Egypt. For ill, because insofar as these developed and militarily powerful civilizations sought from time to time to subdue one another, the land of Israel and adjacent territory often suffered from being sometimes the buffer zone, sometimes the military highway, and sometimes the battleground for these power struggles. From the period of the confederation of Israelite clans during the latter centuries of the second millennium BCE to the fall of the kingdom of Judah to the Babylonians in 597 BCE (or more precisely, over the course of 605 to 597 BCE), the ancient Israelites had to deal with Egyptian, Assyrian, and Babylonian strategic interests—the Israelites being tributary to, allied with, or subdued by one or another of these great powers.

After the outright destruction of Jerusalem by the Babylonians in 586 BCE, this situation did not change; only the cast of imperial powers did. Consequently, with the possible exception of nearly a century of Hasmonean-led, Judah-ite home rule from about the mid-second century BCE to almost the mid-first century BCE, the Jews of the land of Israel were, from Ezra and Nehemiah's era to the Muslim conquest of the Middle East, ruled by a succession of enveloping empires. Over that period, the Judah-ite homeland was subject to Persian-Median kings (principally the Achaemenid dynasty); Alexander the Great of Macedon; Alexander's successing Hellenistic empires (notably, the Ptolemies to the south and the Seleucids to the north); Rome; and the Byzantine-Roman state.[1]

So much for the political, military, and administrative positioning of the land of Israel among powerful neighbors who had designs on one another. What about the cultural side of matters?

Before Alexander's conquest of Asia Minor and the Near East, ancient Israel, as already intimated, was significantly influenced by the relatively advanced cultures of Mesopotamia and Egypt. The influences of Mesopotamian literature, language, and law are evident in biblical literature. For example, that the biblical creation and flood narratives echo the Mesopotamian Enuma Elish and Gilgamesh epics has been written about since the latter nineteenth century. And the same may be said of

---

1. For a very brief period just before the Muslim conquest in the seventh century, the Sassanid-Persian Empire wrested the land of Israel from Byzantine rule.

resemblances of many laws in Hammurabi's law code (c. mid-eighteenth century BCE) and injunctions in the biblical book of the covenant in Exod 21:1—22:16. As regards Egyptian cultural and literary influence, one may, for example, point to the still ongoing scholarly debate as to whether a chunk of the biblical book of Proverbs is only indirectly dependent or directly dependent upon the Egyptian wisdom text called the Teachings of Amenemope.[2] For our purposes, it does not matter whether Proverbs is imitation or outright plagiarism; it is but one of many attestations that the literati of the land of Israel breathed in the cultural air of their Egyptian counterparts, as well as that of the Mesopotamians.

After Alexander's conquest, the culture of the Near East, the land of Israel included, may be said to be tripartite. Some proportion of the population (especially rural inhabitants) clung to their *local*, pre-Alexander cultural patterns. More "urbane" segments of the population in the Near East fell into two broad categories. One group, the outright hellenists, adopted and pressed for the adoption of predominantly Macedonian-Greek culture. Such groups were strongly allied—politically, culturally, socially, and economically—with the ethnic Greeks and Macedonians who had settled in the Near East after Alexander's conquest in the many new or reconstituted, self-governing, Greek-Macedonian constitutional cities (the *polis*), such as Alexandria in Egypt. Other Greek cities were strung as pearls across the northern land of Israel and adjacent regions. And from the books of the Maccabees, we may consider that an influential party in second-century BCE Jerusalem petitioned the Seleucid monarch for a charter to reconstitute Jerusalem as a constitutional Greek *polis*. In contrast, other more or less urbane groups in the Near East fell somewhere in between the former two—a kind of mushy middle, spread out along a continuum—neither fully rejecting their native cultures nor rejecting that of the Greeks and Macedonians. Some ideologically embraced Hellenism, but did so by expressly reinterpreting their native heritage and practices to be exemplars (and even antecedents) of the best that Hellenism had to offer. A first-century CE Alexandrian Jew, Philo, was such a one. He touted his reinvented Moses and the biblical tradition as having anticipated by many centuries Plato, Middle Platonists, and Stoics. What is the implied inference? *Post hoc, ergo propter hoc*; Plato et al. adapted their philosophy from Moses' teachings. Other urbane groups ideologically rejected hellenization, but as an urbane social stratum in a cosmopolitan, somewhat pluralistic context, these groups had to temper that ideology by adopting enough Hellenism to survive and thrive. I think this would describe the early rabbis' "comfort level" with

---

2. Ruffle, "Teaching of Amenemope"; Emerton, "Teaching of Amenemope."

Hellenism, and it may have worked well for them, because most/many of the early rabbinic movement's members lived and sought to serve in what I earlier called second-tier cities and towns in the land of Israel.[3]

The Hellenistic kingdoms in the Near East gave way to Roman rule just before the mid-first century BCE. Rome did not attempt to "latinize" the eastern regions of its expanding territory. Instead, the Romans viewed ongoing hellenization of the East as a means of strengthening the unity of its empire in these regions. (This is why the primary language of the Byzantine-Roman Empire was Greek, not Latin.) And so the aforementioned dynamics that ensued after Alexander's conquest largely continued under Roman domination, and is reflected in modern scholars' use of the adjective "Greco-Roman" as a modifier of "culture" when characterizing the first and subsequent several centuries CE.

What is the significance of these cultural dynamics for our understanding of the land of Israel at the time of the formation of the early rabbinic group? Well, as a result of Alexander's conquest and its aftermath, the land of Israel in the time of the early rabbinic group was a specific, local, Near Eastern, Levantine society that, (1) for more than a millennium, had been the (sometimes involuntary) beneficiary of ancient Egyptian and ancient Mesopotamian cultural forces, and that, (2) for the next five hundred years, had been steeped—administratively, legally, linguistically, and culturally—first, in the Hellenistic and, second, in the Greco-Roman worlds. That the early rabbis were, relatively speaking, resistors of hellenization and romanization (just as King Josiah, centuries before, attempted to wipe out foreign cults in favor of the worship of YHWH alone at his one temple in Jerusalem) cannot expunge these facts. Why? Because, metaphorically speaking, the Greco-Roman versions of Near Eastern cultures constituted the sea upon which the boat of Judah-ite society floated, even if the rabbis did not want that much seawater in the boat. And so, in this chapter we consider what/whether aspects of that greater Greco-Roman, Near Eastern world, that encompassing sea, *also* offer cultural constructs and social profiles in light of which the profile and ideology of the early rabbis in the land of Israel might have been experienced as having currency. Because the "big" world of the eastern Mediterranean and Mesopotamia had become "small" as a result of a "globalization" of sorts.[4]

3. A point stressed by both Miller, *Sages and Commoners*, and Lapin, *Rabbis as Romans*.

4. And indeed, it is alleged by ancient writers that this globalization (and not just the impetus to secure an empire) was Alexander's goal. This aspiration is said to be captured in Alexander's alleged intention to bring about an *oikoumene*, one "inhabited" world, from which the church's term "ecumenical" is derived.

Now, that bigger world is wide and complex, however small it may have become. And this is not a book about either Greco-Roman or Near Eastern culture. So, in discussing both Greco-Roman and Near Eastern society, I shall confine our discussion to a few avenues that seem to me potentially relevant to coming to grips with what the early rabbis were, or, rather, what the early rabbis were (or might have been perceived as) *like*. These avenues all have to do with institutionalized authority and established local, regional, and imperial administrative roles either in the Greco-Roman/Near Eastern world generally, or in minority, diaspora Jewish communities that were situated in many of the Roman-ruled urban centers *outside* the land of Israel.

That the land of Israel at the time of the early rabbis "floated" in a mixed Greco-Roman and Near Eastern cultural, social, and administrative sea, as I have already stated, is a claim that is as easy to understand as it is prima facie credible. So, only a few illustrations of this state of affairs will suffice to make the point in general. As noted earlier in this volume, in the Roman imperial period, many towns in the land of Israel had majority *non-Jewish* populations, especially so after the two failed Jewish revolts against Roman rule in the first and second centuries CE. These hellenized, mostly Near Eastern non-Jews spoke Greek, or Greek and Aramaic, depending on their ancestry, and their presence (and cultural influence) in the homeland was, in fact, an abiding consideration and concern in many Mishnah tractates.[5] That said, even Jews in the homeland in this era spoke Greek and Aramaic (the latter beginning to eclipse Hebrew as a lingua franca, as opposed to a lingua *sacra*).[6] For example, "Jewish" inscriptions in the homeland abundantly use Greek (and Aramaic). Or consider the modern archaeological find in caves of the Judean desert of a first-century CE fragment of a *Greek* translation of the biblical book of the Minor Prophets (sometimes called "the Twelve"),[7] or that one of the caves at the Qumran site (the literary repository of the deeply millenarian, anti-Roman, Jewish Dead Sea Sect) contained some dozen and a half Greek texts,[8] or that Middle (sometimes called mishnaic or rabbinic) Hebrew is itself significantly influenced by Greek and is infused by many Greek loanwords (such as "Sanhedrin," from *synedrion*, meaning "seated assembly/council"). All in all, Judah-ites in their homeland, and the early

5. This is not limited to, but is especially evident in, those Mishnah passages that concern themselves with the indirect, largely unintentional participation in pagan religious practice.

6. It was probably not until the fourth (or fifth) century CE that the use of Hebrew in daily speech had ceased altogether in the land of Israel.

7. Schiffman, "Review."

8. Tov, "Nature of Greek Texts."

rabbis among them, were bathed in a local Near Eastern version of Greco-Roman culture. Moreover, among those pouring the water into the bath were their diaspora Jewish brethren,[9] not only their gentile Greco-Roman neighbors and rulers. Permit me, therefore, to say just a bit about why one might consider this last mentioned claim.

Simply put, it is not hard to point to considerable and sustained "cultural commerce" between Jews/Judah-ites of the Greco-Roman diaspora and those residing in the homeland, both preceding and during the nascent period of the early rabbinic movement. Consider, for example, the apostle Paul *before* his "conversion" to the Jesus movement. He was born a Greek-speaking, diaspora Jew (from Tarsus in Asia Minor); possessed the privileges of full Roman citizenship; studied (in Hebrew and Aramaic) in Jerusalem at the feet of prominent scholars of the Pharisaic party; and was sent by Jerusalem's authorities to convey their advice to adjacent diaspora Jewish communities (e.g., in Damascus) on how to deal with Jews who were part of the Jesus movement. And, indeed, after his conversion to the Jesus movement, he continued to mediate between the policies of the Jesus movement's leaders situated in Jerusalem, on the one hand, and the aspirations and challenges of communities of Jesus' followers outside the land of Israel, on the other. What was at stake in this mediation? It is whether the Jesus movement would remain a largely "native," Judah-ite one, or a more hellenized/romanized group encompassing Jews and gentiles in the urban centers around the eastern Mediterranean—homeland *versus* diaspora, or homeland *and* diaspora.

Or consider the book of Acts's narrative of the events of the Pentecost festival following Jesus' execution. Jews poured into Jerusalem as pilgrims, not only from other parts of Judea but also from numerous diaspora Jewish communities. It appears that many of these diaspora pilgrims, while in Jerusalem, were based in synagogues established there by their respective diaspora communities to host "their" pilgrims. Since these aspects of the Pentecost story in Acts are largely incidental to the narrator's main purpose, they are all the more compelling as evidence about the cultural commerce between homeland Jews and diaspora Jews.

Or consider our by now familiar scribe, Joshua/Jesus Ben Sira, of second-century BCE Judea/Jerusalem, whose grandson, living in Alexandria, Egypt, translates his grandfather's literary oeuvre from the original Hebrew (or Aramaic) to Greek for the consumption of Greek-speaking, diaspora Jews. But why harp on the translation of Ben Sira's work, when

9. Among the most seminal modern scholarly works on the penetration of Greek language and culture in the works of the early rabbis themselves in land of Israel are the classic studies of Lieberman, *Greek in Jewish Palestine.*

we know of the several Greek translations of Hebrew Scripture that circulated among diaspora Jews in the Greco-Roman world. Moreover, some of these translations were known to and used by Jews in the homeland as well, even though the early rabbis, on balance, frowned upon the use of Greek, but not Aramaic, translations of Scripture.

What has all/any of this to do with the cultural currency and, therefore, the plausibility of aspects of the early rabbinic profile?

To be sure, the early rabbis, standing in the shadow of Josiah and Ezra (formally) rejected non-Judah-ite Near Eastern culture, whether of Mesopotamia, Egypt, or the Levant, because it was a vehicle for devotion to foreign gods. This is so despite the rabbis' benign acceptance of Aramaic. Nor were the early rabbis fans of Greek, because they (rightly) understood it to be a fast track to Greco-Roman culture generally, and to Greco-Roman *religious* culture and thought specifically. So, the rabbis preferred that homeland Jews limit their use of Greek, and the rabbis eschewed completely the Greco-Roman culture and the Near Eastern culture associated with Greek. The rabbis tolerated the homeland patriarchs' expertise in Greek (and Greek learning) as a necessary evil, but only to the degree that the patriarchs might play their role as liaisons between Jews and the imperial authorities. And by the latter fourth century CE, the rabbis were increasingly critical of the patriarchate, expressly because of what they perceived to be the excessive hellenization/romanization of the office holders. I would imagine that the early rabbis would have been incensed that the mid-fourth-century, Jewish patriarch of the land of Israel corresponded (seemingly often) in Greek with the renowned pagan teacher of advanced rhetoric Libanius, who resided in Antioch. The correspondence, one of which survives among Libanius's writings, appears to have nothing to do with the patriarchate's mandate and everything to do with the *cultural and personal affinity* shared by these two highly educated and urbane "pen pals."

Yet, paradoxically, despite all of this, early rabbinic literature displays the abundant influence of Greek language, Greco-Roman culture, and Roman law. The rabbis' *imperméables* (French for "raincoats"), donned against all things Greco-Roman or Near Eastern pagan, were hardly impermeable. And it should not be shocking that some well-recognized, institutionalized roles in Greco-Roman and Near Eastern administration, or in (largely Greek-speaking) diaspora Jewish communities, may have bolstered the currency of aspects of the early rabbis' profile. In this chapter two such roles will be featured. One is that of the scribe as an established administrative professional not only inside the Judah-ite homeland (about which much has already been said in ch. 5), but also in the lands surrounding the land of Israel, including within the organization of Greco-Roman, diaspora Jewish communities. The other role is that of the Roman jurist, a quasi-professional profile of legal expertise that arose in the city of Rome itself, but the training in which expertise spread to several notable Roman imperial cities. Some of these schools for jurists of Roman law were situated in the eastern Mediterranean. One famous school of Roman law was in Berytus (today, Beirut). The school in Berytus was founded sometime in the second century CE, and its mandate was specifically (re) confirmed by the emperor Septimius Severus (ruled 193–211 CE), an alleged friend of Rabbi Judah the Patriarch, to whom the authorship of Mishnah is attributed by the early rabbis. Indeed, two of Rome's most renowned jurists, Papinian and Ulpian, were Phoenicians/Syrians and had been teachers of law in Berytus, a mere hop, skip, and jump from the Galilee of Rabbi Judah.

So, let me begin then with the profile and role of scribes in the eastern Mediterranean and Near Eastern lands surrounding the land of Israel in the half-millennium or so preceding the emergence of our Mishnanians.

Let Me Introduce Ahiqar, the Scribe

Permit me one of my shaggy-dog stories—in fact, a shaggy-dog story about a shaggy-dog story on the "best-selling" list for 1000 to 1500 years. The main character in the story is named Ahiqar.

Ahiqar is probably a fictional figure. But fictional or not, the stories in which he appears among the principal characters are certainly fictional. And the works in which he appears as a main figure tell us a lot that is relevant to this chapter's agenda. Why? Because he is a fictionalized version of "real," established authority figures and roles, in the same sense that the primary character in a detective novel is a fictionalized version of real detectives. In both instances, the fiction would be unintelligible without some familiarity with the real. Moreover, the real, historical scribes, of which Ahiqar is a romanticization, appear to be both transcultural and transnational in sway and provenance, not only at the time of the early rabbis but also during the many centuries that preceded the advent of the early rabbinic movement. And this is part of the reason that the fictional Ahiqar pops up in so many different places in different eras, as I will shortly describe.

In the many fictional accounts of Ahiqar, he is portrayed as a scribe whose talents have resulted in his being appointed the most able and trusted civil and military administrator at the court in Nineveh of the Sargonic dynastic kings of the Neo-Assyrian Empire in the latter part of the eighth century and the seventh century BCE. His story typically involves betrayal by his nephew, adopted heir, and protogee, Nadan (or Nadab), who for a time succeeds Ahiqar at the royal court (on Ahiqar's previous recommendation, no less). Ahiqar is saved from execution and is eventually elevated anew to his former position. Nadan, of course, gets his just deserts. That is the narrative aspect of the Ahiqar literary tradition.

The other aspect of the Ahiqar literature is a collection of maxims, epigrams, proverbs, and riddles that convey the proper attitude, values, and comportment of the worthy scribe. These teachings bear a strong family resemblance to the type of maxims and proverbs found in the biblical book of Proverbs[10] and the book of Joshua/Jesus Ben Sira/Sirach (the second-century BCE Jewish work of Judean provenance that the early church often bundled with its Old Testament collection).[11] We might well say that Ahiqar as a figure and purveyor of wisdom teachings is a non-Jewish/pagan, fictionalized, and romanticized antecedent of the very much Jewish, Torah-true, historical, and real Joshua/Jesus Ben Sira (with whom you are familiar from ch. 5), since, as I shall shortly explain, the fiction of Ahiqar and his wisdom teachings appear to have originated about three to four centuries earlier than Ben Sira's career in Jerusalem. Only in the book of Tobit (also an originally second-century BCE Hebrew or Aramaic text, which in translation was included in the early church's Apocrypha to the Old Testament) are Ahiqar and his evil nephew of Israelite ancestry.

So, based on the surviving literary evidence, we may well ask: Who loved, told, and recast the story of the Ahiqar, the royal Assyrian court scribe-administrator? Many, it seems, and over an extended period of time. The romance of Ahiqar appears in medieval manuscripts in many languages (Old Turkish, Arabic, Slavonic, Armenian, and Syriac) and circulated among Christians and Muslims. Earlier, the story of Ahiqar and the maxims attributed to him were beloved among pagans, Christians, and Jews,[12] since scholars have long concluded that the extant medieval versions are based on older Syriac, Greek, Hebrew, and/or Aramaic versions of the Ahiqar romance and associated maxims dating from the first several centuries CE and originating from Jewish and/or early Christian authors. In none of these posited (but no longer extant) earlier texts of

---

10. Of course, not only Mesopotamian scribal wisdom literature influenced Judean wisdom texts (and the Hebrew Bible generally); Egyptian wisdom literature is often seen as reflected in Israelite/Jewish wisdom compositions. See Emerton, "Teaching of Amenemope"; Ruffle, "Teaching of Amenemope." Ruffle is well known for arguing that the biblical book of Proverbs is not literarily dependent on the Egyptian text *Teaching of Amenemope* but is strongly influenced in general by Egyptian wisdom texts. Emerton takes Ruffle to task, arguing for more direct influence of Amenemope on Proverbs.

11. Greenfield, "Wisdom of Ahiqar."

12. Conybeare et al., *Story of Ahikar.*

Ahiqar, according to these scholars, is Ahiqar understood to be a Jew. That said, and as already mentioned, in the second-century BCE book of Tobit, Ahiqar and his evil heir are depicted as Jews/Israelites. In this way, the author of the Tobit romance can anchor his Jewish heros, Tobit and his son, in what is, evidently, an already well-known and much beloved story about the (pagan) scribe and courtier, Ahiqar. This, then, is what we knew of the literary history of the figure of Ahiqar and of the maxims attributed to him, before a remarkable discovery was unearthed.

In the latter decades of the nineteenth century, a stunning archaeological find was made in Egypt. Caches of ancient papyri were discovered in Upper (that is, southern) Egypt at what had long ago been the twin settlements of Elephantine and Syene (near today's Aswan). Here Egyptian pharaohs, followed by Assyrian, Persian-Achaemenid, Macedonian-Greek, and ultimately Roman rulers, controlled and defended the southern borders of Egypt. From just before and during the Neo-Assyrian imperial era in the late eighth and seventh centuries BCE onwards, these twin outposts were inhabited by an ethnically mixed group—including, among others, native Egyptians, Judeans, Arameans, Persians, and (later) Greeks/Macedonians—some of whom (including the Judeans) garrisoned the area as mercenary troops working for whichever Egyptian native or foreign imperial ruler controlled Egypt.

The ancient papyri discovered at Elephantine-Syene tell us much about the daily lives of the inhabitants of the outpost over many centuries. In fact, the oldest documents found there are in hieratic and date from the late third and second millennia BCE. Most of the documents (in Aramaic, Demotic, Greek, and Coptic) span the fifth century BCE to the Muslim conquest. And, amazingly lucky for us, among the fifth-century BCE Aramaic texts found at Elephantine-Syene is an incomplete version of the story and maxims of (a very much pagan) Ahiqar, written (no less) by a bona fide Judah-ite scribe living in Elephantine.[13] This is the earliest attested (even if fragmentary) version of Ahiqar—a text, transcribed in fifth-century BCE Upper Egypt by a Jewish scribe for a (presumably) Jewish, Aramaic-speaking audience, celebrating the (fictitious) story and wisdom of a non-Jewish scribe-administrator, depicted as a high-ranking official in the royal court of late eighth- and seventh-century BCE Assyrian kings.

What do all of these versions, spanning more than 1500 years, about a fictional scribe-courtier tell us? They tell us that across a vast geography (that is, the Near East and eastern Mediterranean lands) and an equally

---

13. Conybeare et al., *Story of Ahikar*, 168–73; Cowley, *Aramaic Papyri*; Porton and Yardeni, *Textbook of Aramaic Documents*.

impressive span of time (from at least the fifth century BCE to the medieval period), the image of the wise, learned, and accomplished scribe as a senior, trusted, and authoritative government administrator was a well-understood, established, and "believable" fictional figure. And this is so, because such a figure had verisimilitude. That is, the fictional figure was a "take" on what was known to have been an established profile *in the real-life world*,[14] as I suggested at the outset of this discussion. Were this not the case, the story of the fictionalized Ahiqar would not have been as compelling a piece of fiction for Jews, non-Jews, and (eventually) for Christians and Muslims across the lands of the Near East and eastern Mediterranean.

The image of Ahiqar and the literary-historical journeys of the story of this fictional character are fascinating indicators of the existence of the professional profile of the sage-scribe and its associated roles—a profile and related roles that are truly transnational and transtemporal in scope in the Near East. When Shaphan the scribe serves as a courtier of Josiah, king of Judah; when Ezra the scribe (and priest) serves as the Persian king's representative in Jerusalem and the land of Yehud/Judah; and when Joshua/Jesus Ben Sira the scribe recruits students to his school with promises of high-paying administrative roles in Jerusalem's administration of the land of Israel, they are all exemplars of *real-life* authorities in Judah-ite society that are themselves instances of a *real-life and long-standing* professional profile of scribes in eastern Mediterranean and Near Eastern lands that underpins the *fictional* figure of Ahiqar.

All this said, to be forthright, we would not have needed the story of Ahiqar to tell us that the government administrator-scribe was a ubiquitous professional role in evidence throughout the Near East for centuries, indeed for perhaps two millennia or more before Mishnah was produced and promulgated as the core curriculum of another group of scholarly, would-be communal authorities, namely, the early rabbis. Let me explain.

Evidence for scribes associated with both imperial and temple administrations, at various levels from local to national, comes from Egypt's Old, Middle, and New Kingdoms, from Egypt's Late Period,[15] as well as from Hellenistic Egypt and the period of Roman rule. We know this from texts and inscriptions written in hieroglyphics, hieratic, Aramaic, Demotic, Greek, and Coptic. A similar body of evidence about scribal roles comes from Mesopotamia (that is, from Sumerian, Akkadian-Babylonian, Assyrian, Neo-Assyrian, Neo-Babylonian, and Achaemenid-Persian dynasties),

14. See Heltzer and Avishur, "Term *sofer mahir*"; see also Greenfield, "Wisdom of Ahiqar."

15. See, e.g., the list of known scribal wisdom literature/teachings from Egypt in Buzov, "Notes," esp. 61.

again spanning the Bronze and Iron Ages. And the same may be said of scribes in the once significant Hittite Empire in eastern Asia Minor and the northern Levant in the late Bronze Age.[16]

What shared characteristics constitute the enduring, "international" profile of these scribes, of which Judah-ite scribes were an instance? Obviously, literacy! The invention of writing, which is the foundation of literacy, was a significant development in the Near East. The impetus for this invention was twofold. As relatively large temple complexes were established in increasingly populous cities with an extensive hinterland of rural villages, some means of keeping a record of the sacrificial animals and other temple/priestly dues and votive gifts to the deity became first desirable and subsequently necessary. The other impetus, soon to follow upon the first, had to do with the emergence of larger political-administrative entities, usually monarchies, that united what previously had been numerous small, local, independent settlements.[17] These, in turn, burgeoned into empires in the Near East. Emerging empires faced administrative challenges that simply could not be easily met by oral culture. Record-keeping became increasingly important. And this spilled over into cultic knowledge and lore; temple priests had for millennia relied on oral tradition to pass down priestly knowledge and norms of ritual practice. The invention of writing not only allowed temple officials to keep accounts of offerings and gifts, perhaps the initial impetus to develop a written script, but also to preserve priestly knowledge and tradition, and to systematize it. The same courtly and priestly impetus to develop and/or adopt writing is evident in ancient Israel in the Iron Age. Israelites were just a little late to this game in comparison to their Mesopotamian and Egyptian neighbors.

The invention of writing in antiquity was as revolutionary for society and culture as was the use, millennia later, of moveable type and printing in fifteenth-century Europe, or the advent of the personal computer and the internet in the late twentieth century. It is remarkable how written documents became a virtual necessity, for example, in Mesopotamia in the second millennium BCE, even among a population the majority of which could neither read nor write. Routinely, properly witnessed or "notarized" bills of sale for property, deeds of loan for investment, marriage agreements, and many other types of written documents were deemed superior proof of claims in legal disputes, even if few could read these documents, and fewer still could write them. Oral testimony that could not be substantiated by written documentation was treated as an inferior level of proof of claim, even when the

16. See Roux, *Ancient Iraq*, esp. 328–42.
17. See, e.g., Noegel, "New Observations."

witnesses could be produced. In other words, an increasingly complex society might presuppose written records, as do, for example, the Babylonian laws of Hammurabi (c. 1750 BCE), even when most people are somewhat to completely illiterate. This leads me to another related point.

Literacy is not a "all-or-nothing" social phenomenon. In the ancient world, or even today for that matter, one is not simply either literate or illiterate. In ancient times, one may have been able to read but been unable to write, since writing is a different and highly technical skill that differs substantially from reading.[18] Or one may be able to read simple things having to do with daily life, like a receipt for purchase or a simple letter, and, perhaps, one may be able to sign one's name. But this is a far cry from reading (and understanding) an astronomical, medical, religious, or legal text, or being able to compose such texts (as opposed to merely copying them). Similarly, one may be able to read (or write) numbers, but it takes significantly more learning to do the mathematics needed to design and build monumental buildings and infrastructure, or to order the necessary amounts of building materials and labor force, or to calculate in advance the next solar or lunar eclipse. The individual residents of ancient Egypt or of Mesopotamia, as well as of interconnecting Levantine lands, possessed varying degrees of literacy—from not at all (the majority), to rudimentary (a minority), to functional (a smaller minority), to advanced and highly advanced (very few). And it is clear that scribal capacities and knowledge also existed on a continuum, from functional literacy (let us say, required to read, compose, and write a proper contract or deed of sale) to highly advanced levels of literacy (such as the ability to read, interpret, and author a treatise on wisdom, law, medicine, mathematics, or astronomy). And so, scribes occupied a range of social functions, also on a continuum—at the level of the neighborhood, town, region, province, or nation—depending on the level of their training and experience.

The other thing to be noted about scribes over these many centuries and across this significant geographical range in the ancient Near East and eastern Mediterranean lands is that they were, *as scribes*, rarely if ever at the very pinnacle or apex of civil or religious authority, locally, regionally, or nationally.[19]

18. In the ancient world, in order to write one needed to have knowledge not only of the system of writing signs—hieroglyphic, hieratic, or Demotic in Egypt, or cuneiform in Mesopotamia—but also of how to prepare the materials on which and with which one wrote—e.g., papyrus, parchment, clay tablets, reeds and styluses, and inks.

19. Insofar as the early rabbis' profile (and claimed authority) derived from their scholarship, not their birth and lineage, what I have just said about scribes may well shed light on how Mishnah explicitly and implicitly depicts the authority of the disciples of the sages in relation to other authority figures depicted in Mishnah. This consideration sheds light, perhaps, on what Goldscheider has observed in his "Religious

By long-standing tradition and convention, birth and lineage, not learning and advanced literacy, tended overwhelmingly to determine who was at the very apex of authority. The village elders or chieftains, the priests of the local or national shrines and temples, the kings and their council of nobles—all of these tended to owe their positions to birth and lineage (enhanced by personal, individual traits and accomplishments, of course).

Scribes, whether positioned locally or nationally, were *at the service* of those at the apex of power (as retainers), even when, as was often the case, these scribes were trusted and were afforded high levels of authority, responsibility, and accountability. This is not to say that some scribes could not also be of noble birth, in which case such a one would have more opportunity. And it is certainly the case that scribes tended *not* to be of lower or poorer classes. Remember (as intimated in earlier chapters of this book) that advanced literacy and advanced learning require a leisure and freedom from arduous manual labour, and a dedication of time to education, which only scions of reasonably wealthy families enjoy. We have already seen that Joshua/Jesus Ben Sira says just this. And many centuries before him, an ancient Egyptian scribe extolled the virtues of pursuing the scribal professions by reminding his intended readers (novice scribes) that their hands will not be calloused by manual labour nor their clothes be sullied with dirt; but they will be afforded much important work to do, from which they will amass wealth.

This role of the *very* literate, ancient scribe as the highly positioned retainer to others at the apex of power by reason of their birth and lineage is very well attested in papyri of Late Period through Ptolemaic-Hellenistic-era Egypt.[20] The Macedonian-Greek "pharaohs" ruled their territory (which included many islands of the eastern Mediterranean) from soon after Alexander the Great's death until the Roman conquest of Egypt in 30 BCE. The pharaohs of this period presided over two distinct systems of government. One system operated in the Greek/Macedonian-founded cities that dotted the Ptolemies' empire. These cities had been granted charters/constitutions to operate as self-governing (quasi-democratic) settlements on the Greek city-state model (the *polis*). While these cities owed their self-governing status to the Ptolemaic king/pharaoh, they were not (technically) ruled by the king's court. But the inhabitants of the rest of the Ptolemaic territory (which at its height of expansion in the third century BCE included the land of Judah) were the direct subjects of the imperial ruler and of the ruler's administration. To rule and administer this significant territory, the

---

Authority in Mishnah."

20. See, e.g., Papadopoulou, "Administration of Egypt."

Greek-Macedonian Ptolemies adopted and adapted systems of imperial administration that had been in use before Alexander's conquest, during the late New Kingdom and the Late Period of Egypt. And in that system, we can clearly perceive the roles into which various echelons of the cadre of scribes fit as specialized service personnel, as retainers to those in power, and as trusted, highly placed bureaucrats with authority.

Let me illustrate this by reference (once more) to just a few of the ancient papyri documents found at Elephantine-Syrene, because a "picture" (of sorts) is worth a thousand words.

Among the papyri are several from, or addressed to, Arsames, a Persian noble. Persian-Achaemenid imperial forces had conquered Egypt in the latter decades of the sixth century BCE. Near the end of the fifth century BCE, let us say, very roughly around the time of the careers of Ezra and Nehemiah in the land of Judah/Yehud, Arsames ruled Egypt as its satrap, the highest-ranking provincial authority, appointed by and governing in the name of the Persian-Achaemenid King of Kings. One such papyrus bearing Arsames's name involves the repair of a ship at Elephantine-Syrene at the state's expense.[21] (It is a fascinating document for anyone interested in ancient shipbuilding, since the materials to be bought for the repair are listed in detail.) The papyrus is in the form of a letter, or perhaps a copy of a letter, written in Aramaic, and bears a number of other names of interest to us. The official issuer of the letter is Arsames himself. But Arsames's hand did not produce it. The letter (or copy) was written by a scribe, Nabuakab, whose name appears at the end; Nabuakab appears to have been Aramean. Another scribe, Anani, a Jew, is mentioned in the letter too. The title by which Anani is designated is very interesting. Anani is not depicted as a scribe who prepares and notarizes letters and other documents, as is the case with Nabuakab. Rather, he is named at the papyrus's conclusion in this manner: "Anani the scribe is chancellor." That is, Anani the scribe is a (local or regional) senior administrative official living in Elephantine-Syrene. And it is under Anani's orders that what Arsames has authorized is to be implemented. Anani, then, is a scribe of a very different order (and authority and responsibility) than Nabuakab, a scribe who prepares and who notarizes documents. In a hierarchy, if you will, Anani the scribe sits somewhere between Nabuakab, the scribe who prepares and notarizes letters, and someone like our fictitious Ahiqar, the scribe who is depicted as the chief civil servant of the Assyrian king. Somewhere in this graduated echelon of scribal roles, positions, and responsibilities sits Ezra in the land of Judah/Yehud, a near-contemporary of Anani, and Joshua/Jesus Ben Sira, the Jerusalemite scribe who lived several centuries later.

21. #B11, in Porton et al., *Elephantine Papyri in English* (1996), 115–21.

Indulge me the presentation of another picture that speaks volumes, again from a late fifth-century BCE Aramaic papyrus from Elephantine-Syene.[22] Again Arsames is mentioned. As Porton points out, Arsames must have been visiting Elephantine, and during the visit issued orders in response to petitions brought to him. Before (or upon) his departure, Arsames wanted his decision(s) on the matter(s) put in writing and addressed to him, as an official record or as an *aide-mémoire*. The resulting document has not survived in its entirety, but several of the remaining lines bear upon our discussion of scribal roles in service to the highest (usually noble) authority of the province or satrapy. The name of the scribe who prepared the document is not recoverable. But the scribe designates himself as being in service to Sinerish the herald and their (that is, other heralds') colleagues. Heralds are a cadre of state officials of some sort. Let me now cite the opening salutation and the concluding seal/address of the surviving text, because they permit us to glimpse various groups of state officialdom. At the beginning of the missive, we read:

> [To our lord Arsa]mes, your servants Achaemenes and his colleagues, Bagadana and his colleagues, and the scribes of the province.

And at the letter's conclusion,[23] one finds:

> [To] (sealing) our lord Arsames who is in Egypt, your [serv]ants Achaemenes and his colleagues the heralds, Bagadana and his colleagues the judges, Peteese and his colleagues the scribes of the province of Pamunparai (?), Harwodj and his colleagues the scribes of the provin[ce of . . .].

Here we find references to two of the provinces within the larger satrapy ruled by Arsames in the name of the Achaemenid-Persian king, as well as to what appear to be senior provincial-government officials and their respective administrative cadres (heralds, judges, and scribes) who are these senior officials' "colleagues." In other words, groups of scribes are routinely ranked among the upper civil service of the imperial provincial government in the satrapy.

In another early fifth-century BCE Aramaic papyrus from Elephantine-Syene, we again read of a cadre of scribes who have bureaucratic decision-making authority within Egypt. The papyrus is a letter sent from

22. #B10, in Porton et al., *Elephantine Papyri in English* (1996), 113–14.

23. These "conclusions," which are often on the reverse side of the papyrus, are like the address written on the exterior of today's envelopes and refer to the recipient(s) and the sender(s).

Jewish parents residing in Migdol, in Lower (northern) Egypt, to their son, who has recently traveled to Elephantine-Syene. It seems the son was owed a payment or salary from the state for services rendered, and neither he nor his parents had received what was due before the son left for the south. The parents sought redress on their son's behalf and have received instructions, which they now pass on to their son.

> Now from the day that you went out from Egypt[,] allotment has not been given to us/you here. And when we complained to the officials about your allotment here in Migdol [in Lower Egypt], thus was said to us, saying: "About this, [you complain before] the scribes and it will be given to you."[24]

Once again, the scribes in question are not just technical experts in the preparation of documents; they are bureaucrats in the ranks of government who exercise bureaucratic decisionary authority to consider and approve claims, and to authorize and effect redress.

To sum up matters so far, fifth-century BCE papyri from Upper Egypt reveal to us several subgroups (if you will) of the larger professional cadre of scribes. One subgroup, of which Nabuakab is an example, prepares/writes official documents in the appropriate form(s). Some may have done so in service to the local or provincial government. As a number of other papyri from Elephantine-Syene indicate, many such scribes also wrote documents for private individuals and their transactions (e.g., marriage contracts, assignments of property, etc.), and ensured that these documents bore the names of appropriate (and an appropriate number of) witnesses.[25]

Yet another subgroup of scribes populated the ranks, sometimes the senior ranks, of the government (provincial) civil service; the "scribes of the province of Pamunparai," associated with Peteese, and another cadre of "scribes of the province of . . . ," colleagues of Harwodj, are such groups. Finally, certain individual scribes have advanced to be in charge of various government functions in local, regional, or provincial jurisdictions. The Jewish scribe Anani, "who is chancellor," is such a one. And I strongly suspect the aforementioned Peteese and Harwodj are as well, since their scribal colleagues seem to be under their charge within provincial government.

These roles of scribes, not only as professionals who prepare and write documents for others within government administrations or for private transactions but also as part of the cadre of professional, government administrators, carry forward into the Hellenistic-Ptolemaic and early Roman

24. #B8, in Porton et al., *Elephantine Papyri in English* (1996), 107–8.

25. I should point out that many of the witnesses signed their own names in their own hand to such documents.

periods in Egypt. The Ptolemies divided their empire, which for a time included Egypt plus the southern Levant (and within it, the land of Judah) and a number of the islands of the eastern Mediterranean, into "nomes" (provinces?), "toparchies" (regions within provinces?), and "komarchies" (villages or towns and their hinterlands). These were all subject to direct imperial rule, as opposed to the constitutional cities, which as noted earlier, governed themselves via their local councils (*boule*) by reason of charters granted them by the king/pharaoh. Each nome, toparchy, and komarchy was governed by a ruler (*archon*) whose appointment was made by, or whose status was recognized by, the central imperial government, if not by the king/pharaoh himself. And I have little doubt that these positions were held by local, regional, or provincial "nobility," for even a local village/town chieftain was a noble to the local inhabitants. But it also appears that each such *archon* was served by an appropriately scaled professional civil service, which included a (chief) scribe (*grammateus*), often supported by a cadre of functionaries, some of whom were also scribes by profession.[26]

Why is this feature of Ptolemaic government and administration important for this chapter and this volume's discussions? Well, long after the land of Israel was no longer under Ptolemaic rule, these basic structures of governance and administration continued to be used in the Judah-ite homeland. Many of these structures and offices persisted through the successive periods of Seleucid, homegrown Hasmonean, Roman-Herodian, and Roman provincial rule in Judea.[27] Josephus tells us of several royal courtiers during the period of Herod's rule who fell out of favor with Alexander, Herod's son and presumptive heir. These royal courtiers were threatened with demotion in the king's government to the level of "village scribes," presumably the lowest echelon of Herod's administration, both because of, and notwithstanding, the fact that "they had been highly educated."[28] In other words, this passage in Josephus is filled with cruel irony; for highborn royal courtiers, functioning as village scribes would have been beneath them, although they had had an education that made them more than competent for the threatened, demoted role. In *Antiquities*, Josephus writes about Jewish revolutionaries' abduction of the scribe of Eleazar the *strategos* (meaning either a military commander or civil governor in the Greco-Roman era),

---

26. See, e.g., Papadopoulou, "Administration of Egypt."

27. Jones, *Cities*, 272–73, is referenced in the excellent discussion of the evidence concerning Judean scribes in Schams, *Jewish Scribes*, 135–36. It is Schams (135–43) who has collected the evidence about scribes in the writings of Josephus to which I refer in the remainder of this paragraph.

28. Josephus, *War* 1.479.

who himself was the son of the high priest, Ananias.[29] And Josephus also introduces us to Aristeus, "the scribe [*grammateus*] of the [city] council [*boule*]" of Jerusalem during the Great Revolt against Rome.[30]

Why mention these examples, since we have already discussed scribes in Judean society in chapter 5? I do so to illustrate what Christine Schams so aptly concludes on the strength of the evidence: "Josephus' notion of scribes in his society [that is, in the land of Israel] seems to agree with the general Graeco-Roman notion of scribes as officials in various positions of government and administration."[31] And it is apt that I remind you once again why this assertion should interest us. My argument is this. The professional profile of scribes in the land of Israel during the more than five centuries that precede the emergence of the early rabbinic group draws upon the image, skills, and duties of scribes in the adjacent Near Eastern and eastern Mediterranean lands generally. Consequently, not only do already well-established norms for scribal prowess, roles, and authority in the Judean homeland help provide currency for the early rabbis' profiles and aspirations as communal authorities based on their high literacy and scholarship of halakha, so do centuries-old and enduring norms for scribal authority and roles throughout the larger region, of which the land of Israel is a part.

This brings me to my last piece of evidence for the role(s) of scribes as professional administrators near the time of, or in the period leading up to, the emergence of the Mishnanian rabbis. Let me say something of the scribe (*grammateus*) as an administrative official of the assembly-association (*synagogue*) in the Jewish communities of the Greco-Roman Jewish diaspora.

The life and organization of diaspora Jewish communities in the Roman imperial era is reasonably well documented. For example, early Christian texts comment frequently upon organized Jewish life in the diaspora. Josephus preserves what he alleges to be edicts issued by Roman authorities affirming rights afforded to Jews residing as minorities in many of the cities of the Mediterranean basin.[32] Additionally, Philo of Alexandria writes about Jewish life and Jewish communal institutions in his native city under Roman rule.[33] Roman law codes preserve edicts that concern Jews and their associations around the empire. And numerous inscriptions, some of which are tomb epitaphs, shed light on Jewish life in the Greco-Roman diaspora.

29. Josephus, *Antiquities* 20.208–209.
30. Josephus, *War* 5.432.
31. Schams, *Jewish Scribes*, 143.
32. Josephus, *Antiquities* 14.185–267.
33. Philo, *Flaccus* and *Embassy to Gaius*.

From this evidence, and notwithstanding local differences, a fairly consistent picture emerges about the structural organization of Jewish diaspora communities in the Greco-Roman world.[34] On the whole, the organized synagogue-assembly of the Jews was, in large part, modeled on the normative system of city governance and administration in the Roman Empire, and, to some degree, also replicated the typical Greco-Roman "voluntary associations" (*collegia*). Within the Roman imperial-era city, the community of Jews was organized as a corporate entity, with a membership, governance structure, physical infrastructure, and self-mandated responsibilities and services for its members.

Like Roman-era cities of the late second to sixth centuries CE, at the apex of the synagogue-assembly's governance structure was its senate/council (*gerousia*). On this body sat designated notables ("elder," *presbyter*, and "ruler of the assembly," *archon* and *archisynagogos*), one of whom was chosen as the council's president ("ruler of the senate," *gerousiarch*). Seats on the council often passed from father to son.[35] Several designated members of the community's senate ("father-ruler," *patriarches*) assumed, for a period of time, governance-oversight over the various assets, functions, and services of the organized Jewish community. Imperial legislation of the fourth and subsequent centuries confirms that such onerous service to the organized Jewish community absolved a patriarch from comparable service to the host city (presumably because doing such "double duty" would be financially crushing). And it also appears that distinguished, multigenerational service and benefaction to the community resulted in family members being designated "fathers" and "mothers of the assembly" as an honorific.

The assets of a Greco-Roman diaspora Jewish community were financial and physical. The community collected levies from its members and received voluntary donations to build and maintain its infrastructure and to underwrite its services to members. The principal physical infrastructure of the synagogue-assembly was its building, which was multifunctional. It served as the seat of the council, the gathering place for the community, the assembly's treasury, its archives, the location of its health services, soup kitchen, court of arbitration, and schoolhouse—all in one.

The community gathered in its building to observe Sabbaths, festivals, and holy days; observance included hymns, prayers, scriptural readings, and scriptural lessons. A "library" for scriptural scrolls was maintained in the

34. The content of the several paragraphs that follow relies upon my previously published studies on Jews and Judaism in the Greco-Roman diaspora. See Lightstone, "Roman Diaspora Judaism," and *Commerce of the Sacred*.

35. As indicated, in my view, when these titles appear as epitaphs on the tombs of deceased children.

building. The community distributed money to the poor from its communal treasury and provided meals to the destitute from the building's kitchen. The assembly's judges and tribunals arbitrated disputes, and the community's healers dispensed medicines, potions, and amulets. And the synagogue-assembly provided burial services for members.

Above I outlined the typical *governance* structure of Greco-Roman diaspora Jewish communities. That structure was in the hands of the community's notables—probably multigenerational, inherited positions that stayed within certain eminent families. What of the *administrative* structure of the community? Was the community served by a "professional" administrative bureaucracy of sorts? Two such professionals appear in the inscriptional and literary evidence: the *hazzan* (transliterated in Greek from the Hebrew/Aramaic[36]) and the scribe (*grammateus*). It is not clear what precise administrative functions either official performed in the community's civil service—only that they played professional administrative roles. But, once more, it is likely that the scribe's high level of literacy was the profile that qualified one for the duties performed as a professional retainer to the notable families at the apex of power in the community, namely, the elders/rulers of the synagogue, presidents of the senate/council, and patriarchs.

So, in sum, highly literate and highly educated scribes—whether in the Greco-Roman, Near Eastern, and eastern Mediterranean lands generally, in the Greco-Roman, Jewish diaspora communities, or in the land of Israel itself—all exhibit a profile that was deemed to have qualified them as competent and authoritative professional administrators and retainers to those members of the local, regional, and provincial nobility who were at the apex of power. All this gave an air of plausibility and legitimacy to the early rabbis' scholarly profile and to their aspirations to be authoritative deciders (and administrators?) of the halakha within the patriarch's noble (even if delimited) rule of the Judah-ites of the land of Israel. But it is not only the image and role of scribes across the lands of the eastern Mediterranean and Near East that provided well-established antecedents to what the rabbis were and wished to be seen as like. The emergence of quasi-professional legal experts, first in Rome in the Republican era, and subsequently across the Roman Empire, may well have provided additional cultural currency for what the Mishnanian rabbis were. These Roman legal experts were the jurists, whose heyday was the late second or early first centuries BCE through the first third of the third century CE—let us say, from the time of the grandson-translator of the book of Joshua/Jesus Ben Sira the

---

36. The term *hazzan* seems derived from the Aramaic verb root *hzy*, meaning "to see"—hence, "[over]see."

scribe to the careers of the sons of Rabbi Judah the Patriarch, to whom the early rabbis attribute Mishnah's authorship.

"Ask Me a Very Difficult Legal Question about a Complex Set of Circumstances, and I Will Tell You How One Should Rule according to the Law, and Why"—Roman Jurists as Legitimating Antecedents for What the Rabbis Were

Ready for a another shaggy-dog story? In the scholarly historical literature of the late nineteenth and early twentieth centuries, one often encounters the view that the Romans of the Roman Republican era had a certain "genius for law." One is, therefore, tempted to imagine that every Roman citizen of that early period was a passable expert in the law and a skilled amateur advocate, capable of convincingly arguing their cases for themselves before the courts, on the benches of which sat their fellow citizens as knowledgeable amateur judges. As it turns out, this is a somewhat idealized stereotype of what early Romans were and of what early Roman society was like. But this stereotype, unlike many others, stands on some well-established facts about how the early Roman judicial system functioned and about the roles individual Roman citizens had to play in judicial actions. To put matters most succinctly, the entire early Roman judicial system operated (technically) via "amateurism." And it is only with time—indeed, many centuries—that more and more parts of the judicial system (and legal profession) "professionalized," ultimately administered from the mid-third century CE on by imperial government bureaucrats with formal legal training in recognized law schools. This relatively late professionalization began, paradoxically, with the rise of amateur jurists.[37] They were truly expert, independent, but, technically speaking, amateur legal scholars, whose heyday lasted just a little more than 300 to 350 years (but whose impact lived on thereafter).[38] Let me explain.

37. See, e.g., Schiavone, *Iuris*, 29–30, 318–37, 341ff.; Schulz, *History*, 28–161; Nicholas, *Introduction to Roman Law*, 28–37. Let us say "amateur" in the sense that most highly trained Olympic athletes were (still) amateurs in the 1950s.

38. E.g., in the mid-sixth-century CE, that is, three centuries after the era of the jurists drew to a close, the Byzantine-Roman emperor Justinian commissioned the production of the *Digest* as one of the companion documents to his *Civil Code*. As noted later in this chapter, the *Digest* collated by topic extracts cited from the writings of the jurists. The legal works commissioned by Justinian (the *Civil Code*, *Digest*, *Institutes*, and *Novellae*) had an enduring influence on law in the West throughout the medieval to early modern periods. Indeed, when the German states and principalities united in the nineteenth century, requiring a unified federal law, the works

What is generally understood to be the first formal Roman law code, the Twelve Tables, was passed as statute law by an assembly of the people in the mid-fifth century BCE[39]—around the time of the careers of Ezra the scribe and Nehemiah in Jerusalem/Yehud and their promotion/imposition of the Torah of Moses in Judah-ite society. It is already evident (indeed, assumed) in the Twelve Tables that individual, private Roman citizens were themselves expected to initiate and prosecute judicial actions for wrongs done to them, debts owed, and for many types of crimes of which they were the victims. Judicial actions and prosecution by *state* authorities and magistrates (as opposed to those legal actions undertaken by private citizens) tended to be reserved for alleged crimes against the state and for capital crimes, as these were punished by execution, stripping of citizenship, confiscation of all property, or banishment. Therefore, crimes against the state and capital crimes excepted, wronged citizens were (formally) their own amateur police, detectives, prosecutors, and lawyers. With the appropriate authorization from governing authorities/magistrates, specifically from the yearly appointed praetors, wronged citizens who were victims of alleged crimes had powers of arrest and detention, pending the appearance of the parties in court, unless in the interim the parties resolved their conflicts and claims by submitting voluntarily to extrajudicial arbitration.[40]

---

commissioned by Justinian provided one important starting point. For this reason, late nineteenth- and early twentieth-century legal education in Germany routinely required the study of Justinian's commissioned legal compilations—almost 1400 years after these were produced.

39. Originally promulgated (it is alleged) by being inscribed on bronze (according to Livy), the Code of the Twelve Tables has not itself survived as a whole, as it were. However, so many pieces of it have been cited and commented upon in other ancient Roman texts that it has not been a difficult task for modern scholars to reconstruct the content of the Twelve Tables.

40. These voluntary arbitrations, even of criminal matters, had the legal force of a regular court judgment. Later in the history, first, of the Roman Republic and, subsequently, of the early Roman Empire, this provision for the legal recognition of voluntary arbitration gave Roman authorities a means of recognizing the jurisdiction of non-Roman courts operating according to local legal norms in the lands that came under Roman rule. It was also the legal means by which the courts of local Jewish communities in the Greco-Roman diaspora were afforded jurisdictional status, namely as voluntary arbitration tribunals, the judgments of which were, if necessary, enforceable by Roman authorities and courts. When in 212 CE the Roman emperor granted full Roman citizenship to almost all free men and women in the empire, all of these newly minted citizens and their descendants became subject to Roman civil law (technically), rendering their local traditional legal systems mute. This did not sit well with many provincials throughout the empire who wished to perpetuate their traditional national and ethnic norms. Again, the legal status of voluntary arbitration, with some limitations and restrictions imposed, became the means of granting continued application of now delimited, local, ethnic law to parties who wished to be subject to it. Justinian's

The Twelve Tables recognizes that many (especially poorer) individuals may not have had the education or financial means either to undertake judicial action against wrongdoers or to defend themselves against their accusers. After all, education was a privilege that required some leisure and the means to pay for it. And the code also acknowledges that many persons did not have the confidence (or ability) to argue effectively in the courts. Such persons could have their wealthier "patrons" act on their behalf, so long as these patrons provided guaranteed "surety" against the outcome—for example, the responsibility to pay some or all of the fines or costs of restitution that might result from the judgment. As one might expect, some wealthy patrons became well known for their skill in advocating the cases of their clients. That said, in all of this, the entire judicial system and processes lay in the hands of (sometimes skilled and knowledgeable) amateurs—especially upper-class amateurs of means (that is, mostly patricians, sometimes members of the equestrian class, and at times the more wealthy among the plebeians). Indeed, even the judges of the tribunals before whom the cases were heard were nothing more than amateurs—citizens (often well-respected ones, but at times not) doing their duty to the state at the request of the praetor. And the annually appointed praetors, who administered the judicial system, were themselves no professionals either. Yet these amateurs were responsible for the judicial system's day-to-day operation, for issuing and (later) maintaining a body of "edicts" that supplemented or that established and (re) interpreted the meaning and scope of application of "statute" laws that applied to Roman citizens (*ius civile*), as well as the body of laws that applied to noncitizen sojourners and resident aliens (*ius gentium*) in Rome.

So, with so much (technical or formal) amateurism pervading the early Roman legal and judicial system, how did the system manage? On the basis of standard forms and formularies for various legal actions—essentially an elaborate "fill-in-the-blanks" process, much of it communicated (originally) orally. Once a litigant had been provided by the praetor with what was considered to be the appropriate form/formulary for the circumstances of the case, the litigant could proceed to bring the (figuratively speaking)

Civil Code (bk. 1, title 9, rescript 8) preserves a (re) confirmation, dated 398 CE, to just such a delimited arrangement for Jewish arbitration tribunals operating in the Jewish communities of the Roman world (see Frier, *Codex of Justinian*, 231). See also Rabello, *Introduction to the History*, ch. 7, 141ff., on "Jewish and Roman Jurisdiction"; and Rabello, "Civil Jewish Jurisdiction." In the latter half of the fourth century CE, John Chrysostom, at the time a presbyter of the church in Antioch, complains that some of his (gentile) Christian congregants prefer to use the local Jewish synagogue-based courts to litigate their disputes with one another. See Meeks and Wilken, *Jews and Christians*; and Fredriksen and Irshai, "Christian Anti-Judaism."

"filled-in" form/formulary to court, as a set of instructions to the citizen judges on how the case is to be tried, under which laws, and with what redress or punishment, if the respondent was deemed guilty. In other words, the circumstances had to be made to fit into the framework of established forms/formularies for some legal action.[41] And if it could not, then the case was not "actionable" at all (and presumably some extrajuridical way would have to be followed to address the dispute).

All this begs the question: What persons in the early Republican period constituted the "brain trust" of these standard, established forms/formularies for legal actions; of their appropriate use; and of the authoritative interpretation of laws generally? As we have already seen so frequently in this volume, that brain trust initially were those persons in charge of the temples of Rome, the pontifices (who tended to be from the most noble of the noble families of the Republic).[42] In learning what one needed to know to be a pontifex, one (or some, at least) needed *also* to acquire the requisite expertise to be the "guardians" of legal forms/formularies and of their proper use by the praetor, the citizen judge (*iudex*), and the individual litigant (or their stand-in patron-advocate).

As Republican Rome's territorial holdings expanded, and as, in lockstep, the city of Rome itself grew in size and complexity—socially, culturally, economically, and politically—all amateurism in government, military command, administration, and judicial systems came under strain. The political and social turmoil of the last century of the Republican system reflects this strain and was an interim attempt by several powerful individuals to address it. The eventual result was the emergence and development of one-man rule that characterized the Roman Empire. In the arena of the judicial system and legal actions, matters yielded slowly but inexorably to increased professionalism (of a sort) between the second century BCE and the early third

41. The last "commentary" of Gaius's second-century CE legal "textbook," the *Institutes*, discusses actions, forms, and formularies. Gaius proffers a telling example that illustrates what I have just written. Permit me to paraphrase part of Gaius's "lesson." If, hypothetically speaking, Tom accuses Harry of entering his, Tom's, property and cutting down his vines (all without prior permission), Tom may not take legal action against Harry *for cutting down Tom's vines*. Why? There is no action, form, or formulary for such a case, because the closest relevant statute, Gaius points out, specifically concerns cutting someone's *tree(s)* down without prior permission. The praetor, on the strength of his or some prior praetor's "edict," would, however, authorize that the case of Tom against Harry proceed using the form/formulary for trespassing and cutting down trees, even though the "trees" in question are actually vines. So, the case would proceed on the *established* legal fiction that vines are trees.

42. See Bryen, "Responsa" (preprint), 4.

century CE. Expertise in the law, originally the purview of the pontifices,[43] began near the end of the Republican period (1) slowly to emerge from that circle and include other (educated and still often noble) Romans, and (2) to express itself differently, not as guardians of prescribed appropriate legal interpretations and the use of forms/formularies (which increasingly and eventually fell into disuse) but as reasoned legal advice (*responsum/responsa*) about how complex disputes/circumstances should be decided under the law.[44] This advice was sought from individual jurists, who upon request provided it to the praetors, citizen judges, or individual litigants. Over these three and a half or so centuries, the role of the *quasi*-professional (in the sense of not formally/technically remunerated) legal expert, the jurist (*iuris consultus*), emerged, took hold, and then faded. Why? Because of (1) the eventual bureaucratization of such legal expertise within the imperial administration's salaried civil service from the mid-third century CE, and (2) the parallel emergence of professional, credentialed lawyers as advocates both for the state and for individual litigants.[45]

What (as opposed to who) were the Roman jurists?[46] Let me begin by commenting on how we know anything at all about them. Like the Twelve Tables, of which no complete copy survives, only a minority of the written works of the Roman jurists survived intact and whole from antiquity, while others have been largely or partially reconstructed. (And for that matter, much/most of their legal advice was, it seems, delivered *orally* to those who sought it.)[47] Of the written works that we have (nearly) in whole, and one of the most well-known, is Gaius's *Institutes of Roman Law* (c. mid-second century CE). Gaius's *Institutes* became the most famous Roman introductory legal textbook of ancient times (supplanted only in the mid-sixth century by Justinian's *Institutes*). But while few books by Roman jurists

---

43. See Domingo, "Roman Jurists," 3; Bryen, "Responsa" (preprint), 1–5; Nicholas, *Introduction to Roman Law*, 28–37; Schulz, *History*, 99–161.

44. Bryen, "Responsa" (preprint), 1–5.

45. This eventual professionalization of legal expertise is, in my opinion, aptly reflected in the introductions provided by the sixth-century CE Byzantine-Roman emperor Justinian to the editions of the *Digest*, which he commissioned. In these introductions Justinian, among other things, prescribes the (new) five-year-long curriculum for a state-recognized legal education. See Watson, *Digest of Justinian*, 1:1–55; see also Schiavone, *Ius*, 29–30; 318–37; 341ff.

46. On the emergence (and eventual decline) of the Roman jurists, see Bryen, "Responsa" (preprint), 1–17; Bauman, *Lawyers in Roman Transitional Politics*; Bauman, *Lawyers and Politics in the Early Roman Empire*; Birks, "Rise of Roman Jurists"; Harries, "Legal Education"; Harries, *Cicero and the Jurists*; Schulz, *History*, 38–116; Gordley, *Jurists*, esp. 1–27; Schiavone, *Ius*, 29–30, 318–37, 341ff.

47. Bryen, "Responsa" (prepring), 1–6.

survived (or have been reconstructed nearly) whole, many hundreds of snippets of the writings of Roman jurists were cited, collated, and arranged topically in the great *Digest* of Roman jurists' commentaries to Roman law that was commissioned in the 530s CE by the Byzantine-Roman emperor Justinian. And from these snippets, many writings of the most cited Roman jurists have also been largely or partially reconstructed by modern scholars, thanks to the methods of the *Digest*'s authors. The *Digest* was intended to be (and is) part of a four-part "library" of Roman law prepared under Justinian's guidance: the *Civil Code* (of imperial law up to Justinian), the aforementioned *Institutes* (which updated and expanded Gaius's *Institutes*), the just-mentioned *Digest*, and the *Novellae* (additional imperial edicts promulgated by Justinian himself). Thankfully, Justinian's mandate for the preparation of the *Digest* required that every snippet used from an antecedent jurist's work be meticulously referenced. And among the several prefaces prepared by the *Digest*'s authors (and by Justinian himself) is an allegedly complete list, roughly in chronological order, of all of the jurists cited, as well as a list of each's writings known to the *Digest*'s compilers. So, what do we know about what these Roman jurists were, and in what sense might what they were have provided currency for the profile and would-be roles of the early rabbis as legal experts of their halakha?

As I have already intimated, one might say that the Roman jurists arose in order to correct for, to counterbalance, and/or to supplement the ingrained amateurism of the Roman legal and judicial system. How so? In the last century or century and a half of the Roman Republican era, a few highly educated (and, understandably, wealthy) Romans, interested both in scholarship for its own sake perhaps and in public service, turned their intellectual skills to the intense study of Roman law. As stated earlier, their hard-acquired, advanced expertise in law began to be sought out by the amateurs operating and involved in Rome's judicial system, processes, and legal actions. In short, the emerging group of jurists were turned to as largely pro bono consultants, as their Latin designation, *iuris consultum*, itself implies. Technically and practically, these jurists operated independently and outside of the formal judicial and legislative processes—at least, they did so initially. Eventually, the judicial system, that is, those who formally operated it, had to decide upon the status and use of these jurist's legal advice to those who sought it. Plaintiffs might seek out such counsel. So might the praetors on how, or whether, a case might be actionable. And Roman citizens doing their civic duty as justices (appointed by the praetor) to hear and adjudicate a case also might seek the opinion of one or more jurists. Nothing obliged anyone to request the advice of a jurist. And (initially) upon receiving such advice, no one *formally* part of the judicial processes of the state—the praetors, judges, and litigants—was *obliged* to act or find in accordance with that advice. In other words, in the late Republican era, jurists had no *formal*, institutionalized authority, and so neither did their legal opinions. Rather, the authority of a jurist's opinion on a given case rested entirely on respect for, and the self-evidence of, "his" legal expertise, founded on dedicated scholarship of Rome's legal texts and traditions. Let me repeat the point, because it deserves repeating: this was an authority (and power) that (initially) lay outside of any formal systems and institutions of Roman governance and administration. And indeed, the early jurists celebrated and guarded their independent status and the resulting independence (*libertas*) of their legal opinions.[48] Indeed, the largely pro bono basis upon which the jurists' opinions were provided was viewed as an important part of the "guarantee" that the advice given was truly objective and independent of the interests of any of the parties involved in the judicial process.

Only in the imperial period did that independence slowly erode. Some modern scholars assert that Augustus, the first Roman emperor, began the formal recognition of some jurists' opinions as authoritative legal pronouncements (*ius respondendi*), essentially credentializing these jurists and giving their views a formal legal status, rather than just free advice. Other modern scholars are of the view that the state imprimatur of select jurists' advice occurred later in the imperial period.[49] It is believed by some legal historians that it was Hadrian in the second century who obligated judges to abide by the advice of jurists, *if* it was sought.[50] In any case, what one has before one is this: highly competent, technically amateur, for a long time independent, expert legal scholars advised (on request only) the less competent amateurs who were actually involved in judicial processes. Indeed, to risk being repetitious, their credibility and that of their opinions hinged in part on the recognition of their legal scholarship and in part upon their real or perceived independence from organized government and the formal administration of the legal system—experts from the periphery, so to speak, even though jurists tended to be from the wealthier classes (often from among the equestrian class).

Why did the jurists disappear near the mid-third century (around the time of the sons of Rabbi Judah the Patriarch)? Did intense scholarship

48. Bryen, "Responsa" (preprint), 10.

49. See the excellent discussions in Tuori, "*Ius respondendi*," and in Bryen, "Responsa" (preprint), 10ff.

50. If the judge sought the advice of two (or more) jurists, and if the judge received conflicting opinions, he was free to choose one such opinion to follow in the case being tried. But having sought a jurist's opinion, the judge, it seems, was no longer free to go his own way.

of Roman law erode? Did those involved in the judicial system as its administrators, litigants, or judges cease to need recourse to greater legal
expertise than what they personally possessed for difficult complex cases?
On all counts, no! What changed is that that intense legal scholarship and
expertise ceased in incremental stages to be *independent* of the institutions
of the state and increasingly became an expertise exercised by a specialized
part of the cadre of the imperial civil service.[51] In short, juristic expertise
became routinized, bureaucratized, and professionalized—as happened to
so much of the workings of imperial governance in the late second and
subsequent centuries CE. Let me say more about this progressive formal
involvement of jurists in state administration and governance (leading,
seemingly paradoxically, to jurists' eventual disappearance), because it
bears comparison with the status and social position of our Mishnanians
and of their relationship to the office and administration of Rabbi Judah
the Patriarch at precisely the same period, that is, the last decades of the
second century CE and the first decades of the third.[52]

Beginning especially in the period of the Severan imperial dynasty
near the end of the second century, some of the most renowned independent
jurists began, for example, to be appointed to one of the most important and
powerful posts of the central imperial administration, that is, as one of the
(usually) two praetorian prefects. Traditionally, the praetorian prefects were
senior military administrators. It is generally understood that Septimius
Severus (reigned 193–211 CE) began to reserve one of the two posts for
a legal expert, chosen from among the independent jurists. The famous,
Phoenician-born and -raised jurist Ulpian held this post. And for a time he
was even the sole praetorian prefect (the other position remaining vacant).[53]

51. An excellent encapsulation of this trend is found in Schiavone, *Ius*, 341ff.

52. In this volume I have refrained from making judgments about the impact (or
lack thereof, depending on the instance) of Roman law on early rabbinic halakha. No
doubt there are a number of instances where that seems to be the case, but it is a case
that must be made on a "case-by-case" basis. What is undeniable, as stated earlier in this
chapter, is that the early rabbis swam in a sea of Roman dominance, which included Roman law. This view is elegantly expressed by Natalie B. Dohrmann in her introduction
to the reprinted edition of B. Cohen, *Jewish and Roman Law*, 1:xiv (emphasis added):

> Even if rabbinic laws *in [all] their particulars* are not by-products of Ro-
> man influence, rabbis themselves certainly were. They were Roman in
> several senses; they were subordinate to Roman power [and law] and
> were products of a Roman world. This reality should not be ignored,
> especially, and perhaps most centrally, as the rabbis are the authors of
> a discourse [primarily a legal discourse] that takes power as its primary
> idiom. Rabbinic law is itself a Roman discourse.

53. See Honoré, *Ulpian*, 19ff.; Schiavone, *Ius*, 318–37.

Other prominent, late second-century and early third-century jurists were also appointed to this position, notably Papinian, a Syrian in origin. The practice continued during the reign of Caracalla (reigned 198–217 CE, initially as co-emperor with Septimius Severus). Interestingly, Ulpian and others appointed to this lofty imperial post were expected by the emperors to continue to exercise their independent legal judgment in fulfilling their imperial duties.[54] But it is easy to understand why, several decades into the third century, subsequent emperors might care little for one of their most important imperial administrators performing duties independently of imperial policy and political interests. And it is also easy to understand why, additionally, legal expertise and legal experts generally were formally and systematically integrated into the ranks of the imperial bureaucracy, leading to the end of the period of the independent jurists within what had become a decidedly "top-down," vertically integrated state system, modeled, to a degree, on military command and administrative structures.[55] So complete was the eventual bureaucratization and professionalization of legal expertise in the imperial system that by the mid-sixth century, Emperor Justinian himself, in his allegedly personally authored introduction to "his" *Civil Code*, specifies the several years-long curriculum for imperial-sanctioned law schools in which future "lawyers" of the empire were trained. The legal academy at Berytus/Beirut was (still in Justinian's era) such a school, and was especially highly regarded by Justinian.

What, in their heyday, did independent Roman jurists produce? As I have already stated, many of their legal opinions are believed to have been provided orally to those seeking their advice on a particular case. Some

54. My use of the term "independent" requires some additional clarification as regards Ulpian's "methods." As with Roman jurists of the preceding several centuries, independence means "outside" of the formal systems of the administration of the justice system; for earlier Roman jurists this implied remaining "unpaid" for their work, lest payment led to suspicions that a jurist was "in someone's pocket," as the expression goes. For Ulpian it is clear that independence does *not* mean without regard to earlier jurists opinions. Schiavone, *Ius*, 349, affirms that citation of earlier jurists' opinions was an "essential aspect of the Ulpian doctrine" (trans. from the Italian my own).

At the risk of overemphasizing the significance of a potential parallel, early rabbinic literature is somewhat unique in the history of Judah-ite literature for the manner and frequency in which it refers to the opinions of earlier, individual, named authorities (as opposed to citing accepted Scripture, which practice had become almost ubiquitous among Judah-ite authors). True, Mishnah refers to attributed opinions almost exclusively when presenting opposing rulings for a single set of posited circumstances. (And Tosefta's materials largely do the same.) But the forms of critical Mishnah analysis reflected or modeled in the Jerusalem Talmud (c. 400) and the Babylonian Talmud (c. 600) routinely "cite" earlier, named rabbinic authorities' views as proofs or as rebuttals (just as Ulpian, e.g., requires).

55. See Schiavone, *Ius*, 341ff., esp. 344.

of these opinions have been preserved, because jurists at times collected their own responses and committed them to writing, or their secretaries or students did so. Jurists sometimes wrote commentaries or short treatises on specific laws or on (parts of?) the praetor's Edict, this apart from being asked about a specific case. A few jurists wrote "textbooks" intended to introduce Roman law to would-be jurists. Gaius's *Institutes of Roman Law*, written in the mid-second century CE, is undoubtedly among the more famous of these. As I have already stated, Gaius's textbook was displaced in the sixth century when Justinian commissioned the production of "his" *Institutes* (albeit using Gaius's as a model).

All of this said, I wish to stress to you that the primary service and output of a jurist was to advise on how the law should be applied *in the particular set of circumstances of individual cases* brought to them. And to appreciate this role of the jurist, permit me to concoct a case.

> Sam has three sons (Frank, Harry, and Gerry) and two daughters (Jane and Janet) by his first wife, Alice. Jane is married; Janet is not, and is still a minor. Alice dies. Sam remarries Betty, who has had a son (Robert) by her previous, now deceased, first husband, Brian. Robert and Sam develop a very close father-son-like relationship, jointly operating Sam's business affairs (with Sam's biological sons). But Sam never formally adopted Robert as a son, although Betty claims that Sam had intended to do so.
>
> Such are the circumstances when Sam dies without having left a will. His estate consists of a house, in which Betty is still living, a fair degree of silver and gold coins, investments, and a significant amount of good farmland just outside the city.
>
> Sam's children, Betty's son, Robert, by her first husband, Brian, and Betty are now at odds about how the estate should be divided, and as to whether Betty can continue to live in the house indefinitely (and with what continued financial support, provided by whom). Moreover, Janet, still a minor, is in the charge of whom, and her future dowry is to paid by whom from what?

The disputants have all ended up in court. And the citizen judges charged with hearing the case have turned to a jurist for advice on how to rule. The jurist's explicit role is to provide a definitive legal opinion, bringing to bear all of the relevant laws and their normative interpretations that might apply to this complex case's circumstances. What is *not* demanded (or relevant) is a systematic treatise on inheritance law or on custody law. Nor is what is required an essay on legal philosophy. Neither of these will help the litigants or the judge(s) deciding the case—in all of its specificity, complexity and concreteness. Such was the typical and normative role of the independent Roman jurist, which he would discharge without payment for services rendered.

Where does each successive generation of jurists come from? No doubt, some jurists were brilliant autodidacts, especially in the late second and early first centuries BCE. But, increasingly, renowned jurists had students who wished to follow in their footsteps. And since this required some form of legal education, however structured or institutionalized, there emerged competing "schools" of law—not (initially) in the sense of academies, but rather in the sense of schools of legal opinion. Two such well-known schools emerged in the early imperial period, that of the Proculians and the Sabinians.[56] In the second and subsequent centuries CE, actual legal academies begin to appear, not only in Rome but also (and significantly) around the empire. As mentioned, one of the earliest and more renowned was the legal academy founded at Berytus/Beirut sometime in the second century CE and (re) confirmed by the Emperor Septimius Severus. That said, a legal academy of lesser stature than that at Berytus was situated at some point in Caesarea in the land of Israel; in the mid-sixth century it (was) closed, along with many others. Three and a half centuries after the reign of Septimus Severus, in the era of Justinian, the legal academy at Berytus was still going strong and still had a stellar reputation, in Justinian's opinion.[57] When Justinian mentions other legal academies, such as those at Alexandria in Egypt and at Caesarea in the land of Israel, he does so only insofar has he wishes to extol Berytus's legal academy and the academy in Constantinople itself by comparison. Why? Because some of the members of the editorial team commissioned by Justinian to prepare his *Code*, *Digest*, and *Institutes* had been "professors" of law at Berytus's legal academy.

How were law students prepared for their vocations as future independent jurists? Gaius's production of his *Institutes of Roman Law* is an indication that by the mid-second century CE, part of that education was served by introductory lectures and textbooks.[58] If Gaius's work stands as an exemplar, such *Institutes* are organized by broad topical headings—for example, property, personal status, etc.—and under each topical rubric an

56. On these schools as schools of legal opinion and interpretation, see Stein, "Interpretation and Legal Reasoning"; "Roman Jurists' Conception"; and "Two Schools of Jurists."

57. See Jolowicz, *Historical Introduction*, 473ff. In fact, Justinian closes a number of these "other" law schools.

58. From the list of jurists and of their written works that appear at the beginning of Justinian's *Digest*, it is apparent that Gaius was not the only jurist to write such introductory textbooks. Gaius's *Institutes* certainly became the "go-to" textbook at some point. As a result it has survived while others have not. As stated, Gaius's *Institutes* provided the basis for Justinian's *Institutes*, and the latter was intended to replace the former.

attempt is made to construct a coherent account of the basic legal principles that underlie the laws and to present some of the more important laws. But it is clear from a reading of Gaius's *Institutes* that (1) such a textbook was not (and probably could not be) a comprehensive compendium of Roman law, and that (2) the attempt to see laws as expressions of coherent and enduring legal principles was a pedagogical construct attempting to tease out or to impose an order and logic upon what arose historically and sometimes haphazardly.

If by the mid-second century CE, when Gaius wrote his *Institutes*, introductory textbooks had their place in the training of jurists at an *introductory* level, such textbooks could hardly, in themselves, have prepared would-be jurists to offer professional, authoritative advice (with reasons) in cases resembling the concocted one I defined earlier. So, an important element of the education and continuing education of jurists, it would appear, involved the consideration of complex *hypothetical* cases, like my invented one perhaps, in order to determine how these should/would be decided under the law.[59] And jurists often organized debates about cases, real and/ or hypothetical. What the existence of such debates serves to indicate is that different approaches might (legitimately?) be taken regarding one and the same case, and that the respective legal merits or validity of each approach might be subject to analysis and discussion.

Of what relevance is the profile, skills, knowledge, and training of Roman jurists to understanding the profile of the early rabbis, or to grasping why and how the early rabbis' profile might be seen by late second and early third-century CE Judah-ites as having a currency that would/might make rabbis appropriate go-to, authoritative sources for halakhic decisions? Well to begin with the negative, I know of no appeals in early rabbinic literature to the profile of Roman jurists as a model for their own, even though it is undeniable that some Roman law is reflected in the early rabbis' halakha. Second, and in the same negative vein, Mishnah, the core curricular text of the early rabbis, and Gaius's *Institutes*, an almost contemporaneous literary work, display little to no resemblance to one another.[60] Whereas the *Institutes* is replete with presentations of first principles and of underlying normative,

59. In comparing legal education in the law schools of the late third century CE onward to legal studies in the earlier classical period of the Roman jurists, Jolowicz, *Historical Introduction*, 474, writes that these later schools' methods "differed widely from the system of [legal education of jurists in] classical times when, after the student had mastered the elements, his further education consisted chiefly in the discussion of cases."

60. My master's student of many years ago, Loiuse Mayer, demonstrated this in her thesis; see Mayer, "Jewish and Roman Law."

legal frameworks for Roman law, the Mishnah is notorious, as you have seen, for assuming that the Mishnah student has all these (pre) requisites in hand (or immediate recourse to a rabbinic master who can supply these as needed). Whereas the *Institutes* is a systematic, well-structured introduction to Roman legal principles, the logic of Mishnah's passages is grounded in the presentation of series of individual, often entirely hypothetical cases, for each of which one and often two (opposed) rulings are given. The Mishnah student must engage the Mishnah text by exploring the possible legal logic, legal principles, and antecedent law that would reveal the appropriateness of the rulings given in Mishnah. In other words, Mishnah demands that the Mishnah student *reconstruct* as halakhic thinking what Gaius's *Institutes* expressly provides the student jurists of Roman law by articulating in advance all relevant underlying legal principles.

Now let us consider the other side of the equation, the positive. That which is requested of the Roman jurist as a service seems very much like what the rabbis appear to have hoped their profile would elicit—that complex individual cases would routinely be brought to individual legal experts for an independent, authoritative opinion or ruling. Indeed, the argument of chapter 3 of this book is that the profile and expertise that derives from engaged Mishnah study made early rabbis expert halakhic thinkers. To what end? Precisely to be able provide authoritative legal rulings and opinions. What is more, as noted earlier, Roman jurists, almost all of whom were upper class, celebrated, nevertheless, their *independence*, qua jurists, from the Roman state's systems of governance and administration. (At least such was the state of affairs until sometime in the latter half of the third century CE, when independent Roman jurists "disappeared" in the face of the ubiquitous use of a cadre of legal experts within the imperial administrative bureaucracy itself.) The authority of jurists derived from recognition of their superior legal scholarship, not from any offices they may have held as members of the Roman upper crust. Similarly, the early rabbis' claim to authority rested on their halakha-Torah scholarship (and *its* pedigree going back to Moses). That authority was not due to holding offices as part of the traditional, largely genealogically grounded governing elite of Judah-ite society at the local or trans-local levels—even though some early rabbis might have been part of this elite. This is what makes the early rabbinic lionizing of Rabbi Judah the Patriarch, to whom the rabbis attribute Mishnah's authorship, so interesting. As we have seen earlier in this book, he is said to have been *both* at the pinnacle of Judah-ite nobility,[61] a friend

---

61. The later Jewish patriarchs of the land of Israel, mostly descendants of Judah, claimed to be descendants of King David, as did their contemporaries, the Jewish exilarchs of the Babylonian Jewish community. Needless to point out, the Gospel of

of Roman emperors, *and* at the pinnacle of halakha-Torah scholarship. His office as the Roman-sanctioned Jewish patriarch of the land of Israel rests on the former, that is, his nobility of blood (and the high culture that goes with it); but his moral authority as Rabbi Judah rests, according to the rabbis, on his alleged expertise in the halakha.

It is in light of the observations of the preceding paragraphs that I note the argument put forward by Naftali Cohn.[62] The implications of Cohn's analyses are that not only do the early mishnaic rabbis *look* like Roman jurists (as we have just discussed), but the early rabbis also expressly *think of themselves* as like Roman jurists. As I have stated earlier in this book, much of the contrived, hypothetical cases that Mishnah rules upon relate to an ideal world that no longer exists, one in which the Jerusalem temple, its institutions, and its personnel still operate, although all of these disappeared in 70 CE. According to Cohn, it is significant that when rabbis place themselves anachronistically in what he calls this "memory" of temple operations portrayed in Mishnah's "narrative," rabbis never see their rabbinic predecessors as the actual officers of these temple institutions. Rather, rabbis see their predecessor disciples of the sages as ritual/legal experts dictating their legal views to those who (largely by right of birth) operate the temple and perform its cultic rites. Cohn likens this to the place of the independent Roman jurists who provided legal opinions to the officers and institutions of the Roman state's judicial system. And, in his view, what Mishnah thereby accomplishes is this: the inherent authority of the temple institutions and practices, even though they are gone after 70 CE, is implicitly portrayed as resting (or if you prefer, as having rested) with the earliest rabbis, *if* one (and, more importantly, if a contemporary Judah-ite) accepts the anachronistic retrojection of rabbis instructing temple officers on proper practice according to the halakha.

What do I make of Cohn's views? I agree that Mishnanian rabbis in many ways look like jurists—independent, scholarly legal experts providing their opinions to those who are formally officers of the state and justice systems. But this is not limited just to the memory of the temple in Mishnah. It entirely pervades Mishnah's imagined, ideal/idealized world. Take, for example, the Mishnah passage we discussed in chapter 3 about a

---

Matthew makes the same claim for Jesus. And most ambitious is a full-page advertisement that I saw in a Canadian newspaper in the mid-1960s during what Canadians of the day called "the great flag debates." A Canadian group of pro-monarchy royalists published an alleged genealogy for Queen Elizabeth II indicating that she, too, was descended from King David.

62. Cohn, *Memory of the Temple*, esp. 17–38, 119–22; see also Cohn, "Rabbis as Jurists."

duly constituted court that (hypothetically) issues an injunction that violates a law of the Torah (m. Horayot 1:1). This Mishnah passage assumes/ imagines, among other things, that rabbis (sages or disciples of the sages), who presumably would not make such an egregious error, do *not* sit, qua rabbis, on these courts either as a matter of routine or policy. Then, in the second half of the passage at m. Horayot 1:1, Mishnah considers an altered set of circumstances; Mishnah hypothesizes that one of the sitting members of the court *happens* to have completed rabbinic training (that is, is "worthy of" rabbinic credentials). Now what is the ruling? Is it the same or different? So here, too, and in many of the imagined circumstances that Mishnah considers, officers of the village, town, region, or state are not routinely rabbis (or legal scholars of any persuasion). Rather, rabbis, qua rabbis, are independent of these officers/offices. Yet Mishnah passages (that is, rabbinic sages) rule upon these hypothetical cases—as they would if, hypothetically, rabbis were there and were asked for their legal opinion, which, you will remember from earlier chapters, rabbis are supposed to provide pro bono. In sum, rabbis look like Roman jurists, and Mishnah study instils an expertise in rabbis very much akin to the expertise that Roman jurists were sought out to exercise. Moreover, Mishnah study instils this expertise in much the same manner as jurists were educated, that is, by analyzing many real and/or hypothetical cases, after having mastered the core prerequisite knowledge to do so.[63]

But did rabbis think of themselves as Judah-ite versions of Roman jurists? And why might we think any other Judah-ites would see them this way? Concerning the first question, early rabbinic tradition has absolutely nothing explicit to say. And this contrasts dramatically with what the rabbis repeatedly say about the allegedly substantial, extra-scriptural halakhic legacy they claim to have received from the Judah-ite scribes of the preceding era(s), as we have noted in previous chapters. So the answer to this question might be: if the rabbis were self-aware of their resemblance to Roman jurists and, moreover, were aware that the demands of Mishnah study resembled how Roman jurists were themselves (in part) trained, they have chosen not to remark upon it—this notwithstanding the fact that Roman jurists, and indeed at least one major academy to train them, were present in the Levant at Beirut/Berytus (if not closer still at Caesarea) at the time of Mishnah's composition and promulgation. I tend to disdain arguments from silence. That said, one might well understand why the early rabbis, who generally resisted romanization/hellenization, would celebrate the legacy they alleged

---

63. To be fair, my phrasing of this sentence is, not coincidentally, reminiscent of how Jolowicz, *Historical Introduction*, 474, describes the education of Roman jurists in their classical heyday, a period that largely overlaps with that of the Tannaim.

to have received from Judah-ite scribes but eschew any mention of how the expertise of the early rabbinic profile is (partially/additionally) modeled upon that of Roman jurists (*if* that is the case).

What about the second question: Would the early rabbis' contemporary Judah-ites see the disciples of the sages as *like* Roman jurists? It is hard to know. (The only Judah-ites who have left us writings and who are not rabbis tend to be Christian writers. And they say next to nothing at all about the early rabbis before Jerome's era.) To be sure, "if it looks like a duck, and walks like a duck, and quacks like a duck . . . ." But, strictly speaking, it simply does not suffice to say: if I were there at that time, I would definitely see the likeness; rabbis are Judah-ite "jurists" of the halakha. That said, I am prepared to venture the following argument. First, as I have asserted above, rabbis in important respects *do* look like Roman jurists. Second, in the late second century CE, jurists would have been present in the land of Israel, even if only in those towns and cities that had substantial or majority non-Jewish populations, like Caesarea, Sepphoris, and Tiberias, Roman provincial centers. Third, many Jews, including some rabbis, lived in these majority non-Jewish urban areas of the land. Fourth, and as I have already remarked several times, as early as the latter second century CE, one of the major academies for the training of Roman jurists operated nearby in Berytus/Beirut; in the subsequent centuries, similar legal academies operated in Caesarea and Alexandria as well, although they never seem to have attained the reputation of the legal academy in Berytus. Fifth, in 212 CE, during the lifetime of Rabbi Judah the Patriarch and near the date of Mishnah's production and initial promulgation, most "free" inhabitants of the Roman Empire, including those living in the land of Israel, were granted Roman citizenship and became *increasingly* subject to Rome's civil law (*ius civile*). This would immediately have necessitated the sorting out of what aspects of Judah-ite life would henceforth be regulated by Roman law, adjudicated in Roman courts, and which aspects would/could remain (voluntarily or involuntarily) under the aegis of traditional Judah-ite law and norms, with disputes arbitrated by Jewish tribunals. It is almost unimaginable that, as a result of the changes in 212 CE, many Judah-ites would not have become increasingly aware of Roman law, of Roman judicial processes, and, hence, of the recourse one might have to authoritative Roman jurists. Given this, it is likely that *both* rabbis *and* Judah-ites would have come to perceive a likeness of the early rabbinic profile of skills as scholars of the halakha, on the one hand, to Roman jurists' legal scholarship and skills, on the other hand. Such a likeness, if and when perceived, would also have provided currency (that is, an air of prima facie legitimacy and authority) to the halakhacist component of the early rabbinic profile, even if the rabbis, for ideological reasons, would not have remarked on their jurist-like nature as analytic halakhic thinkers and consultants.[64]

Rabbinic Scribes or Rabbinic Jurists: Scholar-Bureaucrats or Independent Scholar-Consultants

This chapter is the second in which we have together addressed the question what did the early rabbis think (or might others have perceived) they were *like*? We have considered as likenesses roles and profiles of authoritative "scholar figures" in the lands outside of and surrounding the territory of the land of Israel. Why? Because these lands were the social and cultural sea in which the Judah-ites swam. Two such figures assumed prominence in this chapter's discussions.

One was the enduring figure of Near Eastern scribes. Because of their advanced literacy and learning, many scribes took up positions in the administration and bureaucracy at all levels of governance—local, regional, provincial, and even in temple/cultic settings. Scribes were never, or hardly ever, at the very apex of government and administration. The positions at the apex in village, town, city, regional, provincial, and imperial administrations were usually occupied by persons of high(er) birth—the traditional nobility (or what counted as such locally). Even a hereditary village chieftain's authority was greater than that of the village scribes. Scribes, by reason of their learning, but not their birth per se, served the nobility within the latter's

---

64. As an addendum or footnote to the foregoing section of the chapter, I am inclined to note several other similarities between Roman jurists and early rabbis. Earlier I stated that over the first and second centuries CE Roman jurists tended to self-sort into two "schools" of Roman legal tradition and interpretation, the Proculians and the Sabinians. Peter G. Stein attempts to sort out the differences that defined one school from the other (see above the references in n56). Stein admits that such a scholarly exercise has been fraught with debate and disagreement. But his attempt to do so often reminds me of scholarly attempts by modern scholars of early rabbinic literature to sort out what distinguished the Hillelites ("House of Hillel") and the Shammaites ("House of Shammai"), and, in some respects, to define the Pharisees over against the Sadducees. With respect to the schools of jurists, Stein distinguishes more conservative, literal approaches to the interpretation of law, on the one hand, and more open, adaptive approaches, on the other. Moreover, Stein notes that jurists' approach to the scope for interpretation of law also depended on whether the law in question was *lex*, that is, "written" statute law, or *ius*, that is, legal norms legitimated by long-standing tradition (but not formally made *lex* and *officially* promulgated in written form). This distinction between written law and law whose standing rests on tradition also bears comparison to early rabbinic notions (or Pharisaic ones, according to Josephus) of a biblical/scriptural law that is supplemented by an extra-biblical body of law that is handed down from generation to generation.

bureaucracies. This did not mean that scribes tended to be from peasant stock. Advanced learning required financial means. So scribes tended to be from families of means—even families of successive generations of scribes. But they were not traditional rulers (or priesthoods).

As we have discussed, the early rabbis expressly saw themselves as heirs of generations of Judah-ite scribes, who themselves were significantly modeled on the scribes of Egypt and Mesopotamia. But the institutions of governance and administration in which Judah-ite scribes served, just like their counterparts did in Egypt and Mesopotamia, were largely wiped away in the aftermath of the revolts against Roman rule in the land of Israel. What arose in the land of Israel in the latter decades of the second century CE was the Jewish/Judah-ite patriarchate as a pale remnant of Judah-ite self-rule, limited, mostly likely, to (some?) specifically Judaic matters. Insofar as the rabbis saw themselves as *like* scribes and considered themselves the scholarly heirs of Judah-ite scribes, the rabbis would have expected to serve in the patriarch's administrative apparatus at the local and regional levels. That is, they would have seen themselves as eminently qualified to be "scholar-bureaucrats" of the patriarchate. And there can be no doubt that the early rabbis "cozied up to" the early patriarchs, particularly Rabbi Judah the Patriarch and his son, Gamaliel III. The fact that Mishnah is attributed to Rabbi Judah probably indicates that the rapprochement between the patriarchs and the early rabbis was a two-way mutual one. But, if I may stray into historical issues more than I have wished to do in this volume, it is equally clear that the early rabbis' ambitions (insofar as they had them) to be appointed to local and regional administrative positions and offices commensurate with their Torah/halakhic scholarship were left substantially unfulfilled. There is little evidence of rabbis, qua rabbis, exercising considerable authority over Jews in the land of Israel until the fifth or sixth centuries CE (by which time many of the powers and privileges of the patriarch had been withdrawn by the Byzantine-Roman emperor). One simply cannot square the lack of evidence for substantial rabbinic authority in the land of Israel before the fifth or sixth centuries with notions that the early rabbis had in fact filled the ranks of the patriarchal administration and offices from the late second century CE onwards. So, perhaps we might think of the early rabbis as "administratively unrequited" scholar-scribes. Of course, this begs the question who *did* fill the posts and offices of local and regional administrations under the broader aegis of the patriarch? My answer is twofold: (1) I do not know; (2) the early rabbis' competitors (whose writings, insofar as there were any, seem not to have survived the eventual "triumph" of the rabbinic movement).

This state of affairs jibes well with something else that we have noted about the rabbis in this book: that, generally speaking, they seem not to have made their living being rabbis. Rather, would-be rabbis had the means (and leisure) to study, and so did fully fledged rabbis. Their services as expert halakhic thinkers were offered to those who voluntarily sought their advice or services. Perhaps rabbis sometimes received gifts and honoraria in return (like Roman jurists sometimes did). But the early rabbis' livelihoods seem not to have been predicated on this any more than the authority of their opinions was grounded in possessing offices in some administration (which only a few rabbis held). Indeed, the early rabbis, as you have already learned, were forbidden to demand payment for their halakhic opinions (or to seek wealth by means of Torah study). In others words, as regards their halakhic legal expertise in particular, they provided services on exactly the same independent, largely pro bono basis as Roman jurists did, before the jurists' intellectual heirs came to be subsumed within the Roman imperial civil service sometime in the third century CE and onwards.

Did *some* rabbis, as independent halakhic experts, expect appointments to lofty positions in the patriarch's administration in the Severan era, expressly because some famous jurists, like Ulpian and his several successors, rose to such levels in Roman imperial administration? Perhaps. After all, it is highly likely that even Judah-ites in the land of Israel would have been aware of the monumental novelty of a Roman jurist becoming a praetorian prefect, arguably one of the most powerful administrative positions in the central imperial government. And it is even more likely that Rabbi Judah the Patriarch and his circle would have been aware of such a development. (Perhaps Judah's circle promoted him to the Severan emperors, of which Judah is said to have been a friend, as a kind of Jewish Ulpian, this in addition to his qualifications as a Judah-ite noble.) All this said, few Roman jurists were elevated *as jurists* to high position in the Roman imperial administration at the end of the second century CE and first decades of the third. And few rabbis (too few, in the rabbis' view) seem to have been appointed to senior administrative functions in the patriarchy of Rabbi Judah or his successors.

So, the rabbis may have desired to be *like* scribes (and/or like the Roman jurist Ulpian), but most had to content themselves with being *like* (almost all other) Roman jurists, exercising jurist-like authority, based *not* on position or office but on recognized superior legal scholarship, put to use independently of the state's institutions. In the case of the early rabbis, that scholarship was grounded (1) in thorough knowledge of Scripture and its interpretative tradition, (2) on expert knowledge of an extra-scriptural body of law and legal traditions (assumed but not always articulated in Mishnah), and (3) on an analytic prowess in halakhic thinking inculcated and honed by the lifelong study of Mishnah. All other aspects of the repertoire of early rabbinic skills—shamanistic arts, compelling preaching, mystical practices, etc.—were secondary to the three pillars just enumerated. These three constituted the essential and normative profile of the early rabbis and, together with their mythologizations of their knowledge and their Mishnah as grounded in a chain of tradition linking each rabbi to Moses "our rabbi," provided the basis for their social formation as a distinctive group within Judah-ite society in the late second and third centuries CE.

Afterword

How Did We Get Here,
and to Where Did We Get?

ALL HUMAN COMMUNITIES TEND to seek a shared understanding of whence they came in order to better glimpse whither they may go as a group. Moderns who are academically oriented similarly ask: What past streams and eddies of culture and society interacted in what ways to produce our current socially constructed cultural worlds—worlds that significantly direct and constrain what we are and do as individuals and groups?[1]

For many millennia, human communities mythologized their past. In fact, mythologization has never really ceased to be an important component of how communities interpret and legitimate who and what they are to the themselves and to others. After all, even modern nation-states fashion mythologies about their origins. That said, as early as the fifth century BCE, Greek writers, such as Herodotus (of Halicarnassus) and Thucydides (of Athens), began to pursue historiography as a complement not only to mythology but also to chronicles (that is, lists of alleged important events and persons). Historiography was born more than two and a half millennia ago not only from curiosity about our pasts but also from the realization that understanding the societies and cultures of *our* pasts, including our past mythologizations, contributes to better understanding what we are today (and what culturally and socially either impels us or constrains us to

1. The wording of this question resembles closely, and is informed by, how Emile Durkheim, one of the founders of modern sociology, defined a "social fact."

build certain types of futures together). Modern academic historiography, coupled with social scientific perspectives and approaches to the evidence of the past, stands within this long scholarly tradition.

My motivation to write, and (I would suspect) your decision to read, this volume's social-scientifically informed exploration of the past itself arises from a desire to understand why so much of Western society and culture is as it has been, and what trajectory was taken to get here. In this book's preface, I noted that much had changed in the West—defined, for our purposes, as the Near East and the lands surrounding the Mediterranean— over the course of the first eight or so centuries CE. I stated that, quite astonishingly, over this period of time, the entire region became largely judaized. Developments that at their inception probably seemed relatively insignificant, other than to those most directly affected, eventually wiped away the worship of the gods, their cultic centers, and their associated institutions and authorities in favor of the worship of the God of Israel, YHWH, and in favor of those who spoke and ruled in YHWH's name.

What were these seemingly relatively insignificant events? An inspiring, first-century CE Jewish preacher, Jesus, was executed in Jerusalem, leaving the small group of his closest followers to pick up the pieces. Soon thereafter, the temple to the God of Israel in Jerusalem was destroyed (on the face of it, just one of many cultic sites to many gods that would have been laid waste during the many military sieges of the last centuries BCE and the first several centuries CE). And another charismatic preacher, Mohammed, living just beyond the fringes of Sassanid-Persian and Roman-Byzantine rule, taught and vigorously promoted a religious culture that distilled elements of early seventh-century Eastern Christianity and contemporary Near Eastern Judaism. It is as if the flapping of the wings of three butterflies somehow interacted to produce a whirlwind that carried away much of the classical Western world and radically transformed what remained of it.

In many respects, it was a moment of crisis among Judaic communities in the land of Israel in the latter first and early second centuries CE that astonishingly and somewhat inexplicably birthed this whirlwind. For without the destruction of the Jerusalem temple and the demise of all the institutions grounded in its operation, what would have happened to the early Jesus movement? And without this crisis in Judaic society, which "made room," as it were, for the early rabbis, what early seventh-century Near Eastern Judaism would have provided a model for the Islamic faith and for Sharia law (as the conceptual and cultural counterpart to rabbinic halakha)?

Consequently, this book has examined *what only in retrospect* may be deemed to be a transformation of institutions of authority in Judaic society that is rooted in changes about which the first evidence appears in the late second and/or early third centuries CE in the form of the Mishnah. Within organized Judaic life over the next approximately eight hundred years, authority structures become so radically transformed that a new class of religious-legal scholars, who touted a literature of their own making and who addressed one another and whom others addressed by the honorific title "rabbi," became the highest arbiters of Jewish religious and civil practices in almost every Jewish community in the lands around the Mediterranean and the Near East. That is why this book has focused on the earliest phase and locus at which the social formation of the rabbis may be clearly discerned, described, and understood, that is, to repeat myself, just before and after the turn of the third century CE in the land of Israel.

Thus far this afterword has briefly revisited this book's preface. For you, the reader, that was fully six chapters ago. What have you discovered in the interim, and where have those six chapters taken us, that is, you and me?

For six chapters, our exploration has been driven by just two queries. We began by considering the question *what* were the early rabbis of the late second to mid-third-centuries CE, the period of the early rabbinic movement's *substantial*, initial social formation and institutionalization? And after having explored this first question in chapters 2, 3, and 4, we turned in chapters 5 and 6 to a second query, namely, what might the early rabbis, and other contemporary Judah-ites, have thought they, the rabbis, were *like*?

As you have learned, the title "rabbi" is an honorific meaning "my master"—not in the sense of "my lord" (Latin: *dominus*) but "my teacher" (Latin: *doctore*). Moreover, the early rabbis referred to members of their group collectively as the sages (*hakham*, sg.; *hakhamim*, pl.) and as disciples of the sages (*talmid hakham*, sg.; *talmidei hakhamim*, pl.). To inquire *what* the early rabbis were is to explore what constituted and legitimated their claimed mastery and sagesse. Claimed mastery of what and over whom? Our discussion led us to consider the expertise and profile that characterized members of the early rabbinic social formation as a distinctive (self-styled) elite group in Judah-ite society in the land of Israel. That initial query also impelled us to seek to understand how the early rabbis conceived of and promoted the special *legitimacy* of their distinctive group profile. In service of these ends, they *mythologized* their group identity, their most important text, the Mishnah (produced near the turn of the third century CE), and the person, Rabbi Judah the Patriarch, whom they revered as Mishnah's author. If it is "all about Mishnah," so to speak, what is it about Mishnah that is so pivotal to understanding the early rabbis' distinguishing profile?

You now know that the lifelong study of Mishnah was the principal shared group activity of members and would-be members of the early rabbinic group. If social solidarity and identity are, in part, forged and maintained in group life and common activities, Mishnah study, almost always undertaken with others (teachers, colleagues, and fellow students), was undoubtedly the most significant, socially binding activity of members of the early rabbinic cadre.[2] Mishnah study enjoyed this preeminence of place in the rabbinic curriculum and group life for some four hundred years. And even the text that eventually supplanted Mishnah as the core object of rabbinic study, namely, the Babylonian Talmud (produced c. 600 CE), is itself framed as Mishnah study (albeit of a very particular sort).[3] That is why I characterized the members of the early rabbinic movement of the period just before and after the turn of the third century CE as the Mishna-nians. Early rabbis are Mishnanian rabbis. Yes, some (many?) early rabbis, acting as local sages, provided services that any local wise man of the pe-riod would likely have been expected to dispense; they interpreted dreams, provided anti-demon prophylactics, etc. And as highly educated, religious literati, some rabbis pursued mystical speculation and contemplation, the purpose of which was to experience spiritual, out-of-body journeys through the seven heavens (aka heavenly palaces) to glimpse the scenes described by the prophets Ezekiel and Isaiah. But none of this *made* a rabbi a rabbi; Mishnah study (pursued together with others) and everything required by the engaged analysis of the Mishnah did. How so?

By reason of the enduring preeminence of Mishnah study among the early rabbis, the (*pre*) *requisites* of Mishnah study and the *skills induced* by the engaged analysis of Mishnah's passages, chapters, and tractates charac-terized the distinctive profile of the early rabbis as a special cadre of literati. In important respects, therefore, Mishnah and Mishnah study made and shaped the social identity of the early rabbinic group. Let me briefly review what you have learned in these respects.

Mishnah's content is overwhelmingly legal. Yet, as you have learned, Mishnah is not a systematic introduction to early rabbinic law in the sense that the almost contemporary *Institutes* of Gaius introduces Roman law. For each grand topic in the *Institutes* (e.g., property, personal status, etc.), Gaius presents the system of Roman law "from the ground up," starting with

2. Ben-Zion, in "Quest for Social Identity" and *Roadmap to the Heavens*, lists other "group activities" that served to socially bind members of the early rabbinic group together (e.g., periodically dining together, praying together, visiting one an-other, celebrating and mourning with one another). This may indeed be the case, and all such activities would help reinforce social identity. But none of these, in my opinion, equals the place of Mishnah study with others in reinforcing a distinctively rabbinic group identity.

3. See chs. 7 and 8 of Lightstone, *In the Seat of Moses*, 284–423, for an introduction to the dominant literary conventions that define how both the Jerusalem and Babylo-nian Talmuds engage the Mishnah text.

basic legal principles and concepts and building up from there. In contrast, Mishnah's passages tend to present (and even spin out) topically organized series of largely hypothetical cases of varying complexity. For each such case or series of cases, Mishnah proffers a ruling or, frequently, two opposing rulings. Moreover, the cases often pertain to an imagined world in which the temple and all of its institutions still stand and operate. That is why, for this imagined world, *all* of the laws and rituals prescribed in Scripture, even those that require a central temple in Jerusalem, still apply in principle. Since much (even if not all) of that imagined world is a "dream" at the time of Mishnah's composition (because the Jerusalem temple was destroyed some 130 years earlier in 70 CE), Mishnah study is a theoretical exercise of sorts, engaged in for two reasons: (1) because that imagined world is Scripture's world, so to speak; and (2) because Mishnah study, even of an imagined world, both *demands* and *instills* something of ultimate value in its engaged students. It is what Mishnah study demands and instills in its devotees that makes the early rabbinic sages distinctively rabbinic as a group.

So, what does Mishnah study demand? As you have seen, Mishnah study demands as a (pre) requisite a full understanding of all of Scripture's prescriptions and proscriptions. It also demands a thorough understanding of a body of *extra*-scriptural law that is everywhere assumed by, but is rarely fully spelled out in, Mishnah passages. And since no one is born with this knowledge and understanding, Mishnah study, at least for the novice, demands some institutionalized form of master-disciple relationship (although not necessarily institutionalized academies, for the existence of which there is no evidence during this early period of the rabbinic movement's development).[4]

4. By the end of the third century CE, and certainly by the end of the fourth, rabbinic houses of study (*beyt midrash*, sg.) operate in the land of Israel. The emergence of these houses of study marks a greater form of institutionalization than the master-disciple circles that dominated the earlier phases of the development of the rabbinic movement. Large-scale rabbinic academies (yeshiva, sg.) begin to appear in the subsequent centuries, particularly in the fifth or sixth centuries, and most notably in Mesopotamia. In my view, the development of large-scale rabbinic academies rests on the tradition of founding academies for higher learning of Greco-Roman philosophy, mathematics, science, medicine, law, and rhetoric, particularly of the kind that were known in the late Roman imperial and early Roman Byzantine eras. Early Christianity's antipathy to what was seen as "pagan" learning led to the closing of many of these academies in the fifth and sixth centuries, and many of their intellectual refugees were welcomed in the Sassanian-Persian Empire, where in the sixth century, academies of Greco-Roman learning were (well?) established. These non-Jewish academies and perhaps also the rabbinic yeshivot, were, in turn, refashioned and further developed in the early Islamic era, which saw the emergence of the first "university-like" institutions in the West.

In addition, the nature of how Mishnah tends to use language places demands of a particular sort on the Mishnah student. You have learned that Mishnah's passages are often highly laconic (that is, they are missing many essential bits) in several respects. Mishnah only periodically alludes to the underlying scriptural basis for its rulings. The Mishnah student must (first) identify any of these to understand the ruling (or opposing rulings) provided in any one Mishnah passage. Moreover, relevant *extra*-scriptural law is also frequently left unstated. So, Mishnah study demands filling in these missing bits as well. But additionally, the very "sentences" that comprise Mishnah passages are frequently missing language that is absolutely essential to understanding the *complete* set of circumstances of the (hypothetical) cases under consideration. How can one possibly understand the reasoning behind the rulings proffered for the cases, if all of the relevant circumstances are not spelled out?! The answer (as you have learned)—one must often analytically reasons "backwards" from the ruling or two opposing rulings in order logically to fill in the missing bits of the circumstances of the case. Moreover, if a Mishnah passage provides two opposing rulings for the stated, hypothetical circumstances, the Mishnah student must engage in this reconstructive analytical exercise several times over, first, to mentally fill in what is missing; second, to discern why one ruling would/could be correct; and, third, to understand why the opposite ruling would/could be correct. Now this exercise would in every instance beg a further analytic question. Why does the purveyor of one opposing ruling not reason as the other one does? And the analytic exercise goes on accordingly. And only after doing *all* of this is the legal logic of the Mishnah passage made fully apparent.

When the novice Mishnah student first encounters all of these intellectual demands that Mishnah study places on one, the would-be rabbi needs a teacher as a guide. As one advances in one's study of the Mishnah, one is increasingly able to satisfy these analytic demands on one's own or with a fellow student. At a still further point in one's development as a student of Mishnah, one may guide other would-be rabbis in their studies of Mishnah. In other words, because of the specific types of intellectual/analytic demands placed on one by Mishnah study, one eventually, with guidance, gains an equally specific, highly developed set of skills that are instilled (and continue to be honed) as a result of lifelong engagement with the text of the Mishnah. Moreover, the process of acquiring, and later guiding others in the acquisition of, these specific skills helps effect and maintain the social formation of the Mishnanians as a distinctive cadre. This hard-won, shared skill set is a large part of the *profile* that characterizes the rabbis as a group; it is at the core of their shared social identity, just as engaged Mishnah study undertaken with others constitutes a major mode of *social interaction* for members of the early rabbinic cadre.

What is the utility to themselves and/or to others of this skill set? It is to be able to advise (if not to rule) how one might apply the norms of Scripture and of extra-scriptural Judah-ite legal traditions to the particular exigencies of cases defined by even the most complex set of circumstances, whether real or hypothetical in nature. Or one might say: because of the hypothetical, also for the real. To put this in early rabbinic terms, it is the knowledge and skill to decide matters of halakha—how one ought to behave in order to live one's life together with others in accordance with the "Way" of the Torah of Moses, *as understood at least by the early rabbis.* The end of the preceding sentence, the part in italics, begs an essential question: Why submit to the early rabbis' sagesse as opposed to any other Judah-ite sage's wisdom? In essence, this question (if understood rhetorically) is, as we have seen, an element of the Karaites' resistance in the ninth and subsequent centuries CE to what had become in that era increasingly monopolistic rabbinic authority. Without a firm sense of this why, the rabbis could no more justify their legitimacy and authority to themselves than they could promote these to the Judah-ite population at large in the land of Israel. Permit me to unpack this last statement, in light of what you have already learned in the preceding chapters of this book.

Why do the early rabbis think any of this—the lifelong devotion to Mishnah study, the demands of engaged Mishnah study, and the skill set that is instilled by devoted Mishnah study—is (or ought to be) important to themselves or to anyone else? To respond to this multipart query is to understand the early rabbis' *mythologizations* of what they were. Given the undisputed authority of the Hebrew Scriptures, and especially of the Pentateuch, which long before the turn of the third century CE had been designated as the Torah of Moses in Judah-ite circles, expertise in Scripture and its interpretative traditions would have bestowed erudite-sapiential status and authority on a sage, *any* sage. And as you have already learned, the wisdom of the Judah-ite scribes of the five hundred or so years preceding Mishnah's composition was increasingly defined over the intervening centuries as knowledge of the laws of the Torah of Moses. What distinguished the early rabbis as a group, however, was their devotion to Mishnah study specifically. And since Mishnah is an *exclusive* product and possession of the early rabbinic movement in a way that Scripture is not, what legitimates the early rabbis as the products of lifelong Mishnah study must legitimate Mishnah as Scripture-like. And so, certainly by the mid-third century CE, we see evidence of the beginnings of the early rabbinic mythologization of Mishnah and of its acclaimed author, Rabbi Judah the Patriarch, as the perfect literary embodiment and privileged human recipient (Heb. verb root *qbl*) respectively of "torah [-knowledge] from Sinai," revealed by YHWH to Moses, and thereafter transmitted through a designated chain of tradents to Judah. This made Mishnah "torah" (from Moses) as much as the Pentateuch. And it made the students of Mishnah a singular group of Torah scholars and authorities, at least in the eyes of the rabbis themselves, although (initially) in the eyes of few others. These initial mythologizations of Mishnah and of the early rabbinic group were further elaborated over the fourth and subsequent centuries. For example, in the fourth and fifth centuries, rabbinic traditions fully articulate the notion that on Sinai, God revealed *two* Torahs to Moses, a Written Torah, which is embodied in the Pentateuch, and an Oral Torah, transmitted "by mouth," via the already specified chain of tradition, to be cast ultimately and perfectly in Mishnah by Judah. (And, as you have seen, in the tenth century, Sherira historicizes these mythologizations as part of his epistle to the rabbinic sages of Kairouan, who were, it appears, much perturbed by challenges to exclusive rabbinic authority over the halakha, as claimed by the rabbis of that time.)

If the foregoing is the early rabbis' way of *legitimating* what they are, it does not suffice to understand why any of this would be experienced as *plausible*, prima facie, by the rabbis or other Judah-ites just before and after the turn of the third century CE. We may, quite rightly, see the rabbis as a new type of authority emerging in the aftermath of the near total collapse of the systems of authority that were grounded in the Jerusalem temple and its associated institutions. But in ancient societies in particular, it is very often the case that new is not good, unless it is especially "charismatic" (to use Max Weber's categorical "ideal" type). And even in the latter instance, the charismatic had better adhere to some established social model in order to be viewed as legitimate. Generally speaking, therefore, when one considers matters of legitimacy and plausibility in "traditional" societies and cultures, new is bad and old/established is good. Period! The early rabbis' mythologization of Mishnah indeed makes of the new (that is, Mishnah) something old (that is, revelation to Moses on Sinai). But there is more to systems of legitimation and plausibility than simply articulating a self-serving myth. And it is just these considerations that lie behind the second question that was the driver of this book: What might the early rabbis, and other contemporary Judah-ites, have thought they, the rabbis, were *like*? That is, were core aspects of the early rabbinic profile and of their mythologizations enough *like* antecedent, established social profiles and notions to have an air of plausibility and legitimacy?

In chapters 5 and 6 we examined some compelling candidates and models for these likenesses. Chapter 5 looked for these within the cultural history of the land of Israel. Chapter 6 considered likely models from the surrounding regions of the eastern Mediterranean and Near East, of which the land of Israel was an enduring part in cultural and often political respects. As we have seen, both in the land and surrounding it, a cadre of highly literate, exceptionally learned scribes functioned as a class of senior staff, retainers, and bureaucrats to those at the apex of power. The latter tended to occupy their positions by reason of birth and lineage (for example, kings, princes, local nobility, and priests); the former served them by reason of their education. While these cadres of social authority may have overlapped to a degree (that is, when nobility was coupled with learning), they were distinct, with one caveat. Advanced learning required considerable financial means and the associated leisure that wealth allowed one to have. If rabbis are *like* anyone, they are like the well-known, long-standing figure of the scribes. Moreover, we have seen that in the land of Israel over the course of nearly half a millennium preceding Mishnah's production, Judah-ite literature increasingly depicts scholarship of the Torah of Moses as core to scribal learning. Given their mythologization of Mishnah as torah (in the generic sense) from Moses, this is exactly how the early rabbis are depicting themselves. And, indeed, the rabbis attribute much of the extra-scriptural law that is part and parcel of their knowledge to the Judah-ite scribes that preceded the rabbis.

In important respects rabbis not only look like scribes, but (as I have argued) they also looked much like Roman jurists. As halakhic analysts and thinkers who applied their skills to proffering opinions about complex cases defined by confounding circumstances, rabbis did (or aspired to do) precisely what Roman jurists flourishing just before and at the time of Mishnah's production and initial promulgation did. And insofar as the early rabbis offered, or aspired to offer, such services (on demand, as it were) from positions outside of formal institutions of governance and administration at the local and regional levels, the rabbis occupied a social position similar to that of the independent Roman jurist. That some or many of the early rabbis sought (and in some instances were assigned) positions to which the patriarch was empowered to make appointments does not negate the fact that many or most rabbis' aspirations went unrequited in this respect. That is, the rabbis may have wished to occupy important administrative roles *as the scribes had done*, but in this early period, many rabbis would have had to have "settled" for being consulted *as the Roman jurists were*.

Not only would the profile of the early rabbis have been sufficiently like those of other legitimate and established roles to give the early rabbis' characteristic skill set an air of authenticity, legitimacy, and plausibility in their social and cultural setting, but also their mythologization of

Mishnah and of its acclaimed author bears a semblance to notions that already had currency among Judah-ites of their era. As you have learned, notions that the *publicly* circulating Scriptures did not exhaust YHWH's revelation were already de rigueur in some Judah-ite circles. In the minds of many Judah-ites, revelation, including revelation of (new) law that complemented and supplemented Scripture's law, continued in the period after the largely acknowledged cessation of classical prophecy after the careers of Haggai, Zachariah, and Malachi in the early Second Temple era. Especially in Judah-ite apocalyptic literature, additional secret revelations are said to have been given to lionized figures like Daniel and Ezra, who are commanded to reserve these additional, extra-biblical revelations for the wise of some future era. In such instances, these extra-biblical books and teachings are not said to have been transmitted orally. Rather, they are understood to have been written down and either hidden or entrusted to a very small group. Moreover, some Judah-ite evidence from the several centuries preceding the advent of the early rabbis specifies that diligent scribes/sages dedicated to Torah learning may be worthy to receive divine inspiration in support of the counsel they provide others. Ben Sira made such a claim about himself, as you have seen.

In light of all this, it does not seem to be too great a leap or incredulous to claim that what is only now composed in a text, Mishnah, is revelation that had been passed down "by mouth" from one special tradent to another, from Moses to Rabbi Judah the Patriarch, Mishnah's acclaimed author. After all, according to the ancient Judah-ite historian Josephus, the Pharisees, who had enjoyed a substantial following in Judah-ite society and whom the early rabbis (sometimes) claim as their antecedents, distinguished their policies from those of their detractors by claiming that their extra-scriptural ancestral traditions, whether written or not, were (almost?) as legitimate as the laws written in the Torah of Moses.

Such, then, has been this volume's treatment of the two questions that have steered your reading from the preface on. (1) *What* were the early rabbis of the late second to mid-third centuries CE, the period of the early rabbinic movement's substantial, initial, social formation? And (2) What might the early rabbis, and other contemporary Judah-ites of their society, think they, the rabbis, were *like*? By addressing these questions, we have taken a historical snapshot of the early rabbinic movement through the lens of social science perspectives and approaches. We have discussed matters of the early rabbis' social formation, of their distinctive identity and profile, and of the manners in which that identity and profile possessed an air of plausibility and legitimacy in their contemporary social and cultural contexts. By the end of the first millennium CE, the rabbis had become the most authoritative (near monopolistic) purveyors of the halakha, the "Way" Jews, as individuals and communities, were to conduct their affairs and their religion in accordance with Torah in the aftermath of the wiping away of the Jerusalem temple's cult and institutions at the beginning of that millennium. And it was a millennium that not only changed authority structures of Jewish communities but also (and not coincidentally) that judaized the Western world (that is, the Near East and the lands around the Mediterranean) via the Christian and Islamic versions/revisions of the same Judah-ite religion and culture, over which the rabbis claimed mastery.

Appendix[1]

A Brief Account of the Historical Development
of the Early Rabbinic Movement

(extracts from Jack N. Lightstone, *In the Seat of Moses*, chapter 2)

U NLIKE EARLY CHRISTIAN LITERATURE, indeed unlike *earlier* Judaic literature, early rabbinic literature of the late second century through to the dawn of the seventh century eschewed sustained history-like narratives about anything and everything. [As already remarked in the introduction to this current volume, t]here are no "biographies" of the great rabbis of antiq-

---

1. The entirety of this appendix comprises extracts from chapter 2 of my book *In the Seat of Moses*. These extracts are reproduced here for your convenience with the permission of the Westar Institute and Cascade/Wipf and Stock, to whom I extend my thanks. Throughout this appendix, ellipses are used to indicate where I have not reproduced words, sentences, or whole paragraphs from the original text; I do this not only out of a sense of economy but also because what I have removed will largely be familiar to the readers of this current book from its preface and chapter 1. Furthermore, in this appendix, brackets are used to interpolate language that helps integrate these extracts into their new "home" in this volume. I would note as well that I have retained the copyediting norms of the original text, as opposed to recasting these extracts to conform to the copyediting norms of this current book.

All this said, this book on what the early rabbis were stands on its own without a single sentence in this appendix. The latter is offered as a service of sorts, so that those who wish to read a relatively brief account of what I feel may be reliably said about the history and development of the early rabbinic movement will find it here, rather than having to resort to a copy of *In the Seat of Moses*, the principal focus of which is rendering accessible to a nonspecialist audience the major legal/halakhic texts of the early rabbis.

uity; there are no rabbinic-authored histories of the Jews or of the rabbinic group during this period. There is nothing similar to any one of the Gospels, or the Acts of the Apostles, or Eusebius' *Church History*. And no one *outside* the rabbinic movement in antiquity, whether Jew, Christian, or pagan, has incorporated any extended account of the early rabbinic movement or its main luminaries into their narratives. For example, elements of the history of the Jewish people in the first through early fourth centuries are found in Eusebius' *Church History*. But Eusebius, living in the Land of Israel, writes nothing about the rabbinic movement, its makeup, organization, or place within Jewish polity in the Land of Israel. Yet by Eusebius' time, the Mishnah and probably some version(s) of the Tosefta and the Halakhic Midrashim had already been produced and were studied by rabbis. Libanius, a pagan teacher living in Antioch in the latter half of the fourth century, has provided posterity with his active correspondence with the Jewish Patriarch of the Land of Israel of his day. Later in this chapter I shall say something of the relationship of the Patriarch's administration to the early rabbinic movement. But nothing in Libanius' letters to the Patriarch touches upon the early rabbis. Were it not for the voluminous literature that the rabbis themselves composed in antiquity, and, as I argue at several junctures in this chapter, were it not for the rabbis' ultimate success in the seventh through eleventh centuries in establishing their authority over the vast majority of Jewish communities, we might not have even known of the rabbinic movement's existence or the production of their literature from the late second to the dawn of the seventh century. Perhaps a few inscriptions might have aroused speculation—like the one dated to the fourth century CE from a site on today's Golan Heights that reads, "this is the study house of Rabbi Eliezer Ha-Qappar," or another from the ancient Rehov synagogue from the sixth century CE in the Land of Israel that looks like it reflects the substance of several passages in early rabbinic legal texts[2]—but that is all.

In fact [and as the readers of this current book already know], it is not until the tenth century CE that *anyone* attempts to produce an extended "history" of the rabbinic movement and of its principal literature. Rabbi Sherira Gaon, the head of a major rabbinic academy in Pumbeditha in the Muslim-ruled Babylonian Plain, writes such a work. . . . But what are we modern students of religion and society to make of Sherira's work? Certainly, we have to read it as an apology for, and as a defense of, rabbinic authority [as we have done in chapter 2 of the current volume]. . . . Additionally, Sherira is writing many centuries after the events about which his epistle

2. Specifically, texts found in Tosefta Shevi‘it 4:8–11, Sifre Deuteronomy 51, and Jerusalem Talmud Demai 2:1, 22c–d and Shevi‘it 6:1, 36c.

deals, especially when providing an account of the earlier phases of the rabbinic movement. But he does not seem to have access to any additional sources than one has in hand today for the period much before the fifth or early sixth centuries CE. For example, Sherira possesses no elaborated histories covering these early centuries of the rabbinic group's development that have subsequently been lost to modern historians.

To get a sense of how problematic this is for the modern historian of religion, let me paint a fictional scenario. Imagine that the author of Acts had written not in the latter part of the first [or early second] century about the earliest developments of the Jesus movement, but in the tenth century, with no other earlier elaborated historical narrative available to us (or perhaps even to the author of Acts). Historians of Christianity would be working with such a tenth-century Acts with great caution and reserve in terms of assessing what conclusions one could draw on its basis about the development of Christian communities in the first century. As it is, working with a late first-century Acts is not without its historiographical challenges because of the religious-ideological purposes for which the author writes. This is the situation one faces in using Sherira's history of the rabbinic movement and its literature. He seems to have some sources that have not independently survived and been transmitted to modern scholars. But these appear to be chronicles in his academy covering just the several centuries immediately preceding his own era, from the sixth or seventh centuries to the tenth. As stated, and worth repeating, the earlier the period about which he speaks, the more he seems to have no sources that modern scholars do not already have. And these sources are thin gruel of problematic ingredients.

What are these sources which he and modern scholars both possess, because they are already embedded in the early rabbinic literature transmitted to us? They are mainly episodic, very short, often homiletically oriented, or legal-precedent-purposed stories about this or that rabbi or this or that event. These scattered stories were not composed to give an account of the rabbinic movement's history, organization, economic base, or an account of some of its more seminal figures. They usually serve to convey some moral lesson or to establish the authenticity of some legal ruling. That is all. Sherira reads and repurposes such stories as part of a history, as have many early modern and modern scholars, often influenced by Sherira's particular reconstruction. But frankly, many scholars, myself included, recognize how difficult the methodological path is for such an exercise of historical and social reconstruction, and how speculative, qualified, and incomplete is the resulting picture. . . .

[All this said, and in the interest of edifying this volume's readers, the remainder of this appendix] . . . present[s] my best estimate (some may rightly say, "guestimate") of the development of the early rabbinic movement in its historical contexts. As one might predict from what I have said in the preceding paragraphs, I will frequently be "hedging" my remarks, where I feel it inappropriate to firmly come down on one side or another of an issue.

I divide my account into two parts or periods, (a) from the mid- to late second century CE on, and (b) before the mid- to late second century. I do this for a very specific reason. As far as I am concerned, we have no literary works produced by the rabbis before the end of the second century or so, and lots from that period forward. Some *sources* of the Mishnah and the Tosefta are likely earlier, but we do not possess these sources as documents transmitted independently to us. And what antecedent sources or traditions that may be found in Mishnah and Tosefta have been for the most part (re)cast in the idiomatic language and literary forms that characterize Mishnah and Tosefta as a whole.

What do I mean by these statements? If Mishnah (or Tosefta) were compared to the Gospel of Matthew (or Luke), one has for Mishnah (or Tosefta) nothing like a "Gospel of Mark" that (in some earlier version, "proto-Mark") provided the basis for a "Gospel of Matthew" (or a "Gospel of Luke").[3] Moreover, what early rabbinic literature has to say or implies about the rabbinic movement *before* the end of the second century is even likelier to be tendentious mythmaking than what it has to say for the period contemporaneous with these texts' authors, all of which date from c. 200 CE and later. After all, the texts can be said to reflect the rabbinic culture of those who produced and studied them; one cannot say whether they reflect the culture of the rabbinic movement much before the production of Mishnah, the earliest rabbinic composition, at the end of the second century. So, an account of the earlier period is, admittedly, even more speculative.

It is worth noting that the distinction this . . . [appendix] makes between rendering an account of the rabbinic movement (a) from the latter second century on *versus* (b) before and up to the latter second century

---

3. Whether some "core-Tosefta" is actually earlier than and formed the basis of, or model for some proto-Mishnah has been debated regularly over the past twenty years. I do not subscribe to this view for reasons that I have reviewed in passing in [my book *In the Seat of Moses*,] chapter 9 . . . and . . . articulated in chapter 5, notes 4, 14, 16 and 21. Since generally, this book is not concerned with literary-historical issues, unless absolutely germane to its primary purpose, I do not in this volume take up the issue of the literary history (or prehistory) of Tosefta (or of any other early rabbinic legal text). Harry Fox at the end of the 1990s ably summarized the positions on the nature and origins of Tosefta and puts forward his own quite thorough assessment in Fox, "Introducing Tosefta." More recently, scholarly positions of Tosefta's literary-historical relationship with Mishnah have been critically assessed by Brody in *Mishnah*.

has an important analog in what early fifth century and turn of the seventh century rabbinic documents (the two Talmuds) posit about the generations of rabbis that preceded them. These rabbinic texts draw a line in the historical sand not in the latter second century (as I have done) but in the early third century, just *after* Mishnah was produced and promulgated. [As you have already learned in chapter 1 of this volume, r]abbis whom these documents' authors believed lived before and up to the time of the production of Mishnah were called *tanna'im* . . . ; their authority is superior to those that followed them as are all traditions attributed to *tanna'im* or to their era. Rabbinic figures who lived afterward, in the Land of Israel up to the c. 400 CE or in the Mesopotamian-Babylonian Plain until c. 500 CE, were called *amora'im*. . . . The designation *amora'im* served to differentiate them and teachings from their era from "tannaitic" sources that allegedly preceded them, and from materials that postdated "amoraic" traditions. This late antique or early medieval distinction between "tannaitic" and "amoraic" traditions plays out in how rabbinic legal literature produced c. 400 . . . (in the case of the Jerusalem Talmud) and c. 600 (in the case of the Babylonian Talmud) treat the sources and traditions with which they work. . . .

At this juncture, then, I must make confession. . . . Despite having devoted more than forty-five years to the study of the early movement and its literature, there are many historical issues with which I still struggle. I might as well alert you to them in advance. For most of the period of the second to the dawn of the seventh century, I have difficulty offering sound historical judgments about the size of the rabbinic movement,[4] about its level of social importance and authority in Jewish society, about its economic base, and about its forms of organization and institutionalization. I am prepared to say this: they were likely more numerous toward the end of that period, carried more authority within Jewish society in the Land of Israel and in Persian-ruled Babylonia nearer the end of that period, and had larger, more formally organized institutions of rabbinic learning for the training and continuing education of rabbis by the dawn of the seventh century. But [as I have written in the preface and chapters 1 and 2 of this book,] by the end of that period, they likely still did not enjoy a monopoly, or near monopoly, as purveyors of norms and laws about living a Jewish life in a community of

4. For example, Mishnah and Tosefta attribute legal positions to about 120 named rabbis. About twenty of these are unique to Tosefta, and many seem to be rabbis from the very end of the second century or the first decade or two of the third. Does this represent the sum total of all members of the rabbinic movement for the 150 years or so up to about 220 CE? Or are these the VIPs among the membership of the rabbinic movement over that 150-year period, those whose careers where particularly valued by their more numerous rabbinic disciples? One could legitimately go in either direction, in the absence of probative, explicit evidence.

other Jews, within a larger host society of non-Jews. That achievement had likely to wait another several centuries.

The reason I feel compelled to get this off my chest at the outset of my account is simple. Rabbinic literature has a tendency to portray directly and indirectly rabbis as authoritative, and to have *always been* authoritative since the advent of the group, which rabbis of the fourth or fifth century (and later centuries) portray as having happened in the immediate after-math of the destruction of the Temple in the first century (if not in the several decades before 70 CE). [As you already know from reading chapter 1 of this current book, *rabbi*/"my master" and *hakhamim*/"sages"] . . . the terms and titles used to refer to rabbis by the *earliest* rabbinic document, the Mishnah (c. 200 CE), convey this assumption (or more accurately, pretense and perhaps conceit). . . . All of the biblical wisdom literature extols the virtue and talents of "the sage." Could one think of a more socially self-pro-moting term in ancient Judaic culture, if one is referring to someone who is *not* claiming authority and respect by reason of their Levitical-priestly lineage (as did the High Priest and the Hasmonean kings) or monarchic lineage (as Matthew does for Jesus based on a genealogy linking him to the biblical King David)? That the rabbis from the outset offered themselves as the obvious and "natural" alternative authority figures to priests and Jewish nobility in a world changed by the destruction of the Jerusalem Temple in 70 CE and the defeat of Bar Kokhba in 135 CE is not surprising. We just do not know how and when many others accepted the offer. Nor do we know who made competing offers and with how much success. It is unlikely that those with priestly lineage just packed up and ceded authority and influ-ence to others . . . the day after the Temple was destroyed.[5]

So, the account that follows may refer to a relatively small group, loosely organized, and with limited power and authority until nearer the fifth or sixth century CE (or later). Or rabbinic ranks and prestige may have swelled earlier (as their literature often seems self-servingly to por-tray). I have canvassed and read the writings of a number of trusted aca-demic colleagues on these points, and I am less prepared today to defend a particular position on many of these matters than I was ten or twenty years ago. Such are my caveats to what now follows.

---

5. Based on inscriptions from Caesarea, there is evidence of the existence of "priestly courses" in late Roman Israel well after the destruction of the Temple. This was or may have been a system of twenty-four divisions of the ranks of the priests, each stationed at a different town in the Land of Israel, and in turn still performing some vestigial functions related to their priestly authority. See Avi-Yonah, "List."

From the Second Century Forward, the Development of the Early Rabbinic Movement

. . . [As already intimated in the preface, t]he historical processes that led eventually to the general recognition within almost all Jewish communities (first largely concentrated in the Middle East and Mediterranean lands, and by the time of the Crusades also in the Rhine valley of central Europe and in England) that the teachings and rulings of the rabbis . . . were authoritative for all aspects of Jewish life was a long one. That process started with the earliest formation of the rabbinic movement in the Land of Israel, most likely sometime in the second century CE, and progressed over the subsequent seven or so centuries. The rabbis' aspirations to rise to such levels of authority had much to do with the political, social, and cultural dynamics of the Land of Israel (under Roman and Byzantine rule) and of the Mesopotamian-Babylonian Plain (what the rabbis called simply, "Babylonia," under Persian rule). A definite spur to that progress happened at the time, and perhaps as a result, of the early spread of Islamic rule in the seventh and early eighth centuries, first across the Middle East, and thereafter westward across North Africa and into the Iberian Peninsula to the very southwestern boundaries of France.

The ups and downs of the fortunes of the rabbis and of their authority within Jewish circles over those seven centuries were likely many. Sometimes members of the rabbinic class ended up filling power vacuums in Jewish community institutions, vacuums largely created by outside forces. Or they competed with other nonrabbinic "sages" for such positions with, at first, episodic success. When individual rabbis did succeed, they filled bureaucratic-administrative functions in Jewish communities by reason of their high level of Judaic literacy, including their command of Jewish law and practice—of course, as *they*, the rabbis, defined that law and practice.

As I have implied, it is unlikely that they were the only pretenders. Nor can one say whether they comprised even a significant proportion of these functionaries—indeed they likely did not—before the latter part of this four-hundred-year period. Much has to do, on the one hand, with the policies of the Roman Empire, of the late Persian Empire, and of the early Islamic Caliphate toward Jews and the Jewish communities in their respective territories. And it has to do, on the other, with the presence of other, nonrabbinic, highly Judaically literate administrative and legal experts, the extent of which is now obscured because of the rabbinic movement's ultimate success in the seventh and subsequent centuries.

Under Roman Imperial rule, several developments were key. Some I have already mentioned in . . . [chapter 1 of this volume]. In 70 CE, the

Jewish Temple in Jerusalem was destroyed over the course of the Roman defeat of a rebellion by Jewish groups against Roman rule in the Land of Israel. . . . A second rebellion, associated with the leadership of Simeon bar Kuziba, who took on a messianic *nom de guerre* Bar Kokhba ("Son of the Star"), and who appears to have been viewed by a number of his contemporaries as the messiah, ended in 135–36 CE in the Roman defeat of those rebels as well as in the imposition of harsh (in the main, temporary) punitive measures against Jews in the Land of Israel, especially in Judea, the southern portion of the Land.

One measure was not intended to be temporary. Jerusalem . . . was now rebuilt as a Roman garrison city, was renamed Aelia Capitolina, and a Temple to Jupiter was built either near the current site of the Church of the Holy Sepulchre (the more current scholarly view) or in the Mount Moriah area of the Roman city (a once accepted but now questionable view). . . .[6] In short [and as intimated in chapter 1 of this volume], all forms of Judaic religious and civil leadership, and all religious and cultic practices associated with, and dependent upon the functioning of, the Jerusalem Temple and its institutions appeared irrevocably gone, or if not entirely expunged, lacking their former, formal-institutionalized basis and setting. Many of these were enjoined in the Jewish biblical Scriptures, especially in the first five books of those Scriptures (the Pentateuch), which . . . bore the moniker "the Torah of Moses." Consequently, the understanding and use of these Scriptures also became a matter of uncertainty, although sacred Scriptures they continued to be. Moreover, militant Jewish political and national messianism, the attempt to bring about by civil disobedience and military action the era of the messiah in this world and renewed Davidic monarchic rule over the Land of Israel, will have received a very black eye

6. The current Mount Moriah compound in Jerusalem, where the Dome of the Rock and the Al-Aqsa Mosque now stand, derives from the Roman reconstruction of the site after 135 CE during Hadrian's time. This "more or less" coincides with the compound created by Herod's reconstruction of the Temple Mount. As to the exact location of pre-Islamic structures—such as Solomon's Temple, the reconstructed Temple of YHWH in the fifth and subsequent centuries BCE, and Herod's reconstruction of the Jewish Temple—within the Temple Mount or Mount Moriah compound, there is active debate among archaeologists. The compound itself is of substantial size, and, moreover, was increased in size in Herod's major reconstruction of the site, making it one of the largest such sites in the Roman world. In the religiously charged politics of the region today, whether this or that Temple was twenty or fifty meters this way or that within the compound takes on more significance than historians and archeologists would normally assign it. For example, does the Dome of the Rock sit on the site of the Holy of Holies of Herod's Temple to Yahweh? Or is YHWH's Temple's Holy of Holies a little to the south within the same compound, between what is today the Al-Aqsa Mosque and the Dome of the Rock? See Eliav, "Urban Layout."

indeed. Jews and Judaism in the Land of Israel, and to some extent in the Diaspora too,[7] had experienced severe civil, cultural, and religious shocks to the system. And early Christian communities—*especially* those still largely comprised of Jews who were followers of Jesus and his teachings and whose self-definition blended their Judaic and Christian identities, lives, and practices—likely experienced an equal shock.

The (temporary) retaliatory and punitive measures the Romans imposed in Land of Israel after 135 CE were brought to an end sometime in the mid-second century. Later in that century Rome seems[8] formally to have recognized some forms of Jewish communal self-rule and organization in the Land of Israel. Its details are sketchy. But two trends seem to be in force in the latter decades of the second century in areas of substantial Jewish settlement. These were along the coastal plain of the Land of Israel and in the lower and upper Galilee into what today is known as the Golan Heights[, t]he aftermath of the Bar Kokhba rebellion [having] resulted in major migration

---

7. Of course, the modalities of Diaspora Jewry's experiences of the events of 70 and 135 CE were greatly conditioned by the fact that the Temple ceased well before its destruction in 70 CE to be an active reality in their social and religious lives as Jews. Jerusalem was simply too far away. Theirs was a reconstruction of Jewish life *on the foundations of* a biblical tradition that placed the Temple at its center, but that is hardly the same.

8. The state after 70 CE and 135 CE of formalized leadership and authority over Palestinian Jewish society, whether endowed with Roman authority or not, . . . is a much-debated issue. The debate revolves explicitly or implicitly around a series of interrelated questions, answers to which can be given with too little certainty. My take . . . is just one navigation through this minefield among other possible ones, and I can only say that I prefer it marginally to others based on the evidence. I do not capture the scholarly debate in the body of the text of this chapter. . . . Let me, however, spell out, at the very least, what some of the major, still-burning questions are: (1) When exactly did the rabbinic movement coalesce into some institutionalized entity or group in Roman Palestine? (2) When did the Jewish Patriarchate arise as a formally or informally recognized institution of Jewish leadership in Roman Palestine? (3) Whence did the power and authority of the Patriarchate derive—from the Roman state, by prestige (only) within the Jewish communities of Roman Palestine—over whom and what? (4) What is the relationship of the rabbis and/or the Patriarch to other forms of Jewish communal leadership in Roman Palestine—city and town elders, city and town councils, city magistrates/magistracies? What were the powers and authority of the rabbis in Roman Palestine—formally or informally—over whom and what? Does the evidence evoke different answers to some of these questions depending upon the time period examined—in Palestine, between 70 CE and 135 CE, or 135 CE to c. 200 CE, or c. 200 CE to 400 CE, or after c. 400 CE (all of which time frames correspond to known changes in Roman Palestine)? Moreover, a similar set of questions may be articulated, *mutandis mutandi*, for the rabbinic movement and the Exilarchate (the office of the Resh Galuta) in the Mesopotamian-Babylonian Plain under Persian rule. And, as intimated, specific answers to all of these questions have been vigorously debated by modern scholars.

of Jewish survivors from the territory around Jerusalem (in Judea) to these other regions of the Land of Israel long inhabited by Jews.

One form of Jewish self-administration was at the local level and may have already existed for some time. The Jews of local towns and cities with substantial Jewish populations seem to have been in the charge of councils of elders, on which sat local gentry. Synagogues, whatever, wherever, and whenever their origins,[9] came in a number of locales to function as the seat of these governing councils and related institutions, not just as gathering places for prayers or the reading of Scriptures (as attested in the Gospels and in Acts). So, in a gradual transformation that in time frame paralleled rabbinism's early development in the Land of Israel from the late second to the fifth and into the sixth centuries, the synagogue came to be the seat of both communal religious practice and local Jewish civil administration (just as they were in this time frame outside of the Land of Israel in the Graeco-Roman Jewish Diaspora). In Roman terms, synagogues over this period came to house under one roof the functions that in a typical Roman city would be handled by the council building (*hostilia* or *bouleterion*), the temple(s), and the facility for public civic and judicial proceedings (the *basilica*).

As noted, the emergence in the Land of Israel over these centuries of such a form of Jewish communal organization was not a newfangled or unique development. It is attested in evidence concerning Jewish communities outside the Land of Israel in Roman-ruled lands dating at least as far back as the mid-first century CE. And it is well attested in these "diaspora" Jewish communities thereafter. For example, in the first century, the aristocratic Alexandrian Jewish philosopher Philo (in *Legatio* and *Flaccum*) remarks upon the centrality of such councils and their presidents or "rulers" for the Jews in Alexandria. Alexandrian Jews boasted a number of synagogues with their respective councils and council presidents, and the Jewish population of the city as a whole also seems to have had a super-council and president (comprised of representatives from individual synagogue councils). Alleged Roman edicts of the early Caesars (mentioned in Josephus' *Antiquities of the Jews* (Book XIV, 183–267), subsequent Roman edicts dating from the fourth, fifth, and sixth centuries and preserved in Roman legal texts, inscriptional evidence from Jewish communities around the Mediterranean basin, and references in early Christian literature (such as John Chrysostom's fourth-century sermons, *Against the Jews*) all corroborate this depiction of local Jewish communal organization and governance in the Roman Mediterranean lands. And as regards the Land of Israel, such forms of local communal organization are consistent with passages in early rabbinic literature itself. As I shall

9. See Levine, *Ancient Synagogue*.

discuss shortly, the members of the nascent rabbinic movement or class or guild (whatever the appropriate designation) in the Land of Israel would have had to find their way within, between, on top of, or around such established forms of communal governance to exercise any authority.

The second form of Jewish self-rule in the Land of Israel was the Jewish Patriarchate. Its precise origins are obscure, and there is some dispute about the full range of its civil and religious authority and powers, especially over matters beyond Jewish ritual observance and its coordination within the Land. But the Patriarchate's established presence near the end of the second century, headquartered in the lower Galilee, is clear.

It is uncertain to what degree the Jewish Patriarchate in the Land of Israel operated under some form of official *license* from the Roman Imperial government at the end of the second and during the first decades of the third century. But the Patriarch certainly operated with Roman acquiescence and recognition, as well as by some form of broad acceptance on the part of Jews in the Land. Indeed, it seems that by the fourth century CE (and probably somewhat earlier as well), the Jewish Patriarch was formally addressed using titles and honorifics generally reserved for Roman senators and Imperial officials. He was, it seems, properly addressed as "the illustrious Patriarch" or "most illustrious Patriarch." For example, in his correspondence with the Patriarch, the fourth-century Antiochene pagan educator and orator Libanius uses such titles in addressing him. Rome at some point permitted the monies raised annually in Jewish communities in the Land of Israel and the Diaspora to be sent in whole or in part to support the Jewish Patriarch's administration. And when in the early fifth century the powers and privileges of the Patriarch were revoked by Imperial decree, one of the privileges that was removed was the Patriarch's status as honorary prefect of Rome, as was the power to levy or collect funds from Jewish communities in the Land and abroad to support the Patriarchate.

The Patriarch's administration seems to have had some pan-communal responsibilities and authority over a number of defined Jewish religious and distinctively Jewish civil matters and perhaps over other matters devolved to it (officially or by benign neglect) by the Roman-Imperial provincial administration. The third-century Caesarean Christian writer Origen (who refers to the Patriarch by the term "ethnarch") complains that the powers routinely exercised by the Patriarch in the Land of Israel are extensive and exceed his formal authority. The Patriarchate's relationship to local Jewish community elites and their local councils seems to have operated on the basis of some agreed-upon division of powers and responsibilities, the details of which, and the official basis for which, one cannot today completely reconstruct. Perhaps the division of responsibilities that was *de rigueur* in the empire between the Roman Imperial provincial administration and local city and town government was a justificatory parallel for the division between the Patriarchate's roles and those of the local Jewish council.

The Jewish Patriarchs constituted a dynasty. Son succeeded father until the Patriarchate's authority was whittled down and ultimately revoked in the . . . fifth century CE by the now well Christianized Roman Imperial government. The Patriarch's family were likely Jewish aristocrats of some renown. Early rabbinic literature attributes to the Patriarch's dynasty a pedigree going back to King David, just as the Gospel of Matthew does for Jesus. . . . In so doing, rabbinic literature likely reflects the Patriarchal family's own genealogical claim for itself. The Hebrew and Aramaic titles for the Patriarch, *nasi* and *nesia* respectively, mean literally "the Prince."

Early rabbinic literature, however, also and always refers to the Patriarch using the honorific "rabbi," the same honorific by which the early rabbis addressed one another. Moreover, at some point in the third or fourth century, the early rabbis attributed the production of the first rabbinic *magnum opus*—the Mishnah, composed near the turn of the third century—to one of the Patriarchs, "Rabbi" Judah "the Prince." Rabbi Judah the Prince (or simply, *Rebbi*, as rabbinic literature starting with Tosefta often refers to him) held office during the last decades of the second century CE and the first several of the third century. It is unlikely that Judah wrote the Mishnah, or indeed that Mishnah was the work of any single author. But *attributing* the composition of Mishnah to a Patriarch, "Rabbi" Judah, is a significant statement about what the early rabbinic movement wished the relationship to be between themselves and the Patriarchate. Moreover, it constitutes a statement that the rabbinic movement saw the Patriarchs as fully rabbinized, in my view an overstatement.

The rabbinic attempt, from the early or mid-third century on, to portray the Patriarchs as their "brothers" in the rabbinic movement is indeed extensive. Like other major rabbinic figures, Judah the Patriarch is depicted as teaching illustrious students who thereafter themselves become renowned rabbinic masters. And Judah's (alleged?) immediate ancestors—such as Gamaliel the Elder (known to us from New Testament literature as well), Simeon ben Gamaliel I, Gamaliel II, Simeon ben Gamaliel II—all appear in Mishnah and Tosefta as typical renowned rabbinic figures to whom legal positions are attributed, just as these texts do with other named rabbinic figures. It is all the more curious, then (and perhaps significant), that Judah's . . . descendants and successors in the Patriarch's office nowhere figure in rabbinic literature as prominently as Judah, at least not as "rabbis" fully engaged in typically rabbinic teaching and learning.

That said, the relationship between the rise of the early rabbinic movement in the Land of Israel sometime in the second century CE and the establishment of the Patriarchate also in the (late?) second century is unclear. What is likely is that they are in some sense codevelopments that somehow became intertwined (at the very least for the rabbis)—the rabbis as a "wannabe" professional-like, social formation, the Patriarchate as an institution of administration with some (and growing) *de facto* powers recognized by Rome. The rabbis, initially, seemed to desire a close relationship with the Patriarch, and by reason of it some sought or expected appointments of various sorts. The members of the early rabbinic movement promoted their candidacy for professional posts in the Patriarch's administration and for those appointments in local Jewish communities in the Land of Israel over which rabbinic literature assumes the Patriarchate had sway. To what degree were the rabbinic sentiment and ambitions equally reciprocated and satisfied by successive Patriarchs from the end of the second century CE to the . . . fifth century, when Rome abrogated the powers of the Patriarch? That is difficult to surmise. Did the rabbis define or seek to define the Patriarch as their "patron" and themselves as his "clients" in the Roman sense of these terms? Perhaps so. In any case, it is reasonably certain that the early rabbinic group tried to hitch its wagon in some fashion to the Patriarchate, on the one hand, and sought to either "rabbinize" the Patriarch or claimed to have "rabbinized" the Patriarch, on the other. Why, otherwise, would the rabbis not only have called the Patriarch rabbi but also have attributed the composition of *their* Mishnah to an illustrious member of the Patriarchal dynasty, "Rabbi" Judah? In any case, by the mid-fourth century, the rabbis seemed to have soured somewhat on the Patriarchs, whom they portrayed, among other things, as highly hellenized and romanized.[10] Is this souring a result of sour grapes? Perhaps.

What was the urban and rural social topography in which the early rabbinic movement in the Land of Israel developed? As I have stated, after the failure of the Bar Kokhba rebellion, many Jews in the region of Judea migrated to join brethren in communities in the coastal plain and in lower and upper Galilee (which then seems to have included at least part of the Golan, the high plain east and northeast of the Sea of Galilee). Local Jewish governance, the Patriarchate, along with an aspiring rabbinic class seeking to find its place in the former two spheres, all inhabited a social-geographical landscape that was anything but uniformly Jewish.

In Hellenistic and early Roman times, a number of "Greek cities" were founded in the Land of Israel; non-Jews from adjacent territories migrated

10. A point emphasized by Lee I. Levine in conversation with me in the fall of 2017.

into the Land, increasingly so after the Bar Kokhba rebellion, attracted to the more highly Hellenized Romanized urban centers. Rabbinic literature knows of "(primarily?) Jewish towns," "(primarily?) Gentile towns" and towns with both substantial Jewish and non-Jewish populations.[11] The Land of Israel in the late second and early third centuries might well be described as follows: larger urban centers with mixed populations displaying the cultural, economic, and organizational traits of other major cities in the eastern end of the Roman Empire; smaller cities and towns, whether primarily Gentile, or Jewish, or Samaritan (in the case of the territory between Judea and Galilee and east of the coastal plain); a substantial agricultural hinterland around larger and smaller urban centers, comprising smaller freehold farms, tenant farmers, and wealthy landed gentry with substantial agricultural lands as well as (second) dwellings in a nearby urban center.

While urbanization in the Land of Israel had been a steady ongoing process from Hellenistic times, it seems, then, to have accelerated in the late second and early third centuries, as attested by the archaeological remains of substantial urban building projects and urban infrastructure, including monumental structures dating from this period. This appears to have been a period of "investment" by Roman authorities in the region's development, further bolstered by Rome's granting in 212 CE by the edict of Caracalla of Roman citizenship to all free inhabitants of the empire.[12]

The latter third and especially fourth centuries may well have been a period of economic (and, therefore, of cultural) decline in the Galilee, the very center of Jewish settlement (and of rabbinic activity) in Land of Israel. A major earthquake and the revolt of Gallus, both mid-fourth-century occurrences in the region, will only have made matters worse. It appears, many settlements in the region between Sepphoris and Tiberias seem to

11. It is important to take cognizance of the fact that the Roman-ruled Land of Israel in the aftermath of the Bar Kokhba rebellion (if not before) had a remarkably robust pagan culture intermingled with the "native" Jewish one. Evidence for this comes from the many pagan cults and cultic sites in the Land of Israel from c. 200 CE to 400 CE (when, of course, the Christianization of the Roman Empire begins to reshape and curtail pagan culture throughout the empire). See Belayche, *Iudaea-Palaestina*.

12. In conversation with me in the fall of 2017, Lee I. Levine emphasized these developments as pivotal contextual elements for the development of the rabbinic movement and of the Patriarchate. Think for a moment what bestowing Roman citizenship on all Jews in the Land of Israel (and beyond) would have meant in terms of the legal jurisdictions and processes under which the Jews now fell! Ironically, in the fifth and sixth centuries now-Christian Roman emperors sought to reverse the process in a manner of speaking; Imperial edicts order that disputes among Jews be arbitrated in Jewish communal tribunals. This was part of an emerging Roman policy increasingly to separate the Jewish and Christian populations of the Roman Empire, so that Jews would not influence Christians.

have lost substantial population. And some scholars posit that the intellectual rigor of the rabbinic movement in the Land of Israel was dealt a serious blow in this period, while, in parallel, the Roman support for the stature and authority of the Patriarchate diminished near the end of the fourth century, culminating in Rome's abrogation of many/most of the Patriarch's formal, legal powers in the early fifth century. Some attribute to the conditions of this fourth century "crisis"-period the impetus to commence work on producing the Jerusalem Talmud (or Yerushalmi), which work is generally thought to have been completed (or abandoned in its more or less current state) by the beginning of the fifth or so century.

Yet, by the fifth and sixth centuries we encounter the expansion, renewal, or building of many synagogues in the Galilee and the beginning of a renewed period of homeland-based, Jewish literary activity, the editing of major Haggadic-Midrashic collections of earlier rabbinic homiletic (as opposed to legal) materials,[13] and the beginning of the production of liturgical poetry (the *piyyutim*). None of this is to say that agriculture ceased to be the backbone of the economy, even during the posited decline of the fourth century. Local, translocal, and transregional trade seems still to have dealt largely in agriculture-based products.

Forms of Jewish governance and formal Jewish communal organization, as well as the nascent and aspiring early rabbinic movement, had to find their places in this diverse, evolving landscape. We do not really know when the Patriarchate began. In my opinion, early rabbinic literature quite anachronistically assigns its origins in the first century (or earlier). But something seems to have given it considerable impetus in the last decades of the second century, during the Patriarchate of Judah the Prince, even if some may assign its origins to an earlier date. And these are precisely the decades that the nascent rabbinic movement is sufficiently institutionalized to produce their first literary oeuvre, the Mishnah. In the social topography of the Land of Israel just described, both the rabbinic movement and the Patriarchate are both situated in tier 2 and tier 3 urban settings, like Usha and Beit Shearim (. . . in the Galilee), or, in the case of many rabbis, in still smaller towns. In the early third century the Patriarchate (perhaps under an aged Judah the Patriarch, perhaps under his successor) moves to Sepphoris, a tier 1, highly Hellenized and Romanized city. Later in the third century, the Patriarch's court moves to another tier 1 urban center, Tiberias.

It is evident too that over this time frame some prominent members of the early rabbinic movement situate themselves in the largest urban centers

13. A distinction discussed further in chapters 3 and 6 [of Lightstone, *In the Seat of Moses*].

as well, in Caesarea, Sepphoris and Tiberias. The work on the "Jerusalem" Talmud (composed c. 400 or in the several subsequent decades) was likely completed in Tiberias.[14] But it seems that many rabbis did not migrate to these larger centers, continuing rather to live in the smaller cities and towns of the coastal plain, of the lower and upper Galilee, and of the Golan, surrounded by and serving a still largely agrarian economy. Certainly, when Mishnah, Tosefta and later rabbinic literature name the centers of gravity of the nascent rabbinic group, they repeatedly mention Yavneh and Lod on the coastal plain (when speaking of the decades before Bar Kokhba) and Usha and Beit Shearim (after Bar Kokhba).

Thus, the early rabbis and even Judah the Patriarch were by Roman standards Roman provincials and townsfolk within a larger, encompassing, rural-agricultural milieu.[15] To Roman officials, the Patriarchs of the end of the second century and the beginning of the third would have looked like prestigious, wealthy country/provincial gentry. As the Patriarchate became more closely associated in the third century with the major urban centers of Sepphoris and, later, Tiberias, and as their privileges and rank, like honorary prefect, came to be defined in typically Roman terms, it is understandable that many members of the rabbinic movement, whose literature often displays overt aversion to Hellenization and Romanization, would have viewed the later Patriarchs with more jaundiced eyes.

Within the general "landscape" in the Land of Israel in which the early rabbinic group coalesced and operated, what precisely did rabbis do, for whom, for what recompense (if any), by reason of what (claimed) expertise, and on what authority? And where did they seek to fit or position themselves, likely in competition with others (whose identity and affiliations are now

14. The hypothesis that some of the civil-tort sections of the Jerusalem Talmud were drafted earlier in Caesarea was put forward and defended by Saul Lieberman. Jacob Neusner has forcefully challenged Lieberman's conclusions on the grounds that those characteristics that are alleged to set these sections of the Jerusalem Talmud apart from the whole, also set these same tractates of the Babylonian Talmud apart from the rest of the BT. Consequently, in Neusner's view, these sections' distinguishing characteristics, in so far as they are significant at all, must be attributed to some other factors, not to their origins in Caesarea.

15. Hayim Lapin makes the point that emerging or aspirational rabbinic power and authority in Roman Palestine is best understood within the context of typical eastern Roman-Imperial social and political order, in which wealthy landowners take up their duties in the councils and magistracies of their towns and cities, served by (what Lee Levine would call) a "retainer class" of administrative-legal experts and what others might call a class of "scribes." See, for example, Lapin, "Hegemony and Its Discontents." See also Levine, *Rabbinic Class*, 38–42, 167–75. On where rabbis fit, and do not fit, within the Roman social and cultural world, see Schwartz, *Were the Jews*, 110–64.

obscured), within the well-established systems for local governance by local gentry ("elders") and within the panlocal institution of the Patriarchate?

Whatever the origins of the rabbinic movement in the second century CE in the Land of Israel, over the course of the next 200 years, the rabbis in part seem increasingly to have promoted themselves as possessing professional-like qualifications by reason of their learning, learning they characterized particularly as "torah" (singular, indefinite in English grammar), which in biblical terminology means revelatory or divine teaching. The rabbis' claimed knowledge of torah extends well beyond expertise in the Judaic Scriptures and their interpretation. It encompasses all aspects of Halakha, the "way" one lives a Judaic life with others in accordance with God's will. Halakha was wide-ranging in its scope. It concerned religious rites and purity law; civil, criminal, and family law; judicial and administrative process. The rabbis' "torah" knowledge also provided the basis for many other activities, including teaching, preaching, medical practices, methods of demon-avoidance and exorcism, incantations, and dream interpretation [all of which is more extensively discussed in chapters 2 through 4 of the current book].

The relationship (portrayed, sought, or fantasized) with the Patriarchate appears to support the aspirations of the rabbis to act as a profession-like cadre to implement their Halakha within organized and institutionalized community settings. Moreover, contemporary developments in Roman provincial governance paralleled and perhaps provided a model for such aspirations. During the latter part of the second century CE and the third, Roman Imperial provinces were in the process of "professionalizing" the ranks of its civil, provincial administrations rather than continuing to rely on the appointment of Italian and provincial gentry, who were at best skilled amateurs. To the degree that the Patriarch in the Land of Israel may at times have responded to the aspirations of the members of the rabbinic movement by placing some of them, rather than their competitors, in various positions, he may have been imitating a contemporary trend in Roman Imperial provincial governance.

Moreover, historically speaking, it is hard to know what to make of occasional third-, fourth-, and fifth-century references in early rabbinic literature to a supposedly late first-, second-, or early third-century institution of the Patriarch's "Court" or "Council" (*beit din*), the sitting members of which were said to be, in whole or in part, rabbis. Are these few references an anachronistic retrojection into earlier times of a state of affairs in the third, fourth, or early fifth centuries? Are they merely self-serving fictions about the late first, second, and early third centuries? If they are the latter, which I suspect, then such portrayals of an early period of Patriarchal and rabbinic codependency may nevertheless still reflect something of closer relationships between the rabbis and the Patriarchate that entailed at the turn of the third century but had largely fractured by the fourth century.

While the early rabbinic movement sought relations with, and appointments from, the Patriarch, and from local Jewish administrations, as judges, agents of the courts, civil administrators, teachers, and sometimes preachers, this, as I have already implied, was not their only means, and maybe not their principal means, of exercising their expertise and authority, let alone of earning a living. [As I have remarked and further discuss in the current book, c]ore steady income for rabbis likely did not come from any of these activities, any more than it did for community leaders and authorities generally in the cities and towns of the Roman Empire. According to early rabbinic literature, rabbis seem to have had businesses and enterprises unrelated to their activities as rabbis. Some were very wealthy as a result; others were not. [I have already intimated in this book's introductory chapter and repeat the point in subsequent chapters] . . . that the time and dedication involved in becoming a rabbi, and mastering the requisite body of knowledge . . . is likely to have been something that mostly those of sufficient independent economic means could pursue. [As we shall see, t]he rabbinic mythology about Rabbi Aqiva starting out his life in poverty (and therefore ignorance) works to aggrandize Aqiva's rabbinic stature only if Aqiva is understood to be the exception, not the rule.

Additionally [and, again, further discussed in chapters 3, 4 and 5 of this volume], rabbis offered services based on their rabbinic skills and knowledge as independent operators and contractors to the Jewish population at large. As I already stated, rabbis seem to have promoted themselves as service providers and arbiters in all sorts of matters in which they could render opinions or reconcile conflicts in light of their Torah learning and teachings. The Talmuds show that the range of what rabbis subsumed under their Torah-based learning was wide indeed. I have already mentioned that that range includes claimed expertise about potions, amulets, dream interpretation, demon avoidance and exorcism, and incantations. [As chapter 4 elaborates, i]t is likely that no late antique "sage" was worth his salt without claimed prowess in these domains. (Indeed, Acts depicts Paul as possessing such gifts, and implies that these gifts corroborate his authority to preach the gospel.)

Such services included mystical and gnostic praxa undertaken by some rabbis[, an aspect of some rabbis' skills profiles that this current volume addresses in chapter 4].[16] . . . Mere echoes only of these pursuits are contained

16. See, e.g., these classic and accessible works: Scholem, *Jewish Gnosticism*, and

in the Talmuds. But they are certainly there. . . . [T]he practice by some rabbis of trance-inducing techniques to effect heavenly journeys and visions, and to garner, thereby, special knowledge, is neither new in Judaic circles nor unique to rabbis. [As discussed in chapter 5 of the current book,] Jewish Apocalyptic literature, such as 4 Ezra and the Book of Enoch, and the non-rabbinic, late-antique Jewish text referred to as Sefer Ha-Razim (the Book of Mysteries) demonstrate this. And again Paul, this time in his own writings, seems to make similar claims when he states in 2 Corinthians 12:2 that he was ". . . in Christ . . . caught up to the third heaven . . . ." A late antique holy man is a late antique holy man, whether a rabbi or not. To act or claim otherwise is to cede ground to the competition, as Acts portrays Paul refusing to do to the sons of Sceva, a Jewish "priest" (Acts 19:13–14).

Of course, rabbis also taught disciple-students, who would constitute the next generation of rabbis [as you will already have gathered from this current book's introductory chapter]. The institutional arrangements for rabbinic education range from circles comprising a single master and his students—much like Libanius' arrangement with his students of rhetoric in Antioch—to the development by the sixth century of larger rabbinic academies with an institutional head and organized faculty—much like the last major academies of pagan learning in the eastern Roman Empire, some of which in the sixth century were transplanted into Persian Imperial territory at the invitation of the emperor, Kushro Noshirwan. Earlier evidence for such organized rabbinic academies is largely absent. Third- and fourth-century rabbinic documents refer to rabbinic "Houses of Study" (*beit midrash* in the singular). How much more structured and "permanent" a House of Study was than a master-disciple circle is difficult to say. On the Golan Heights at Kfar Dvora, just east of the Galilee, archeologists discovered a likely fourth-century inscription on what had probably been the stone lintel of a doorway; the inscription reads, "This is the house of study of Rabbi Eliezer Ha-Qappar." A Bar-Qappara is known to us from early rabbinic literature as an important rabbi in the Galilee in the early third century. Whether or not the Eliezer of the fourth-century inscription is the Bar-Qappara otherwise known to us from the early third, the inscription has some significance as an attestation to the formalization and institutionalization of rabbinic learning in the Land of Israel by the fourth century. It implies the existence of something more highly institutionalized, with some institutional longevity, than what is usually imagined when one refers to master-disciple circles.

What does any of the foregoing say or imply about the material and economic basis for the rabbinic movement or of its individual members?

Blumenthal, *Understanding Jewish Mysticism*, vol. 1.

I have noted that the mythology about Rabbi Aqiva implies that rarely could someone from humble economic origins aspire to become a rabbi. And the third-century addition to the Mishnah, Tractate Avot (3:21) provides an aphorism, "If there is no [economic basis for purchasing] flour [to make bread], there [can be] no torah [learning]." It is entirely consistent with my depiction thus far of rabbinic activities and roles that many (perhaps most) rabbis seemed to have had other, nonrabbinic-related forms of principal employment and income, and offered their services as rabbinic arbiters, service providers, and teachers "on the side," as it were. Some were skilled artisans; some were landholders; others were merchants and traders. (Again, the case of Paul offers an apt parallel. Paul was a skilled artisan and practised his skills to support himself while teaching and preaching. But before his conversion, he was for a time in the "employ" of the Jerusalem Temple authorities as their agent.) A number of rabbis were simply wealthy in their own right. In all, rabbis' economic security achieved in conventional pursuits allowed them to provide services as rabbis and to engage in teaching and study.

Certain rabbis became more renowned than others in offering opinions, rendering judgments, and arbitrating disputes for those who voluntarily sought them out, rather than seeking recourse at the formal courts. For this to work, not only those who voluntarily sought their services, but others, would have had to come to recognize the legitimacy of the rabbis' decisions. If this were not the case, the value to the clients would have been much diminished. Such "independent operations" were often done for a fee or honorarium paid to literati, teachers, scribes, sages, and other holy men in the Levant, Egypt, and the Middle East, and had been so for centuries. [And even though, as discussed in chapters 3, 4 and 6 of this book, rabbis were not supposed to take a professional "salary" for such services, i]t is likely that rabbis, too, accepted and expected such [token or honorary] payment.

Thus far, I have primarily framed my account within the social, economic, and historical context of the Land of Israel in the late Roman period. The rabbinic movement first developed in the Land of Israel, and to some degree was, as already stated, a co-development of the Jewish Patriarchate there. [And this is the particular rabbinic group and era, upon which this current volume focuses.]But sometime in the third century, some members of the rabbinic movement began operating in the Jewish communities of the Persian-ruled, Mesopotamian-Babylonian Plain. If it is accurate to call the rabbis' relationship with and their attempt to "rabbinize" the Patriarch's dynasty in the Land of Israel a deliberate strategy that by the fourth century had failed, then it would be accurate to assert that they used a similar strategy, perhaps with more success by the sixth century, in insinuating themselves into the operations of the Jewish Exilarch (in Aramaic, the *Resh Galuta,* "head of the community in Exile") in Persian-ruled Babylonia. The Babylonian-Jewish Exilarchate was probably an older institution than the Jewish Patriarchate in the Land of Israel. Persian Imperial rule over its domains was by policy less centralized than Roman Imperial rule, and part of Persian policy was to grant ethnic-religious groups in its domains some fair degree of autonomy and self-rule, by appointment of, and with reporting lines to, the Imperial throne. Rabbis in Babylonia began training their own cadre of rabbinic recruits, imported traditions and knowledge over the course of the third into the fifth centuries from their counterparts in the Land of Israel, and over some unspecifiable period of time seemed to have ultimately rabbinized the Exilarch's dynasty. If early medieval rabbinic sources are to be believed, by the time of the Islamic conquest of the Persian Empire in the seventh century, the norm was that the Exilarch's successor had to have acquired a complete rabbinic education before assuming the office of his father, and the heads of the larger rabbinic academies in Babylonia-Mesopotamia claimed the authority to exercise some sort of veto power over the Persian emperor's choice of Exilarch from among members of the dynastic family.

The parallels between rabbinic attempts in the period before the Muslim conquest at co-opting of the Exilarchate in Persian Babylonia and their *ultimately* less successful attempts to co-opt the later Patriarchs in the Roman-ruled Land of Israel, whom they began to criticize in the fourth century as overly Romanized, also extends to the demise of both the Patriarchate and the Exilarchate. In the fifth century, the Roman Imperial government, with a century of Christianization under its belt, begins to rescind the powers of the Patriarchate in the Land of Israel, eventually eliminating the office altogether. Although we have too little information about the development, stature, and roles of members of the rabbinic class in a post-Patriarchate era in the Land of Israel, the composition of the Jerusalem Talmud took place sometime near the end of the Patriarchate. Additionally, anti-Judaic Roman Imperial policy increased over the course of the fifth century and into the sixth from the reigns of Theodosius II to Justinian and his successors, negatively affecting the vitality of the rabbinic group and its institutions in the Land of Israel.

In Mesopotamia-Babylonia the powers of the Exilarchate fell victim to something else entirely. In the sixth and into the seventh centuries, the Persian emperor revised models of Imperial government. Persian governance became more centralized based upon Roman-Byzantine models of administration. As a result, the position of Exilarch, while not eliminated, became more of an honorific and ceremonial one, and power and authority over matters of Jewish life to some large extent seems to have passed to the heads of the several large rabbinic academies that had (recently?) developed, likely in the sixth century. Unlike developments in the Land of Israel under Roman rule in the fifth century, these changes in Persian ruled Babylonia seem not to be part of any specifically anti-Judaic policy. The advancement of rabbinic institutions and learning continued unabated in Babylonia (unlike the situation in the Land of Israel) with the Babylonian Talmud being composed sometime near the turn of the seventh century.

Thus far, I have said little about the ideology that buttressed the early rabbinic group and its claims to authority, other than to say they laid claim to "torah" learning. [Most of chapter 2 and a portion of chapter 5 of the current book deal with this matter in some detail. But a "short" account here is also integral to this survey of the *historical* development of the rabbinic movement from the early third to early seventh centuries.] How, then, did the rabbis in the Land of Israel and Babylonia justify and legitimate their authority, that of their teachings, and the legitimacy of their emerging literature in the face of whatever resistance or competition they faced? After all, for many centuries the Torah of Moses, identified as the first five books of the Judaic Bible, the biblical books of the Prophets, and other writings widely recognized in Judaic communities as scriptural were the basis of authority. Even the writings of the early Church acknowledge this state of affairs. The earliest rabbinic group may not have had any formally-accepted, well-articulated ideology grounding their own sense of authority, or that of their traditions or of their first literary compositions. Perhaps it sufficed within their own circles to be conscious of being dedicated to honing their skills to apply Torah-based law. . . . But at some point, there seemed to be felt the need to say more about the basis of their enterprise and the authority of the traditions and teachings that they articulated and contemplated. What they came to say about that authority seems to have developed in stages.

[As is treated extensively in chapter 2 of this book, t]he earliest articulation of a "myth" about themselves and their authority is likely the one found in Tractate Avot, which is probably a mid- to late-third-century addition to the Mishnah. Avot articulates an ethos of earnest and dedicated discipleship and master-disciple relations. [You will see in chapter 2 how] Avot makes the first master God, and the first disciple Moses, followed by Joshua, and so on down through a chain of generations of masters and disciples to the very rabbis whose names appear in the Mishnah (and the Tosefta). What is passed from master to disciple is "Torah" (divine-based teaching in a more generic sense) not simply "*the* Torah (of Moses)," that is, the first five books of the Judaic Scriptures specifically. In the fourth, fifth and sixth centuries, this emerging myth further develops to become the

ideology of the Oral Torah. [As discussed in chapter 2, i]n this more elaborated form, God on Sinai revealed to Moses two Torahs, one to be written
down by Moses as "Written Torah," that is the Torah of Moses in the Judaic
Scriptures. The other is transmitted orally [as] "Oral Torah" from master
to faithful and diligent disciple through the ages to the rabbis at the latter
end of the chain. Together, the Oral and the Written Torah constitute the
"Whole Torah." In the later articulations of this emergent mythology or
ideology it is made clear that the "Oral Torah" is in dynamic evolution; it
does not seem to be something that is fixed. Thus, the substance of debates
and discussions among rabbinic students and between students and teachers was also part and parcel of "Oral Torah" that Moses received on Sinai.
It is as if acts of authentic rabbinic learning and study taking place in the
Roman era generate content that automatically and retroactively becomes
part of what God revealed to Moses. . . .

The notion of Oral Torah in its full-blown version is a justificatory
mythology and religious ideology that ought not to surprise any historian
of religion. In the history of religions novelty is not valued. Quite the opposite. Antiquity is the basis for legitimacy. Yet novel developments happen all the time in religions. Consequently, one often finds mythologies
and ideologies in religions that articulate how the newfangled is actually
ancient. [In fact, as you will learn in reading chapter 5 of this current
book, e]ven in the history of early Judaism the rabbinic myth or ideology of the dual, Oral and Written, Torah has precursors. . . . [And, s]ome
notion of this dual revelation claimed by some Jews to be their unique
heritage seems to register, too, in a number of early Christian documents,
particularly those registering anti-Judaic polemics. [Discussed in chapter
5 of this volume, t]hese second-to-fourth-century Christian writings refer
to a "second" body of divine teachings (*deuterosis*) claimed to be possessed
by Jews. . . . The implication [rejected by the early Christian authors] is
that the Jews' claim to possess this second body of divine teaching makes
them, not Christians, the true heirs of God's revelation. Patristic writers
disabuse their readers of such notions.

For modern scholars of early rabbinism and its literature, the emerging mythology of dual Torah, the "Written Torah" and "Oral Torah," is
confounded with a vexatious historical-literary debate, about which I have,
after forty-five years in the academic trenches, still not fully made up my
mind. A number of modern academics claim that some rabbinic literature,
most notably the Mishnah, once composed in writing, was transmitted
and studied orally, that is, without a written text in front of the student.
Others have concluded that Mishnah was *both* written *and* promulgated
in written form, but was studied and cited largely from memory by reason

of ideology. Some pretty good evidence suggests this may well have been the case[, and in chapters 2, 3 and 4 of this book I discuss this matter as part and parcel of the shared early Rabbinic identity that bound members of the group to one another]. But there are also scholars who maintain that the text or texts were originally *composed* orally (like Homer's *Iliad*), and only perhaps half a century or more after its/their oral composition were "fixed" in writing. About this I am much less certain. I lean toward the hypothesis, written composition, and written *cum* oral transmission—that is, written texts serving as an authenticating base as needed—coupled with a strong tradition of memorization, oral use and citation in the context of the early study of Mishnah in the third and perhaps part of the fourth century. After that, my best judgment is that Mishnah both circulated and was used in written form, although rabbis still knew much of it by heart and often quoted it by heart. Did the mythology of Oral Torah spur this tradition of memorization and oral-use in study (or spur oral composition, for those scholars who see matters that way), or vice versa? To this question I can offer no definitive answer.

What happens to the rabbinic movement immediately *after* . . . the turn of the seventh century?

In the middle of the seventh century, the Persian Empire fell to the armies of Islam. The early Islamic Caliphate presented both a challenge and an opportunity for the rabbis. Islam inherited from Christianity much of the latter's supercessionist attitudes to Jews and Judaisms, and the early Caliphate adopted, but often tempered, some late Roman anti-Jewish/anti-Judaic policies, applying them first to Christians in the House of Islam and then to Jews. As a result, neither Jews nor the rabbis in the lands ruled by the Caliphate experienced anything close to the active suppression of Jewish culture and learning that had taken hold in the Christian-ruled territories of the early medieval period.

In fact, the Caliphate needed to consider who would exercise authority over proper Judaic practice, and ultimately, they seem to have supported the rabbis over against the rabbis' competition among Jewish literati . . . . In so doing, the Caliphate effectively made the heads of the large rabbinic academies in Babylonia, who already may have exercised considerable moral authority over the rabbis of Babylonia-Mesopotamia, into the *de facto* arbiters over disputes and questions about Judaic practice in Jewish communities across the rapidly expanding Muslim-ruled territory. With that, the die was cast[, notwithstanding vocal and obviously Judaically learned resistance movements, chief among them the Karaites, who withstood the entrenchment of the authority of the rabbis. Indeed, as elaborated in chapter 2 of this volume, the "resisters'" critiques of rabbinic claims to authority forced medieval rabbis such as Sherira Gaon to consolidate and justify rabbinic mythologizing with "histories" of the rabbinic movement. Nevertheless, as stated in the preface to this book, w]ithin several centuries of the rise of Islam, virtually all Jewish communities, even those in Christian lands, recognized the authority of the rabbis in the domains of life over which they claimed expertise as arbiters of a life lived in accordance with Torah-teachings. Under Torah-teachings was now subsumed not only the teachings of the Hebrew biblical Scriptures but also all rabbinic instruction, interpretation, and literature, understood as well to be part and parcel of the Torah of Moses revealed on Sinai. Only early modernity, the enlightenment, secularism, and eighteenth-century pietism in the form of the early Hasidic movement, all nearly a millennium later, presented truly serious challenges to rabbinic authority.

From the Second Century CE Backward, the Historical and Cultural Origins of the Early Rabbinic Movement

Having concluded one [account of] . . . the development of the early rabbinic movement, guild, or class from the latter second century to the dawn of the seventh, I will now begin another. Let us consider the origins of the rabbinic group in the decades, century, or centuries leading up to the latter second century.

To this juncture, I have intimated that the rabbinic movement coalesced sometime in the second century. I have pointed to the aftermath of the failure of the Bar Kokhba rebellion in 135 CE as a pivotal point of some sort in that development. However, it is improbable that the rabbinic movement appeared out of nowhere and spontaneously on the social stage of the Land of Israel at that moment. After all, by the end of the second century the rabbinic movement had coalesced sufficiently to produce a magnum opus, the Mishnah, which they immediately promulgated as the most important focus of rabbinic study, and the mastery of which was quintessential to membership in the rabbinic movement[, as we discuss at length in chapters 3 and 4 of the current book]. These developments in and of themselves bespeak a certain level of institutionalization and organization that could not have happened overnight. Moreover, [as you will, or will have read at length in chapters 5 and 6 of this volume,] such newly formed organized groups within any social setting arise out of a social and cultural background that would have rendered the nature, identity, preoccupations, and activities and aspirations of the group plausible and appropriate, at least in the eyes of its members and arguably in the eyes of some (significant) others. Much in the Land of Israel's culture and society in the early Roman period would have made the early rabbis in the second century culturally and socially believable figures, or it is unlikely that the early rabbis would have exhibited the traits and preoccupations that mark them as a distinctive (quasi-occupational) group.

The foregoing may seem like an odd, convoluted, and rather indirect way to formulate the issue of the origins of the early rabbinic group. Admittedly, it is. But I have resorted to it for a reason. Simply put, we lack evidence that is both explicit and reliable about the historical and social origins of the early rabbinic movement much earlier than several decades prior to the authorship and promulgation of the Mishnah. However, that does not prevent us from attempting to surmise what the most plausible cultural and historical "soil" was from which the early rabbinic group germinated and sprouted.

Let me begin with describing the problems ahead of us. Addressing the early rabbinic group's origins and development in the years preceding the latter part of the second century CE, we find ourselves once again in difficult historiographical straits. On the one hand, if we take at face value what the rabbis' documents purport to tell us, we are often confronted with vexatious issues about the historicity of the evidence. At the risk of repeating myself, so much of what rabbinic literature says about its origins, which is not all that very much, comes from documents that are several and more centuries later than the events and personages about which the documents speak. How much did the authors of these documents really know about these earliest stages of the rabbinic movement's development? In addition, much of what these documents do say about the earliest rabbis' activities is obviously stylized, the result of mythologizing, and self-servingly tendentious—or all three at once. Origin stories in these texts are bent upon inculcating a certain perspective in service of bolstering the image and authority of the rabbis. Consequently, these sources tell us a lot about the culture and ideology of the documents' authors, *their* time, and *their* intended audience, but have much less to tell us that is valid about those who preceded by several centuries these authors and their readers.

On the other hand, we know a fair bit about the culture, religion, society, and history of the Jewish community of the Land of Israel in the last two centuries BCE and the first century CE from documents actually authored *during that period*. Many documents collected in what we call the Apocrypha and Pseudepigrapha of the Judaic Bible, the Dead Sea Scrolls, other texts found in the Judean desert, some New Testament literature and other early Christian writings, and the writings of Flavius Josephus all fall into this category. Yes, these documents' authors also have their particular ideological bents. [As I have intimated in the introductory chapter of this current volume,] they too are tendentious. They too will often engage in mythologizing. But they inevitably reflect the views of some group, persons, or person contemporaneous with *their* authorship (just as the rabbinic documents represent the views of their authors). That contemporary scene is the immediate antecedent of the decades in which the nascent rabbinic group appeared. And, additionally, they are at least not offering tendentious and mythologized depictions of the early rabbis, because they are not talking about, let alone for, rabbis at all. We also have archaeological evidence for this period in the Land of Israel. And we know what was going on in the territories adjacent to, and culturally linked with, the Land of Israel in the last several centuries BCE and the first two centuries CE. [In fact, all of this evidence underpins the analyses of chapters 5 and 6 of the current book.]

Consequently, these roughly contemporary bodies of evidence for the period leading up to the mid- to late second century CE, while telling us little or nothing explicitly about the first rabbis, tell us much about the cultural, social, and historical landscape from which and in which the earliest rabbinic movement emerged. As a result, we can perform a kind of triangulation using the very earliest rabbinic documents we have, that is, the Mishnah (c. 200 CE) and the Tosefta (c. 250–425 CE), together with these other, earlier, nonrabbinic bodies of evidence. We may triangulate by asking, first: what do these earliest rabbinic documents *implicitly* reflect about the culture and sociology of the documents' authors and intended readers? And we can, second, try to correlate the answers to these questions with cultural and social parallels or likely cultural and social antecedents attested in these other, earlier bodies of evidence from the centuries immediately preceding the authorship of the Mishnah and the Tosefta[, as we undertake at length in chapters 5 and 6 of this book].

But let me begin by somewhat deviating from the approach that I have just advocated. What, at least, do Mishnah and Tosefta tell us *explicitly* about the rabbinic movement and rabbis that they allege commenced the rabbinic movement?

Mishnah, the earliest rabbinic document, refers to the legal opinions of rabbis and protorabbis which Mishnah's authors place in (a) the mid- to late second century after Bar Kokhba, (b) the early second century before Bar Kokhba and the late first century following the Temple's destruction in 70 CE, and (c) in the generation or generations immediately preceding the destruction of the Temple. Among these pre-70 figures are Hillel and Shammai and their "Houses" (disciples), and Gamaliel (the Elder), mentioned also in early Christian literature as a prominent Pharisee, the teacher of Paul (himself a self-declared Pharisee), and, in Acts, as a moderate voice among Jewish authorities dealing with the followers of the Jesus movement.

Mishnah and Tosefta also attribute legal rulings to a Rabbi Yohanan ben Zakkai, whom Mishnah and Tosefta understand to be a figure straddling the decades before and after the destruction of the Temple in 70 CE. In several of these Mishnah passages (in Tractate Yadayim), Yohanan is portrayed as articulating *specifically labeled* Pharisaic legal positions over against contrary "Sadducean" positions. One such dispute concerns an issue of purity law that also registers in one of the Dead Sea Scrolls (4QMMT). It is later rabbinic texts (in succession Avot, Avot de Rabbi Nathan, the Talmuds, and Lamentations Rabbah) that progressively fashion or refashion a narrative that makes Yohanan ben Zakkai into the founder of the organized rabbinic group in the coastal town of Yavneh during the last phases of, and immediately following, the Roman siege of Jerusalem in 70 CE. Based on such accounts of Yohanan's activity and what is alleged to have occurred at Yavneh, several generations of nineteenth- and twentieth-century historians of Judaism elaborated a picture of a great, ongoing Council of Yavneh (akin to the major Church Councils of the fourth and fifth centuries), where major decisions were made about Judaism's practice after the Temple's destruction and concerning the stabilization of the list of books comprising Hebrew Scriptures. Avot (c. 250), moreover, provides lists of rabbinic figures, organized as successive generations of masters and their disciples, from pre-70 CE rabbinic or protorabbinic authorities to rabbis of the time of Judah the Prince. [Indeed, in chapter 3 of this current book we look at Avot's list of names and put this evidence to use for ends other than writing a "history" of the early rabbinic movement before c. 200 CE.]

As stated—and worth repeating—any attempt to reconstruct [such a] . . . history of the early rabbinic movement much before the middle of the second century CE from such rabbinic sources is difficult because of the nature of the evidence. After all, Mishnah is composed around 200 CE, attributes rulings to these early figures, but otherwise tells us virtually nothing about them. Later rabbinic texts from the third century into the seventh offer short vignettes about some of them, but clearly a fair degree of mythologizing is going on[, a state of affairs discussed in chapters 1 and 2 of this current book]. Moreover, given the dates of these texts, several or more centuries after these early rabbinic and protorabbinic authorities were said to have lived, one may well be circumspect in thinking that these texts' authors had any historical basis at all for their stories and mythologizing. And few academic scholars today support the notion of a Council of Yavneh that looked like or did anything like what nineteenth- and early twentieth-century scholars depicted. Indeed, few would today maintain that a "Council of Yavneh" likely took place at all, even if places like Yavneh and Lod on the coastal plain were centers of activity of the early rabbis sometime between 70 CE and 135 CE. However, to return to the method I have advocated, we may ask[, W]hat may we glean from Mishnah and Tosefta, the earliest rabbinic documents, that does not succumb to later rabbinic texts' mythologizing or these documents' own speculation about rabbinic origins? [And with this question, we have, in fact, segued to the principal topic and focus of this book, *What Were the Early Rabbis?* How so? Because f]irst and foremost, Mishnah and Tosefta reflect a group and group-culture that sees its members and, therefore, its founders as the go-to experts in, and students of, how to live a Jewish life in accordance with the "way" (the Halakha) consistent with Torah teaching. . . . [T]hat "way" encompasses in theory a broad spectrum of individual, group, and societal behavior: prayer, Sabbath and festival practice, cultic sacrifices, agricultural tithes in support of the Levitical-priestly classes and the Jerusalem Temple, and purity law to guard the Temple against the powers of uncleanness. But it also includes family law and laws concerning damages, injury, theft, judicial practice, and legislative processes.

On face value, there are some curious aspects to Mishnah and Tosefta's treatment of agricultural tithes, purity, and sacerdotal law. In the Hebrew Bible, these laws have to do with support of the central Temple cult and its officiating castes, the priests and Levites, and guarding that Temple cult and all who participate in it from the powers of uncleanness. Mishnah and Tosefta were, respectively, composed roughly 130 and 180 or more years after the destruction of the Temple and the cessation of the cult. Yet, about half of Mishnah and Tosefta is dedicated to these topics. The framers of Mishnah and Tosefta, and those assiduously studying these texts and traditions in the early rabbinic group to some significant extent, are imaginatively living in the Land of Israel as it was before 70 CE (or as it might be in some future age in which the Temple and its cult are restored). And yet, neither Mishnah nor Tosefta imagines rabbis to be remnants of the priestly caste, nor do Mishnah and Tosefta appear to be addressing priests. They do portray rabbis as possessing the expertise, and therefore the authority, to direct members of the priestly caste in their functions.

There is another trait of Mishnah's and Tosefta's treatment of purity law (and to some extent of agricultural tithes) that may be relevant to our attempt to triangulate to their social and cultural origins and antecedents. Documents representing Jewish culture and society in the first centuries BCE and CE, including early Christian literature, seem to agree that one must be in a state of purity to participate as a priest, Levite, or lay Israelite/Jew in the Temple cult. If one is a priest, Levite, or lay Jew eating tithed produce, one must also be free from uncleanness. The laws of Mishnah and Tosefta square with this as well. But the laws of both Mishnah and Tosefta exhort Jews to do more than this. They exhort them, within limits that they consider 'reasonable', to eat all meals in a state of cleanness, as if one were eating holy foodstuffs, and they demand that all produce be tithed, that is, the sanctified portion be separated, *before* the produce is consumed as regular daily food. Mishnah and Tosefta, however, assume that many or most Jews neither practice purity rites when they eat regular meals and go about their daily business, nor tithe their produce before using any of it. So, Mishnah and Tosefta must also articulate procedures for dealing with the uncertainties that result from these assumptions.

Finally, while neither Mishnah nor Tosefta spills much ink on what a Jew or a rabbi is to believe, they do insist (in Tractate Sanhedrin) that a life after death in "the world to come" is a basic tenet of Judaism, and that denial of this is tantamount to heresy, bordering on apostasy.

When one compounds (1) these characteristics of Mishnah's and Tosefta's treatment of purity law and tithing with (2) their depiction of Rabbi Yohanan ben Zakkai as the defender of Pharisaic legal positions against those of the Sadducees, (3) these documents' identification of Gamaliel the Elder, a known Pharisee, as one of the early illustrious rabbinic figures, and (4) the insistence on some future postmortem life, one cannot escape seriously considering that based upon what Josephus and early Christian literature have to say about Pharisees (as tendentious as those depictions might be) some strong Pharisaic element is part and parcel of the early development of the rabbinic group. Further than this I do not believe we can responsibly go; we cannot simply identify the early rabbis as remnants of the Pharisees [for reasons that I spell out more fully in chapter 4 of the current volume and with a very different purpose in mind]. . . .

[Having reached this point—indeed, this "impasse," in my opinion—in articulating a history of the early rabbinic movement before the latter decades of the second century CE, I (re)turn in this current book to the alternative inquiries about (a) "what the early rabbis were" and (b) what relevant and compelling models existed in contemporary and antecedent Judaic society in the Land of Israel that likely informed the nature of the early rabbinic group and the characteristic shared profile of its members. For in a very real sense, given the nature of the evidence at hand, the very early history and development of the early rabbinic movement is better sought in these models than in a more conventional historiographical enterprise.]

Bibliography

Akenson, Donald H. *Surpassing Wonder: The Invention of the Bible and the Talmuds*. Montreal: McGill-Queens University Press, 1998.

Albeck, Hanokh. *Mavo LeTalmudim* [Introduction to the Talmuds]. Tel Aviv: Dvir, 1987.

———. *Shishah Sidre Mishnah*. Tel Aviv: Dvir, 1951–1958.

Alexander, Elizabeth Shanks. "The Fixing of the Oral Mishnah and the Displacement of Meaning." *Oral Tradition* 14 (1999) 100–139.

———. "The Orality of Rabbinic Writing." In *The Cambridge Companion to the Talmud*, edited by Charlotte Elisheva Fonrobert and Martin S. Jaffee, 38–57. Cambridge Companions to Religion. Cambridge: Cambridge University Press, 2007.

———. *Transmitting Mishnah: The Shaping Influence of Oral Tradition*. Cambridge: Cambridge University Press, 2009.

Alexander, Philip. "Using Rabbinic Literature as a Source for the History of Late-Roman Palestine: Problems and Issues." In *Rabbinic Texts and the History of Late-Roman Palestine*, edited by Martin Goodman and Philip Alexander, 7–24. Proceedings of the British Academy 165. Oxford: Oxford University Press, 2010.

Alon, Gedalyahu. *Jews, Judaism and the Classical World: Studies in Jewish History in the Times of the Second Temple and Talmud*. Translated by Israel Abrahams. Jerusalem: Magnes, 1977.

Appelbaum, Alan. *The Dynasty of the Jewish Patriarchs*. Texts and Studies in Ancient Judaism 156. Tübingen: Mohr Siebeck, 2013.

———. "Rabbi's Successors: The Later Jewish Patriarchs of the Third Century." *Journal of Jewish Studies* 63 (2012) 1–21.

Astren, Fred. *Karaite Judaism and Historical Understanding*. Columbia: University of South Carolina Press, 2004.

———. *History, Historicization, and Historical Claims in Karaite Jewish Literature*. Berkeley: University of California Press, 1993.

Avery-Peck, Alan J. "The Galilean Charismatic and Rabbinic Piety: The Holy Man in the Talmudic Literature." In *The Historical Jesus in Context*, edited by Amy-Jill Levine et al., 149–65. Princeton: Princeton University Press, 2006.

Avi-Yonah, Michael. *BeYemai Roma UBizantium*. [In Hebrew.] Jerusalem: Mosad Bialik, 1970.

———. *The Jews under Roman and Byzantine Rule: A Political History of Palestine from the Bar Kokhba War to the Arab Conquest*. 1976. Reprint, Jerusalem: Magnes, 1984.

———. "A List of Priestly Courses from Caesarea." *Israel Exploration Journal* 12 (1962) 137–39.

Bagnall, Roger, and William V. Harris. *Studies in Roman Law*. Columbia Studies in the Classical Tradition 13. Leiden: Brill, 1986.

Bar-Ilan, Meir. "Illiteracy as Reflected in the Halakhot concerning the Reading of the Scroll of Esther and the Hallel." [In Hebrew.] *Proceedings of the American Academy of Jewish Research* 54 (1987) 1–12.

———. "Illiteracy in the Land of Israel in the First Centuries CE." In *Essays in the Social Scientific Study of Judaism and Jewish Society*, edited by Simcha Fishbane et al., 2:46–61. Hoboken, NJ: Ktav, 1992.

———. "Literacy among the Jews in Antiquity." *Hebrew Studies* 44 (2003) 217–22.

———. "Scribes and Books in the Late Second Commonwealth and Rabbinic Period." In *Mikra: Text, Translation, Reading, and Interpretation of the Hebrew Bible in Ancient Judaism and Early Christianity*, edited by Martin J. Mulder, Compendia Rerum Iudaicarum ad Novum Testamentum 1, sect. 2: *Literature of the Jewish People in the Period of the Second Temple and the Talmud*, 21–38. Assen: Van Gorcum, 1988.

Bauman, Richard A. *Lawyers and Politics in the Early Roman Empire: A Study of the Relations between the Roman Jurists and the Emperors from Augustus to Hadrian*. Münchener Beiträge zur Papyrusforschung und antiken Rechtsgeschichte 82. Munich: Beck, 1989.

———. *Lawyers in Roman Transitional Politics: A Study of Roman Jurists is the Political Setting in the Late Republic and Triumvirate*. Münchener Beiträge zur Papyrusforschung und antiken Rechtsgeschichte 79. Munich: Beck, 1985.

Becker, Hans-Jürgen, and Christoph Berner. *Avot de-Rabbi Natan: Synoptische Edition beider Versionen*. Texte und Studien zum antiken Judentum 162. Tübingen: Mohr Siebeck, 2006.

Becking, Bob. *Identity in Persian Egypt: The Fate of the Yehudite Community of Elephantine*. University Park, PA: Eisenbrauns, 2020.

Belayche, Nicole. *Iudaea-Palaestina: The Pagan Cults in Roman Palestine (Second to Fourth Century)*. Religion in the Roman Provinces 1. Tübingen: Mohr Siebeck, 2001.

Ben-Zion, Sigalit. "The Quest for Social Identity through Group Interaction: Negotiating Social Position through Imitation, Confrontation and Cooperation; A Focus on the Tannaitic Sages." PhD diss., Norwegian University of Science and Technology, Trondheim, 2006.

———. *A Roadmap to the Heavens: An Anthropological Study of Hegemony among Priests, Sages, and Laymen*. Judaism and Jewish Life. Boston: Academic Studies, 2008.

Berger, Peter. *Invitation to Sociology: A Humanistic Perspective*. San Francisco: Double-day, 1963.

Berman, Joshua. "A Critical Intellectual History of the Historical-Critical Paradigm in Biblical Studies." In *Exploring the Composition of the Pentateuch*, edited by L. S. Becker Jr. et al., Bulletin for Biblical Research Supplement 27, 7–25. University Park, PA: Eisenbrauns, 2020.

Birks, Peter. "The Rise of the Roman Jurists." *Oxford Journal of Legal Studies* 7 (1966) 444–53.

Birks, Peter, and Grant McLeod, trans. *Justinian's Institutes*. With the Latin text of Paul Krueger. Ithaca: Cornell University Press, 1987.

Blumenthal, David. *The Merkabah Tradition and the Zoharic Tradition.* Vol. 1 of *Understanding Jewish Mysticism: A Source Reader.* Library of Judaic Learning 2. New York: Ktav, 1978.

Bottiglieri, Anna, et al. *Antiquissima Iuris Sapietia. Saec. VI–III A.C.* Scriptores Iuris Romani 3. Rome: Erma di Bretschneider, 2019.

Boustan, Ra'anan S. *From Martyr to Mystic: Rabbinic Martyrology and the Making of Merkavah Mysticism.* Tübingen: Mohr Siebeck, 2005.

Boyarin, Daniel. *Border Lines: The Partition of Judaeo-Christianity.* Divinations. Philadelphia: University of Pennsylvania Press, 2004.

———. "The Diadoche of the Rabbis; or Judah the Patriarch at Yavneh." In *Jewish Culture and Society under the Christian Roman Empire*, edited by Richard Kalmin and Seth Schwartz, 285–318. Interdisciplinary Studies in Ancient Culture and Religion 3. Leuven: Peeters, 2003.

———. *A Traveling Homeland: The Babylonian Talmud as Diaspora.* Divinations. Philadelphia: University of Pennsylvania Press, 2015.

Bradbury, Ray. *Fahrenheit 451.* Woodstock, IL: Dramatic, 1986.

Bregman, Marc. "Pseudepigraphy in Rabbinic Literature." Orion Center, 1997. http:// orion.mscc.huji.ac.il/symposiums/2nd/papers/Bregman97.html.

Brody, Robert. "The Epistle of Sherira Gaon." In *Rabbinic Texts and the History of Late-Roman Palestine*, edited by Martin Goodman and Philip Alexander, 253–64. Proceedings of the British Academy 165. Oxford: Oxford University Press, 2010.

———. *Mishnah and Tosefta Studies.* Jerusalem: Magnes, 2014.

Brutti, Massimo. *Iulius Paulus.* Scriptores Iuris Romani 6. Rome: Erma di Bretschneider, 2020.

Bryen, Ari Z. "Responsa." In *The Oxford Handbook of Law and the Humanities*, edited by Simon Stern et al., ch. 37. Oxford: Oxford University Press, 2020. Preprint available at https://www.academia.edu/38175803/Responsa.

Bultmann, Rudolph. *The History of the Synoptic Tradition.* Translated by John Marsh. 2nd ed. San Francisco: Harper & Row, 1963.

Bunn, Edward Devere, Jr. *The Origins of the Western Judicial Systems: The Roman Empire's Praetors. Jurists and Advocates.* El Paso: Cambridge Lighthouse, 2004.

Buzov, Emil. "Notes on Egyptian Wisdom Texts." *Journal of Egyptological Studies* 4 (2015) 49–83.

Cameron, Ron. "The Labours of Burton Mack: Scholarship That's Made a Difference," *Forum* 7 (2018) 21–50. http://www.westarinstitute.org/wp-content/uploads/2018/04/Forum-7-1-FULLTEXT-ChristianitySeminar.pdf.

Chilton, Bruce. *Rabbi Paul: An Intellectual Biography.* New York: Doubleday, 2004.

Choi, Jungwha. *Jewish Leadership in Roman Palestine from 70 CE to 135 CE.* Ancient Judaism and Early Christianity 83. Leiden: Brill, 2013.

Chroust, Anton-Hermann. "Legal Education in Ancient Rome." *Journal of Legal Education* 7 (1955) 509–29.

Cohen, Boaz. *Jewish and Roman Law: A Comparative Study*. 2 vols. New York: Jewish Theological Seminary of America, 1966.

———. *Jewish and Roman Law: A Comparative Study*. Introduction by Natalie B. Dohmann. 2 vols. Reprint, Picataway, NJ: Gorgias, 2018.

Cohen, Shaye J. D. *The Beginnings of Jewishness: Boundaries, Varieties and Uncertainties*. Hellenistic Culture and Society 31. Berkeley: University of California Press, 2001.

———. "Epigraphical Rabbis." *Jewish Quarterly Review* 72 (1981) 1–17.

Cohn, Naftali S. *The Memory of the Temple and the Making of the Rabbis*. Divinations. Philadelphia: University of Pennsylvania Press, 2012.

———. "Rabbis as Jurists: On the Representation of Past and Present Legal Institutions in the Mishnah." *Journal of Jewish Studies* 60 (2009) 245–63.

Conybeare, F. C., et al. *The Story of Ahikar from the Aramaic, Syriac, Arabic, Armenian, Ethiopic, Old Turkish, Greek and Slavonic Versions*. 2nd ed. Cambridge: Cambridge University Press, 1913.

Cook, Stephen L. *On the Question of the "Cessation of Prophecy" in Ancient Judaism*. Texts and Studies in Ancient Judaism 145. Tübingen: Mohr Siebeck, 2011.

Cowley, Arthur Ernest. *Aramaic Papyri of the Fifth Century BC*. Oxford: Clarendon, 1923. Reprint, Eugene, OR: Wipf & Stock, 2005.

Davies, Philip R. *Scribes and Schools: The Canonization of the Hebrew Scriptures*. Library of Ancient Israel. Louisville: Westminster John Knox, 1998.

Davies, W. D., et al., eds. *The Cambridge History of Judaism*. 4 vols. Cambridge: Cambridge University Press, 1984–2006.

Davila, James R. "The Hekhalot Literature and Shamanism." In *Society of Biblical Literature, 1994 Seminar Papers*, 767–89. Atlanta: Scholars, 1994.

Dolgopolski, Sergey. *What Is Talmud?* New York: Fordham University Press, 2009.

Domingo, Rafael. "The Roman Jurists and the Legal Science." 2017. Preprint available at: https://ssrn.com/abstract=2994130.

Durkheim, Emile. *The Rules of Sociological Method and Selected Texts on Sociology and Its Method*. Edited by Steven Lukes. Translated by D. Halls. New York: Free, 1982.

Eisenstadt, David. "Aelia Capitolina: Jerusalem as a Roman Pagan City." Ingeborg Rennert Center for Jerusalem Studies, Bar-Ilan University, 1997. https://www2.biu.ac.il/js/rennert/history_5.html.

Eliav, Yaron Z. "The Urban Layout of Aelia Capitolina: A New View from the Perspective of the Temple Mount." In *The Bar Kokhba War Reconsidered: New Perspectives on the Second Jewish Revolt against Rome*, edited by Peter Schäfer, 241–79. Texts and Studies in Ancient Judaism 100. Tübingen: Mohr Siebeck, 2003.

Elman, Yaakov. "Orality and the Redaction of the Babylonian Talmud." *Oral Tradition* 14 (1999) 52–99.

———. "Orality and the Transmission of Tosefta Pisha in Talmudic Literature." In *Introducing Tosefta: Textual, Intratextual and Intertextual Studies*, edited by Harry Fox and Tirzah Meacham, 123–80. New York: Ktav, 1999.

Emerton, J. A. "The Teaching of Amenemope and Proverbs XXII 17–XXIV 22: Further Reflection on the Longstanding Problem." *Vetus Testamentum* 51 (2001) 431–65.

Eshel, Hanan. "The Bar Kochba Revolt, 132–135 CE." In *The Cambridge History of Judaism*, edited by Steven T. Katz, 4:105–27. Cambridge: Cambridge University Press, 2006.

Eusebius. *Praeparatio Evangelica (Preparation for the Gospel).* Translated by Edwin H. Gifford. 1903. Reprint, Grand Rapids: Baker, 1981.

———. *The Proof of the Gospel, Being the* Demonstratio evangelica *of Eusebius of Cæsarea.* Translated by W. J. Ferrar. London: SPCK, 1920.

Finkelstein, Louis. *Akiba: Scholar, Saint, Martyr.* 1936. Reprint, Lanham, MD: Aronson, 1990.

Fox, Harry. "Introducing Tosefta." In *Introducing Tosefta: Textual, Intratextual and Intertextual Studies,* edited by Harry Fox and Tirzah Meacham, 1–30. New York: Ktav, 1999.

Fox, Harry, and Tirzah Meacham, eds. *Introducing Tosefta: Textual, Intratextual and Intertextual Studies.* New York: Ktav, 1999.

Fredriksen, Paula. "What 'Parting of the Ways?' Jews, Gentiles and the Ancient Mediterranean City." In *The Ways That Never Parted: Jews and Christians in Late Antiquity and the Early Middle Ages,* edited by Adam H. Becker and Annette Yoshiko Reed, 35–64. 2003. Reprint, Minneapolis: Fortress, 2007.

———. *When Christians Were Jews: The First Generation.* New Haven: Yale University Press, 2018.

Fredriksen, Paula, and Oded Irshai. "Christian Anti-Judaism: Polemics and Policies." In *The Cambridge History of Judaism,* edited by Steven T. Katz, 4:977–1034. Cambridge: Cambridge University Press, 2006.

Frey, Joerg. "From Text to Community: Methodological Problems Reconstructing Communities behind Texts." In *Jewish and Christian Communal Identities in the Roman World,* edited by Yair Furstenberg, 167–84. Ancient Judaism and Early Christianity 84. Leiden: Brill, 2016.

Friedman, Shamma. "The Primacy of Tosefta to Mishnah in Synoptic Parallels." In *Introducing Tosefta: Textual, Intratextual and Intertextual Studies,* edited by Harry Fox and Tirzah Meacham, 99–121. New York: Ktav, 1999.

———. *Tosefta Atiqta, Pesah Rishon: Synoptic Parallels of Mishna and Tosefta Analysed with a Methodological Introduction.* Ramat Gan: Bar Ilan University Press, 2002.

Frier, Bruce W., ed. *The Codex of Justinian: A New Annotated Translation with Parallel Latin and Greek Text.* 3 vols. Cambridge: University of Cambridge Press, 2016.

———. *The Rise of the Roman Jurists: Studies in Cicero's Pro Caecina.* Princeton: Princeton University Press, 1985.

Furstenberg, Yair. "Introduction: Shared Dimensions of Jewish and Christian Communal Identity." In *Jewish and Christian Communal Identities in the Roman World,* edited by Yair Furstenberg, 1–21. Ancient Judaism and Early Christianity 84. Leiden: Brill, 2016.

Gafni, Isaiah M. "How Babylonia Became 'Zion': Shifting Identities in Late Antiquity." In *Jewish Identities in Antiquity: Studies in Memory of Menahem Stern,* edited by Lee I. Levine and Daniel R. Schwartz, 333–48. Texts and Studies in Ancient Judaism 130. Tübingen: Mohr Siebeck, 2009.

———. *The Jews of Babylonia in the Talmudic Era.* [In Hebrew.] Jerusalem: Zalman Shazar Center for Jewish History, 1990.

Gilat, Yitzhak D. *R. Eliezer ben Hyrcanus: A Scholar Outcast.* [In Hebrew.] Ramat Gan: Bar-Ilan University Press, 1984.

Goldberg, Abraham. "The Babylonian Talmud." In *The Literature of the Jewish People in the Period of the Second Temple and the Talmud,* edited by Shmuel Safrai, 3:223–66. Assen: Van Gorcum, 1987.

———. "Mishnah: A Study Book of Halakha." In *The Literature of the Jewish People in the Period of the Second Temple and the Talmud*, edited by Shmuel Safrai, 3:211–62. Assen: Van Gorcum, 1987.

———. "The Palestinian Talmud." In *The Literature of the Jewish People in the Period of the Second Temple and the Talmud*, edited by Shmuel Safrai, 3:303–22. Assen: Van Gorcum, 1987.

Goldenberg, Robert. "The Broken Axis: Rabbinic Judaism and the Fall of Jerusalem." *Journal of the American Academy of Religion* 45 (1977) 869–82.

———. "The Destruction of the Jerusalem Temple: Its Meaning and Its Consequences." In *The Cambridge History of Judaism*, edited by Steven T. Katz, 4:191–205. Cambridge: Cambridge University Press, 2006.

———. *The Origins of Judaism: From Canaan to the Rise of Islam.* New York: Cambridge University Press, 2007.

Goldscheider, Calvin. "Religious Authority in the Mishnah. Social Science Perspectives on the Emerging Role of Scholars." In *Exploring Mishnah's World(s): Social Scientific Approaches*, by Simcha Fishbane et al., 119–46. London: Palgrave-Macmillan, 2020.

Goodblatt, David M. *The Monarchic Principle: Studies in Jewish Self-Government in Antiquity.* Texts and Studies in Ancient Judaism 38. Tübingen: Mohr Siebeck, 1994.

———. *Rabbinic Institutions in Sasanian Babylonia.* Studies in Judaism in Late Antiquity 9. Leiden: Brill, 1975.

Goodman, Martin. "A Note on Josephus, the Pharisees and Ancestral Tradition." In *Judaism in the Roman World: Collected Essays*, 117–22. Ancient Judaism and Early Christianity 66. Leiden: Brill, 2007.

———. "The Roman State and Jewish Diaspora Communities in the Antonine Age." In *Jewish and Christian Communal Identities in the Roman World*, edited by Yair Furstenberg, 75–86. Ancient Judaism and Early Christianity 94. Leiden: Brill, 2016.

———. "The Roman State and the Jewish Patriarch." In *The Galilee in Late Antiquity*, edited by Lee I. Levine, 127–39. New York: Jewish Theological Seminary, 1992.

———. *Rome and Jerusalem: The Clash of Ancient Civilizations.* New York: Knopf, 2007.

———. *State and Society in Roman Galilee, AD 132–212.* Totowa, NJ: Rowman & Allanheld, 1983.

———. *State and Society in Roman Galilee, AD 132–212.* 2nd ed. Elstree, UK: Mitchell, 2001.

———. "Texts, Scribes and Power in Roman Judea." In *Literacy and Power in the Ancient World*, edited by Alan K. Bowman and Greg Woolf, 99–108. Cambridge: Cambridge University Press, 1994.

———. "Trajan and the Origins of the Bar Kokhba War." In *The Bar Kokhba War Reconsidered: New Perspectives on the Second Jewish Revolt against Rome*, edited by Peter Schäfer, 23–30. Texts and Studies in Ancient Judaism 100. Tübingen: Mohr Siebeck, 2003.

Goodman, Martin, and Philip Alexander, eds. *Rabbinic Texts and the History of Late-Roman Palestine.* Proceedings of the British Academy 165. Oxford: Oxford University Press, 2010.

Gordley, James. *The Jurists: A Critical History.* Oxford: Oxford University Press, 2013.

Graves, Michael. "The Public Reading of Scripture in Early Judaism." *Journal of the Evangelical Theological Society* 50 (2007) 467–87.

Green, William Scott. "What's in a Name? The Problematic of Rabbinic Biography." In *Approaches to Ancient Judaism: Theory and Practice*, edited by William Scott Green, 77–96. Brown Judaic Studies 1. Missoula, MT: Scholars, 1978.

Greenfield, Jonas C. "The Wisdom of Ahiqar." In *Wisdom in Ancient Israel: Essays in Honour of J. A. Emerton*, edited by John Day et al., 43–52. Cambridge: Cambridge University Press, 1995.

Greengus, Samuel. *Laws in the Bible and in Early Rabbinic Collections: The Legacy of the Ancient Near East*. Eugene, OR: Cascade Books, 2011.

Gruen, Erich S. *The Construct of Identity in Hellenistic Judaism: Essays on Early Jewish Literature and History*. Deuterocanonical and Cognate Literature Studies 29. Berlin: de Gruyter, 2016.

Halivni, David Weiss. *The Formation of the Babylonian Talmud*. Edited and translated by Jeffrey L. Rubenstein. Oxford: Oxford University Press, 2013.

———. *Midrash, Mishnah and Gemara: The Jewish Predilection for Justified Law*. Cambridge: Harvard University Press, 1986.

Harland, Philip A. *Associations, Synagogues, and Congregations: Claiming a Place in Ancient Mediterranean Society*. Minneapolis: Fortress, 2003.

———. *Dynamics of Identity in the World of the Early Christians: Associations, Judeans and Cultural Identities*. New York: T. & T. Clark, 2009.

Harries, Jill. *Cicero and the Jurists: From Citizen's Law to the Lawful State*. London: Duckworth, 2006.

———. "Legal Education and the Training of Lawyers." In *The Oxford Handbook of Roman Law and Society*, edited by Clifford Ando et al., 151–53. Oxford: Oxford University Press, 2016.

Harris, Jay M. "Midrash Halachah." In *The Cambridge History of Judaism*, edited by Steven T. Katz, 4:136–68. Cambridge: Cambridge University Press, 2006.

Hartmann, Benjamin. *The Scribes of Rome: A Cultural and Social History of Scribae*. Cambridge: Cambridge University Press, 2020.

Hauptman, Judith. "Does the Tosefta Precede the Mishnah? Halakhah, Aggada, and Narrative Coherence." *Judaism* 50 (2001) 224–40.

———. *Rereading the Mishnah: A New Approach to Ancient Jewish Texts*. Texts and Studies in Ancient Judaism 109. Tübingen: Mohr Siebeck, 2005.

———. "The Talmudic Rabbi as Holy Man." In *Rabbi-Pastor-Priest: Their Roles and Profiles through the Ages*, edited by Walter Homolka and Heinz-Gunther Schottlen, 1–22. Studia Judaica 64. Berlin: de Gruyter, 2013.

———. "The Tosefta as a Commentary on an Early Mishnah." [In Hebrew.] *Jewish Studies, Internet Journal* 4 (2005) 109–32. https://jewish-faculty.biu.ac.il/files/jewish-faculty/shared/JSIJ4/hauptman.pdf/.

Heltzer, M., and Y. Avishur. "The Term *sofer mahir* as Designating a Courtier in the Old Testament and the Ahiqar Story." *Ugarit-Forschungen* 34 (2002) 17–22.

Herman, Geoffrey. "The Talmud in Its Babylonian Context: Rava and Bar-Sheshakh: Mani and Mihrshah." [In Hebrew.] In *Between Babylonia and the Land of Israel: Studies in Honour of Isaiah M. Gafni*, edited by Geoffrey Herman et al., 65–78. Jerusalem: Zalman Shazar Center for Jewish History, 2016.

Herr, Moshe David. "The Identity of the Jewish People before and after the Destruction of the Second Temple: Continuity or Change?" In *Jewish Identities in Antiquity: Studies in Memory of Menahem Stern*, edited by Lee I. Levine and Daniel R. Schwartz, 211–36. Texts and Studies in Ancient Judaism 130. Tübingen: Mohr Siebeck, 2009.

———. "A Zoroastrian-Sasanian and a Babylonian Talmudic 'Renaissance' at the Beginning of the Third Century: Could this be a Mere Coincidence." [In Hebrew.] In *Between Babylonia and the Land of Israel: Studies in Honour of Isaiah M. Gafni* [in Hebrew], edited by Geoffrey Herman et al., 51–64. Jerusalem: Zalman Shazar Center for Jewish History, 2016.

Hezser, Catherine. "The Jesus Movement as a "Popular" Judaism for the Unlearned." In *Jesus—Gestalt und Gestaltungen: Rezeptionen des Galiläers in Wissenschaft, Kirche und Gesellschaft*, edited by Petra von Gemünden et al., 75–105. Göttingen: Vandenhoek & Ruprecht, 2013.

———. "Jewish Literacy and the Use of Writing in Late Roman Palestine." In *Jewish Culture and Society under the Christian Roman Empire*, edited by Richard Kalmin and Seth Schwartz, Interdisciplinary Studies in Ancient Culture and Religion 3, 149–96. Leuven: Peeters, 2003.

———. *Jewish Literacy in Roman Palestine*. Texts and Studies in Ancient Judaism 81. Tübingen: Mohr Siebeck, 2001.

———. *Oxford Handbook of Jewish Daily Life in Roman Palestine*. Oxford Handbooks in Classics and Ancient History. Oxford: Oxford University Press, 2010.

———. "Social Fragmentation, Plurality of Opinion, and Nonobservance of Halakhah: Rabbis and Community in Late Roman Palestine." *Jewish Studies Quarterly* 1 (1993–1994) 234–51.

———. *The Social Structure of the Rabbinic Movement in Roman Palestine*. Texts and Studies in Ancient Judaism 66. Tübingen: Mohr Siebeck, 1997.

Hidary, Richard. "Classical Rhetorical Arrangement and Reasoning in the Talmud: The Case of Yerushalmi Berakhot 1:1." *Association of Jewish Studies Review* 34 (2010) 33–36.

———. *Rabbis and Classical Rhetoric: Sophistic Education and Oratory in the Talmud and Midrash*. Cambridge: Cambridge University Press, 2018.

Hirshman, Marc. *The Stabilization of Rabbinic Culture, 100 CE—350 CE: Texts in Education and Their Late Antique Context*. Oxford: Oxford University Press, 2009.

Hoffman, Lawrence A. "The Professionalization of the American Rabbinate." In *Rabbi-Pastor-Priest: Their Roles and Profiles through the Ages*, edited by Walter Homolka and Heinz-Gunther Schottlen, 129–56. Studia Judaica 64. Berlin: de Gruyter, 2013.

Honoré, Tony. *Ulpian*. Oxford: Clarendon, 1982.

Horbury, Richard. "Rabbinic Perceptions of Christianity and the History of Roman Palestine." In *Rabbinic Texts and the History of Late-Roman Palestine*, edited by Martin Goodman and Philip Alexander, 353–76. Proceedings of the British Academy 165. Oxford: Oxford University Press, 2010.

Horbury, William. "The New Testament and Rabbinic Study: An Historical Sketch." In *The New Testament and Rabbinic Literature*, edited by Reimund Bieringer et al., 2–40. Journal for the Study of Judaism Supplements 136. Leiden: Brill, 2010.

Horsley, Richard A. *The Revolt of the Scribes: Resistance and Apocalyptic Origins*. Minneapolis: Fortress, 2010.

Houtman, Alberdina. *Mishnah and Tosefta: A Synoptic Comparison of Tractates Berakhot and Shebiit*. 2 vols. Texts and Studies in Ancient Judaism 59. Tübingen: Mohr Siebeck, 1997.

Hunter, Wiliam A. *Introduction to Roman Law*. Revised by F. H. Lawson. London: Sweet, 1959.

Isaac, Benjamin. "Roman Religious Policy and the Bar Kokhba War." In *The Bar Kokhba War Reconsidered: New Perspectives on the Second Jewish Revolt against Rome*, edited by Peter Schäfer, 37–54. Texts and Studies in Ancient Judaism 100. Tübingen: Mohr Siebeck, 2003.

Jackson, Bernard S. *Essays in Jewish and Comparative Legal History*. Studies in Judaism in Late Antiquity 10. Leiden: Brill, 1975.

Jacobs, Louis. *The Talmudic Argument: A Study in Talmudic Reasoning and Methodology*. Cambridge: Cambridge University Press, 1984.

Jaffee, Martin S. "A Rabbinic Ontology of the Written and Spoken Word: On Discipleship, Transformative Knowledge, and the Living Texts of Oral Torah." *Journal of the American Academy of Religion* 65 (1997) 525–49.

———. *Torah in the Mouth: Writing and Oral Tradition in Palestinian Judaism 200 BCE—400 CE*. Oxford: Oxford University Press, 2001.

Jassen, Alex P. *Mediating the Divine: Prophecy and Revelation in the Dead Sea Scrolls and Second Temple Judaism*. Studies on Texts of the Desert of Judah 68. Leiden: Brill, 2007.

———. "Stephen L. Cook. *On the Question of the 'Cessation of Prophecy' in Ancient Judaism*." Journal of Semitic Studies 59 (2014) 450–52.

Jolowicz, H. F. *Historical Introduction to Roman Law*. Cambridge: Cambridge University Press, 1961.

Jones, Arnold Hugh Martin. *Cities of the Eastern Roman Empire*. Oxford: Clarendon, 1971.

———. *The Later Roman Empire: 284-602; A Social, Economic and Administrative Survey*. Norman: University of Oklahoma Press, 1964.

Kahana, Menahem I. "The Halakhic Midrashim." In *The Literature of the Jewish People in the Period of the Second Temple and the Talmud*, edited by Shmuel Safrai et al., 3:3–106. Assen: Van Gorcum, 2006.

Kalmin, Richard. "Holy Men, Rabbis, and Demonic Sages in Late Antiquity." In *Jewish Culture and Society under the Christian Roman Empire*, edited by Richard Kalmin and Seth Schwartz, 211–53. Interdisciplinary Studies in Ancient Culture and Religion 3. Leuven: Peeters, 2003.

———. *Jewish Babylonia between Persia and Roman Palestine*. Oxford: Oxford University Press, 2006.

———. "Problems in the Use of the Babylonian Talmud for the History of Late-Roman Palestine: The Example of Astrology." In *Rabbinic Texts and the History of Late-Roman Palestine*, edited by Martin Goodman and Philip Alexander, 165–84. Proceedings of the British Academy 165. Oxford: Oxford University Press, 2010.

Kalmin, Richard, and Seth Schwartz, eds. *Jewish Culture and Society under the Christian Roman Empire*. Interdisciplinary Studies in Ancient Culture and Religion 3. Leuven: Peeters, 2003.

Karakocali, Ahmet. "Changes in Roman Legal Education." *Online Journal of New Horizons in Education* 6 (2016) 42–45.

Katz, Steven T., ed. *The Late Roman-Rabbinic Period*. Vol. 4 of *The Cambridge History of Judaism*. Cambridge: Cambridge University Press, 2006.

Kohler, Kaufmann, and David Philipson. "Homiletics." *Jewish Encyclopedia*, 1906. https://www.jewishencyclopedia.com/articles/7842-homiletics.

Kraemer, David C. *A History of the Talmud*. Cambridge: Cambridge University Press, 2019.

————. *The Mind of the Talmud: An Intellectual History of the Bavli.* New York: Oxford University Press, 1990.

————. "The Mishnah." In *The Cambridge History of Judaism,* edited by Steven T. Katz, 4:299–315. Cambridge: Cambridge University Press, 2006.

Kulp, Joshua. "Organizational Patterns in the Mishnah in Light of their Toseftan Parallels." *Journal of Jewish Studies* 58 (2007) 52–78.

Kunkel, Wolfgang. *An Introduction to Roman Legal and Constitutional History.* Oxford: Oxford University Press, 1966.

Lapin, Hayim. "Early Rabbinic Civil Law and the Literature of the Second Temple Period." *Jewish Studies Quarterly* 2 (1995) 149–83.

————."Economy and Society." In *Rabbinic Texts and the History of Late-Roman Palestine,* edited by Martin Goodman and Philip Alexander, 389–402. Proceedings of the British Academy 165. Oxford: Oxford University Press, 2010.

————. *Economy, Geography, and Provincial History in Later Roman Palestine.* Texts and Studies in Ancient Judaism 85. Tübingen: Mohr Siebeck, 2001.

————. "Epigraphical Rabbis: A Reconsideration." *Jewish Quarterly Review* 101 (2011) 311–46.

————. "Hegemony and Its Discontents: Rabbis as a Late Antique Provincial Population." In *Jewish Culture and Society under the Christian Roman Empire,* edited by Richard Kalmin and Seth Schwartz, 319–48. Interdisciplinary Studies in Ancient Culture and Religion 3. Leuven: Peeters, 2003.

————. "The Origins and Development of the Rabbinic Movement in the Land of Israel." In *The Cambridge History of Judaism,* edited by Steven T. Katz, 4:206–29. Cambridge: Cambridge University Press, 2006.

————. "The Rabbinic Class Revisited: Rabbis as Judges in Later Roman Palestine." In *"Follow the Wise": Studies in Jewish History and Culture in Honor of Lee I. Levine,* edited by Zev Weiss et al., 255–74. University Park, PA: Eisenbrauns, 2010.

————. *Rabbis as Romans: The Rabbinic Movement in Palestine, 100–400 CE.* Oxford: Oxford University Press, 2012.

Lavee, Moshe. "Rabbinic Literature and the History of Judaism in Late Antiquity: Challenges, Methodologies and New Approaches." In *Rabbinic Texts and the History of Late-Roman Palestine,* edited by Martin Goodman and Philip Alexander, 319–52. Proceedings of the British Academy 165. Oxford: Oxford University Press, 2010.

LeFebvre, Michael. *Collections, Codes, and Torah: The Re-Characterization of Israel's Written Law.* Library of Hebrew Bible/Old Testament Studies 451. New York: T. & T. Clark, 2006.

Leibner, Uzi. "The Settlement Crisis in the Eastern Galilee during the Late Roman and Early Byzantine Periods: Response to Jodi Magness." In *Jewish Identities in Antiquity: Studies in Memory of Menahem Stern,* edited by Lee I. Levine and Daniel R. Schwartz, 314–20. Texts and Studies in Ancient Judaism 100. Tübingen: Mohr Siebeck, 2009.

————. "Settlement Patterns in the Eastern Galilee: Implications Regarding the Transformation of Rabbinic Culture in Late Antiquity." In *Jewish Identities in Antiquity: Studies in Memory of Menahem Stern,* edited by Lee I. Levine and Daniel R. Schwartz, 269–95. Texts and Studies in Ancient Judaism 130. Tübingen: Mohr Siebeck, 2009.

Leesen, Tessa G. *Gaius Meets Cicero: Law and Rhetoric in the Schools Controversies.* Legal History Library 2. Leiden: Brill, 2010.

Levine, David. "Between Leadership and Marginality: Models for Evaluating the Role of the Rabbis in the Early Centuries CE." In *Jewish Identities in Antiquity: Studies in Memory of Menahem Stern*, edited by Lee I. Levine and Daniel R. Schwartz, 195–210. Texts and Studies in Ancient Judaism 130. Tübingen: Mohr Siebeck, 2009.

———. "Is Talmudic Biography Still Possible?" [In Hebrew.] *Jewish Studies* 46 (2009) 61–64.

———. "Rabbi Judah the Patriarch and the Boundaries of Palestinian Cities, a Literary-Historical Study." [In Hebrew.] *Cathedra* 138 (2010) 7–42.

———. "Rabbis, Preachers and Aggadists: An Aspect of Jewish Culture in Third and Fourth Century Palestine." In *"Follow the the Wise": Studies in Jewish History and Culture in Honor of Lee I. Levine*, edited by Zev Weiss et al., 272–94. University Park, PA: Eisenbrauns, 2010.

Levine, Lee I. *The Ancient Synagogue: The First Thousand Years.* New Haven, CT: Yale University Press, 2000.

———. "Introduction: Was There a Crisis in Jewish Settlement in the Eastern Galilee of Late Antiquity." In *Jewish Identities in Antiquity: Studies in Memory of Menahem Stern*, edited by Lee I. Levine and Daniel R. Schwartz, 267–68. Texts and Studies in Ancient Judaism 130. Tübingen: Mohr Siebeck, 2009.

———. "Jewish Identities in Antiquity: An Introductory Essay." In *Jewish Identities in Antiquity: Studies in Memory of Menahem Stern*, edited by Lee I. Levine and Daniel R. Schwartz, 12–40. Texts and Studies in Ancient Judaism 130. Tübingen: Mohr Siebeck, 2009.

———. "The Jewish Patriarch." In *Oxford Classical Dictionary*, Oct. 24, 2018. https:// doi.org/10.1093/acrefore/9780199381135.013.8133.

———. "The Jewish Patriarch (Nasi) in Third Century Palestine." In *Aufstieg und Niedergang der römischen Welt*, edited by Hildegard Temporini and Wolfgang Haase, II.19.2:649–88. Berlin: de Gruyter, 1979.

———. *The Rabbinic Class of Roman Palestine in Late Antiquity.* New York: Jewish Theological Seminary of America, 1989.

———. "The Status of the Patriarchate in the Third and Fourth Centuries: Sources and Methodology." *Journal of Jewish Studies* 47 (1996) 1–32.

Levine, Lee I., and Daniel R. Schwartz, eds. *Jewish Identities in Antiquity: Studies in Memory of Menahem Stern.* Texts and Studies in Ancient Judaism 130. Tübingen: Mohr Siebeck, 2009.

Lieberman, Saul. *Greek in Jewish Palestine/Hellenism in Jewish Palestine.* 1950. Reprint, New York: Jewish Theological Seminary, 2012.

Lightstone, Jack N. *The Commerce of the Sacred: Mediation of the Divine among the Jews in the Greco-Roman Diaspora.* 2nd ed. With a foreword by Willi Braun and updated bibliography by Herbert Basser. New York: Columbia University Press, 2006.

———. *In the Seat of Moses: An Introductory Guide to Early Rabbinic Legal Rhetoric and Literary Conventions.* Westar Studies. Eugene, OR: Cascade, 2020.

———. "Introduction: Challenges and Opportunities in the Social Scientific Study of the Evidence of the Mishnah." In *Exploring Mishnah's World(s): Social Scientific Approaches*, by Simcha Fishbane et al., 1–24. London: Palgrave-Macmillan, 2020.

———. "Is It Meaningful to Talk of *a* Greco-Roman Diaspora Judaism? A Case Study in Taxonomical Issues in the Study of Ancient Judaism." In *Introducing Religion: Essays in Honor of Jonathan Z. Smith*, edited by Willi Braun and Russell T. McCutcheon, 267–81. London: Equinox, 2008.

———. *Mishnah and the Social Formation of the Early Rabbinic Guild: A Socio-Rhetorical Study*. Studies in Christianity and Judaism 11. Waterloo, ON: Wilfrid Laurier University Press, 2002.

———. "Mishnah Kiddushin 4:1–8: Mishnah's (Re-)Conceptualization of Jewish Society in the Hebrew Bible." In *Studies in Judaism, Humanities, and the Social Sciences: Annual Review* 3 (2020) 10–26. https://www.degruyter.com/document/doi/10.26613/sjhss.3.1.60/html?lang=en.

———. "Names without 'Lives': Why No 'Lives of the Rabbis' in Early Rabbinic Judaism." *Studies in Religion* 19 (1990) 43–57.

———. "Naming Names: The Meaning and Significance of Disputes and the Use of Attributions to Named Authorities in Mishnah." In *To Fix Torah in Their Hearts: Essays in Biblical Interpretation and Jewish Studies in Honor of B. Barry Levy*, edited by Jacqueline S. du Toit et al., 86–117. Cincinnati: Hebrew Union College Press, 2019.

———. "The Rabbis' Bible: The Canon of the Hebrew Bible and the Early Rabbinic Guild." In *The Canon Debate: On the Origins and Formation of the Bible*, edited by Lee M. McDonald and James Sanders, 163–84. Peabody, MA: Hendrickson, 2002.

———. *The Rhetoric of the Babylonian Talmud, Its Social Meaning and Context*. Studies in Christianity and Judaism 6. Waterloo, ON: Wilfrid Laurier University Press, 1994.

———. "Roman Diaspora Judaism." In *A Companion to Roman Religion*, edited by Jörg Rüpke, 345–77. Blackwell Companions to the Ancient World 9. Oxford: Blackwell, 2007.

———. "Sociological and Anthropological Approaches to the Study of the Evidence of the Mishnah: A Call to Scholarly Action and a Programmatic Introduction." *Studies in Judaism, Humanities, and the Social Sciences* 2 (2019) 1–16.

———. "Study as a Socially Formative Activity: The Case of Mishnah Study in the Early Rabbinic Group." In *Exploring Mishnah's World(s): Social Scientific Approaches*, by Simcha Fishbane et al., 181–216. London: Palgrave Macmillan, 2020.

———. "Studying Mishnah 'Talmudic-ly': What the Basic Literary-Rhetorical Features of the Talmuds' Legal Compositions and Composite 'Essays' Tell Us about Mishnah Study as an Identity-Informing Activity within Rabbinic Groups at the End of Late Antiquity." In *Exploring Mishnah's World(s): Social Scientific Approaches*, by Simcha Fishbane et al., 259–306. London: Palgrave Macmillan, 2020.

———. "Textual Study and Social Formation: The Case of Mishnah." *Studies in Judaism, Humanities, and the Social Sciences* 1 (2017) 23–44.

———. "Textual Study and Social Formation, Part II: Does the Evidence of Tosefta Confirm That of Mishnah?" *Studies in Judaism, Humanities, and the Social Sciences: Annual Review*, forthcoming.

———. "What Is Mishnah? (1) A Range of Meanings of the Question, and (2) One Illustrative Proposal: Mishnah and Roman Legal Education." In *Studies in Judaism, Humanities, and the Social Sciences: Annual Review* 4 (2021) 3–21.

———. "When Speech Is no Speech: The Problem of Early Rabbinic Rhetoric as Discourse." *Semeia* 34 (1985) 53–58.

—————. "When Tosefta Was Read in Service of Mishnah-Study: What Pervasive Literary-Rhetorical Traits of Toseftan Materials Divulge about the Evolution of Early Rabbinic Group Identity on the Heels of Mishnah's Promulgation." In *Exploring Mishnah's World(s): Social Scientific Approaches*, by Simcha Fishbane et al., 217–58. London: Palgrave Macmillan, 2020.

Linder, Amnon. *The Jews in Imperial Roman Legislation*. Detroit: Wayne State University Press, 1995.

—————. "The Legal Status of the Jews in the Roman Empire." In *The Cambridge History of Judaism*, edited by Steven Katz, 4:128–73. Cambridge: Cambridge University Press, 2006.

Luchetti, Giovanni, et al. *Iulius Paulus. Ad Edictum Libri I–II*. Scriptores Iuris Romani 2. Rome: Erma di Bretschneider, 2018.

Macadam, Henry Innes. "*Studia et Circenses*: Beirut's Roman Law School in Its Colonial, Cultural Context." *ARAM* 13–14 (2001–2002) 193–226.

Mack, Burton L. *A Myth of Innocence: Mark and Christian Origins*. Minneapolis: Fortress, 1991.

—————. "The Quest for Christian Origins." *Forum* 7 (2018) 7–20. http://www.westarinstitute.org/wp-content/uploads/2018/04/Forum-7-1-FULLTEXT-ChristianitySeminar.pdf.

Mack, Burton L., and Vernon K. Robbins. *Patterns of Persuasion in the Gospels*. Foundations & Facets: Literary Facets. 1989. Reprint, Eugene, OR: Wipf & Stock, 2008.

Mandel, Paul. *The Origins of Midrash: From Teaching to Text*. Journal for the Study of Judaism Supplements 80. Leiden: Brill, 2017.

—————. "The Tosefta." In *The Cambridge History of Judaism*, edited by Steven T. Katz, 4:316–35. Cambridge: Cambridge University Press, 2006.

Mayer, Louise A. "Jewish and Roman Law in Second Century CE: A Socio-Anthopological Approach." Master's thesis, Concordia University, 1988.

Meacham, Tirzah. "Tosefta as Template: Yerushalmi Niddah." In *Introducing Tosefta: Textual, Intratextual and Intertextual Studies*, edited by Harry Fox and Tirzah Meacham, 181–220. New York: Ktav, 1999.

Meeks, Wayne A., and Robert L. Wilken. *Jews and Christians in Antioch in the First Four Centuries of the Common Era*. Missoula, MT: Society of Biblical Literature, 1978.

Milikowsky, Chaim. "The *Status Quaestionis* of Research in Rabbinic Literature." In *Rabbinic Texts and the History of Late-Roman Palestine*, edited by Martin Goodman and Philip Alexander, 67–78. Proceedings of the British Academy 165. Oxford: Oxford University Press, 2010.

Millar, Fergus. "The Palestinian Context of Rabbinic Literature." In *Rabbinic Texts and the History of Late-Roman Palestine*, edited by Martin Goodman and Philip Alexander, 25–50. Proceedings of the British Academy 165. Oxford: Oxford University Press, 2010.

Miller, Stuart S. *Sages and Commoners in Late Antique "Erez Israel": A Philological Inquiry into Local Traditions in Talmud Yerushalmi*. Texts and Studies in Ancient Judaism 111. Tübingen: Mohr Siebeck, 2006.

—————. "Stepped Pools, Stone Vessels, and Other Identity Markers of 'Complex Common Judaism.'" *Journal for the Study of Judaism* 41 (2010) 214–43.

Moore, George Foote. *Judaism in the First Centuries of the Christian Era*. 3 vols. 1927–1930. Reprint, Cambridge: Harvard University Press, 1954.

Mor, Menahem. "The Geographical Scope of the Bar Kokhba Revolt." In *The Bar Kokhba War Reconsidered: New Perspectives on the Second Jewish Revolt against Rome*, edited by Peter Schäfer, 107–32. Texts and Studies in Ancient Judaism 100. Tübingen: Mohr Siebeck, 2003.

Moscovitz, Leib. "Legal Fictions in Rabbinic Law and Roman Law: Some Comparative Observations." In *Rabbinic Law in Its Roman and Near Eastern Context*, edited by Catherine Hezser, 105–32. Texts and Studies in Ancient Judaism 97. Tübingen: Mohr Siebeck, 2003.

———. *Talmudic Reasoning*. Texts and Studies in Ancient Judaism 89. Tübingen: Mohr Siebeck, 2002.

Muffs, Yochanan. *Studies in the Aramaic Legal Papyri from Elephantine*. Handbuch der Orientalistik 66. Leidein: Brill, 2003.

Neusner, Jacob. *The Bavli: An Introduction*. South Florida Studies in the History of Judaism 42. Atlanta: Scholars, 1992.

———. *The Bavli That Might Have Been: Tosefta's Theory of Mishnah Commentary Compared with the Bavli's*. South Florida Studies in the History of Judaism 18. Atlanta: Scholars, 1991.

———. *The Bavli's One Voice: Types and Forms of Analytical Discourse and Their Fixed Order of Appearance*. South Florida Studies in the History of Judaism 24. Atlanta: Scholars, 1991.

———. *Conclusions*. Vol. 3 of *Rabbinic Traditions about the Pharisees before 70*. 1971. Reprint, Dove Studies in Bible, Language, and History, Eugene, OR: Wipf & Stock, 2003.

———. "Describing Tosefta: A Systematic Account." In *Introducing Tosefta: Textual, Intratextual and Intertextual Studies*, edited by Harry Fox and Tirzah Meacham, 39–72. New York: Ktav, 1999.

———. *Development of a Legend: Studies on the Traditions Concerning Yohanan ben Zakkai*. Leiden: Brill, 1970.

———. *From Politics to Piety: The Emergence of Pharisaic Judaism*. New York: Ktav, 1979.

———. *A History of the Jews in Babylonia*. 5 vols. Studia Post-biblica 9, 11–12, 14–15. Leiden: Brill, 1965–70.

———. *A History of the Mishnaic Law of Purities, Part 21*. Studies in Judaism in Late Antiquity 6. Leiden: Brill, 1977.

———. *How the Bavli Is Constructed: Identifying the Forests Comprised by the Talmud's Trees*. Studies in Judaism. Lanham, MD: Rowman & Littlefield, 2009.

———. *Introduction to Rabbinic Literature*. New Haven, CT: Yale University Press, 1999.

———. *Judaism in Society: The Evidence of the Yerushalmi; Toward the Natural History of a Religion*. Chicago: University of Chicago Press, 1983.

———. *Judaism, the Classical Statement: The Evidence of the Bavli*. Chicago Studies in the History of Judaism. Reprint, Eugene, OR: Wipf & Stock, 2003.

———. *A Life of Rabbi Yohanan ben Zakkai*. Leiden: Brill, 1962.

———. *The Memorized Torah: The Mnemonic System of Mishnah*. Brown Judaic Studies 96. Chico, CA: Scholars, 1985.

———. "The Mishnah in Roman and Christian Contexts." In *The Mishnah in Contemporary Perspective*, edited by Alan J. Avery-Peck and Jacob Neusner, 1:121–48. Atlanta, GA: SBL, 2002.

————. *Mishnah: Introduction and Reader.* 1992. Reprint, Eugene, OR: Wipf & Stock, 2004.

————. *Rabbinic Traditions about the Pharisees before 70.* 3 Vols. Leiden: Brill, 1971–1973.

————. "The Rabbis and Prophecy." *Review of Rabbinic Literature* 17 (2014) 1–26.

————. *The Reader's Guide to the Talmud.* Brill Reference Library of Ancient Judaism 5. Leiden: Brill, 2001.

————. *Reading and Believing: Ancient Judaism and Contemporary Gullibility.* Brown Judaic Studies 113. Atlanta: Scholars, 1986.

————. *The Rules of Composition of the Talmud of Babylonia.* South Florida Studies in the History of Judaism 13. Atlanta: Scholars, 1991.

————. *Tosefta: An Introduction.* South Florida Studies in the History of Judaism 47. Atlanta: Scholars, 1992.

————. *The Yerushalmi: The Talmud of the Land of Israel: An Introduction.* Library of Classical Judaism. Northvale, NJ: Aronson, 1993.

Neusner, Jacob, and Bruce D. Chilton, eds. *In Quest of the Historical Pharisees.* Waco, TX: Baylor University Press, 2007.

Neusner, Jacob, and William Scott Green. *Writing with Scripture: The Authority and Uses of the Hebrew Bible in the Torah of Formative Judaism.* 1989. Reprint, Eugene, OR: Wipf & Stock, 2003.

Newman, Hillel J. "The Normativity of Rabbinic Judaism: Obstacles on the Path to a New Consensus." In *Jewish Identities in Antiquity: Studies in Memory of Menahem Stern*, edited by Lee I. Levine and Daniel R. Schwartz, 165–71. Texts and Studies in Ancient Judaism 130. Tübingen: Mohr Siebeck, 2009.

Nicholas, Barry. *An Introduction to Roman Law.* Oxford: Clarendon, 1962.

Noegel, Scott B. "New Observations on Scribal Activity in the Ancient Near East." In *Voice, Text, Hypertext: Emerging Practices in Textual Studies*, edited by Raimonda Modiano et al., 133–43. Seattle: University of Washington Press, 2004,

Oppenheimer, Aaron. *Between Rome and Babylon.* Texts and Studies in Ancient Judaism 108. Tübingen: Mohr Siebeck, 2005.

————. *By the Rivers of Babylon: Perspectives on the History of Talmudic Babylonia.* [In Hebrew.] Tel Aviv: Tel Aviv University Press, 2017.

————. "Politics and Administration." In *Rabbinic Texts and the History of Late-Roman Palestine*, edited by Martin Goodman and Philip Alexander, 377–88. Proceedings of the British Academy 165. Oxford: Oxford University Press, 2010.

Papadopoulou, Despina. "The Administration of Egypt in Hellenistic Times: The Rise and Fall of the *oikonomos*." *Anistoriton Journal* 12 (2010) 1–8.

Pervo, Richard I. *Dating Acts: Between the Evangelists and the Apologists.* Westar Institute. Santa Rosa, CA: Polebridge, 2006.

Petuchowski, Jakob J. "The Modern Rabbi." *Commentary*, Feb., 1963. https://www.commentary.org/articles/jakob-petuchowski-2/the-modern-rabbi/.

Porton, Bezalel, and Ada Yardeni. *Textbook of Aramaic Documents from Ancient Egypt.* 4 vols. Jerusalem: Acadamon, 1986–1999.

Porton, Bezalel, et al. *The Elephantine Papyri in English: Three Millennia of Cross-Cultural Continuity and Change.* Documenta et Monumenta Orientis Antiqui 22. Leiden: Brill, 1996.

Porton, Bezalel, et al. *The Elephantine Papyri in English: Three Millennia of Cross-Cultural Continuity and Change.* 2nd rev. ed. Atlanta: Society of Biblical Literature and Leiden: Brill, 2011.

Quack, Joachim Friedric. "The Interaction of Egyptian and Aramaic Literature." In *Judah and the Judeans in the Achaemenid Age: Negotiating Identity in an International Context*, edited by Oded Lipschits et al., 375–401. University Park, PA: Eisenbrauns, 2011.

Rabello, Alfredo Mordechai. "Civil Jewish Jurisdiction in the Days of Emperor Justinian (527–565): Codex Justinianus 1.9.8." *Israel Law Review* 33 (1999) 51–66. https://ssrn.com/abstract=2681188.

———. *An Introduction to the History and Sources of Roman Law*. Oxford: Oxford University Press, 2021.

Rajak, Tessa. "Synagogue and Community in the Graeco-Roman Diaspora." In *Jews in the Hellenistic and Roman Cities*, edited by John R. Bartlett, 22–38. London: Routledge, 2002.

———. "The Synagogue within the Greco-Roman City." In *Jews, Christians, and Polytheists in the Ancient Synagogue: Cultural Interactions during the Greco-Roman Period*, edited by Steven Fine, 161–73. Baltimore Studies in the History of Judaism. London: Routledge, 1999.

Reichman, Ronen. *Mishna und Sifra: Ein literarkritischer Vergleich paralleler Überlieferungen*. Texts and Studies in Ancient Judaism 68. Tübingen: Mohr Siebeck, 1998.

———. "The Tosefta and Its Value for Historical Research: Questioning the Historical Reliability of Case Stories." In *Rabbinic Texts and the History of Late-Roman Palestine*, edited by Martin Goodman and Philip Alexander, 117–28. Proceedings of the British Academy 165. Oxford: Oxford University Press, 2010.

Rosenfeld, Ben-Zion, and Haim Perlmutter. *Social Stratification of the Jewish Population of Roman Palestine in the Period of the Mishnah, 70–250 CE*. Brill Reference Library of Judaism 59. Leiden: Brill, 2020.

Roux, George. *Ancient Iraq*. 2nd ed. New York: Penguin, 1980.

Rubenstein, Jeffrey L. *The Culture of the Babylonian Talmud*. Baltimore: Johns Hopkins University Press, 2003.

———. "Social and Institutional Settings of Rabbinic Literature." In *The Cambridge Companion to the Talmud and Rabbinic Literature*, edited by Charlotte Elisheva Fonrobert and Martin S. Jaffee, 58–74. Cambridge Companions to Religion. Cambridge: Cambridge University Press, 2007.

Rubenstein, Richard E. *Aristotle's Children: How Christians, Muslims, and Jews Rediscovered Ancient Wisdom and Illuminated the Dark Ages*. Orlando: Harcourt, 2003.

Rubenstein, Richard L. "A Rabbi Dies" (1971). In *American Judaism: Adventure in Modernity*, by Jacob Neusner, 48–58. New York: Ktav, 1978.

Ruffle, John. "The Teaching of Amenemope and Its Connection with the Book of Proverbs." *Tyndale Bulletin* 28 (1977) 29–68.

Safrai, Zeev. *The Economy of Roman Palestine*. London: Routledge, 1994.

Safrai, Zeev, and Chana Safrai. "To What Extent Did the Rabbis Determine Public Norms?" In *Jewish Identities in Antiquity: Studies in Memory of Menahem Stern*, edited by Lee I. Levine and Daniel R. Schwartz, 172–94. Texts and Studies in Ancient Judaism 130. Tübingen: Mohr Siebeck, 2009.

Saldarini, Anthony J. *The Fathers according to Rabbi Nathan (Avot de Rabbi Nathan): Version B: Translation and Commentary*. Studies in Judaism in Late Antiquity 11. Leiden: Brill, 1975.

Samely, Alexander. *Forms of Rabbinic Literature and Thought: An Introduction*. Oxford: Oxford University Press, 2007.

Saperstein, Marc. *Jewish Preaching: 1200–1800*. New Haven: Yale University Press, 1989.

————. "Rabbis as Preachers." In *Rabbi-Pastor-Priest: Their Roles and Profiles Through the Ages*, edited by Walter Homolka and Heinz-Gunther Schottlen, 111–28. Studia Judaica 64. Berlin: de Gruyter, 2013.

Satlow, Michael L. "'And on the Earth You Shall Sleep': 'Talmud Torah' and Rabbinic Asceticism." *Journal of Religion* 83 (2003) 204–25.

Schäfer, Peter. "Bar Kokhba and the Rabbis." In *The Bar Kokhba War Reconsidered: New Perspectives on the Second Jewish Revolt against Rome*, edited by Peter Schäfer, 1–22. Texts and Studies in Ancient Judaism 100. Tübingen: Mohr Siebeck, 2003.

————, ed. *The Bar Kokhba War Reconsidered: New Perspectives on the Second Jewish Revolt against Rome*. Texts and Studies in Ancient Judaism 100. Tübingen: Mohr Siebeck, 2003.

————. "Research into Rabbinic Literature: An Attempt to Define the *Status Quaestionis*." In *Rabbinic Texts and the History of Late-Roman Palestine*, edited by Martin Goodman and Philip Alexander, 51–66. Proceedings of the British Academy 165. Oxford: Oxford University Press, 2010.

Schäfer, Peter, and Chaim Milikowsky. "Current Views on the Editing of the Rabbinic Texts of Late Antiquity: Reflections on a Debate after Twenty Years." In *Rabbinic Texts and the History of Late-Roman Palestine*, edited by Martin Goodman and Philip Alexander, 79–89. Proceedings of the British Academy 165. Oxford: Oxford University Press, 2010.

Schams, Christine. *Jewish Scribes in the Second Temple Period*. Journal for the Study of the Old Testament: Supplement Series 291. Sheffield: Sheffield Academic, 1998.

Schechter, Solomon. *Avot de-Rabbi Natan*. Vienna: Knapfelmacher, 1887.

Schiavone, Aldo. *Ius: L'Invenzione del Dritto in Occidente*. Torino: Einaudi, 2005. Eng. ed.: *The Invention of Law in the West*. Translated by Jeremy Carden and Anthony Shugaar. Cambridge: Harvard University Press, 2012.

————. *Nascita della Giurisprudenza: Cultura Aristocratia e Pensiero Giuridico nella Roma Tardo-Repubblicana*. Rome: Laterza, 1978.

————. *Studi sulle Logiche dei Giuristi Romani: Nova Negotia e Transactio da Labeone a Ulpiano*. Naples: Jovene, 1971.

Schiffman, Lawrence H. *From Text to Tradition: A History of Second Temple and Rabbinic Judaism*. New York: Ktav, 1991.

————. *Reclaiming the Dead Sea Scrolls: Their True Meaning for Judaism and Christianity*. Anchor Yale Bible Reference Library. New Haven: Yale University Press, 2009.

————. Review of *The Greek Minor Prophets Scroll from Nahal Hever (8HevXIIGr) (The Seiyal Collection I)*, by Emanuel Tov et al. *Journal of Biblical Literature* 111 (1992) 532–35.

————. *Who Was a Jew? Rabbinic and Halakhic Perspectives on the Jewish Christian Schism*. New York: Ktav, 1985.

Schofer, Jonathan W. *The Making of the Sage: A Study in Rabbinic Ethics*. Madison: University of Wisconsin Press, 2005.

Scholem, Gershom. *Jewish Gnosticism, Merkavah Mysticism, and the Talmudic Tradition*. New York: Jewish Theological Seminary, 2015.

————. *Major Trends in Jewish Mysticism*. New York: Schocken, 1946.

Scott, Frank. *The Queen's Gambit*. Los Gatos, CA: Netflix, 2020.

Schremer, Adiel. "The Religious Orientation of Non-Rabbis in Second-Century Palestine: A Rabbinic Perspective." In *"Follow the the Wise": Studies in Jewish History and Culture in Honor of Lee I. Levine*, edited by Zev Weiss et al., 319–42. University Park, PA: Eisenbrauns, 2010.

Schulz, Fritz. *Classical Roman Law*. Oxford: Clarendon, 1954.

———. *History of Roman Legal Science*. Oxford: Clarendon, 1963.

Schwartz, Daniel R., and Zeev Weiss. *Was 70 CE a Watershed in Jewish History?* Ancient Judaism and Early Christianity 78. Leiden: Brill, 2012.

Schwartz, Seth. *The Ancient Jews: From Alexander to Muhammad*. Key Themes in Ancient History. Cambridge: Cambridge University Press, 2014.

———. *Imperialism and Jewish Society, 200 B.C.E. to 640 C.E.* Jews, Christians, and Muslims from the Ancient to the Modern World. Princeton, NJ: Princeton University Press, 2001.

———. "The Political Geography of Rabbinic Texts." In *The Cambridge Companion to the Talmud and Rabbinic Literature*, edited by Charlotte Elisheva Fonrobert and Martin S. Jaffee, Cambridge Companions to Religion, 75–97. New York: Cambridge University Press, 2007.

———. "'Rabbinic Culture' and Roman Culture." In *Rabbinic Texts and the History of Late-Roman Palestine*, edited by Martin Goodman and Philip Alexander, 283–300. Proceedings of the British Academy 165. Oxford: Oxford University Press, 2010.

———. *Were the Jews a Mediterranean Society? Reciprocity and Solidarity in Ancient Judaism*. Princeton, NJ: Princeton University Press, 2010.

Schweitzer, Albert. *The Quest of the Historical Jesus*. 2nd ed. Translated by John Bowden. Minneapolis: Fortress, 2001.

Simon-Shoshan, Moshe. *Stories of the Law: Narrative Discourse and the Construction of Authority in the Mishnah*. Oxford: Oxford University Press, 2012.

Sivertsev, Alexei. *Households, Sects, and the Origins of the Rabbinic Judaism*. Supplements to the Journal for the Study of Judaism 102. Leiden: Brill, 2005.

Smith, Lionel. Review of *Invention of Law in the West*, by Aldo Schiavone. *Canadian Journal of History* 48 (2013) 479–81.

Smith, Morton. *Jesus the Magician*. San Francisco: Harper & Row, 1978.

Sommer, Benjamin D. "Did Prophecy Cease? Evaluating a Reevaluation." *Journal of Biblical Literature* 115 (1996) 31–47.

Stein, Peter G. "Interpretation and Legal Reasoning in Roman Law." *Chicago-Kent Law Review* 70 (1995) 1539–41.

———. "The Roman Jurists' Conception of Law." In *A Treatise of Legal Philosophy and General Jurisprudence*, edited by A. Pandovani and P. G. Stein, 1–20. Dordrecht: Springer, 2007.

———. "The Two Schools of Jurists in the Early Roman Principate." *Cambridge Law Journal* 31 (1972) 8–31.

Stemberger, Gunter. "Halakhic Midrashim as Historical Sources." In *Rabbinic Texts and the History of Late-Roman Palestine*, edited by Martin Goodman and Philip Alexander, 129–42. Proceedings of the British Academy 165. Oxford: Oxford University Press, 2010.

———. Review of *Mishna und Sifra*, by Ronen Reichman. *Annual of Rabbinic Judaism* 3 (2000) 207–10.

Stern, Sacha. "Rabbi and the Origins of the Patriarchate." *Journal of Jewish Studies* 54 (2003) 193–215.

———. "The Talmud Yerushalmi." In *Rabbinic Texts and the History of Late-Roman Palestine*, edited by Martin Goodman and Philip Alexander, 143–64. Proceedings of the British Academy 165. Oxford: Oxford University Press, 2010.

Stertz, Stephen A. "Appendix: Roman Legal Codification in the Second Century." In *The Mishnah in Contemporary Perspective*, edited by Alan J. Avery-Peck and Jacob Neusner, 1:146–66. Atlanta: SBL, 2002.

Strack, Herman L., et al. *Introduction to the Talmud and Midrash*. 2nd ed. Minneapolis: Fortress, 1996.

Tennenblat, M. A. *Peraqim Hadashim leToldot Eretz-Yisrael ve-Bavel beTequfat Ha-Talmud*. Tel-Aviv: Dvir, 1966.

Tov, Emanuel. "The Nature of the Greek Texts from the Judean Desert." *Novum Testamentum* 43 (2001) 1–11.

Tropper, Amram. "The State of Mishnah Studies." In *Rabbinic Texts and the History of Late-Roman Palestine*, edited by Martin Goodman and Philip Alexander, 91–116. Proceedings of the British Academy 165. Oxford: Oxford University Press, 2010.

Tuori, Kaius. "The *ius respondendi* and the Freedom of Roman Jurisprudence." *Revue Internationale des droits de l'Antiquité* 51 (2004) 295–337.

Urbach, Ephraim E. *The Sages: Their Concepts and Beliefs*. 2 vols. Jerusalem: Magnes, 1975–1979.

Uusimäki, Elisa. *Lived Wisdom in Jewish Antiquity: Studies in Exercise and Exemplarity*. London: T&T Clark, 2021.

———. "Maskil among the Hellenistic Jewish Sages." *Journal of Ancient Judaism* 8 (2017) 42–68.

———. "The Rise of the Jewish Sage in Greek and Jewish Antiquity." *Journal for the Study of Judaism* 49.1 (2018) 1–29.

———. *Turning Proverbs towards Torah: An Analysis of 4Q525*. Studies on the Texts of the Desert of Judah 117. Leiden: Brill, 2016.

Watson, Alan, ed. and trans. *The Digest of Justinian*. Vol 1. Philadelphia: University of Pennsylvania Press, 1985.

———. *The Law of the Ancient Romans*. Dallas: Southern Methodist University Press, 1970.

———. *The Spirit of Roman Law*. The Spirit of the Laws 4. Athens: University of Georgia Press, 2008.

Westrup, C. W. *An Introduction to Early Roman Law*. 2 vols. London: Cumberlege, 1944–1954.

Whybray, R. N. *Wisdom in Proverbs: The Concept of Wisdom in Proverbs 1–9*. Studies in Biblical Theology, 1/45. 1965. Reprint, Eugene, OR: Wipf & Stock, 2009.

Wiebe, Matthew C. "The Wisdom of the Proverbs: An Integrated Reading of the Book." PhD diss., University of Sheffield, 1992.

Wilson, Stephen. *Related Strangers: Jews and Christians, 70–170 CE*. Minneapolis: Fortress, 2004.

Wise, Michael Owen. "Language and Literacy in Roman Judaea: A Study of the Bar Kokhba Documents." PhD diss., University of Minnesota, 2012.

Zaiman, Joel. "The Traditional Study of the Mishnah." In *The Modern Study of the Mishnah*, edited by Jacob Neusner, 1–10. Studia Post-biblica 23. Leiden: Brill, 1973.

Zhakevich, Philip. *Scribal Tools in Ancient Israel: A Study of Biblical Hebrew Terms for Writing Materials and Implements*. University Park, PA: Eisenbrauns, 2020.

Zuckermandel, M. S., ed. *Tosefta: Based in the Erfurt and Vienna Codices*. Jerusalem: Wahrmann, 1970.

Zunz, Leopold. *Die gottesdienstlichen Vorträge der Juden, historisch Entwickelt*. Reprint, Oxford: Oxbow, 2003.

———. *HaDrashot BeYisrael*. Edited by Hanokh Albeck. Jerusalem: Mosad Bialik, 1954.

Subject Index